D0937419

The Earl & the Fairy

Story & Art by Ayuko
Original Concept by Mizue Tani

From Cobalt Series *Hakushaku to Yosei Amai Wana Ni Wa
Kiotsukete (The Earl and the Fairy: Beware of Sweet Traps)*

4

Last time in The Earl & the Fairy

Eight years ago...

→Rosalie stole the Fairy Egg from Edgar when he was young!

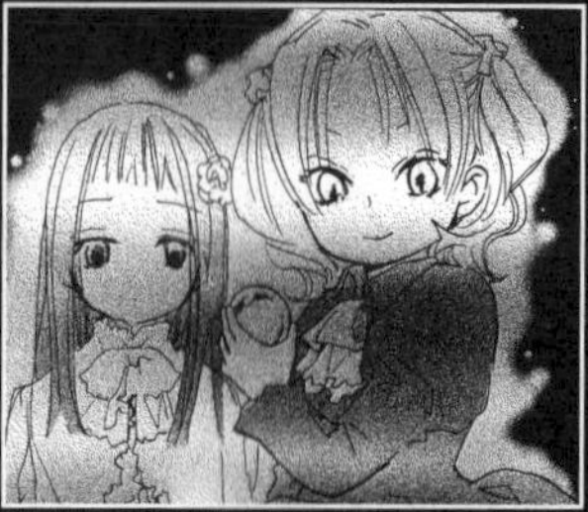

Nineteenth century England. Lydia Carlton has become Lord Ibrazel's official fairy doctor and is investigating the disappearance of Lady Doris Walpole. A type of agate known as a Fairy Egg and the Fogman, an evil creature from the Unseelie Court, may be involved. Meanwhile, Lady Doris's cousin Rosalie has taken a liking to Edgar and views Lydia as her rival. Then a bogey-beast from the Unseelie Court coaxes Rosalie into imprisoning Lydia in a warehouse!

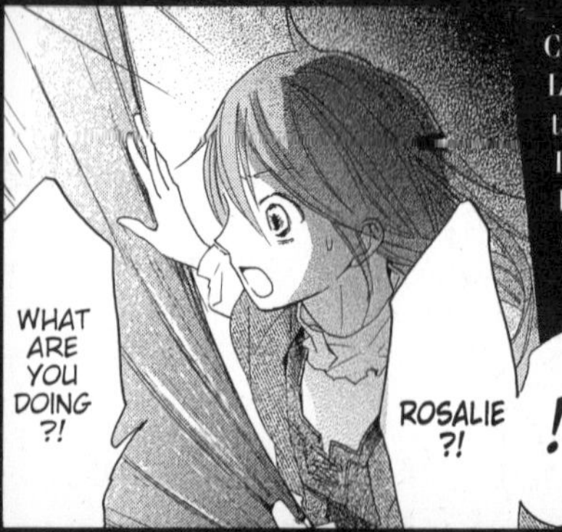
!!
ROSALIE ?!
WHAT ARE YOU DOING ?!

In a fit of jealousy...

←Rosalie imprisons Lydia so she can have Edgar all for herself!

Key Terms

Fairy Egg

An agate with the power to absorb demons. Edgar used to have it, but now it is in Rosalie's hands.

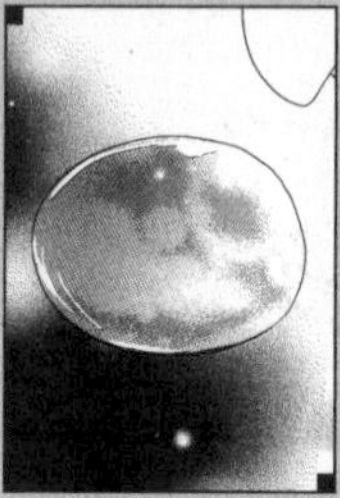

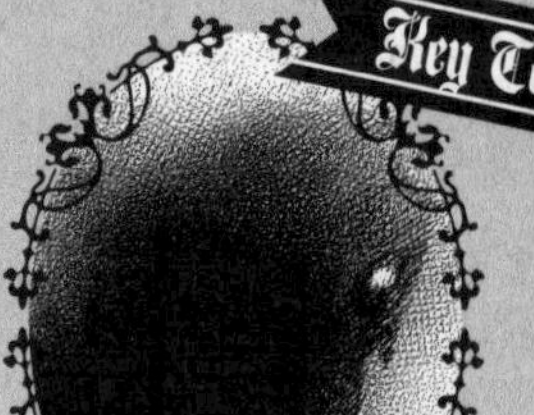

Fogman

A fairy of the Unseelie Court who makes people disappear by swallowing them. He is currently sealed within the Fairy Egg. Is he involved in the disappearance of Lady Doris?

Bogey-beast

A fairy of the Unseelie Court who has been serving Rosalie. His true master, however, is...

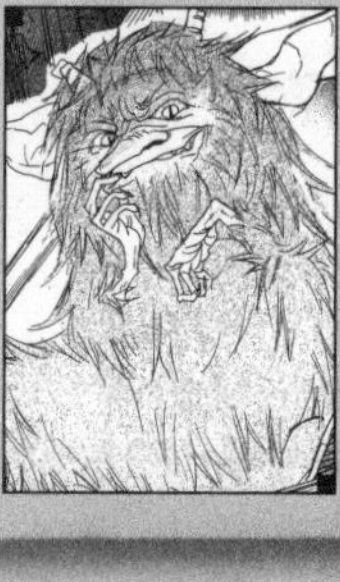

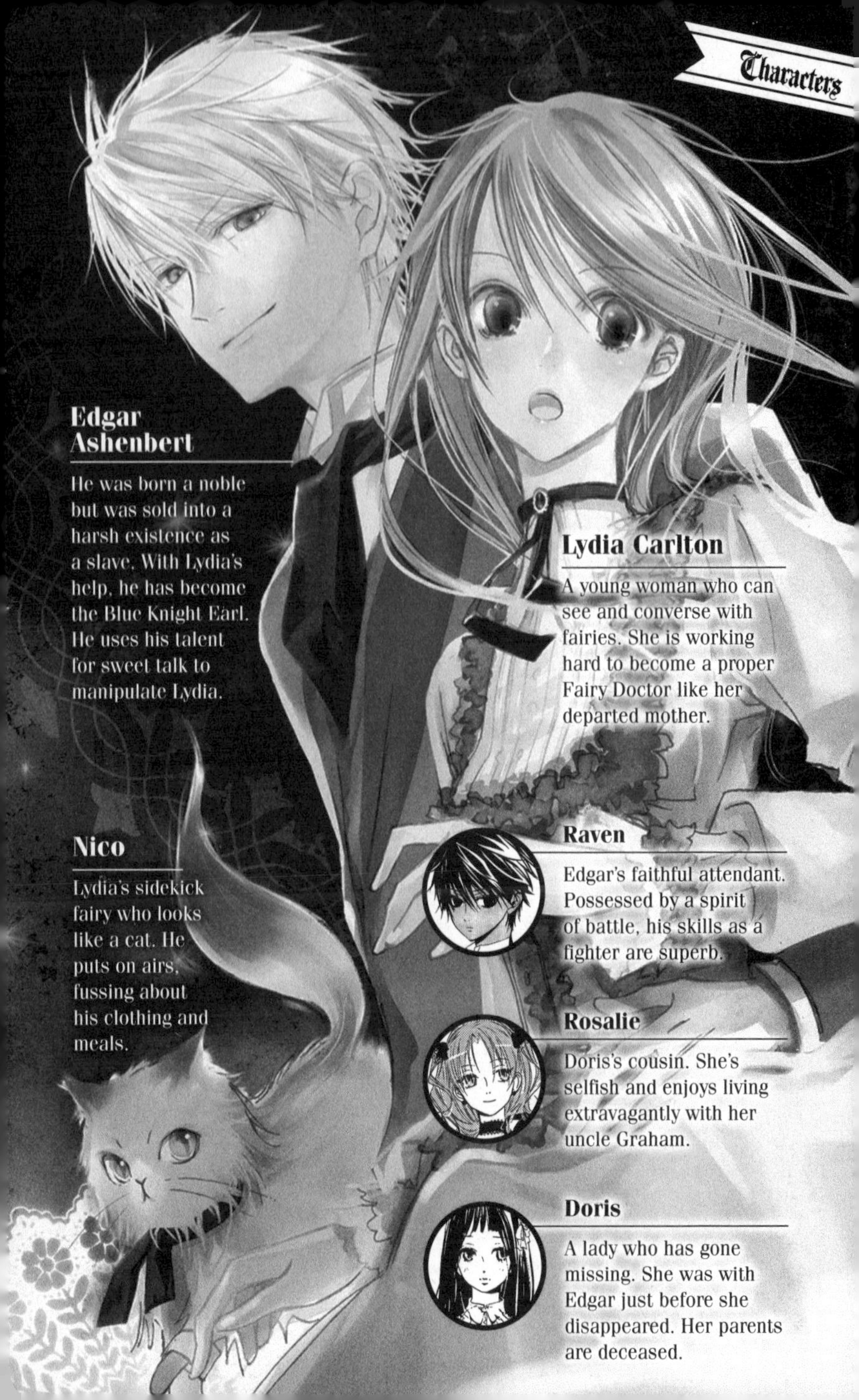

Characters

Edgar Ashenbert

He was born a noble but was sold into a harsh existence as a slave. With Lydia's help, he has become the Blue Knight Earl. He uses his talent for sweet talk to manipulate Lydia.

Lydia Carlton

A young woman who can see and converse with fairies. She is working hard to become a proper Fairy Doctor like her departed mother.

Nico

Lydia's sidekick fairy who looks like a cat. He puts on airs, fussing about his clothing and meals.

Raven

Edgar's faithful attendant. Possessed by a spirit of battle, his skills as a fighter are superb.

Rosalie

Doris's cousin. She's selfish and enjoys living extravagantly with her uncle Graham.

Doris

A lady who has gone missing. She was with Edgar just before she disappeared. Her parents are deceased.

The Earl & the Fairy

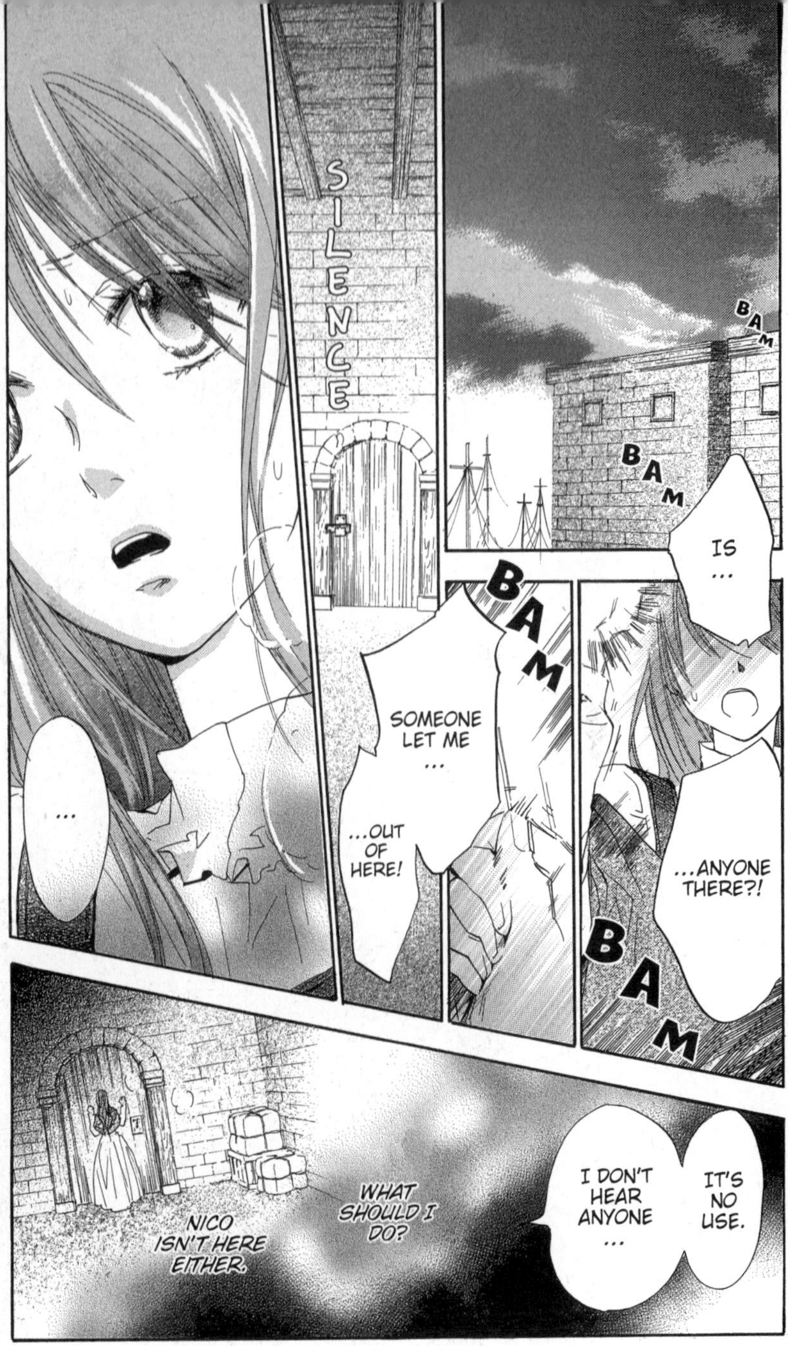
BAM
BAM
IS ...
...ANYONE THERE?!
BAM
BAM
SOMEONE LET ME ...
...OUT OF HERE!
SILENCE
...
IT'S NO USE.
I DON'T HEAR ANYONE ...
WHAT SHOULD I DO?
NICO ISN'T HERE EITHER.

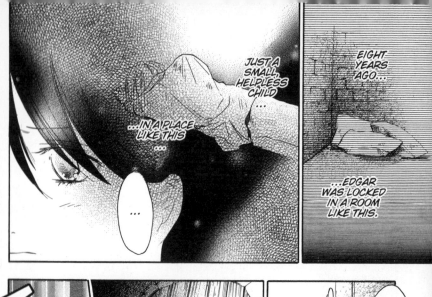

EIGHT YEARS AGO...

...EDGAR WAS LOCKED IN A ROOM LIKE THIS.

JUST A SMALL, HELPLESS CHILD...

...IN A PLACE LIKE THIS...

...

TIME FOR...

...DRASTIC ACTION.

UNGH!

WHAM

EEK!

HUH?

THUD

KRACK

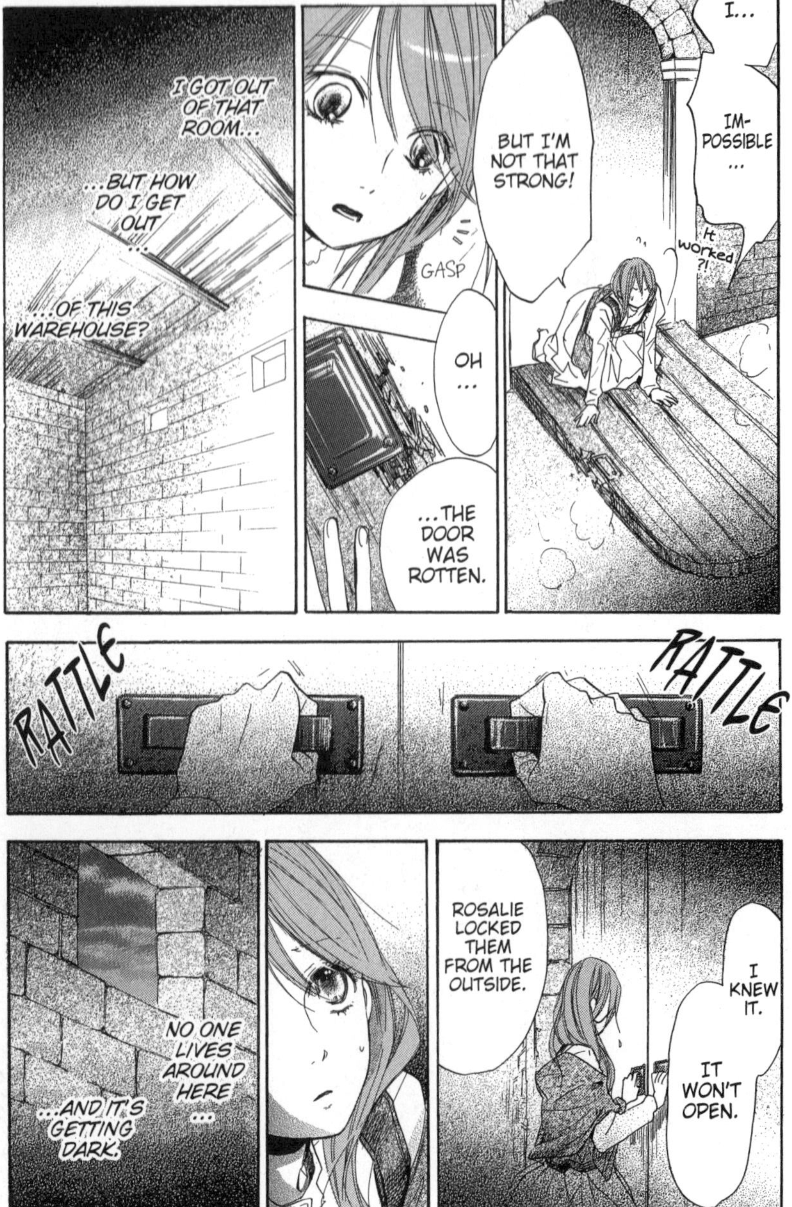
I...
IM-POSSIBLE...
It worked?!
BUT I'M NOT THAT STRONG!
GASP
OH...
...THE DOOR WAS ROTTEN.
I GOT OUT OF THAT ROOM...
...BUT HOW DO I GET OUT...
...OF THIS WAREHOUSE?
RATTLE
RATTLE
I KNEW IT.
IT WON'T OPEN.
ROSALIE LOCKED THEM FROM THE OUTSIDE.
NO ONE LIVES AROUND HERE...
...AND IT'S GETTING DARK.

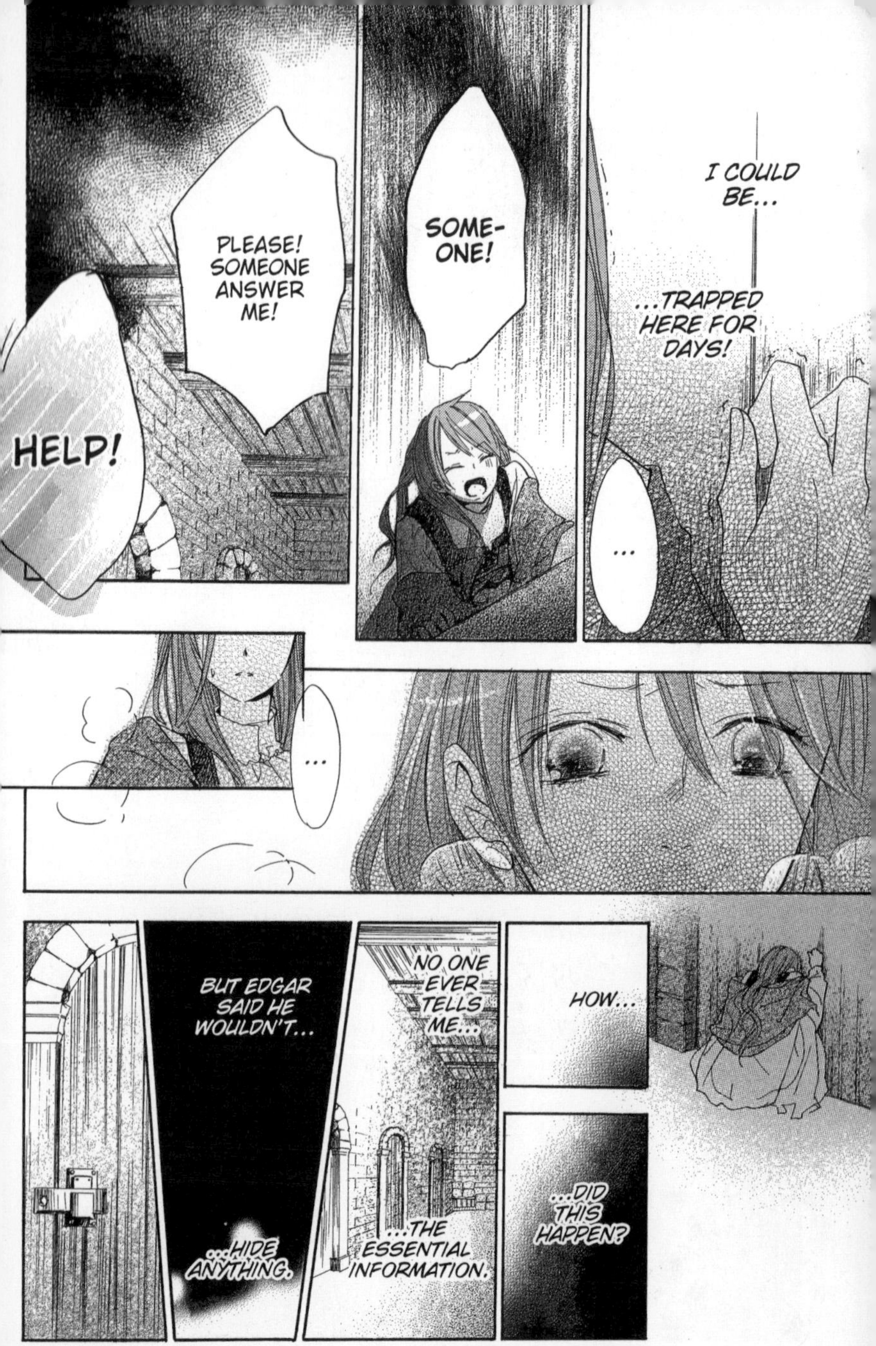
I COULD BE...
...TRAPPED HERE FOR DAYS!
...
SOME-ONE!
PLEASE! SOMEONE ANSWER ME!
HELP!
...
HOW...
...DID THIS HAPPEN?
NO ONE EVER TELLS ME...
...THE ESSENTIAL INFORMATION.
BUT EDGAR SAID HE WOULDN'T...
...HIDE ANYTHING.

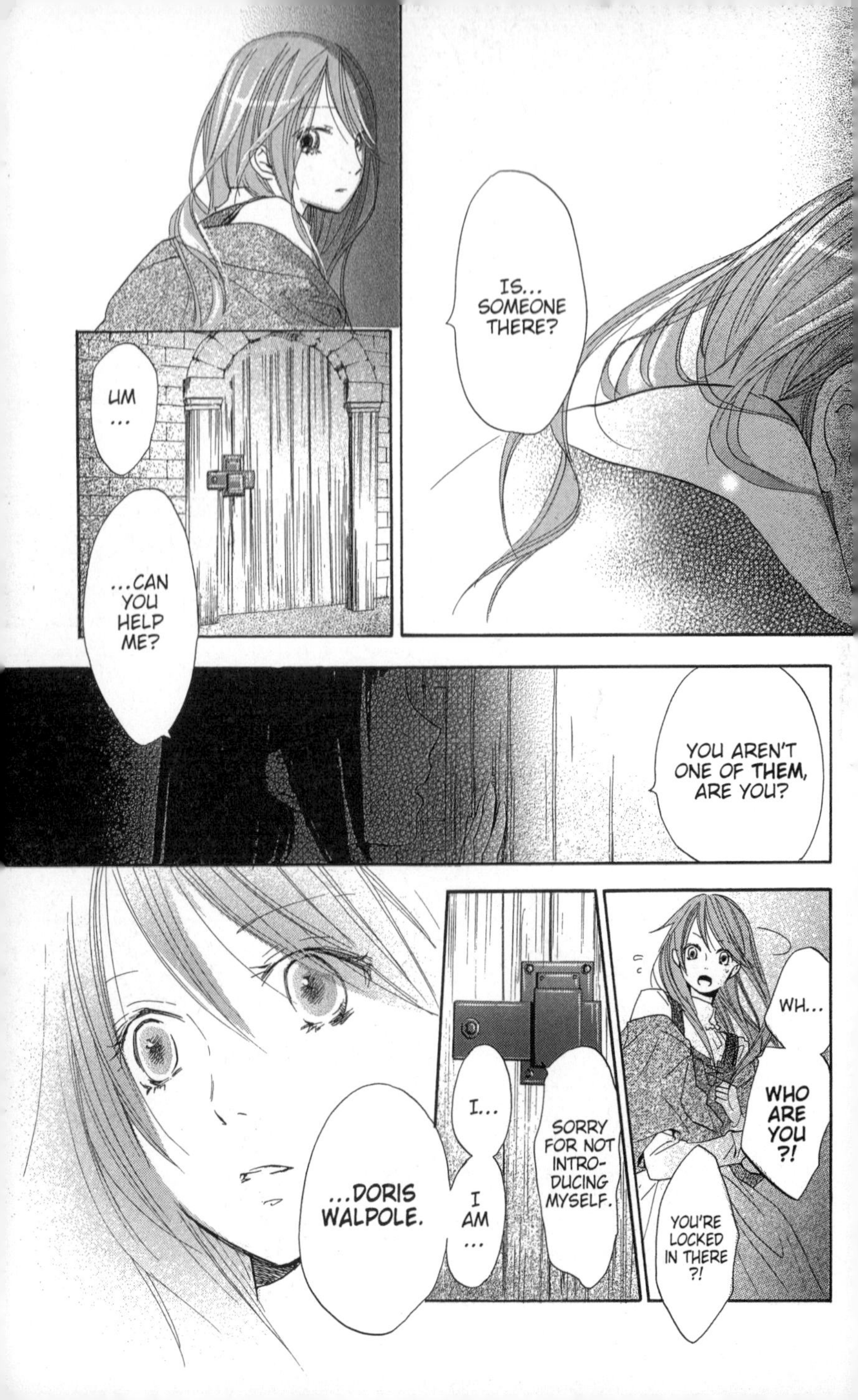
IS... SOMEONE THERE?
UM ...
...CAN YOU HELP ME?
YOU AREN'T ONE OF THEM, ARE YOU?
WH...
WHO ARE YOU?!
YOU'RE LOCKED IN THERE?!
SORRY FOR NOT INTRO-DUCING MYSELF.
I...
I AM ...
...DORIS WALPOLE.

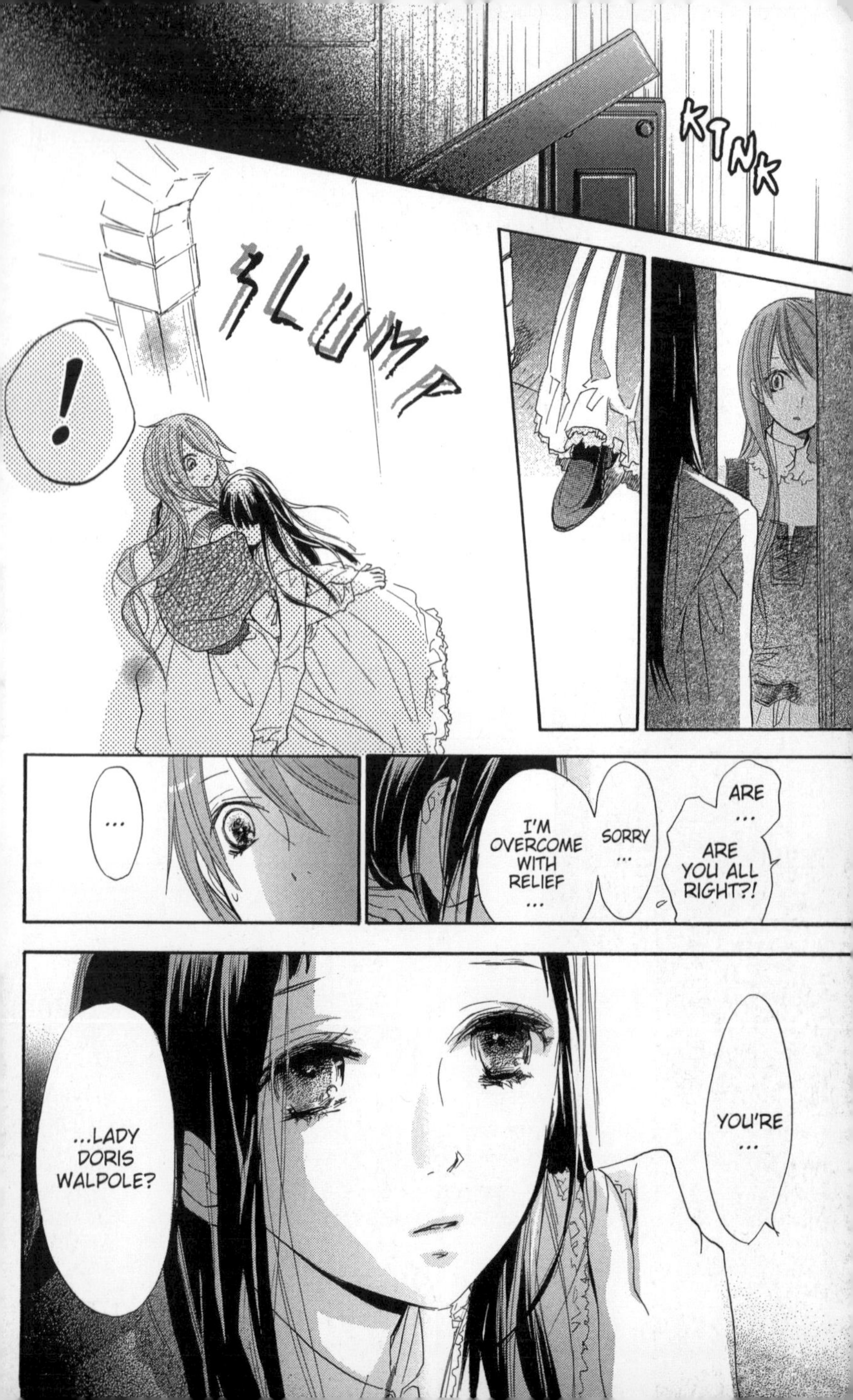
KINK
SLUMP
!
ARE... ARE YOU ALL RIGHT?!
SORRY...
I'M OVERCOME WITH RELIEF...
...
YOU'RE...
...LADY DORIS WALPOLE?

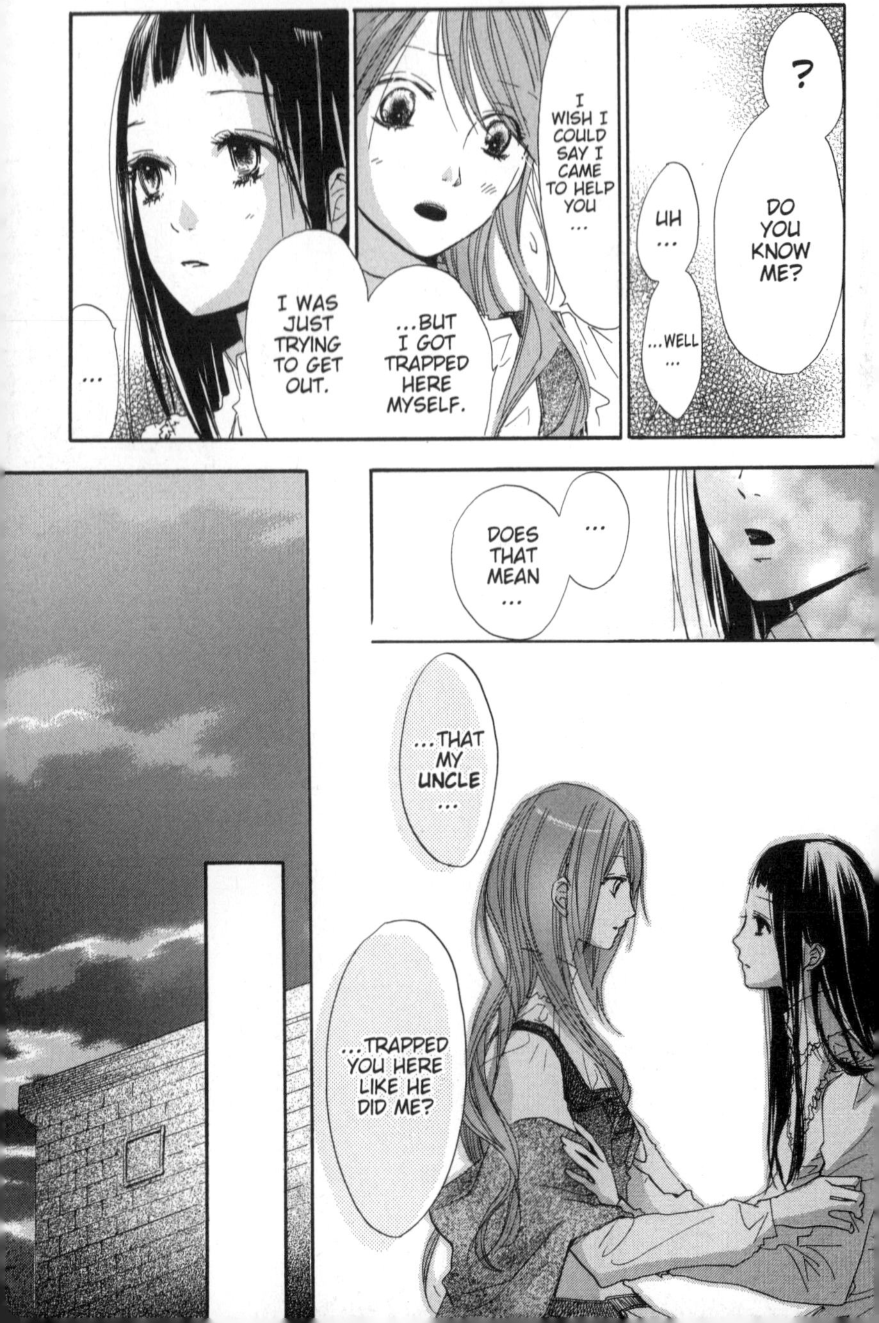
?
DO YOU KNOW ME?
UH...
...WELL...
I WISH I COULD SAY I CAME TO HELP YOU...
I WAS JUST TRYING TO GET OUT.
...BUT I GOT TRAPPED HERE MYSELF.
...
...
DOES THAT MEAN...
...THAT MY UNCLE...
...TRAPPED YOU HERE LIKE HE DID ME?

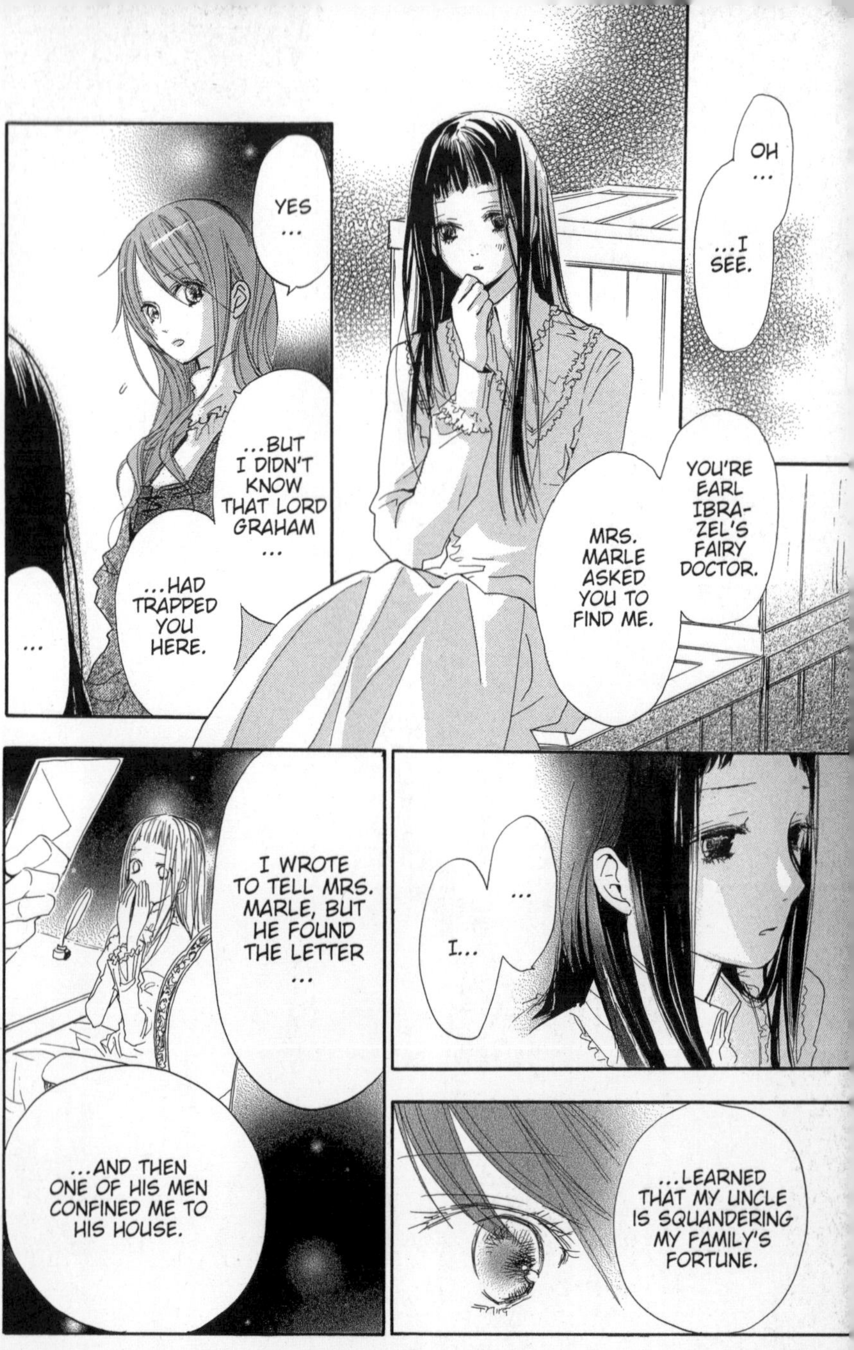
OH ... ...I SEE.
YOU'RE EARL IBRAZEL'S FAIRY DOCTOR.
MRS. MARLE ASKED YOU TO FIND ME.
YES ...
...BUT I DIDN'T KNOW THAT LORD GRAHAM ...
...HAD TRAPPED YOU HERE.
...
... I...
...LEARNED THAT MY UNCLE IS SQUANDERING MY FAMILY'S FORTUNE.
I WROTE TO TELL MRS. MARLE, BUT HE FOUND THE LETTER ...
...AND THEN ONE OF HIS MEN CONFINED ME TO HIS HOUSE.

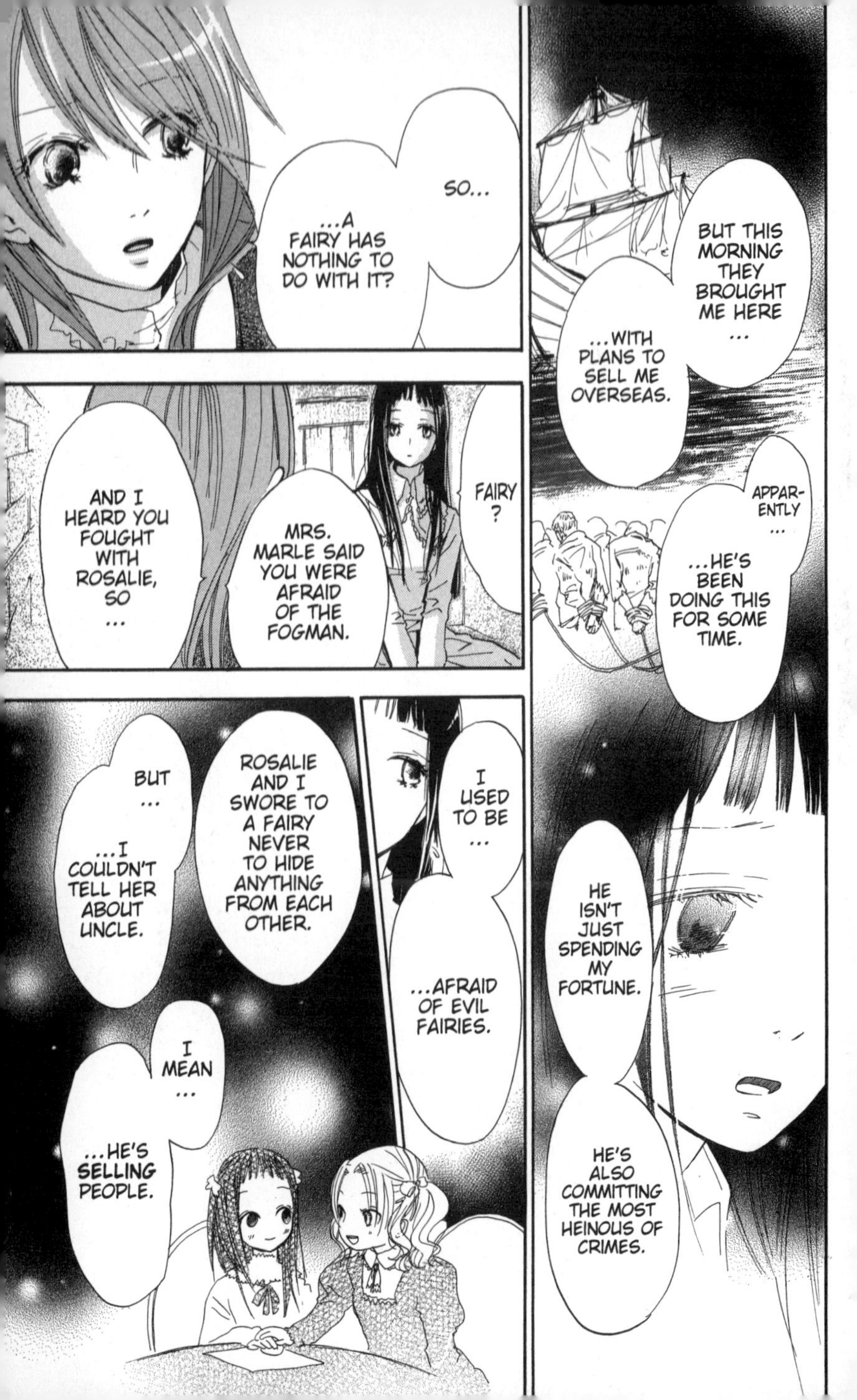
BUT THIS MORNING THEY BROUGHT ME HERE ...
...WITH PLANS TO SELL ME OVERSEAS.
APPAR-ENTLY ...
...HE'S BEEN DOING THIS FOR SOME TIME.
HE ISN'T JUST SPENDING MY FORTUNE.
HE'S ALSO COMMITTING THE MOST HEINOUS OF CRIMES.
SO...
...A FAIRY HAS NOTHING TO DO WITH IT?
FAIRY ?
MRS. MARLE SAID YOU WERE AFRAID OF THE FOGMAN.
AND I HEARD YOU FOUGHT WITH ROSALIE, SO ...
I USED TO BE ...
...AFRAID OF EVIL FAIRIES.
ROSALIE AND I SWORE TO A FAIRY NEVER TO HIDE ANYTHING FROM EACH OTHER.
BUT ...
...I COULDN'T TELL HER ABOUT UNCLE.
I MEAN ...
...HE'S SELLING PEOPLE.

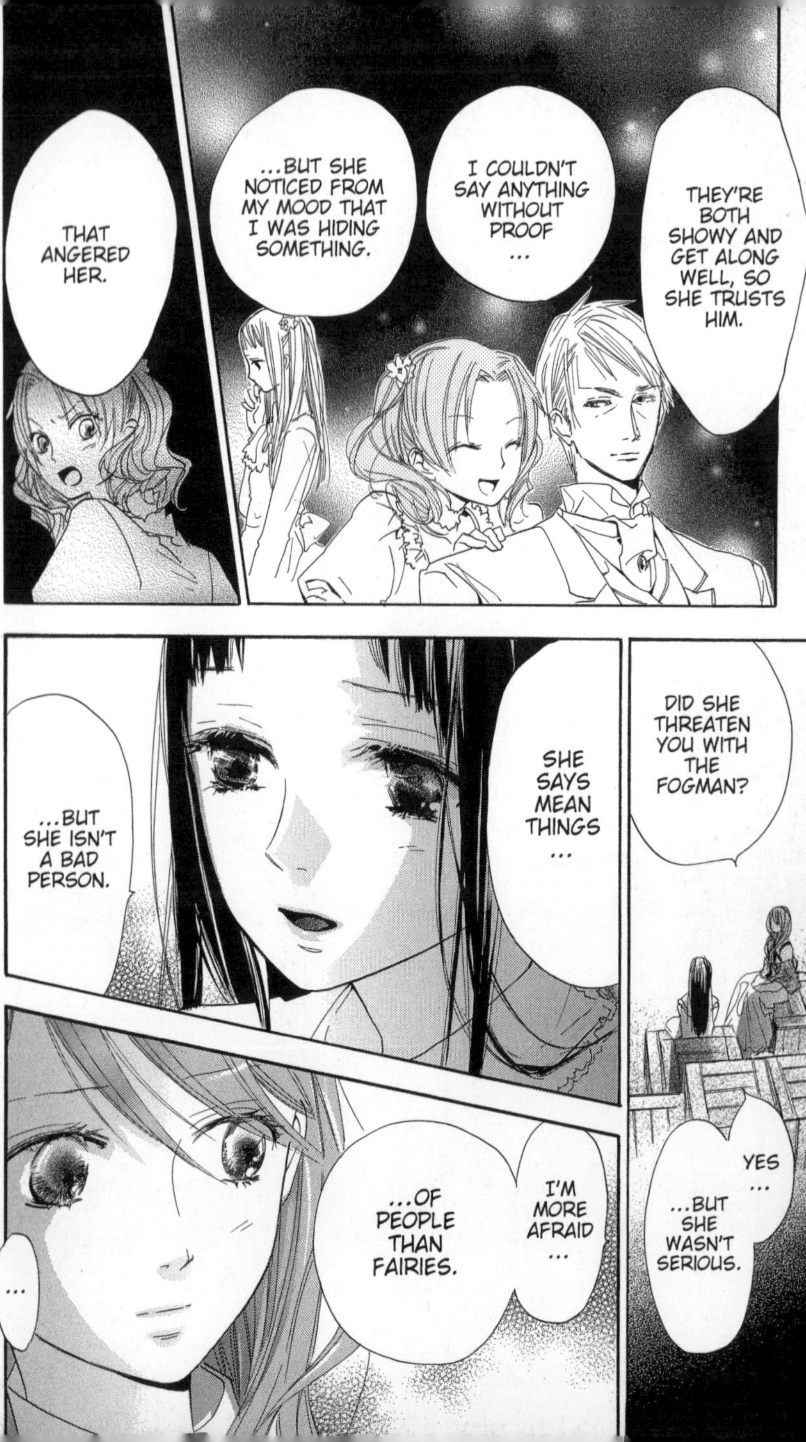
THEY'RE BOTH SHOWY AND GET ALONG WELL, SO SHE TRUSTS HIM.
I COULDN'T SAY ANYTHING WITHOUT PROOF...
...BUT SHE NOTICED FROM MY MOOD THAT I WAS HIDING SOMETHING.
THAT ANGERED HER.
DID SHE THREATEN YOU WITH THE FOGMAN?
YES...
...BUT SHE WASN'T SERIOUS.
SHE SAYS MEAN THINGS...
...BUT SHE ISN'T A BAD PERSON.
I'M MORE AFRAID...
...OF PEOPLE THAN FAIRIES.
...

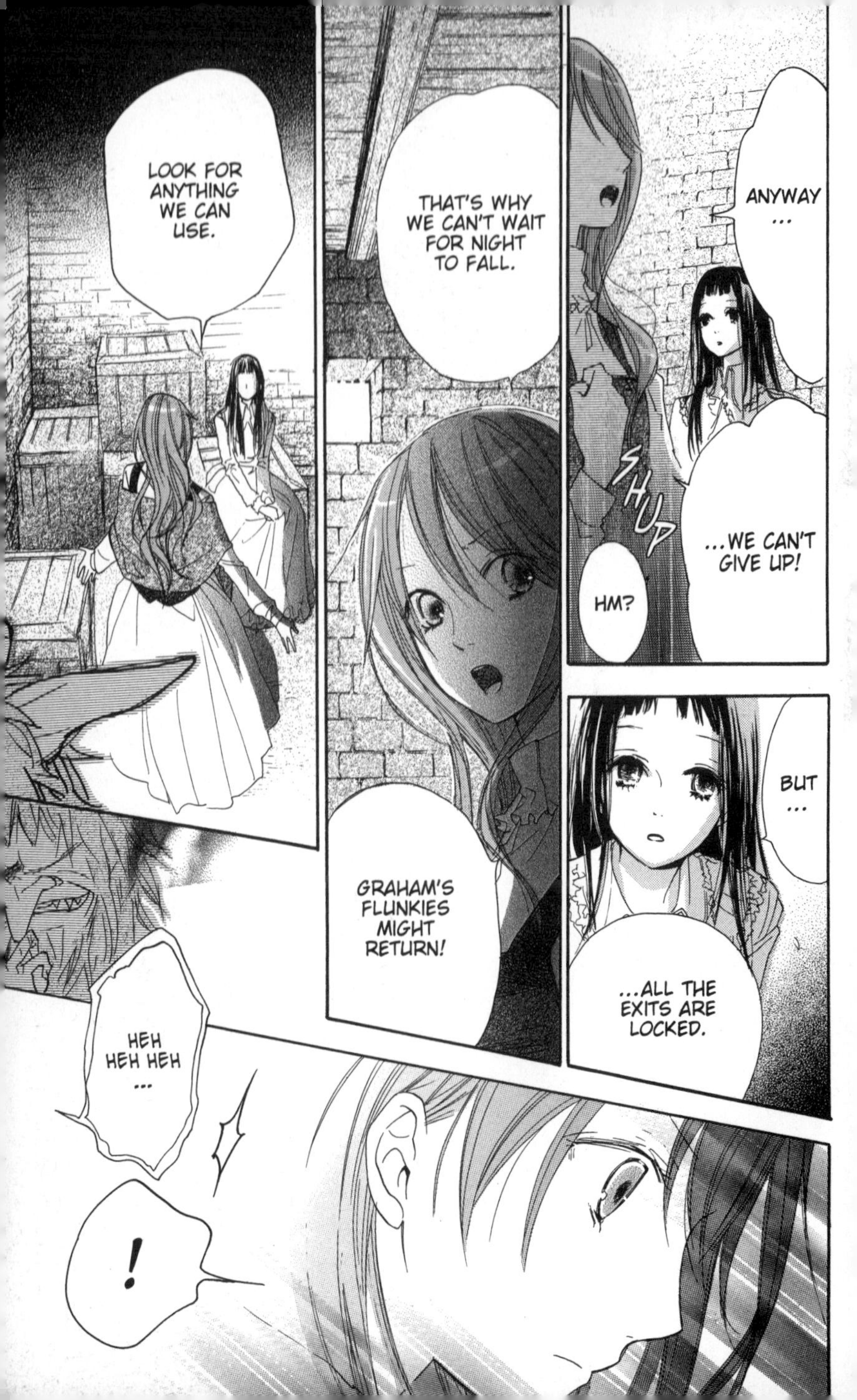
ANYWAY...
SHUP
...WE CAN'T GIVE UP!
HM?
BUT...
...ALL THE EXITS ARE LOCKED.
THAT'S WHY WE CAN'T WAIT FOR NIGHT TO FALL.
GRAHAM'S FLUNKIES MIGHT RETURN!
LOOK FOR ANYTHING WE CAN USE.
HEH HEH HEH...
!

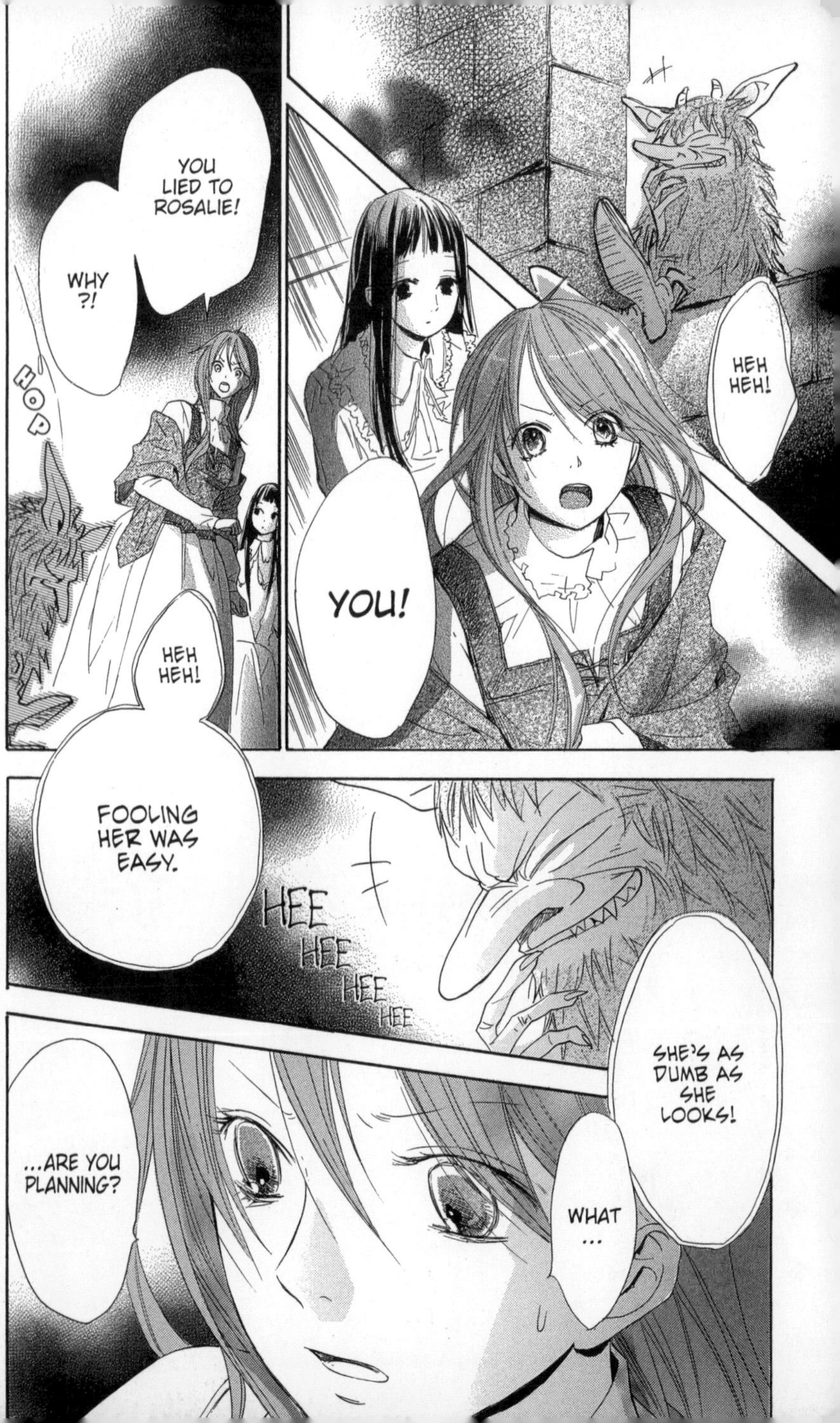
HEH HEH!
YOU!
YOU LIED TO ROSALIE!
WHY?!
HOP
HEH HEH!
FOOLING HER WAS EASY.
HEE HEE HEE HEE
SHE'S AS DUMB AS SHE LOOKS!
WHAT ...
...ARE YOU PLANNING?

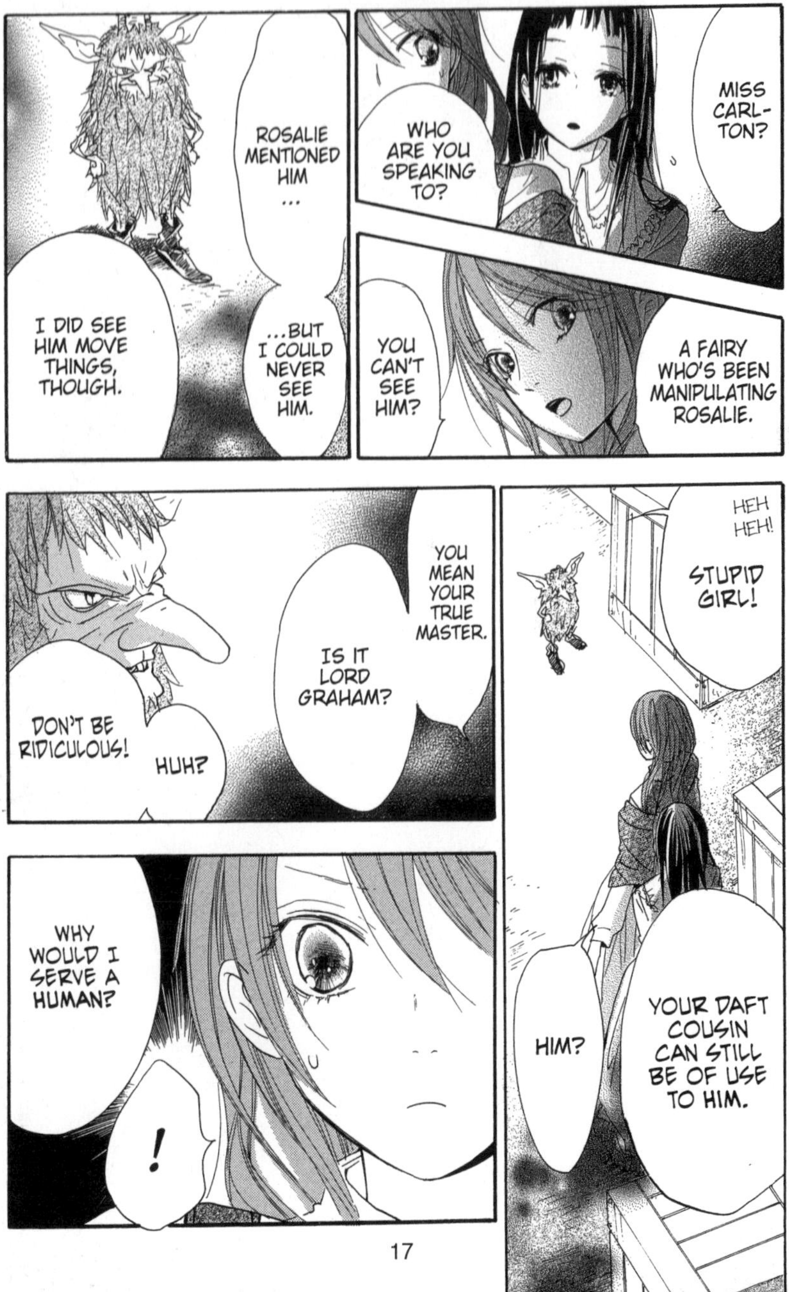
MISS CARL-TON?
WHO ARE YOU SPEAKING TO?
A FAIRY WHO'S BEEN MANIPULATING ROSALIE.
YOU CAN'T SEE HIM?
ROSALIE MENTIONED HIM ...
...BUT I COULD NEVER SEE HIM.
I DID SEE HIM MOVE THINGS, THOUGH.
HEH HEH!
STUPID GIRL!
YOUR DAFT COUSIN CAN STILL BE OF USE TO HIM.
HIM?
YOU MEAN YOUR TRUE MASTER.
IS IT LORD GRAHAM?
HUH?
DON'T BE RIDICULOUS!
WHY WOULD I SERVE A HUMAN?
!

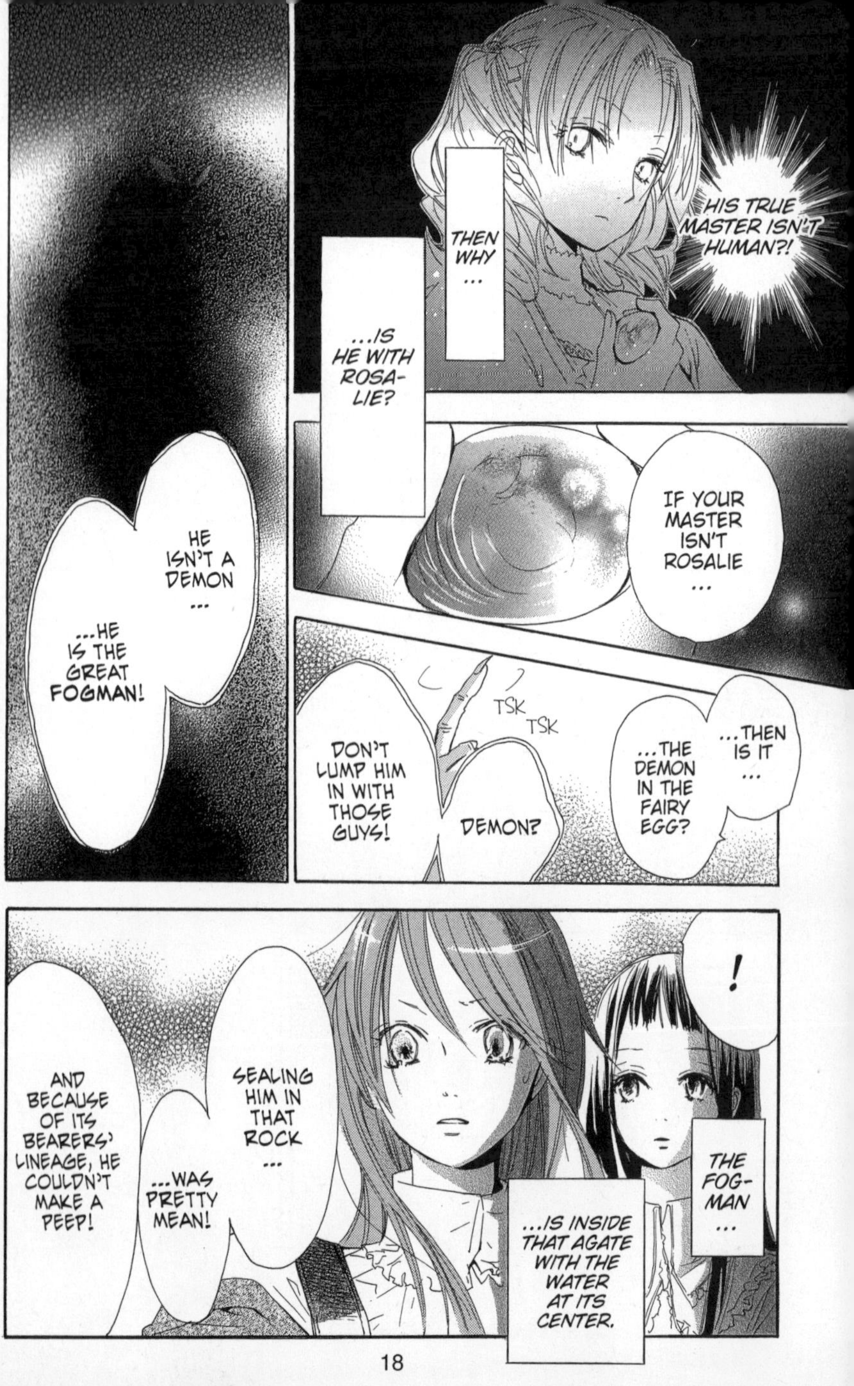
HIS TRUE MASTER ISN'T HUMAN?!
THEN WHY...
...IS HE WITH ROSA-LIE?
IF YOUR MASTER ISN'T ROSALIE...
...THEN IS IT...
...THE DEMON IN THE FAIRY EGG?
TSK TSK
DEMON?
DON'T LUMP HIM IN WITH THOSE GUYS!
HE ISN'T A DEMON...
...HE IS THE GREAT FOGMAN!
!
THE FOG-MAN...
...IS INSIDE THAT AGATE WITH THE WATER AT ITS CENTER.
SEALING HIM IN THAT ROCK...
...WAS PRETTY MEAN!
AND BECAUSE OF ITS BEARERS' LINEAGE, HE COULDN'T MAKE A PEEP!

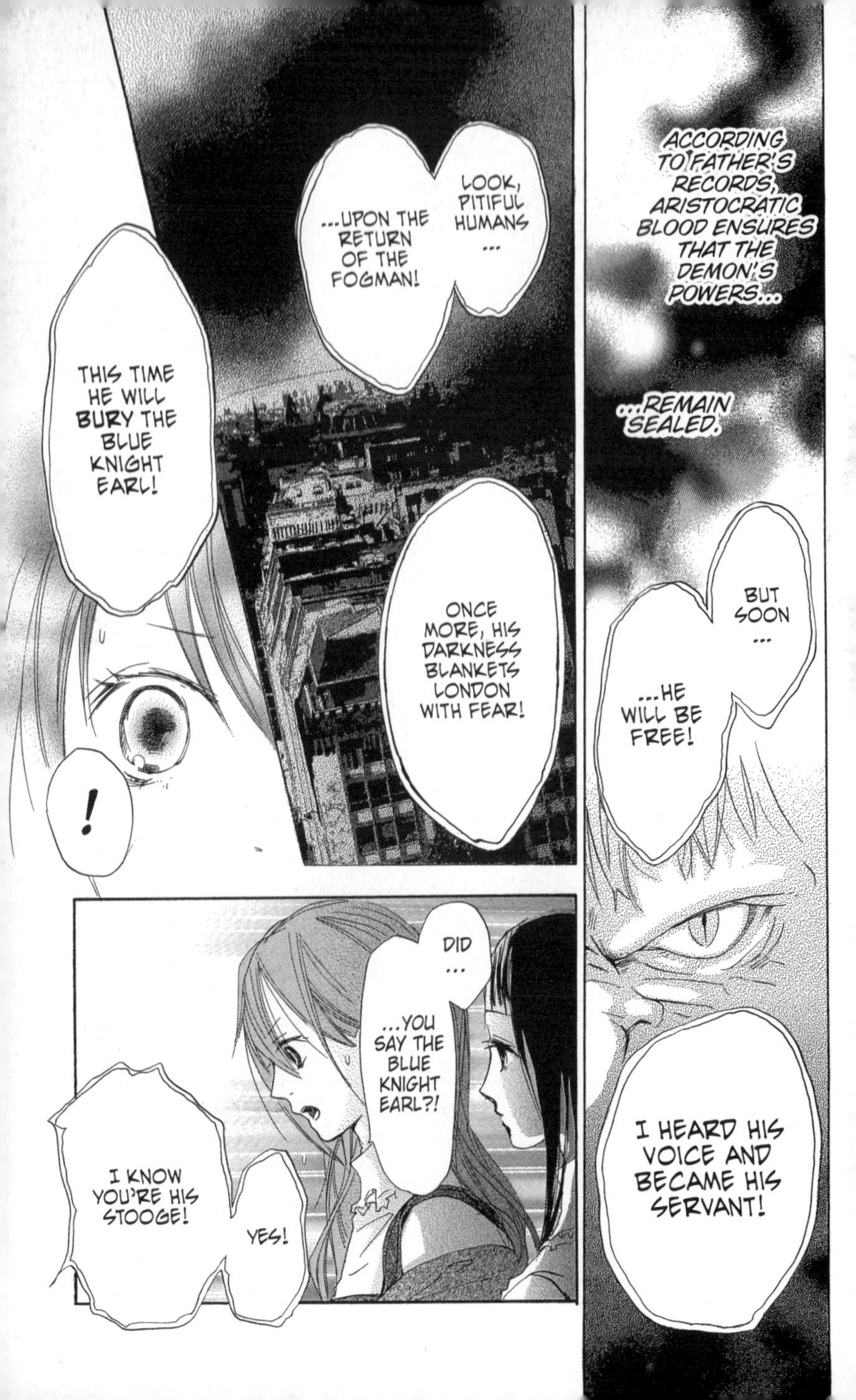
ACCORDING TO FATHER'S RECORDS, ARISTOCRATIC BLOOD ENSURES THAT THE DEMON'S POWERS...
...REMAIN SEALED.
BUT SOON...
...HE WILL BE FREE!
I HEARD HIS VOICE AND BECAME HIS SERVANT!
LOOK, PITIFUL HUMANS...
...UPON THE RETURN OF THE FOGMAN!
ONCE MORE, HIS DARKNESS BLANKETS LONDON WITH FEAR!
THIS TIME HE WILL **BURY** THE BLUE KNIGHT EARL!
!
DID...
...YOU SAY THE BLUE KNIGHT EARL?!
YES!
I KNOW YOU'RE HIS STOOGE!

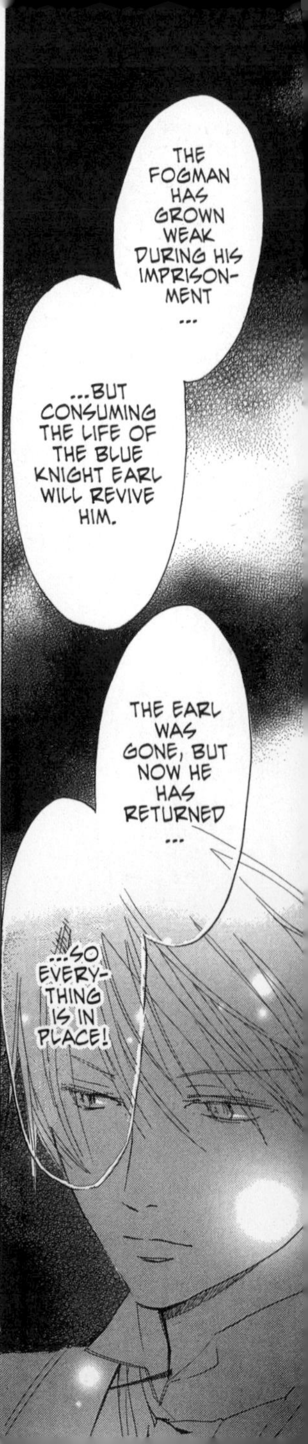
THE FOGMAN HAS GROWN WEAK DURING HIS IMPRISONMENT...
...BUT CONSUMING THE LIFE OF THE BLUE KNIGHT EARL WILL REVIVE HIM.
THE EARL WAS GONE, BUT NOW HE HAS RETURNED...
...SO EVERYTHING IS IN PLACE!

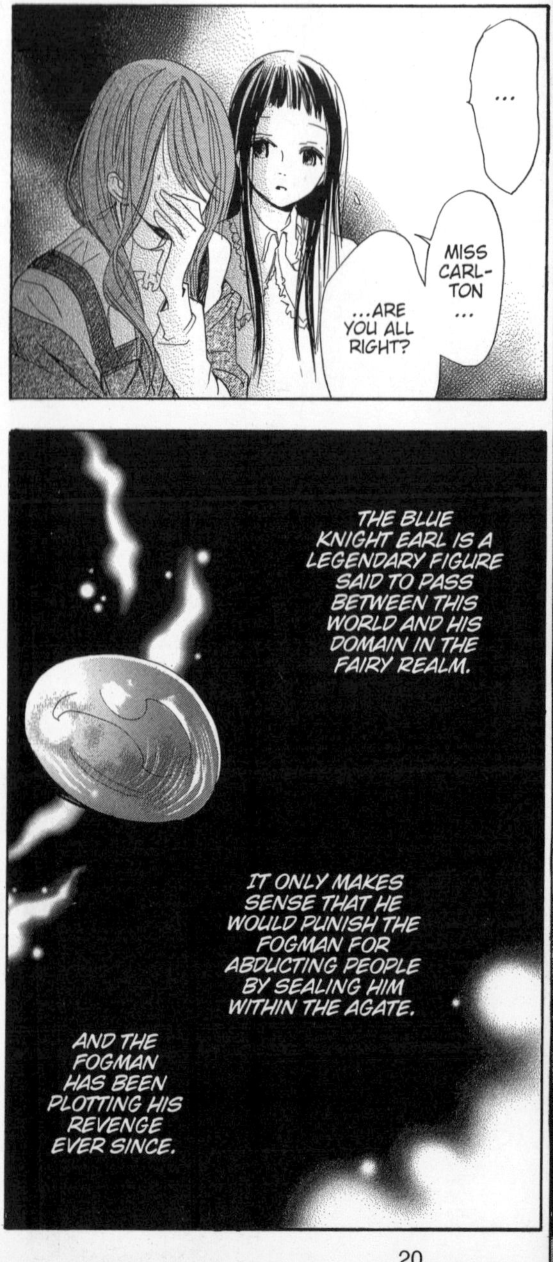
...
MISS CARLTON...
...ARE YOU ALL RIGHT?
THE BLUE KNIGHT EARL IS A LEGENDARY FIGURE SAID TO PASS BETWEEN THIS WORLD AND HIS DOMAIN IN THE FAIRY REALM.
IT ONLY MAKES SENSE THAT HE WOULD PUNISH THE FOGMAN FOR ABDUCTING PEOPLE BY SEALING HIM WITHIN THE AGATE.
AND THE FOGMAN HAS BEEN PLOTTING HIS REVENGE EVER SINCE.

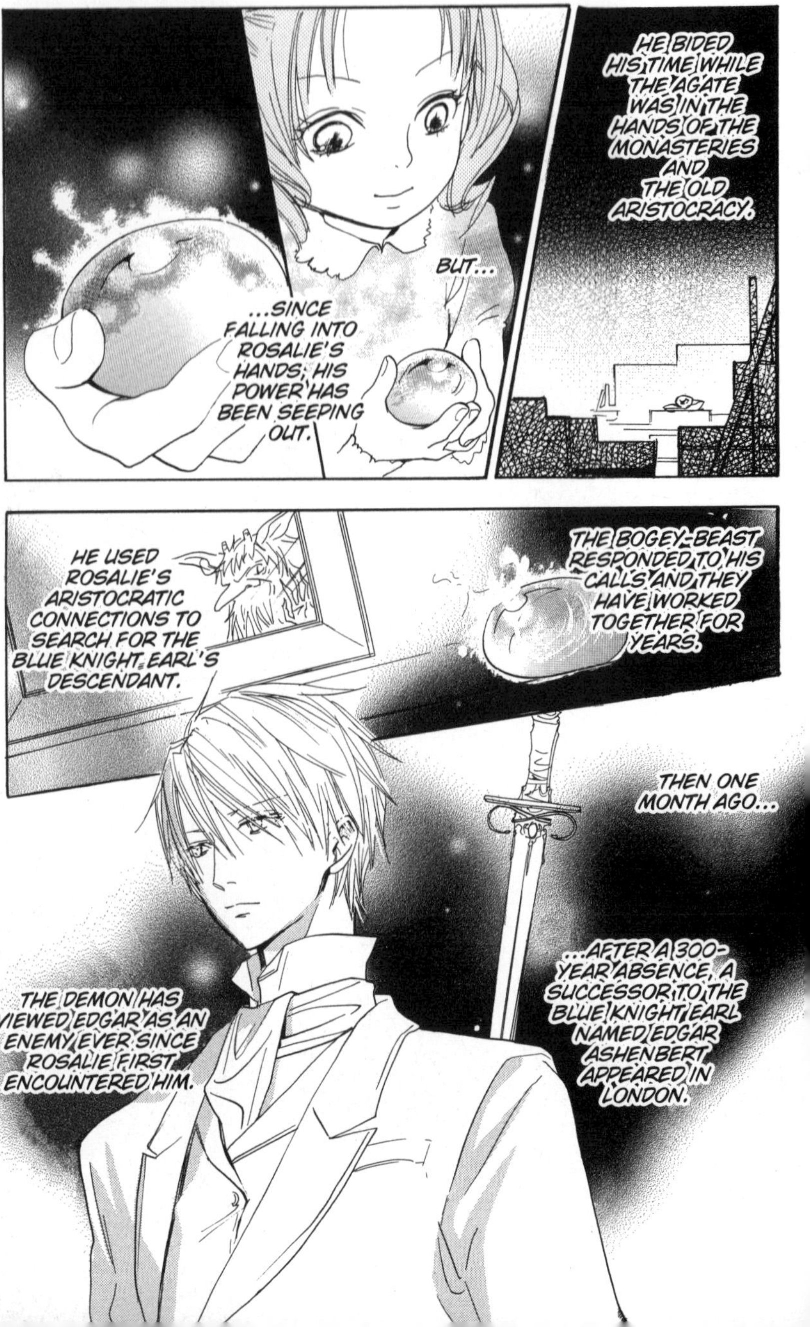
HE BIDED HIS TIME WHILE THE AGATE WAS IN THE HANDS OF THE MONASTERIES AND THE OLD ARISTOCRACY.
BUT...
...SINCE FALLING INTO ROSALIE'S HANDS, HIS POWER HAS BEEN SEEPING OUT.
THE BOGEY-BEAST RESPONDED TO HIS CALLS AND THEY HAVE WORKED TOGETHER FOR YEARS.
HE USED ROSALIE'S ARISTOCRATIC CONNECTIONS TO SEARCH FOR THE BLUE KNIGHT EARL'S DESCENDANT.
THEN ONE MONTH AGO...
...AFTER A 300-YEAR ABSENCE, A SUCCESSOR TO THE BLUE KNIGHT EARL NAMED EDGAR ASHENBERT APPEARED IN LONDON.
THE DEMON HAS VIEWED EDGAR AS AN ENEMY EVER SINCE ROSALIE FIRST ENCOUNTERED HIM.

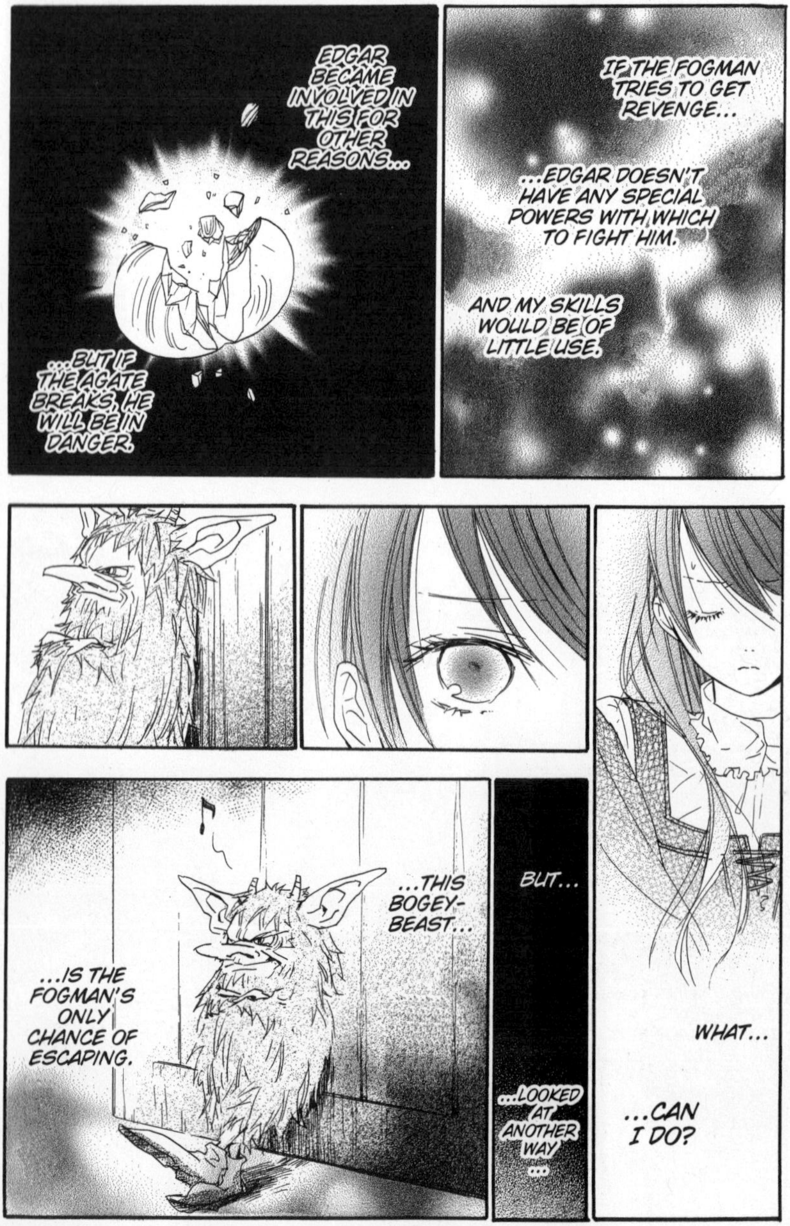
IF THE FOGMAN TRIES TO GET REVENGE...
...EDGAR DOESN'T HAVE ANY SPECIAL POWERS WITH WHICH TO FIGHT HIM.
AND MY SKILLS WOULD BE OF LITTLE USE.
EDGAR BECAME INVOLVED IN THIS FOR OTHER REASONS...
...BUT IF THE AGATE BREAKS, HE WILL BE IN DANGER.
WHAT...
...CAN I DO?
BUT...
...LOOKED AT ANOTHER WAY...
...THIS BOGEY-BEAST...
...IS THE FOGMAN'S ONLY CHANCE OF ESCAPING.

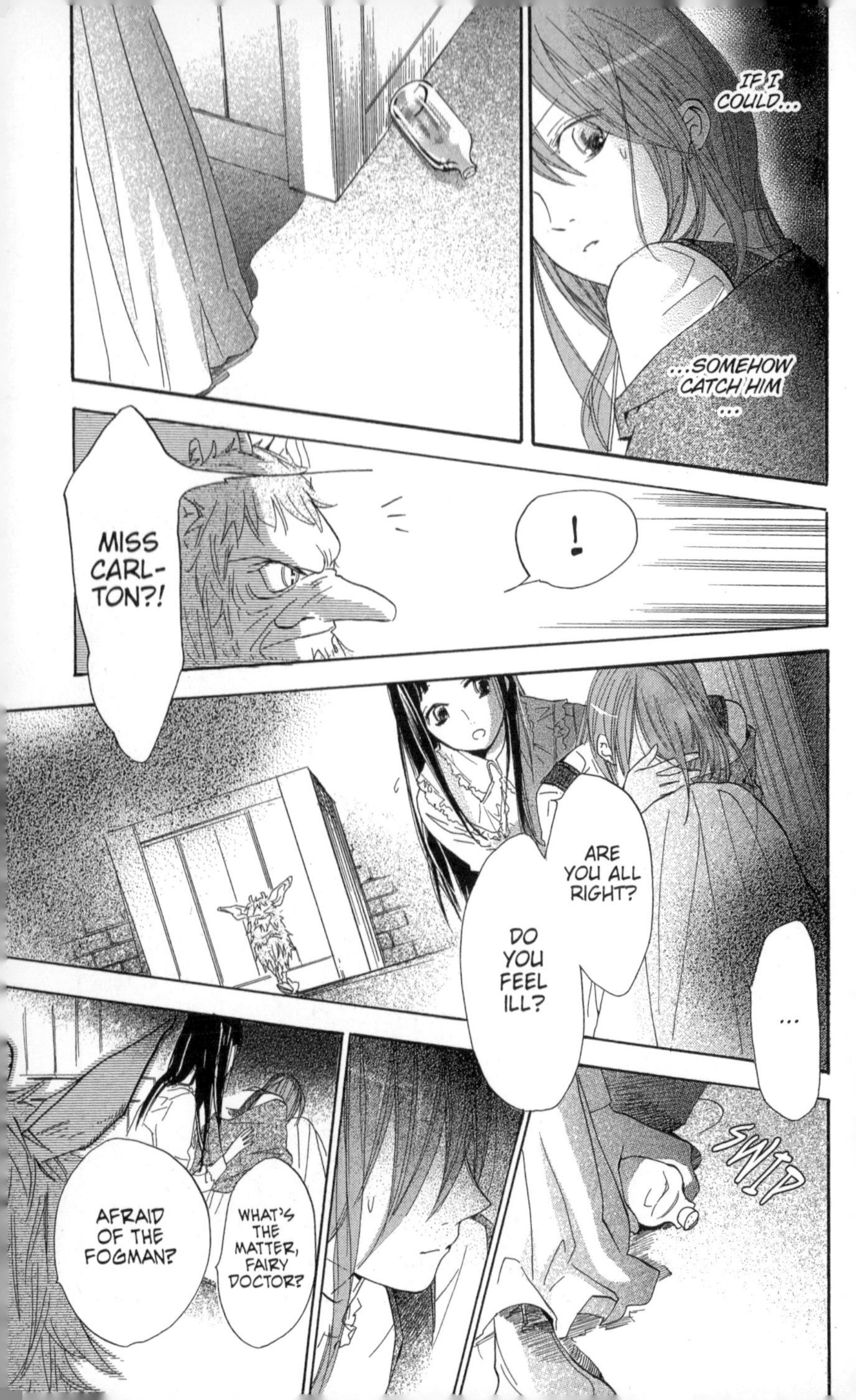
IF I COULD...
...SOMEHOW CATCH HIM ...
!
MISS CARL-TON?!
ARE YOU ALL RIGHT?
DO YOU FEEL ILL?
...
SWIP
WHAT'S THE MATTER, FAIRY DOCTOR?
AFRAID OF THE FOGMAN?

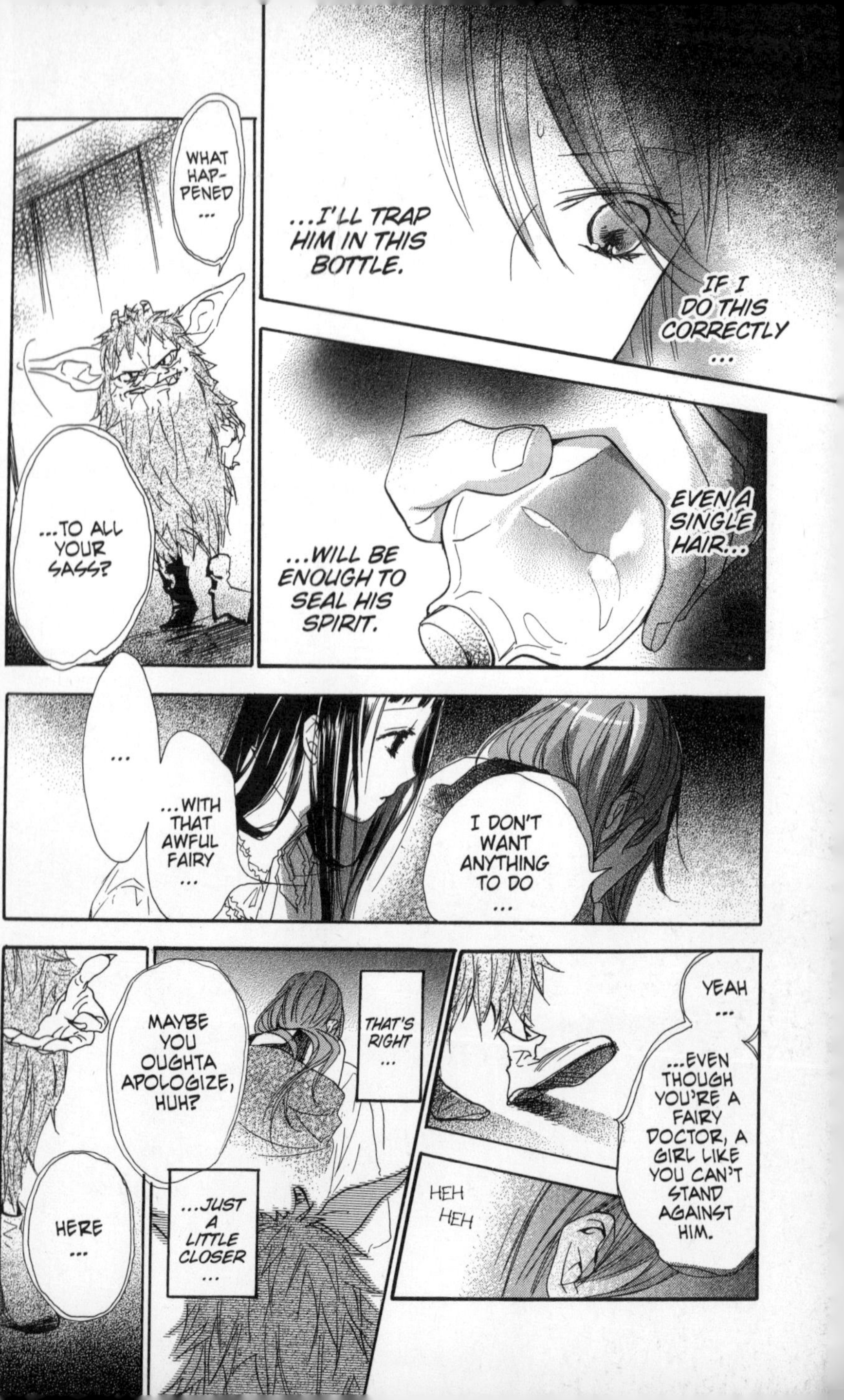
IF I DO THIS CORRECTLY...
...I'LL TRAP HIM IN THIS BOTTLE.
EVEN A SINGLE HAIR...
...WILL BE ENOUGH TO SEAL HIS SPIRIT.
WHAT HAP-PENED...
...TO ALL YOUR SASS?
I DON'T WANT ANYTHING TO DO...
...WITH THAT AWFUL FAIRY...
...
YEAH...
...EVEN THOUGH YOU'RE A FAIRY DOCTOR, A GIRL LIKE YOU CAN'T STAND AGAINST HIM.
HEH HEH
THAT'S RIGHT...
...JUST A LITTLE CLOSER...
MAYBE YOU OUGHTA APOLOGIZE, HUH?
HERE...

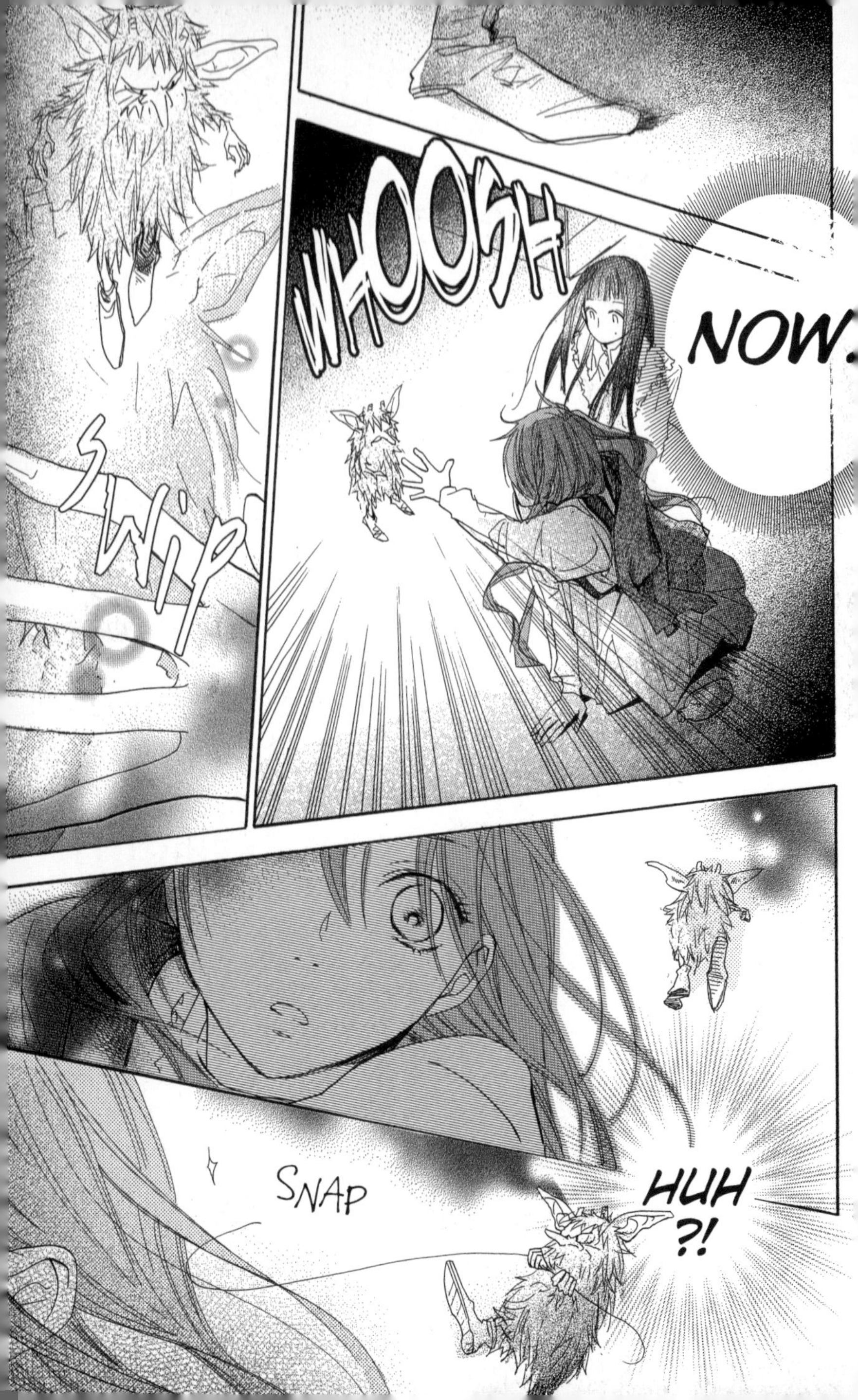
NOW.
WHOOSH
SWIP
HUH ?!
SNAP

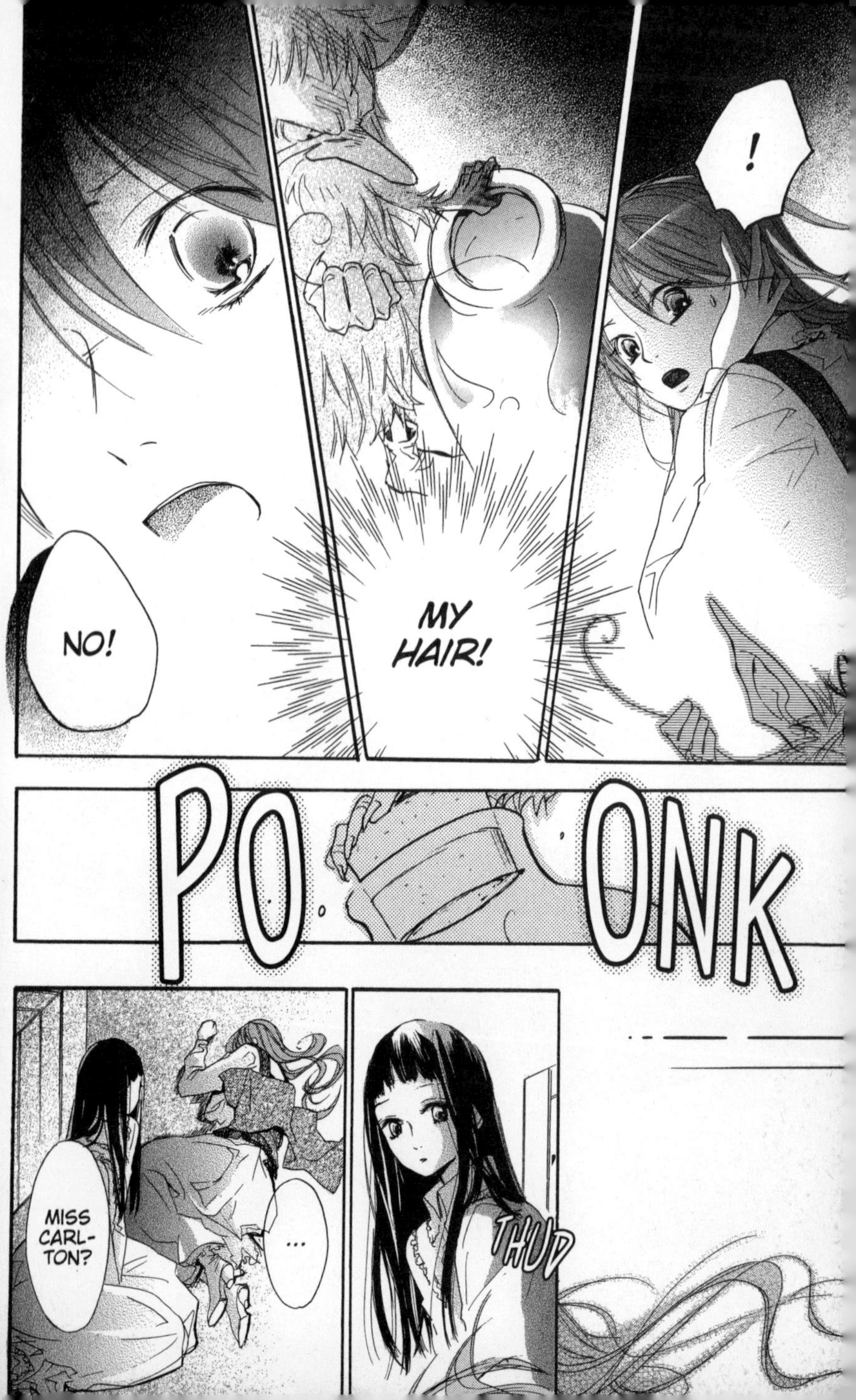
!
MY HAIR!
NO!
PO ONK
THUD
...
MISS CARL-TON?

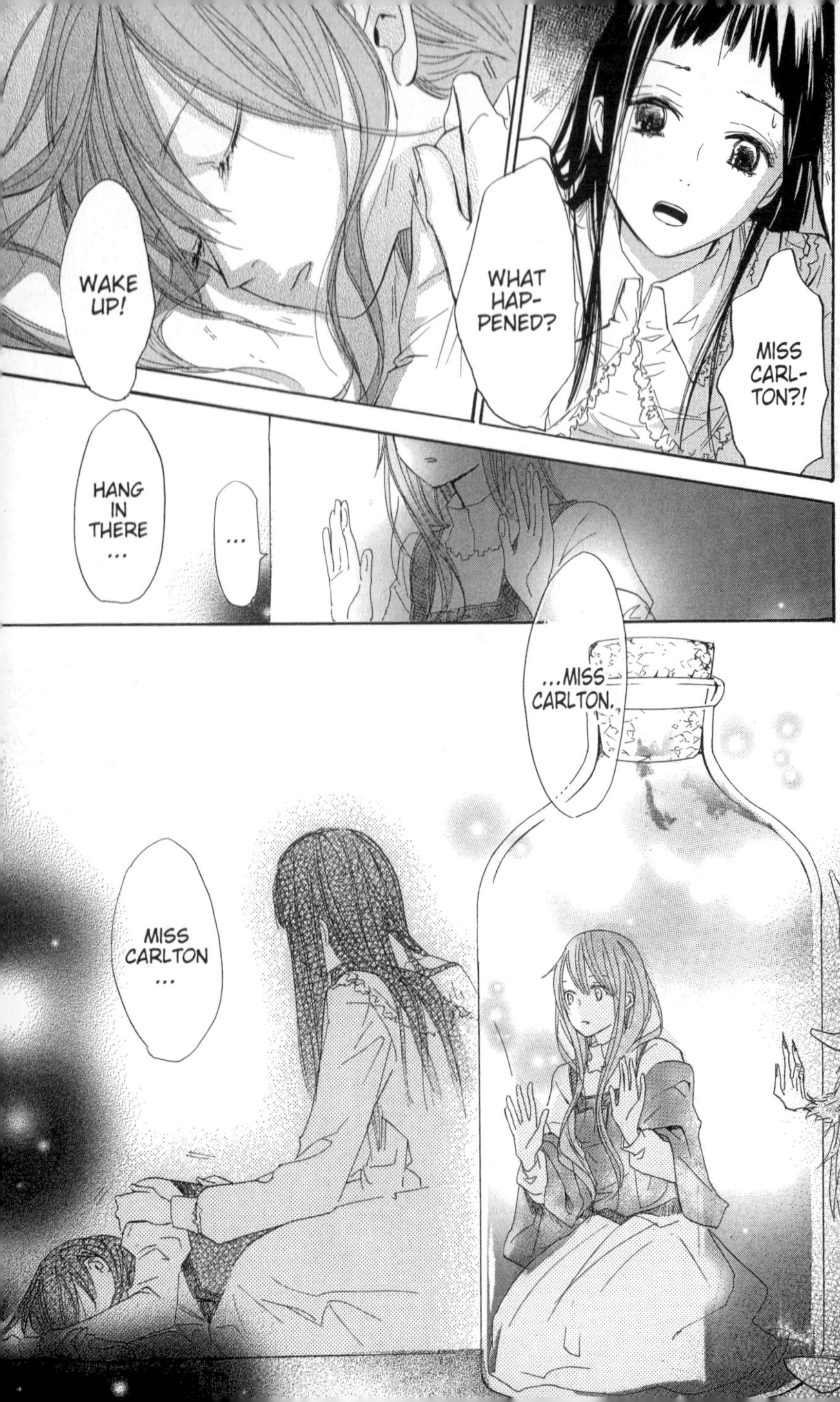
MISS CARL-TON?!
WHAT HAP-PENED?
WAKE UP!
...
HANG IN THERE ...
...MISS CARLTON.
MISS CARLTON ...

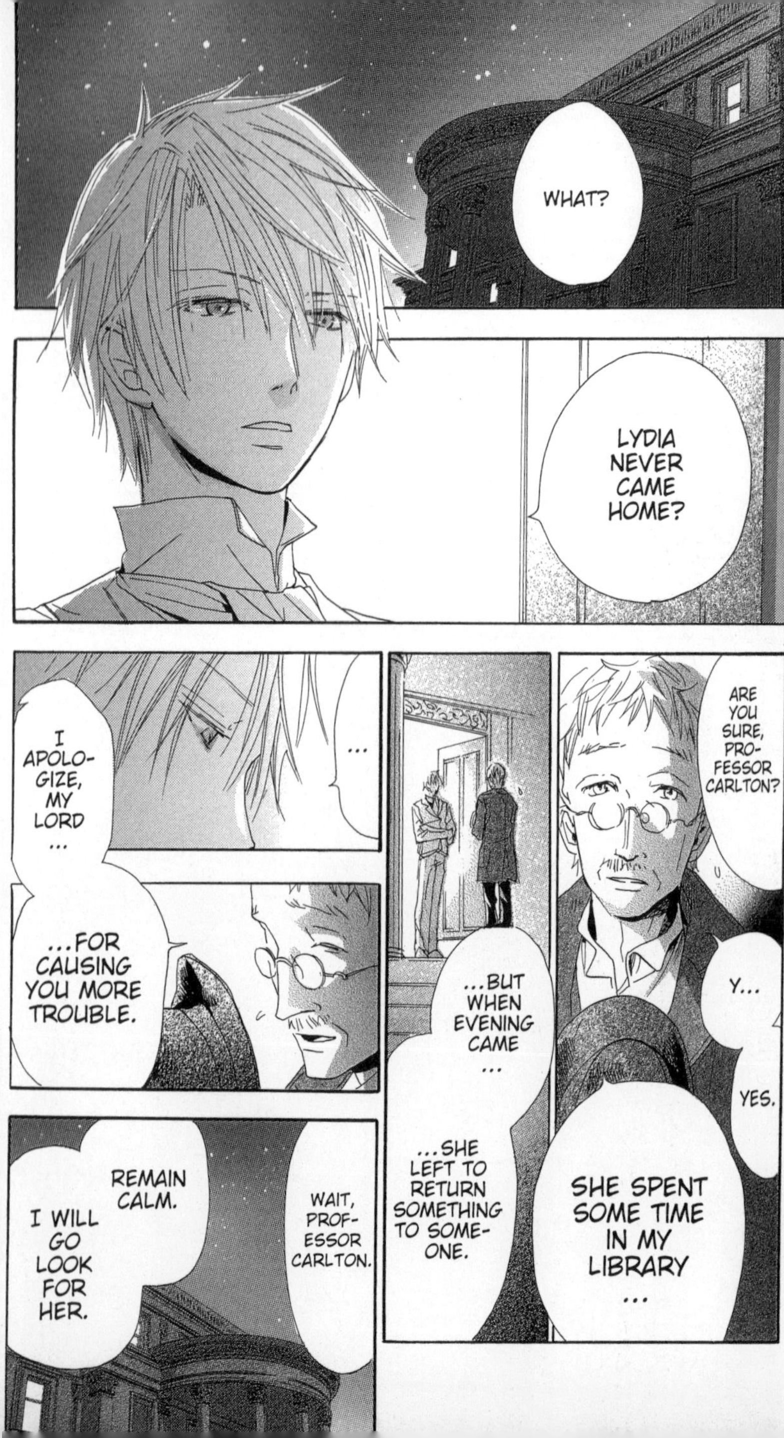
WHAT?
LYDIA NEVER CAME HOME?
ARE YOU SURE, PRO-FESSOR CARLTON?
Y...
YES.
SHE SPENT SOME TIME IN MY LIBRARY...
...BUT WHEN EVENING CAME...
...SHE LEFT TO RETURN SOMETHING TO SOME-ONE.
...
I APOLO-GIZE, MY LORD...
...FOR CAUSING YOU MORE TROUBLE.
WAIT, PROF-ESSOR CARLTON.
REMAIN CALM.
I WILL GO LOOK FOR HER.

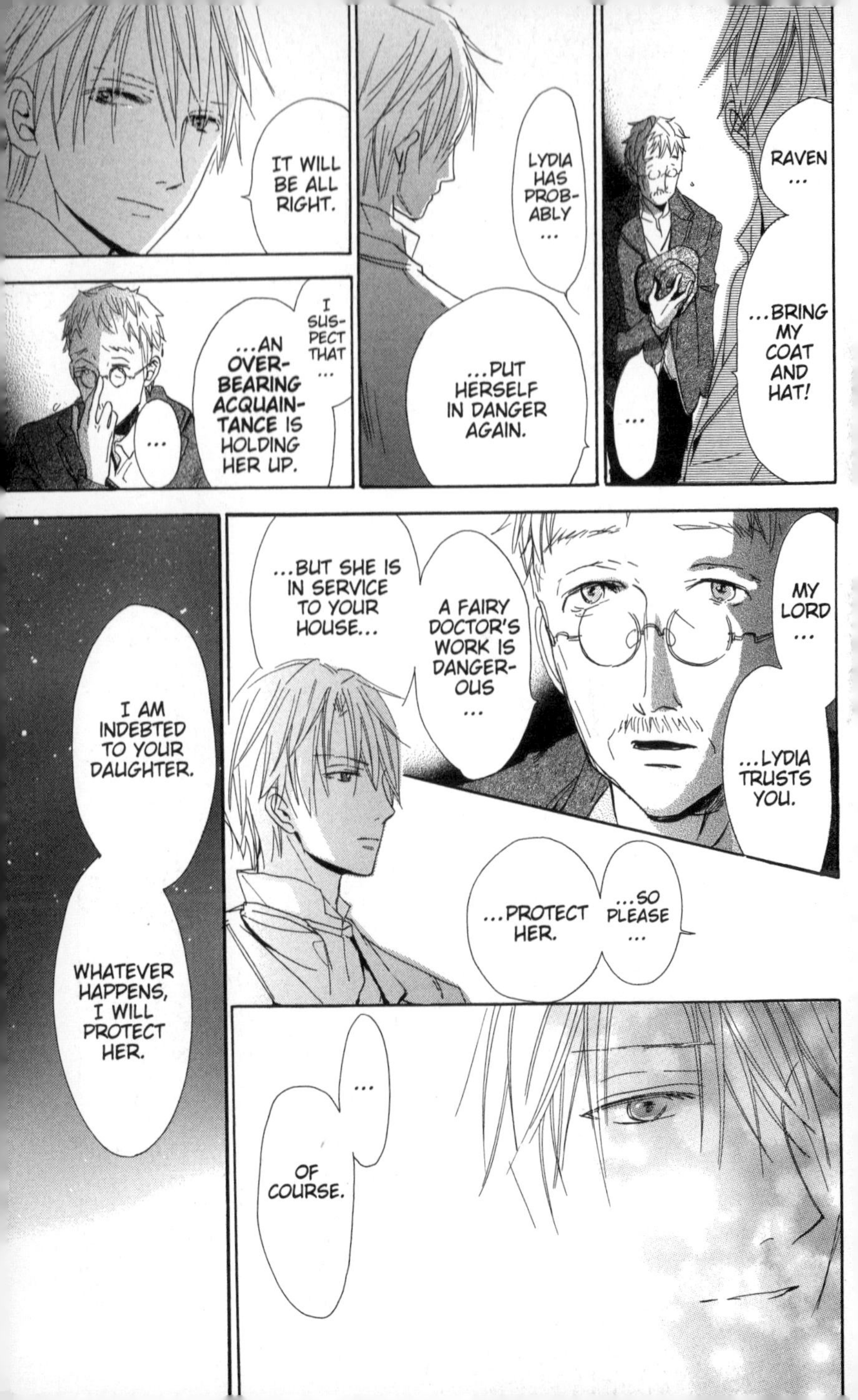
RAVEN ...
...BRING MY COAT AND HAT!
...
LYDIA HAS PROBABLY ...
...PUT HERSELF IN DANGER AGAIN.
IT WILL BE ALL RIGHT.
I SUSPECT THAT ...
...AN OVERBEARING ACQUAINTANCE IS HOLDING HER UP.
...
MY LORD ...
...LYDIA TRUSTS YOU.
A FAIRY DOCTOR'S WORK IS DANGEROUS ...
...BUT SHE IS IN SERVICE TO YOUR HOUSE...
...SO PLEASE ...
...PROTECT HER.
...
OF COURSE.
I AM INDEBTED TO YOUR DAUGHTER.
WHATEVER HAPPENS, I WILL PROTECT HER.

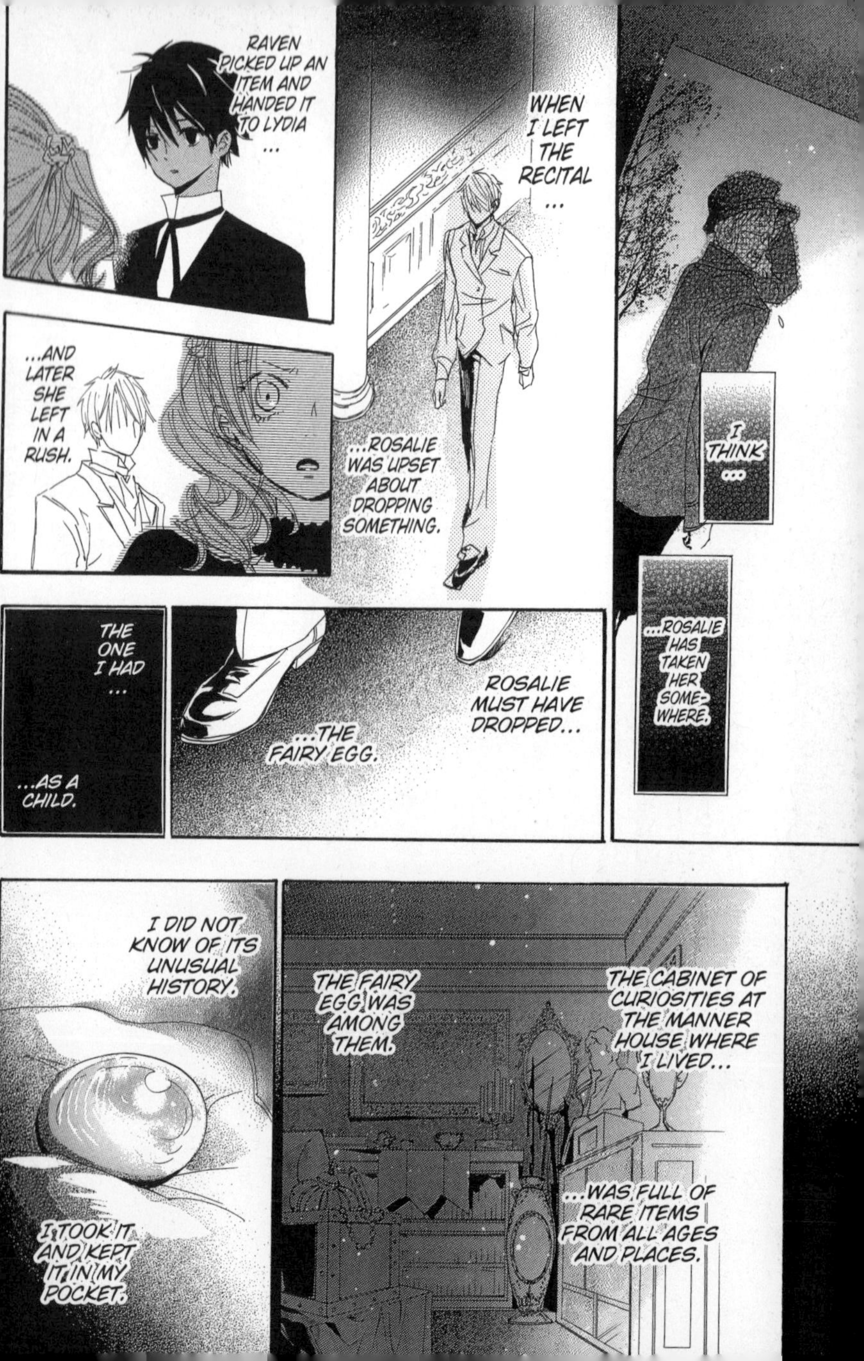
I THINK...
...ROSALIE HAS TAKEN HER SOMEWHERE.
WHEN I LEFT THE RECITAL...
...ROSALIE WAS UPSET ABOUT DROPPING SOMETHING.
RAVEN PICKED UP AN ITEM AND HANDED IT TO LYDIA...
...AND LATER SHE LEFT IN A RUSH.
ROSALIE MUST HAVE DROPPED...
...THE FAIRY EGG.
THE ONE I HAD...
...AS A CHILD.
THE CABINET OF CURIOSITIES AT THE MANNER HOUSE WHERE I LIVED...
...WAS FULL OF RARE ITEMS FROM ALL AGES AND PLACES.
THE FAIRY EGG WAS AMONG THEM.
I DID NOT KNOW OF ITS UNUSUAL HISTORY.
I TOOK IT AND KEPT IT IN MY POCKET.

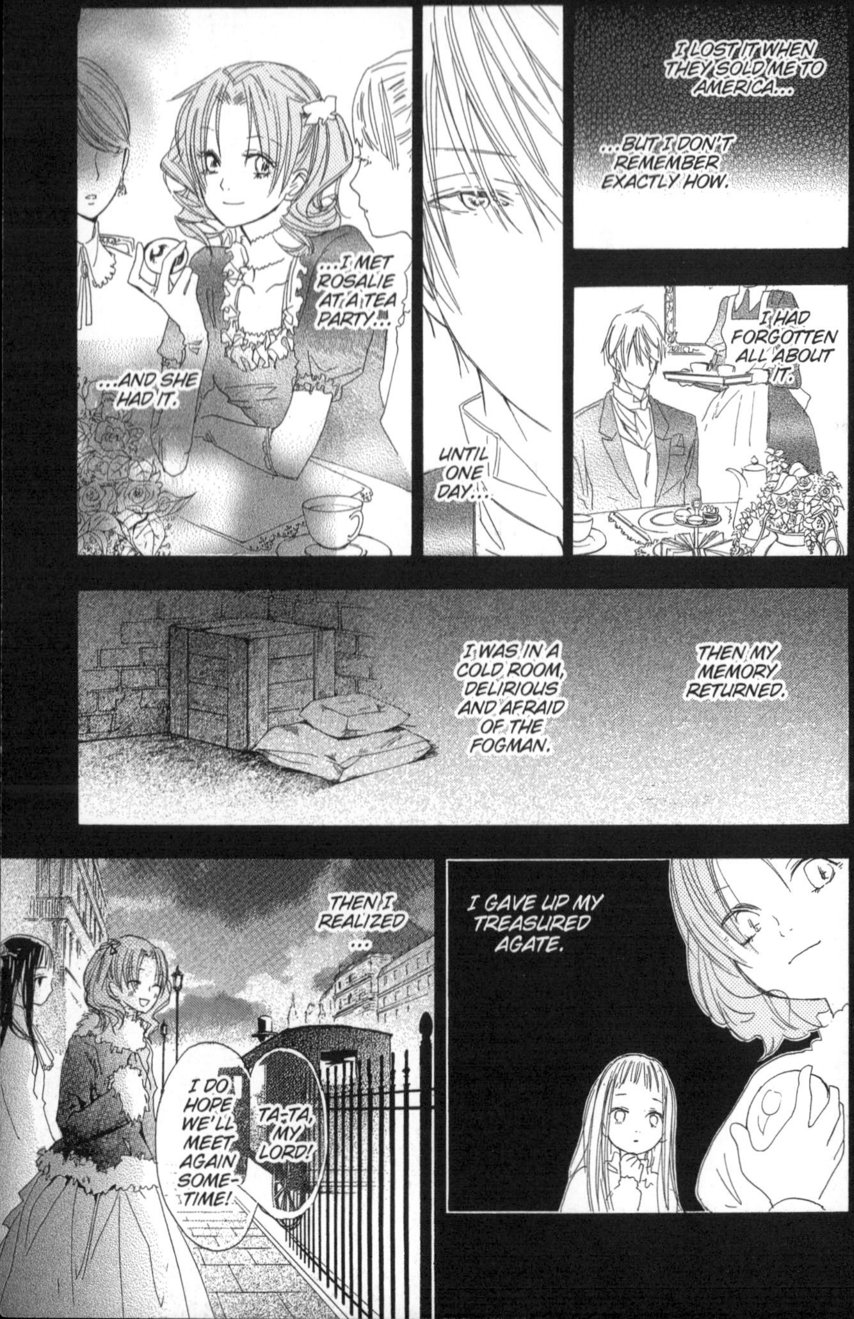
I LOST IT WHEN THEY SOLD ME TO AMERICA...
...BUT I DON'T REMEMBER EXACTLY HOW.
I HAD FORGOTTEN ALL ABOUT IT.
UNTIL ONE DAY...
...I MET ROSALIE AT A TEA PARTY...
...AND SHE HAD IT.
THEN MY MEMORY RETURNED.
I WAS IN A COLD ROOM, DELIRIOUS AND AFRAID OF THE FOGMAN.
I GAVE UP MY TREASURED AGATE.
THEN I REALIZED...
TA-TA, MY LORD!
I DO HOPE WE'LL MEET AGAIN SOMETIME!

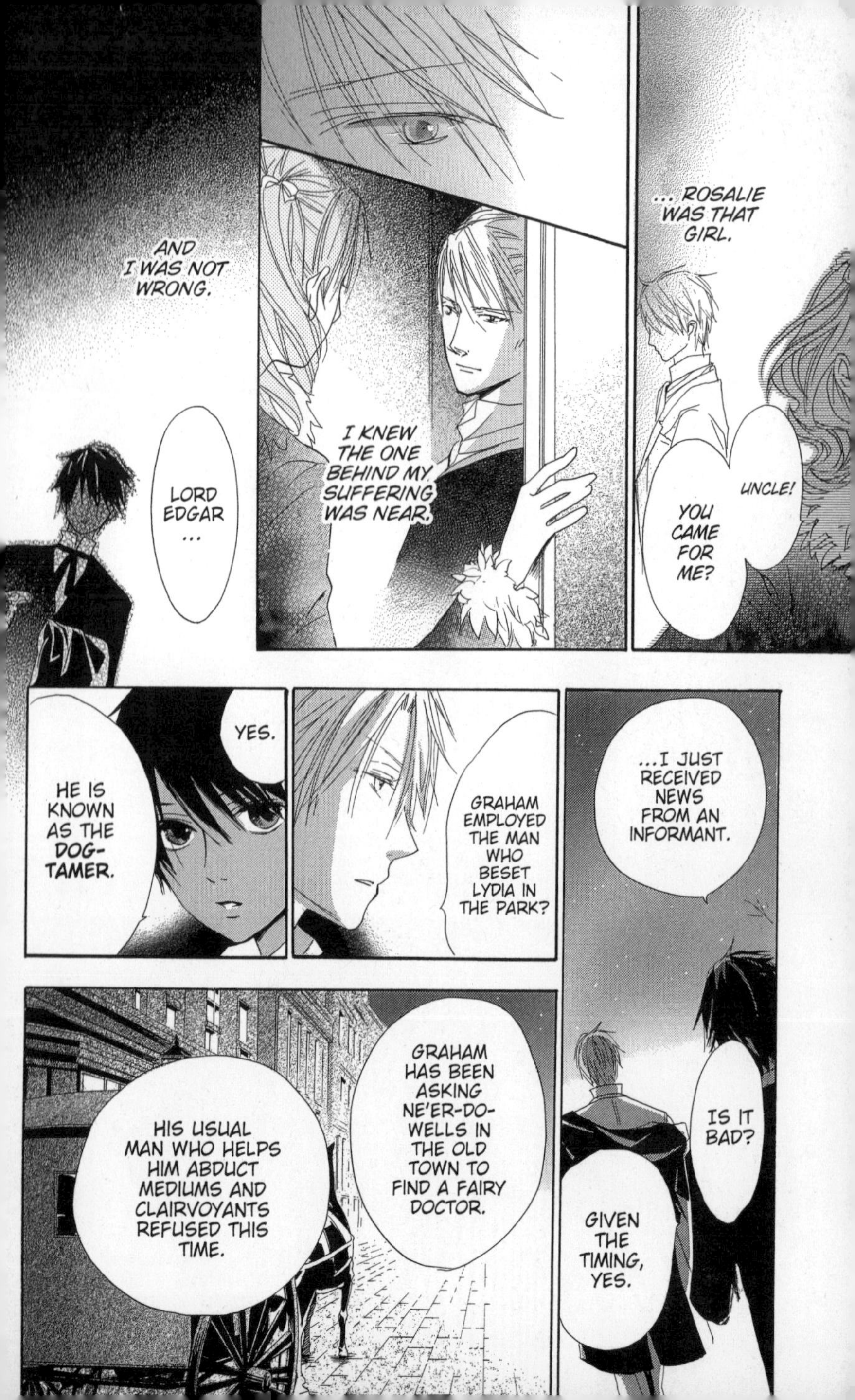
...ROSALIE WAS THAT GIRL.
UNCLE!
YOU CAME FOR ME?
I KNEW THE ONE BEHIND MY SUFFERING WAS NEAR.
AND I WAS NOT WRONG.
LORD EDGAR ...
...I JUST RECEIVED NEWS FROM AN INFORMANT.
IS IT BAD?
GIVEN THE TIMING, YES.
GRAHAM EMPLOYED THE MAN WHO BESET LYDIA IN THE PARK?
YES.
HE IS KNOWN AS THE DOG-TAMER.
GRAHAM HAS BEEN ASKING NE'ER-DO-WELLS IN THE OLD TOWN TO FIND A FAIRY DOCTOR.
HIS USUAL MAN WHO HELPS HIM ABDUCT MEDIUMS AND CLAIRVOYANTS REFUSED THIS TIME.

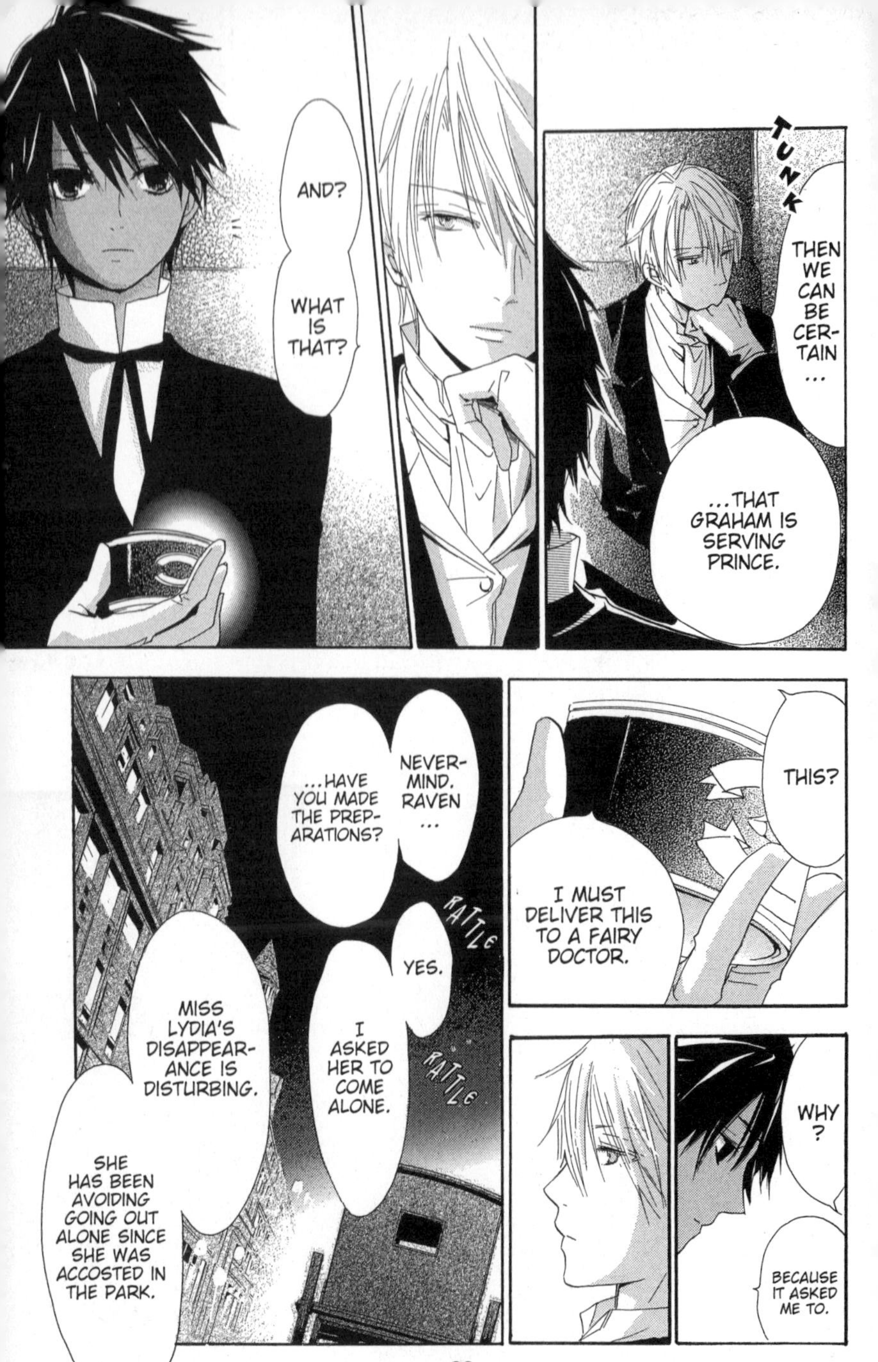
TUNK
THEN WE CAN BE CERTAIN...
...THAT GRAHAM IS SERVING PRINCE.
AND?
WHAT IS THAT?
THIS?
I MUST DELIVER THIS TO A FAIRY DOCTOR.
WHY?
BECAUSE IT ASKED ME TO.
NEVERMIND. RAVEN...
...HAVE YOU MADE THE PREPARATIONS?
RATTLE
YES.
I ASKED HER TO COME ALONE.
RATTLE
MISS LYDIA'S DISAPPEARANCE IS DISTURBING.
SHE HAS BEEN AVOIDING GOING OUT ALONE SINCE SHE WAS ACCOSTED IN THE PARK.

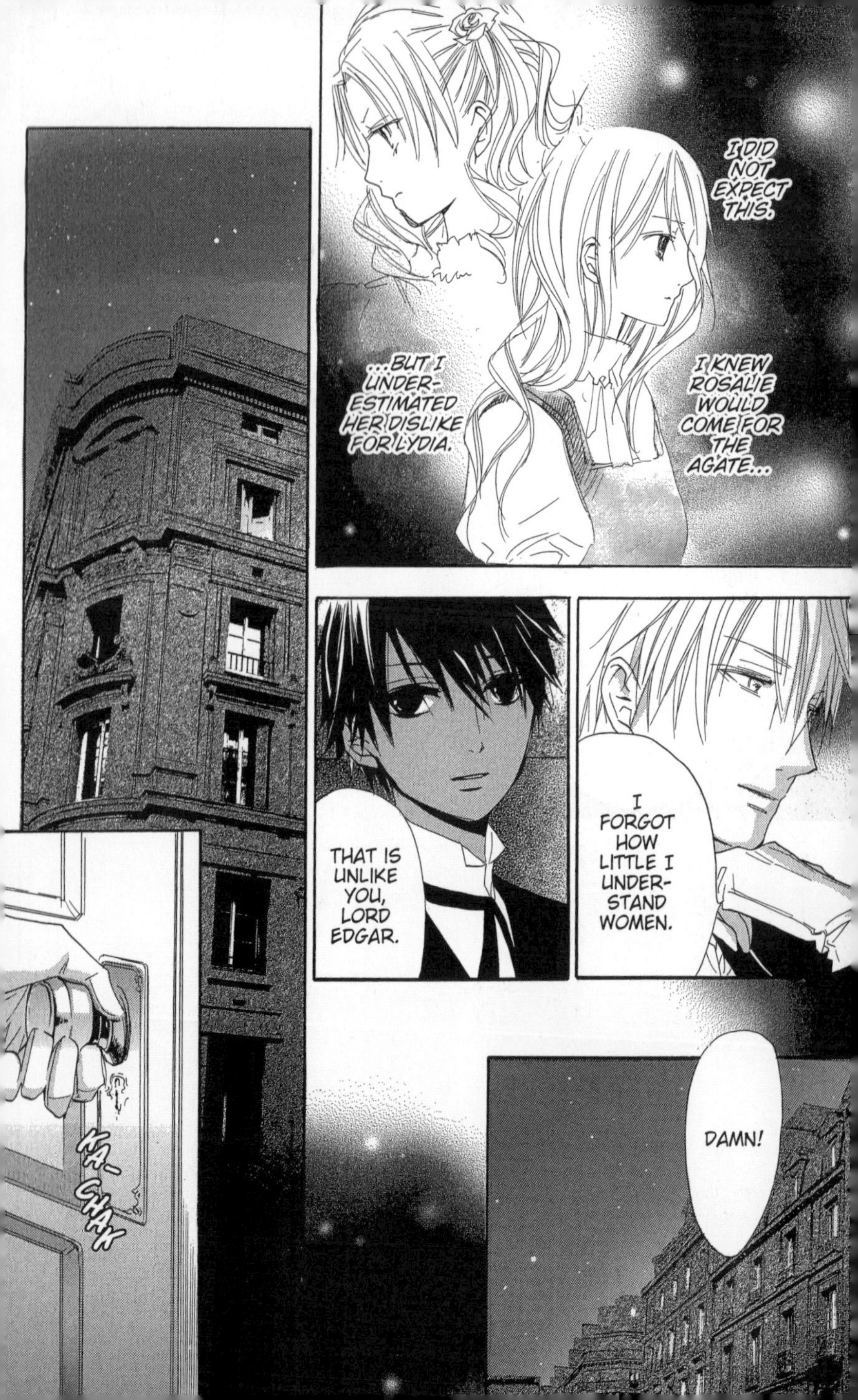
I DID NOT EXPECT THIS.
I KNEW ROSALIE WOULD COME FOR THE AGATE...
...BUT I UNDER-ESTIMATED HER DISLIKE FOR LYDIA.
I FORGOT HOW LITTLE I UNDER-STAND WOMEN.
THAT IS UNLIKE YOU, LORD EDGAR.
DAMN!
KA-CHAK

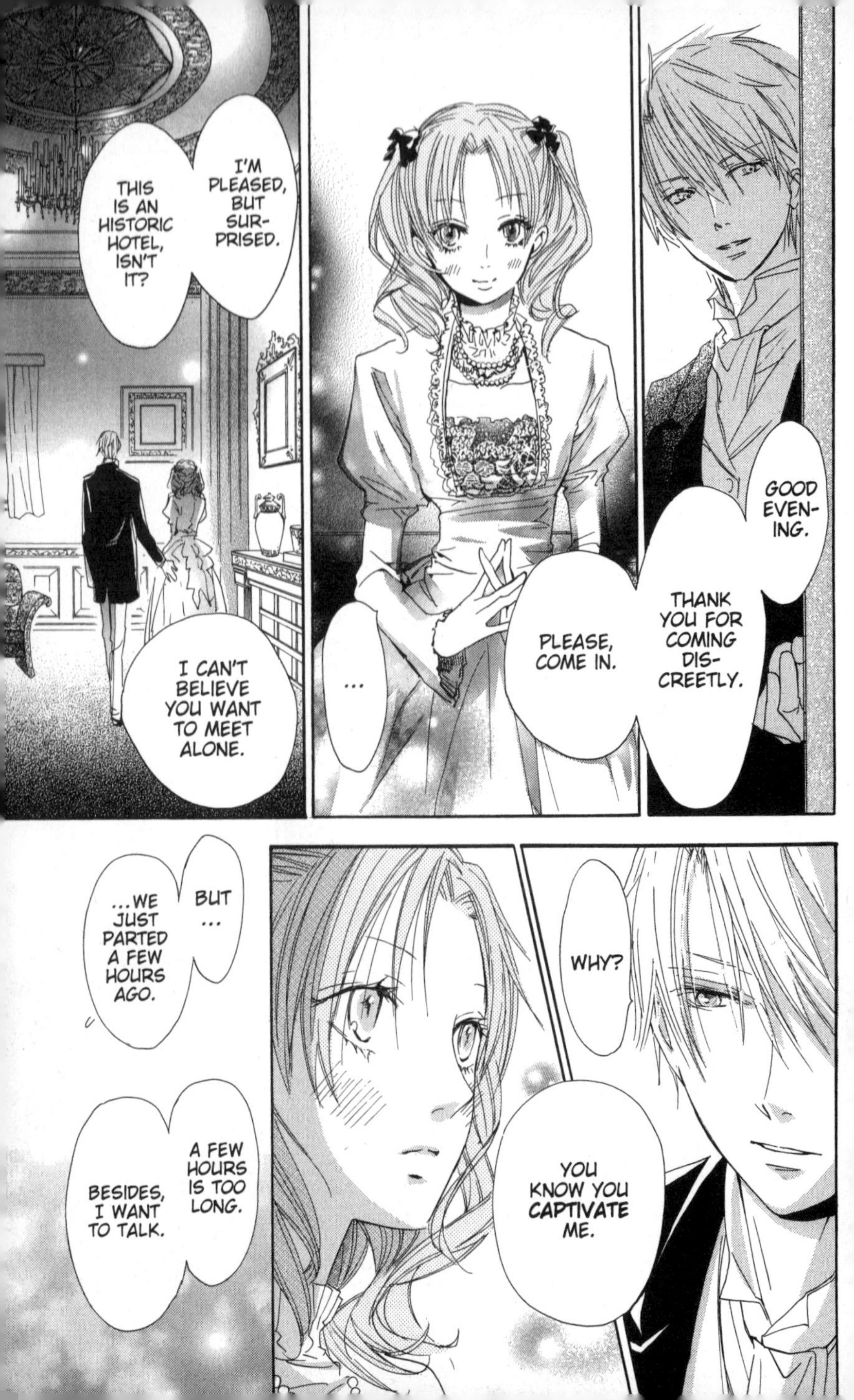
GOOD EVENING.
THANK YOU FOR COMING DISCREETLY.
PLEASE, COME IN.
...
I'M PLEASED, BUT SURPRISED.
THIS IS AN HISTORIC HOTEL, ISN'T IT?
I CAN'T BELIEVE YOU WANT TO MEET ALONE.
WHY?
YOU KNOW YOU CAPTIVATE ME.
BUT...
...WE JUST PARTED A FEW HOURS AGO.
A FEW HOURS IS TOO LONG.
BESIDES, I WANT TO TALK.

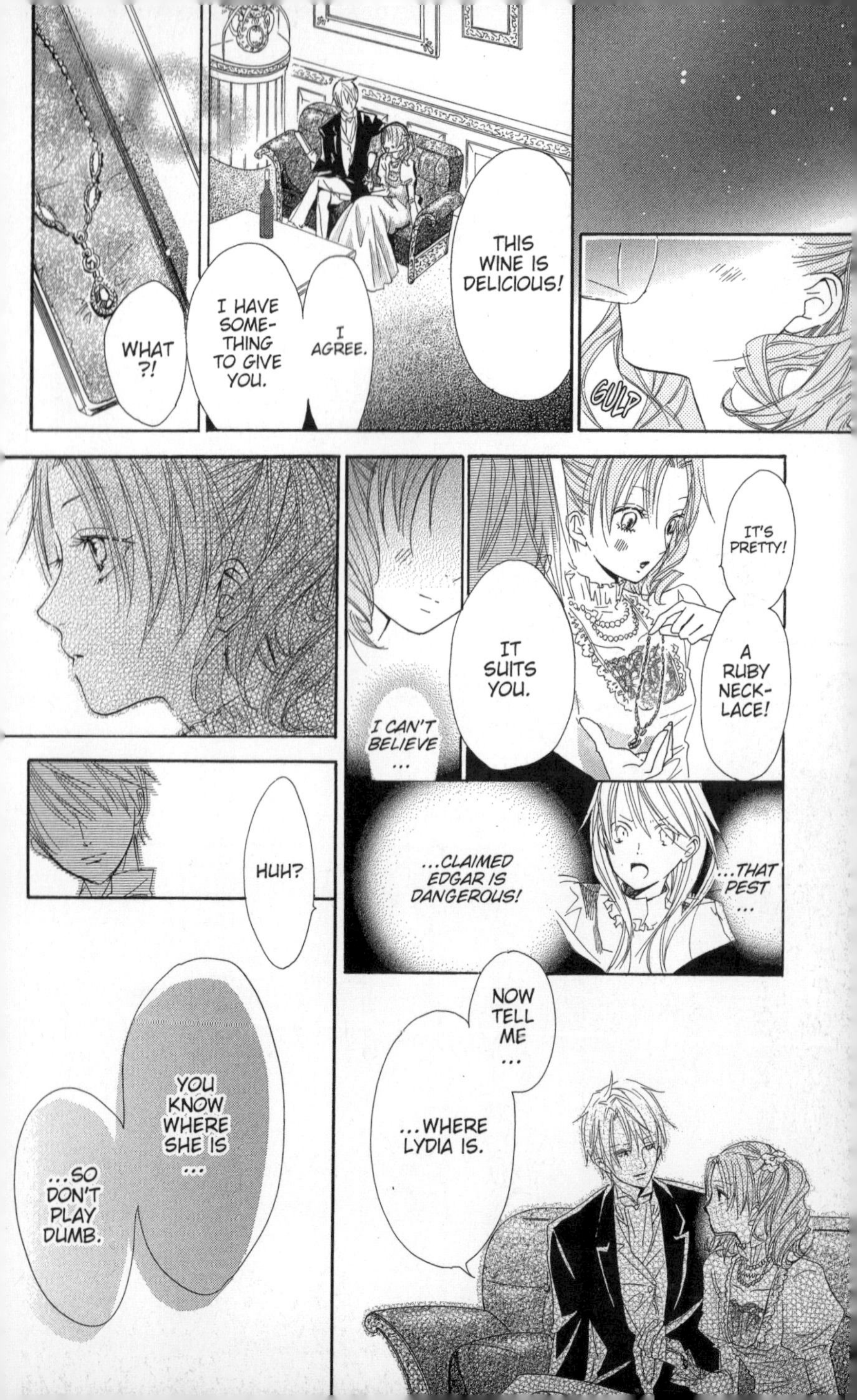
GULP
THIS WINE IS DELICIOUS!
I AGREE.
I HAVE SOMETHING TO GIVE YOU.
WHAT?!
IT'S PRETTY!
A RUBY NECKLACE!
IT SUITS YOU.
I CAN'T BELIEVE...
...THAT PEST...
...CLAIMED EDGAR IS DANGEROUS!
HUH?
NOW TELL ME...
...WHERE LYDIA IS.
YOU KNOW WHERE SHE IS...
...SO DON'T PLAY DUMB.

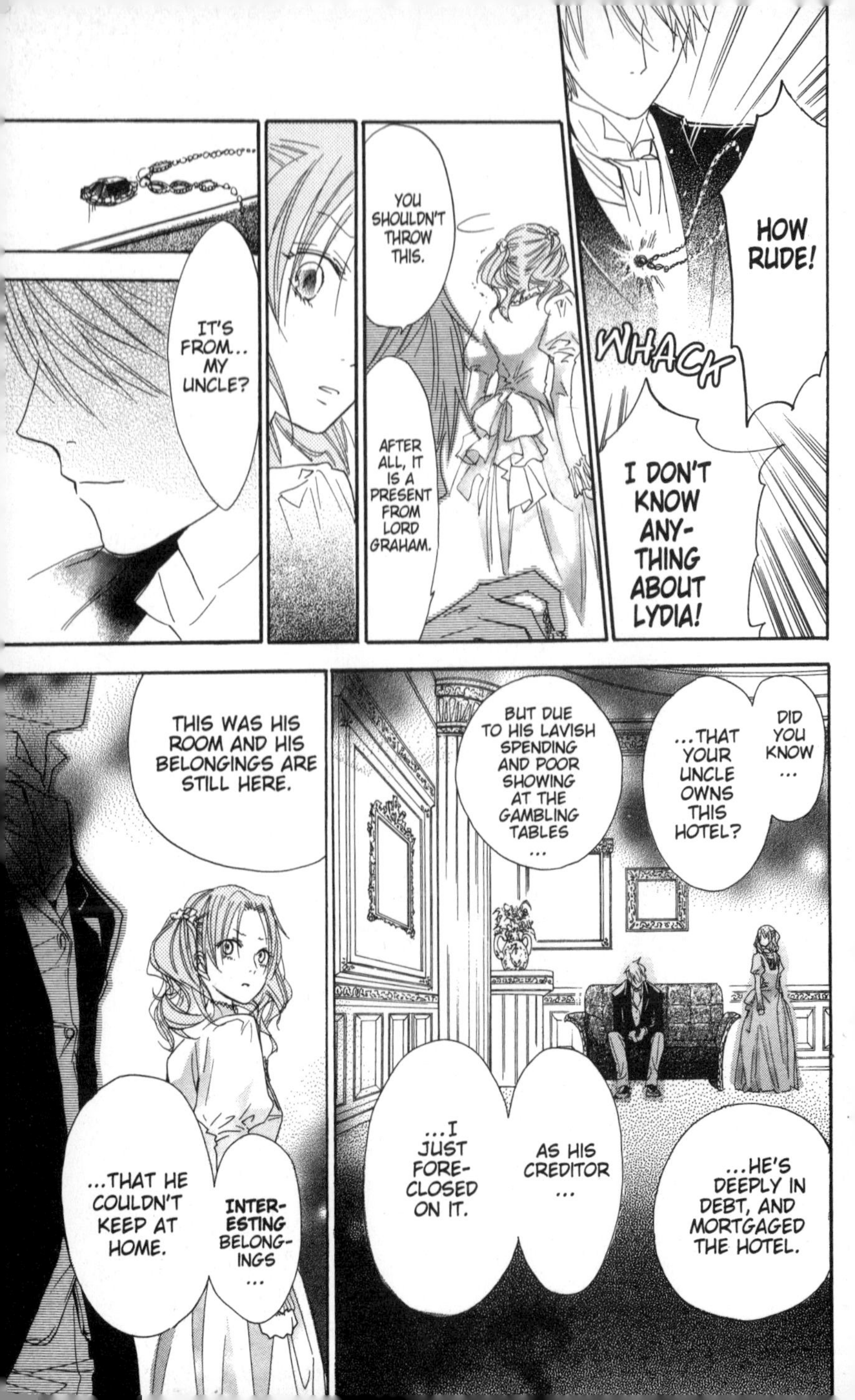
HOW RUDE!
WHACK
I DON'T KNOW ANY-THING ABOUT LYDIA!
YOU SHOULDN'T THROW THIS.
AFTER ALL, IT IS A PRESENT FROM LORD GRAHAM.
IT'S FROM... MY UNCLE?
DID YOU KNOW...
...THAT YOUR UNCLE OWNS THIS HOTEL?
BUT DUE TO HIS LAVISH SPENDING AND POOR SHOWING AT THE GAMBLING TABLES...
...HE'S DEEPLY IN DEBT, AND MORTGAGED THE HOTEL.
AS HIS CREDITOR...
...I JUST FORE-CLOSED ON IT.
THIS WAS HIS ROOM AND HIS BELONGINGS ARE STILL HERE.
INTER-ESTING BELONG-INGS...
...THAT HE COULDN'T KEEP AT HOME.

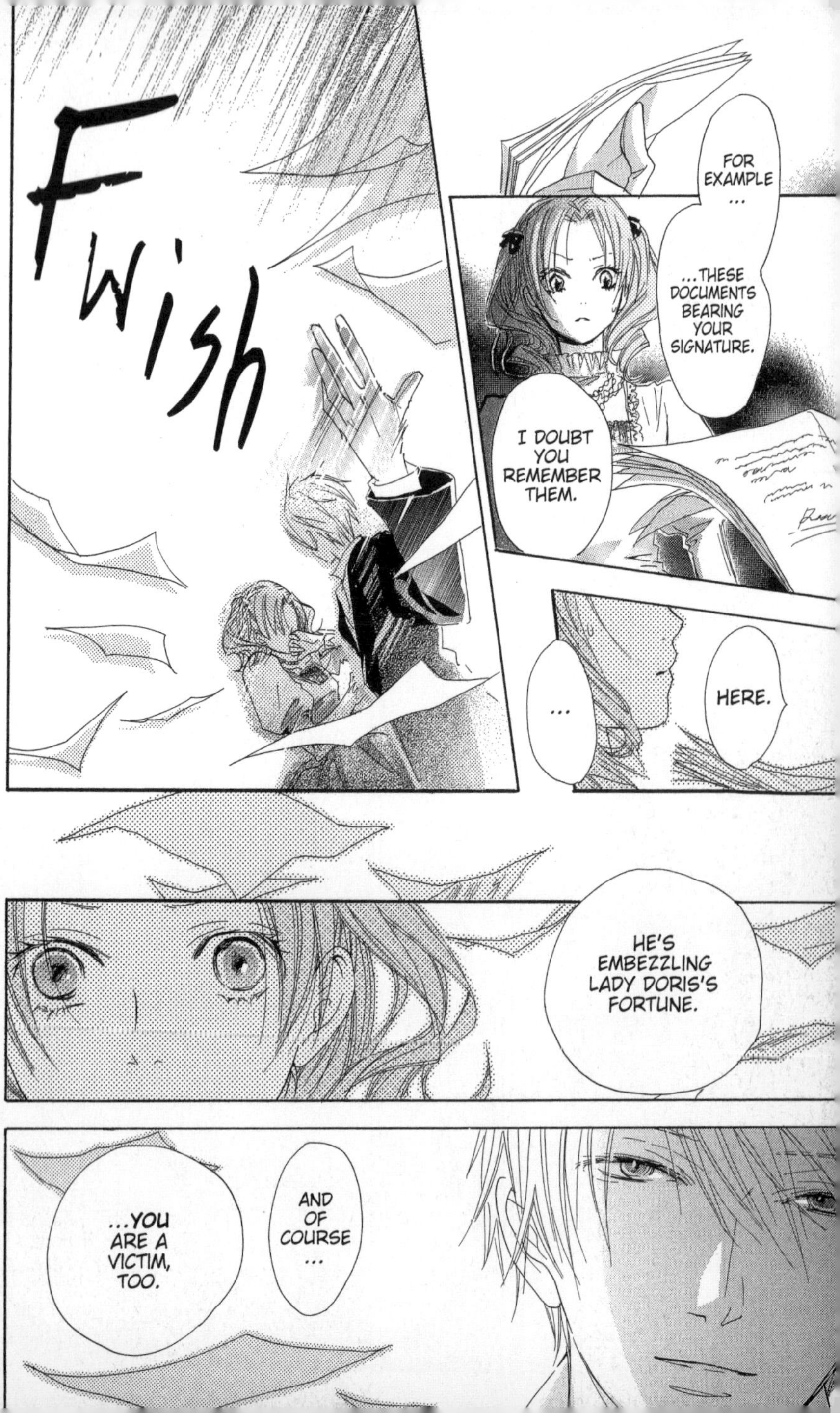
FOR EXAMPLE...
...THESE DOCUMENTS BEARING YOUR SIGNATURE.
I DOUBT YOU REMEMBER THEM.
HERE.
...
FWISH
HE'S EMBEZZLING LADY DORIS'S FORTUNE.
AND OF COURSE...
...YOU ARE A VICTIM, TOO.

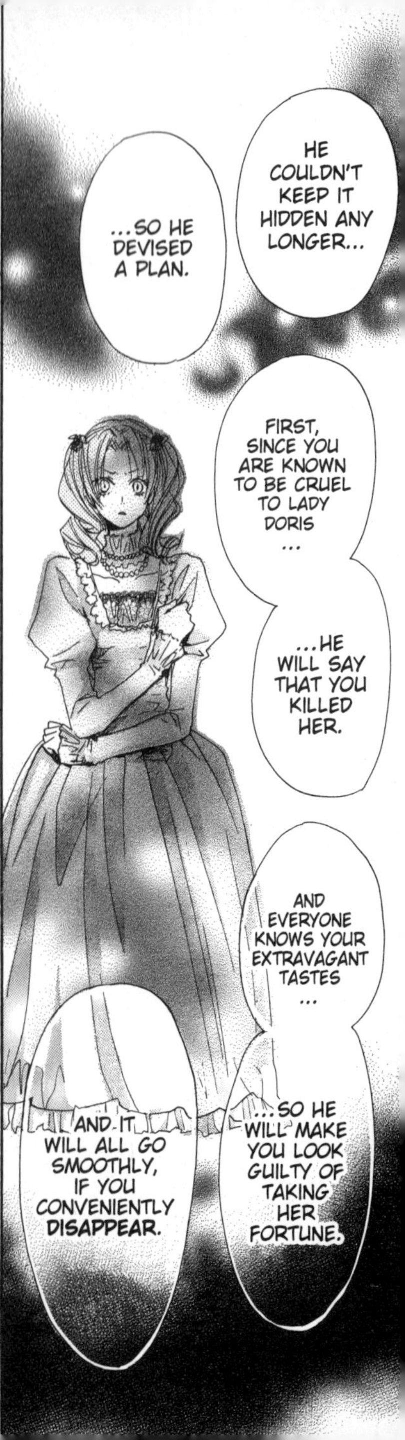
HE COULDN'T KEEP IT HIDDEN ANY LONGER...
...SO HE DEVISED A PLAN.
FIRST, SINCE YOU ARE KNOWN TO BE CRUEL TO LADY DORIS ...
...HE WILL SAY THAT YOU KILLED HER.
AND EVERYONE KNOWS YOUR EXTRAVAGANT TASTES ...
...SO HE WILL MAKE YOU LOOK GUILTY OF TAKING HER FORTUNE.
AND IT WILL ALL GO SMOOTHLY, IF YOU CONVENIENTLY **DISAPPEAR**.
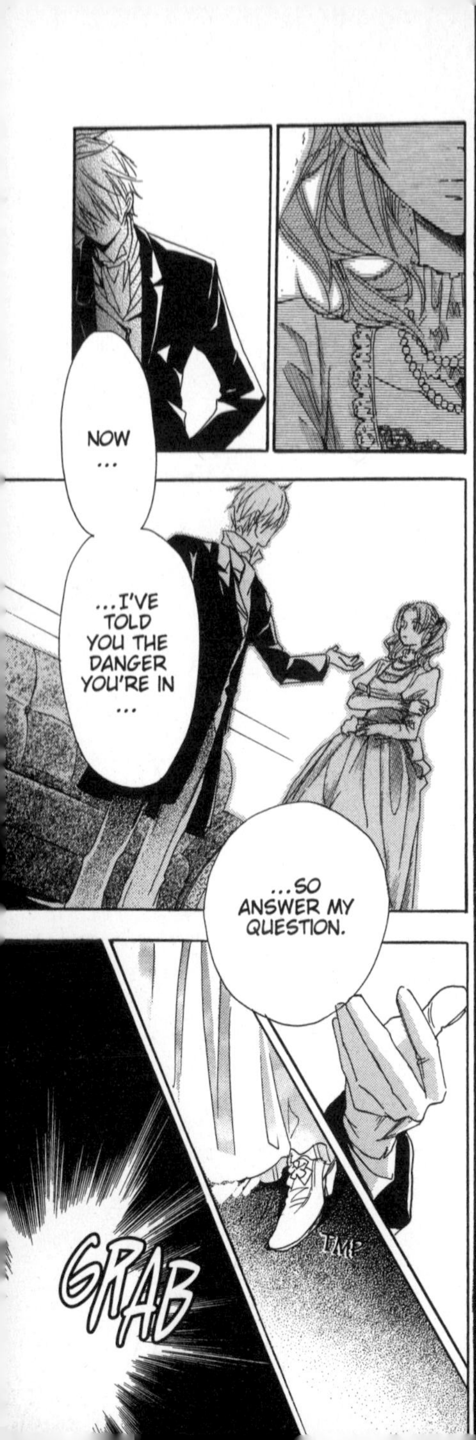
NOW ...
...I'VE TOLD YOU THE DANGER YOU'RE IN ...
...SO ANSWER MY QUESTION.
TMP
GRAB

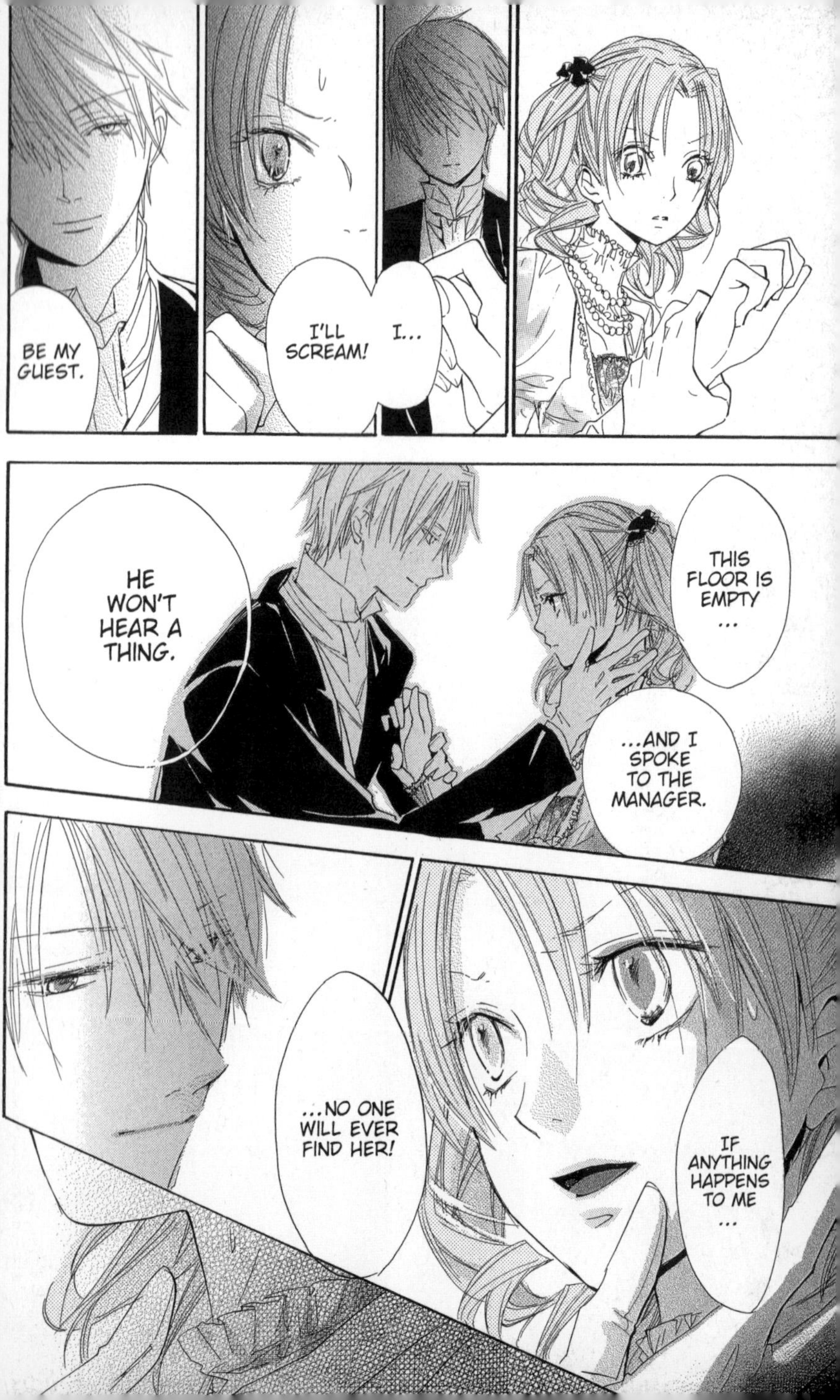
I...
I'LL SCREAM!
BE MY GUEST.
THIS FLOOR IS EMPTY ...
...AND I SPOKE TO THE MANAGER.
HE WON'T HEAR A THING.
IF ANYTHING HAPPENS TO ME ...
...NO ONE WILL EVER FIND HER!

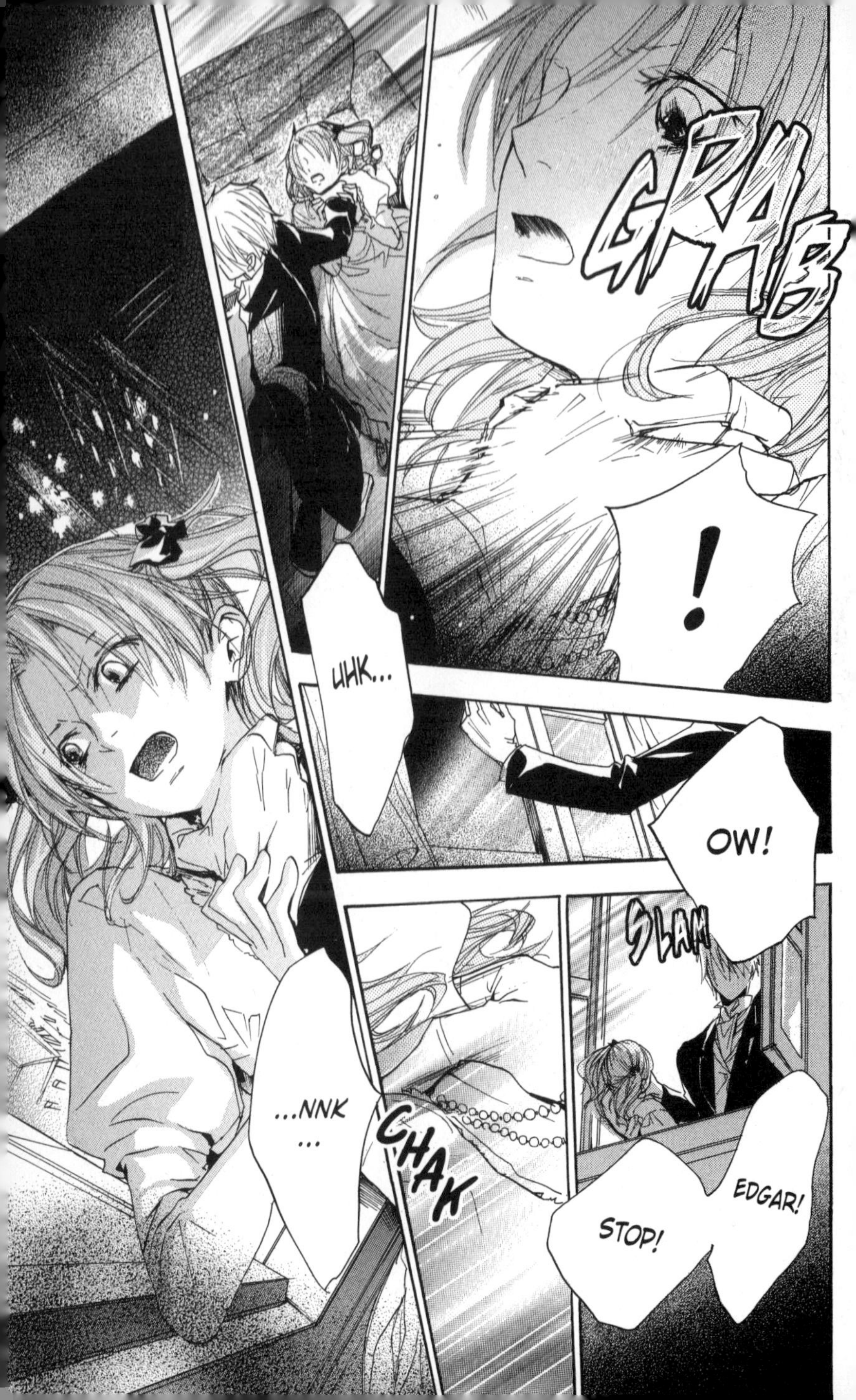
GRAB
!
UHK...
OW!
SLAM
EDGAR!
STOP!
CHAK
...NNK
...

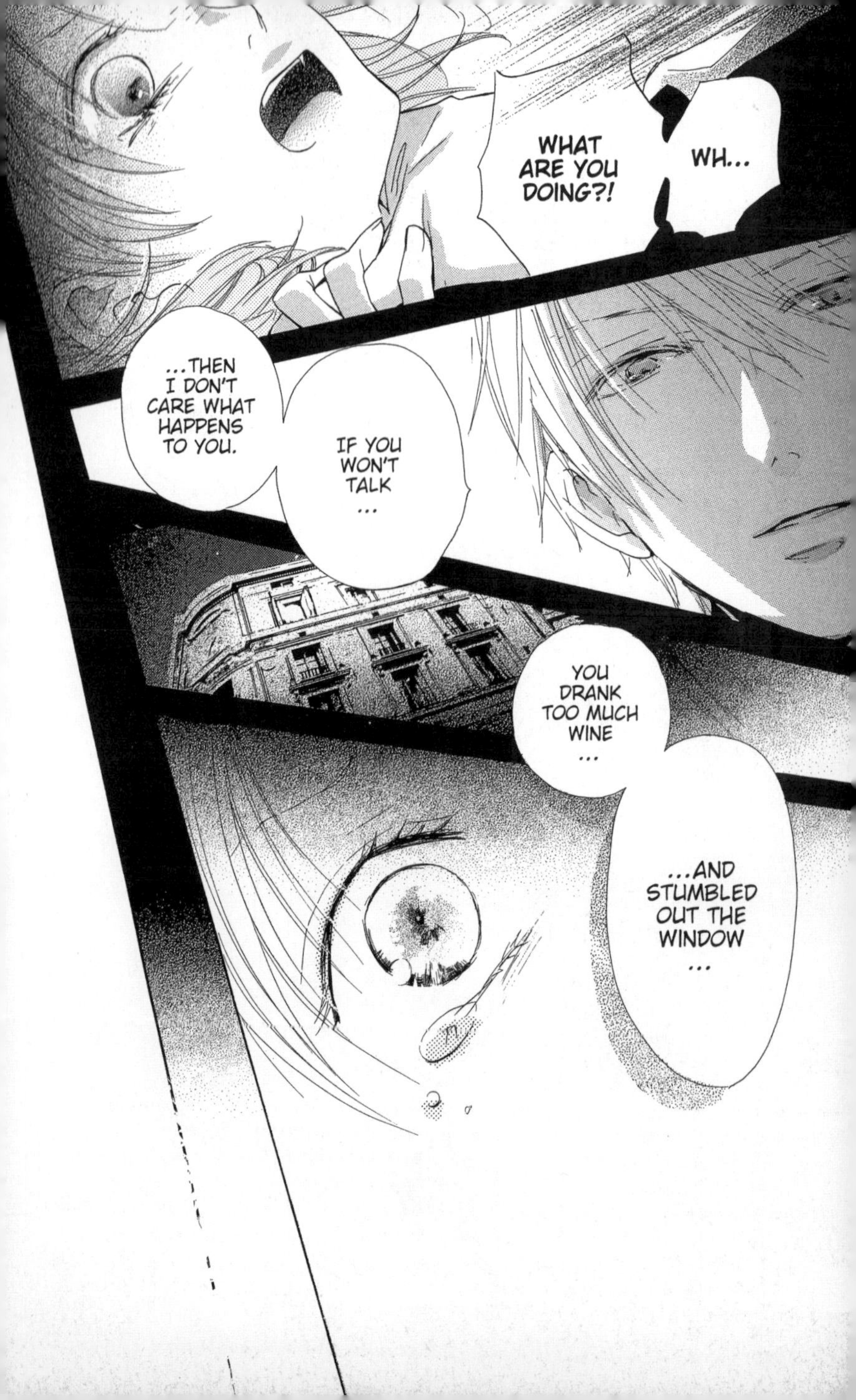
WH...
WHAT ARE YOU DOING?!
IF YOU WON'T TALK ...
...THEN I DON'T CARE WHAT HAPPENS TO YOU.
YOU DRANK TOO MUCH WINE ...
...AND STUMBLED OUT THE WINDOW ...

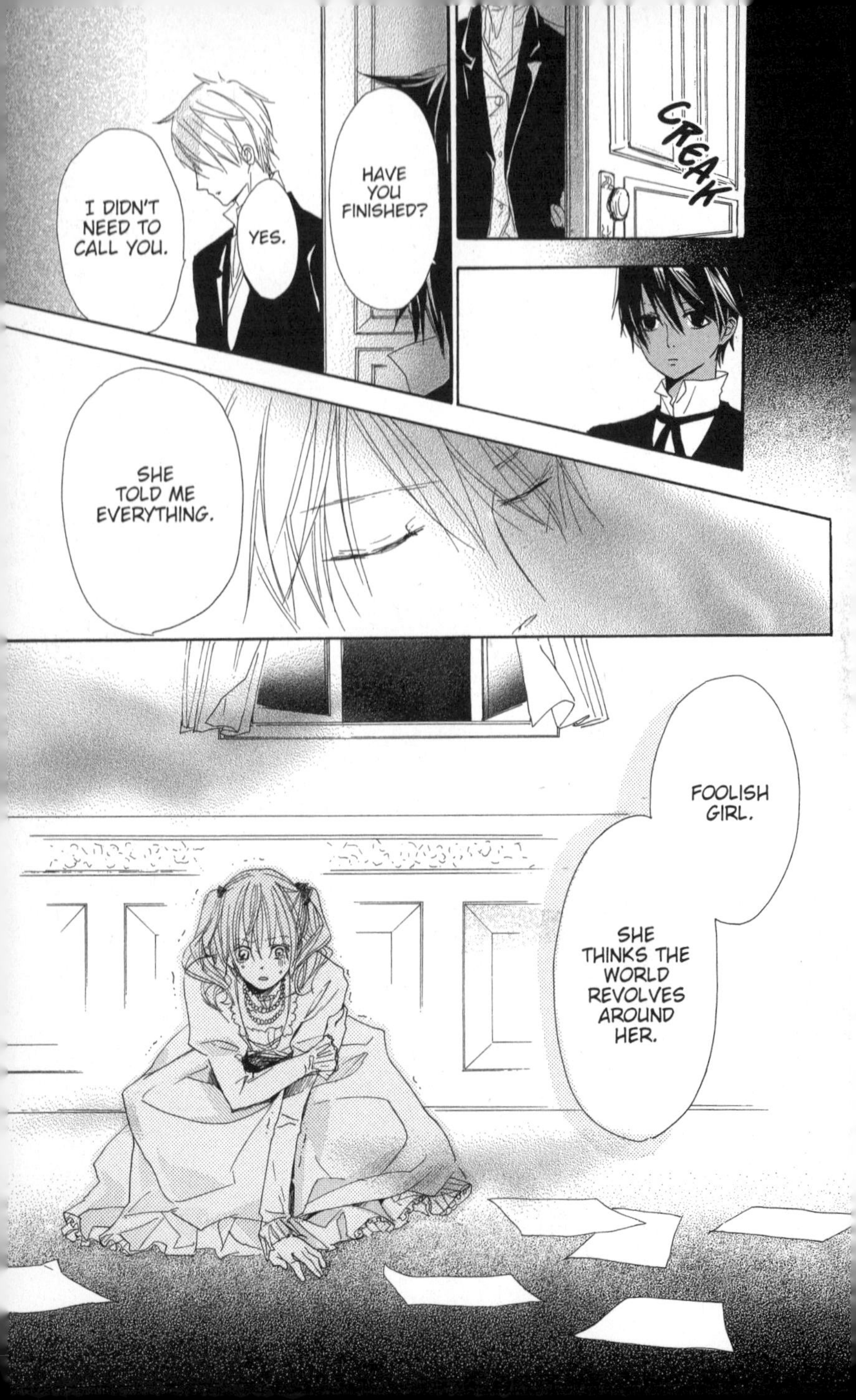
CREAK
HAVE YOU FINISHED?
YES.
I DIDN'T NEED TO CALL YOU.
SHE TOLD ME EVERYTHING.
FOOLISH GIRL.
SHE THINKS THE WORLD REVOLVES AROUND HER.

The Earl & the Fairy

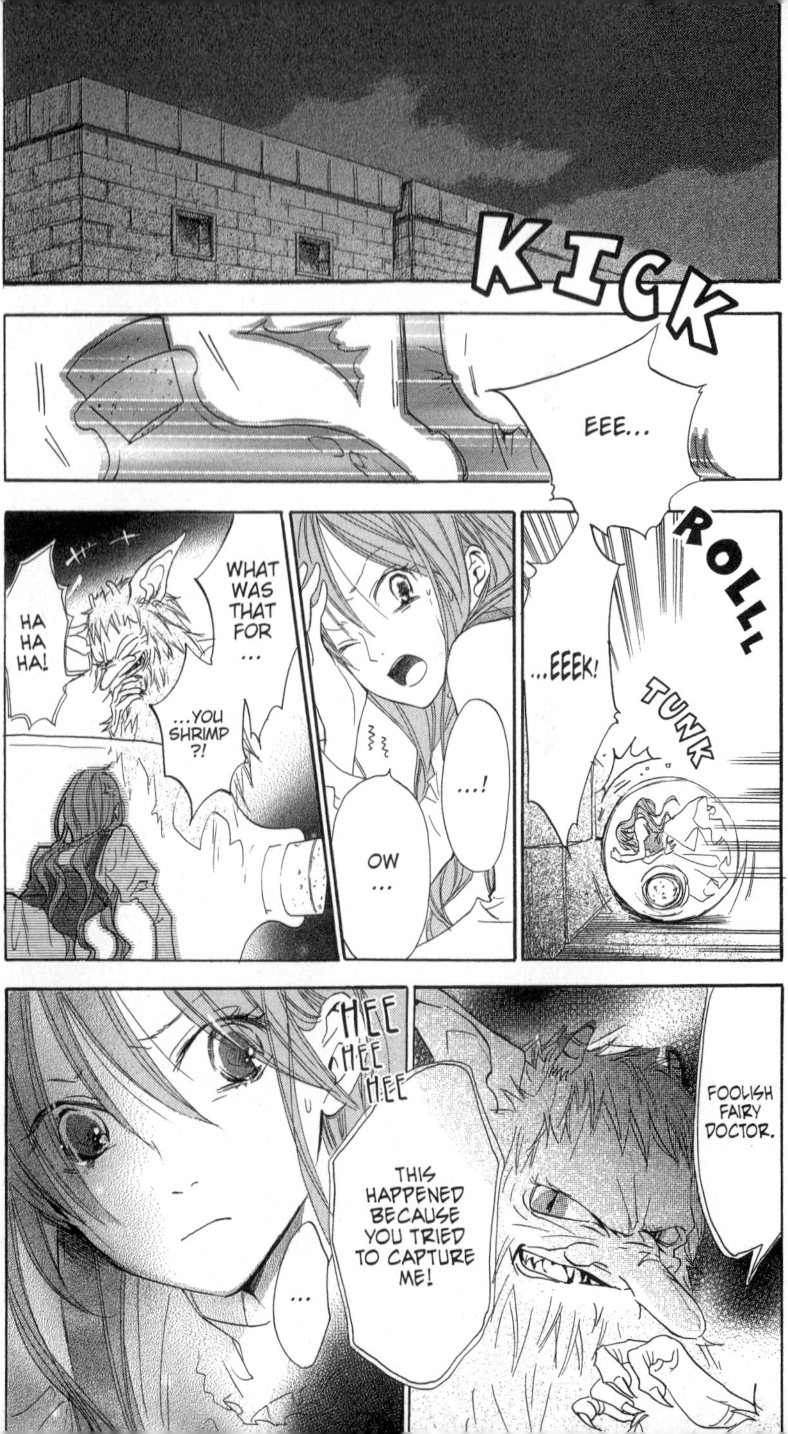
KICK
EEE...
ROLL
...EEEK!
TUNK
...!
OW...
WHAT WAS THAT FOR...
HA HA HA!
...YOU SHRIMP?!
FOOLISH FAIRY DOCTOR.
HEE HEE HEE
THIS HAPPENED BECAUSE YOU TRIED TO CAPTURE ME!
...

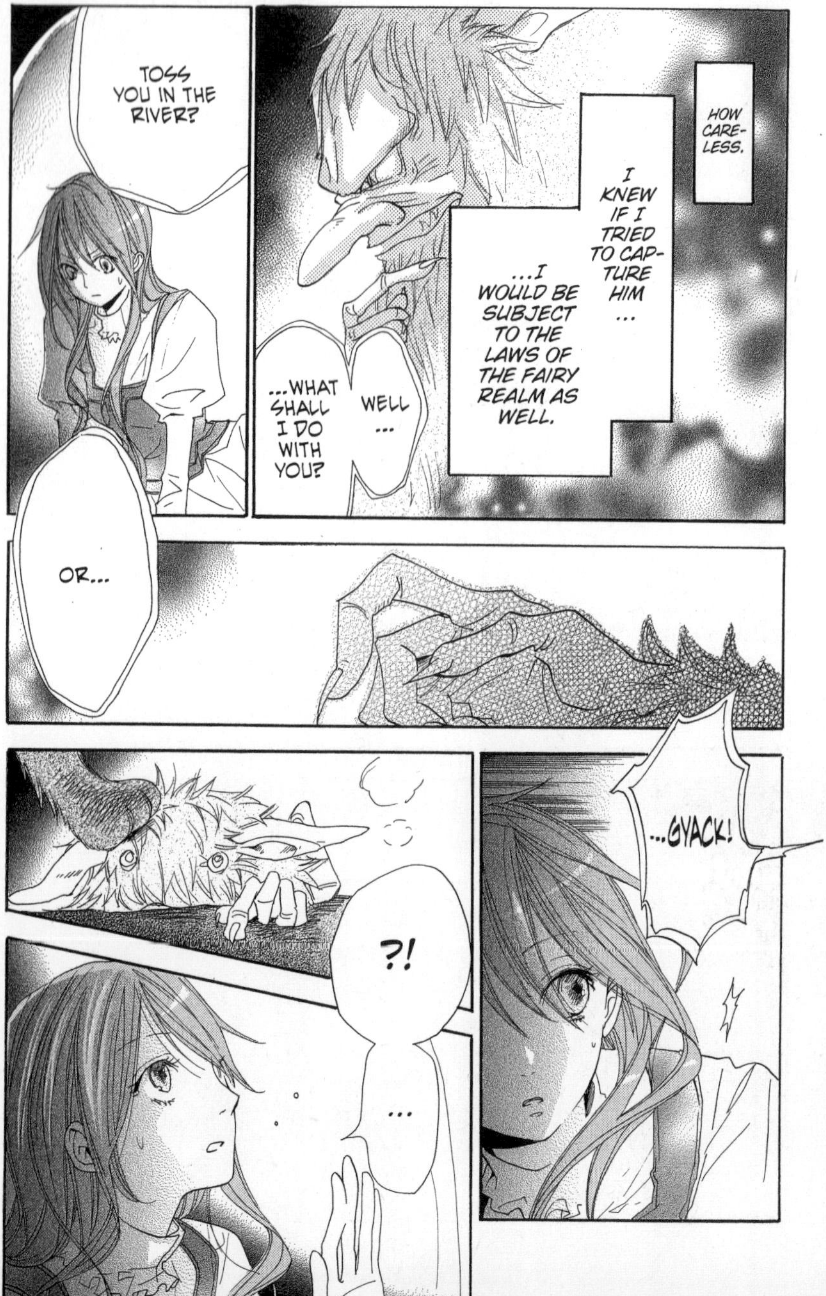
HOW CARE-LESS.
I KNEW IF I TRIED TO CAPTURE HIM...
...I WOULD BE SUBJECT TO THE LAWS OF THE FAIRY REALM AS WELL.
WELL...
...WHAT SHALL I DO WITH YOU?
TOSS YOU IN THE RIVER?
OR...
...GYACK!
?!
...

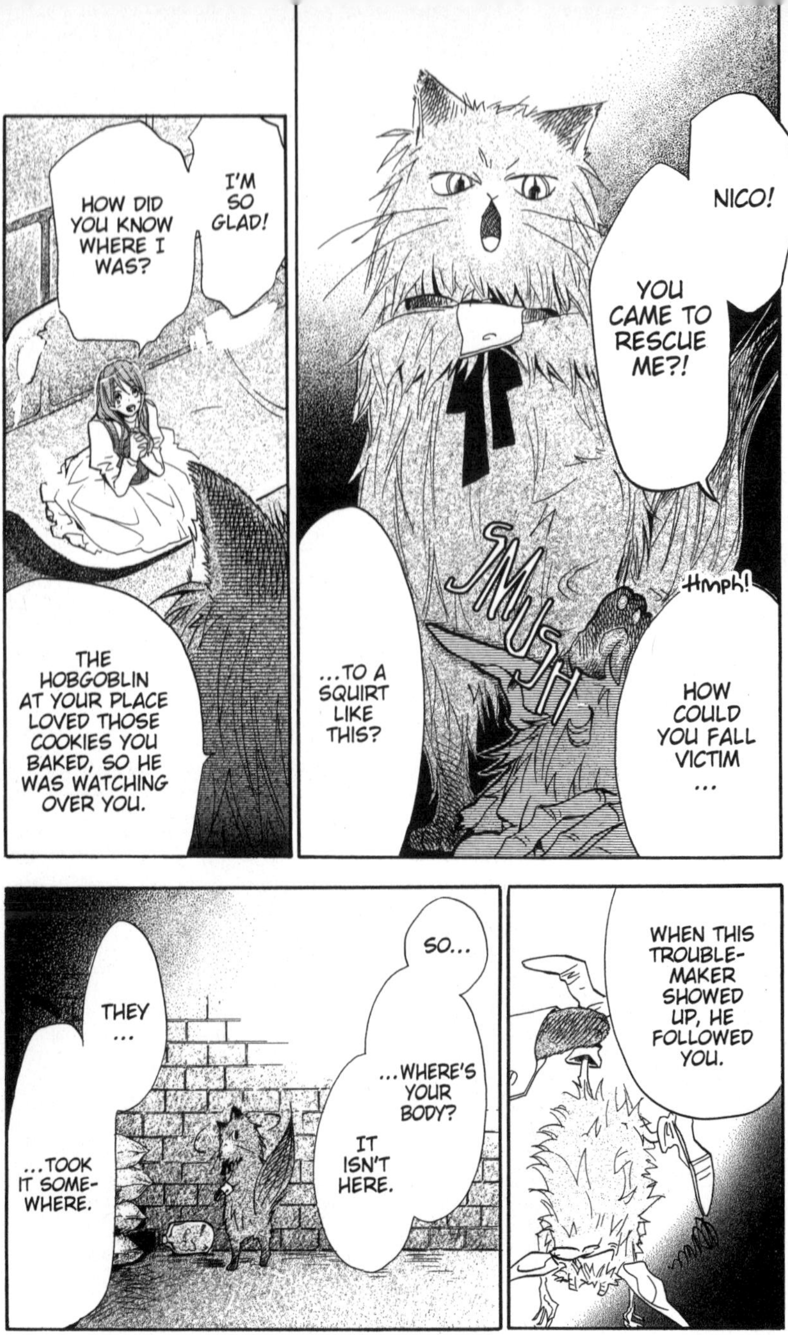
NICO!
YOU CAME TO RESCUE ME?!
Hmph!
HOW COULD YOU FALL VICTIM ...
SMUSH
...TO A SQUIRT LIKE THIS?
I'M SO GLAD!
HOW DID YOU KNOW WHERE I WAS?
THE HOBGOBLIN AT YOUR PLACE LOVED THOSE COOKIES YOU BAKED, SO HE WAS WATCHING OVER YOU.
WHEN THIS TROUBLE-MAKER SHOWED UP, HE FOLLOWED YOU.
SO...
...WHERE'S YOUR BODY?
IT ISN'T HERE.
THEY ...
...TOOK IT SOME-WHERE.

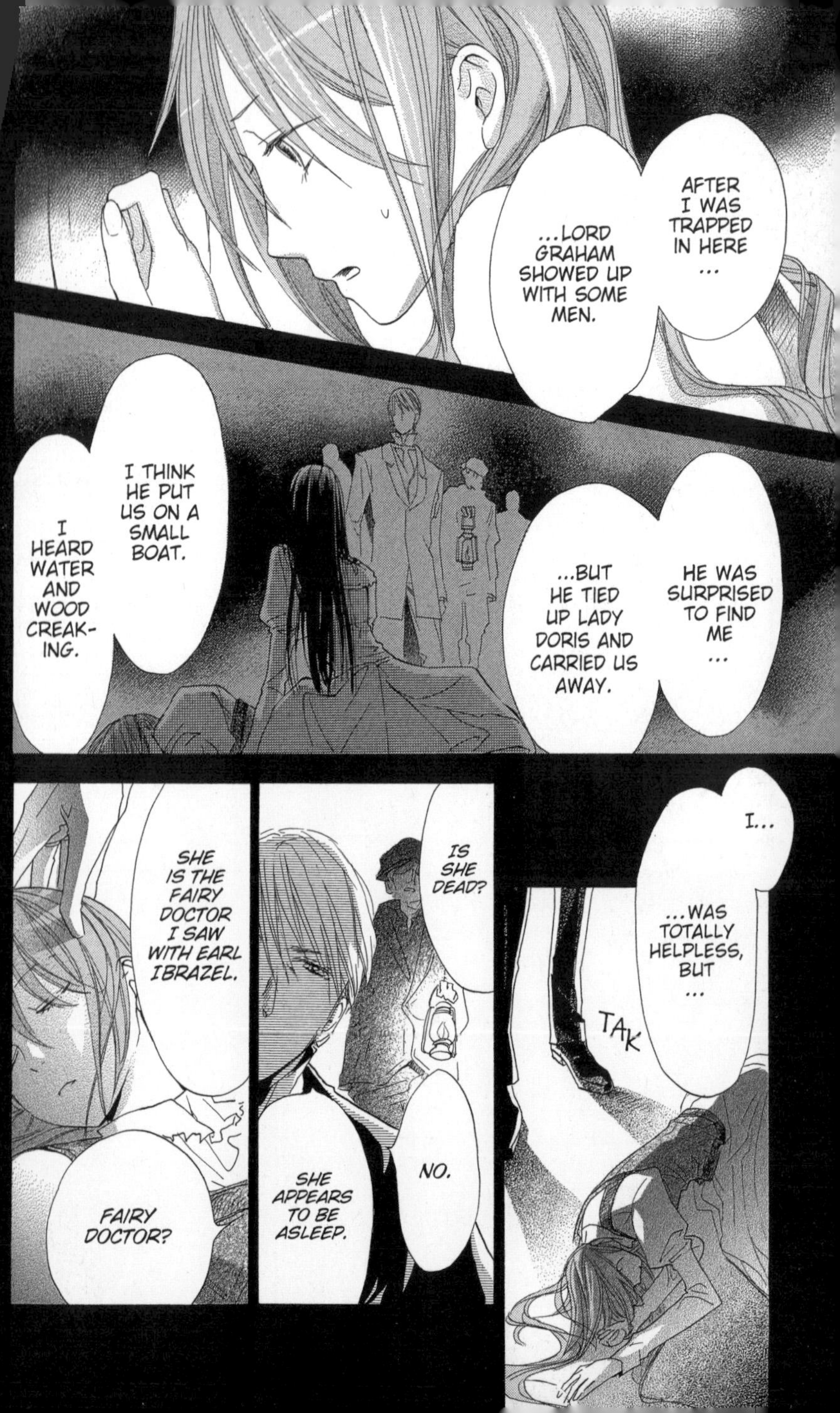
AFTER I WAS TRAPPED IN HERE...
...LORD GRAHAM SHOWED UP WITH SOME MEN.
HE WAS SURPRISED TO FIND ME...
...BUT HE TIED UP LADY DORIS AND CARRIED US AWAY.
I THINK HE PUT US ON A SMALL BOAT.
I HEARD WATER AND WOOD CREAK-ING.
I...
...WAS TOTALLY HELPLESS, BUT...
TAK
IS SHE DEAD?
NO.
SHE APPEARS TO BE ASLEEP.
SHE IS THE FAIRY DOCTOR I SAW WITH EARL IBRAZEL.
FAIRY DOCTOR?

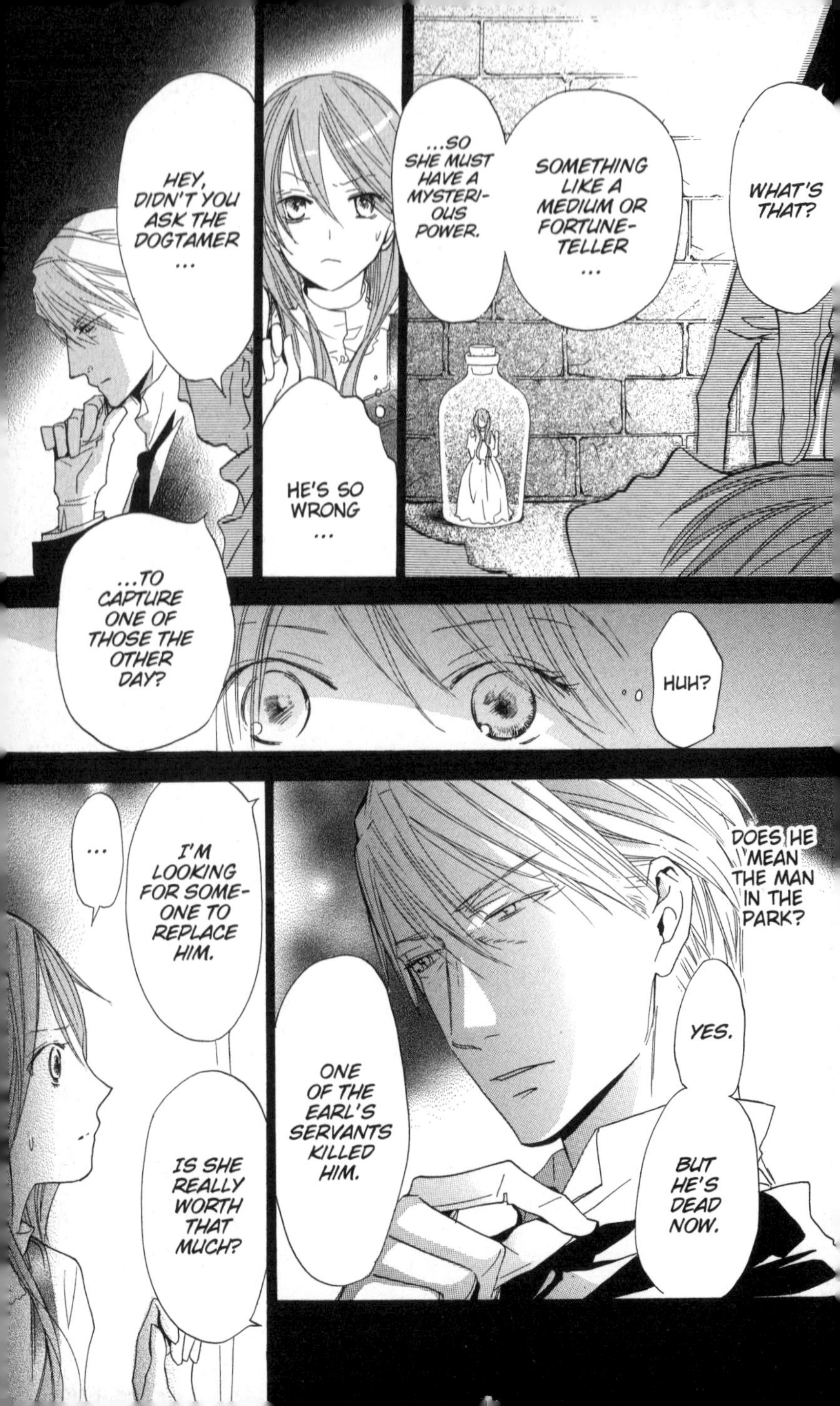
WHAT'S THAT?
SOMETHING LIKE A MEDIUM OR FORTUNE-TELLER...
...SO SHE MUST HAVE A MYSTERIOUS POWER.
HE'S SO WRONG...
HEY, DIDN'T YOU ASK THE DOGTAMER...
...TO CAPTURE ONE OF THOSE THE OTHER DAY?
HUH?
DOES HE MEAN THE MAN IN THE PARK?
YES.
BUT HE'S DEAD NOW.
ONE OF THE EARL'S SERVANTS KILLED HIM.
I'M LOOKING FOR SOMEONE TO REPLACE HIM.
...
IS SHE REALLY WORTH THAT MUCH?

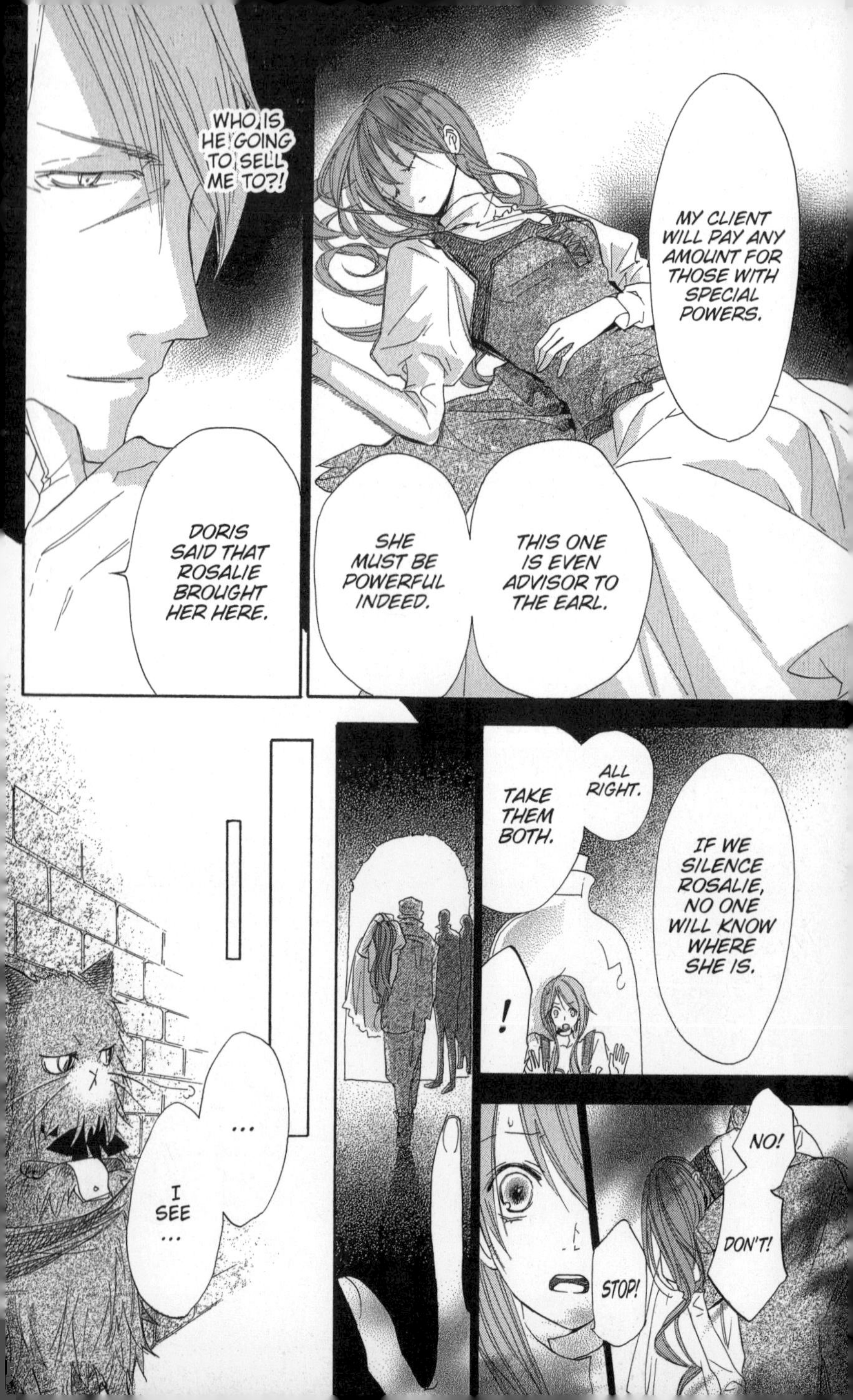
MY CLIENT WILL PAY ANY AMOUNT FOR THOSE WITH SPECIAL POWERS.
THIS ONE IS EVEN ADVISOR TO THE EARL.
SHE MUST BE POWERFUL INDEED.
WHO IS HE GOING TO SELL ME TO?!
DORIS SAID THAT ROSALIE BROUGHT HER HERE.
IF WE SILENCE ROSALIE, NO ONE WILL KNOW WHERE SHE IS.
ALL RIGHT.
TAKE THEM BOTH.
!
NO!
DON'T!
STOP!
...
I SEE ...

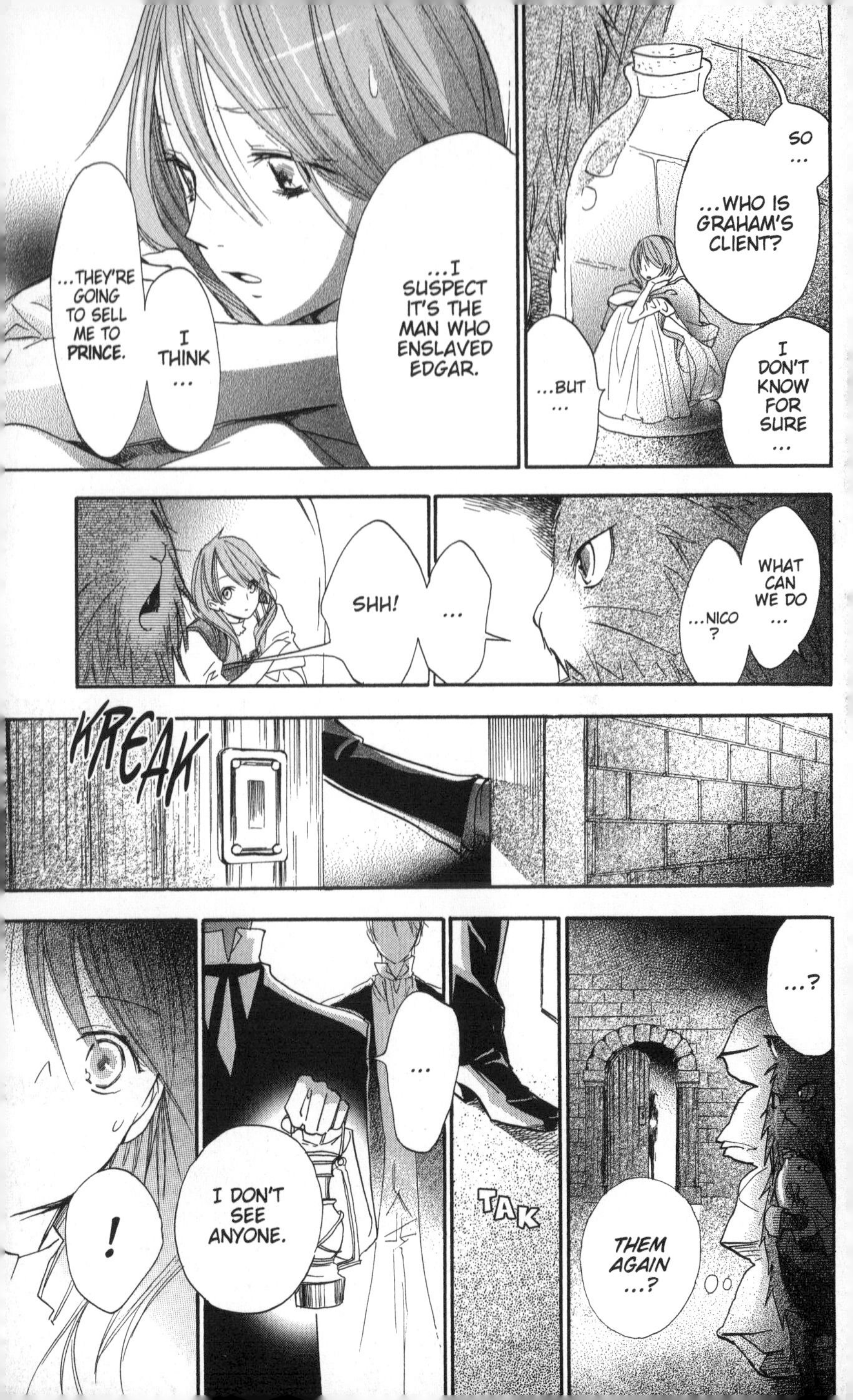
SO ...
...WHO IS GRAHAM'S CLIENT?
I DON'T KNOW FOR SURE ...
...BUT ...
...I SUSPECT IT'S THE MAN WHO ENSLAVED EDGAR.
I THINK ...
...THEY'RE GOING TO SELL ME TO PRINCE.
WHAT CAN WE DO ...
...NICO ?
...
SHH!
KREAK
...?
THEM AGAIN ...?
TAK
...
I DON'T SEE ANYONE.
!

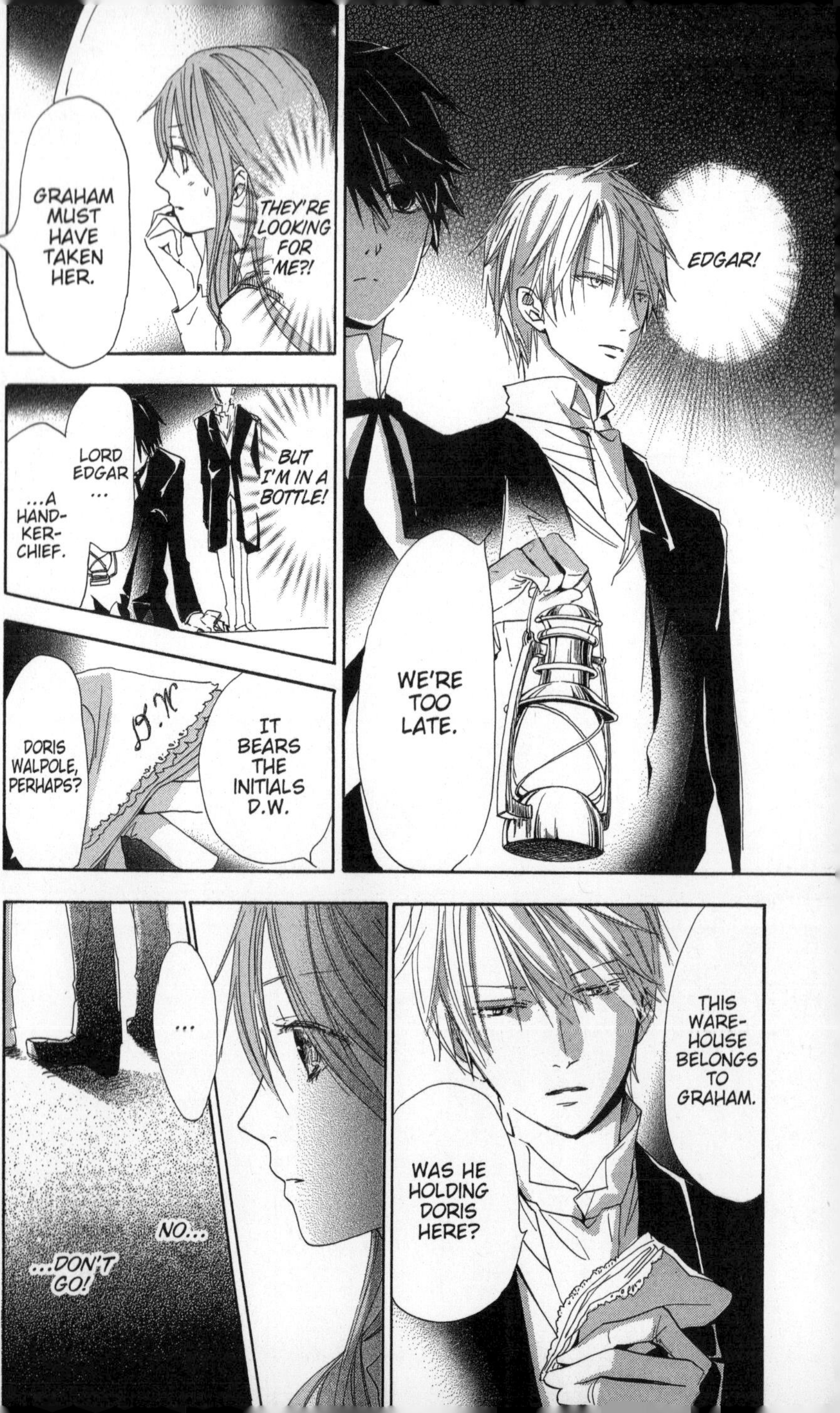
EDGAR!
WE'RE TOO LATE.
THEY'RE LOOKING FOR ME?!
GRAHAM MUST HAVE TAKEN HER.
BUT I'M IN A BOTTLE!
LORD EDGAR ...
...A HANDKERCHIEF.
IT BEARS THE INITIALS D.W.
DORIS WALPOLE, PERHAPS?
THIS WAREHOUSE BELONGS TO GRAHAM.
WAS HE HOLDING DORIS HERE?
...
NO...
...DON'T GO!

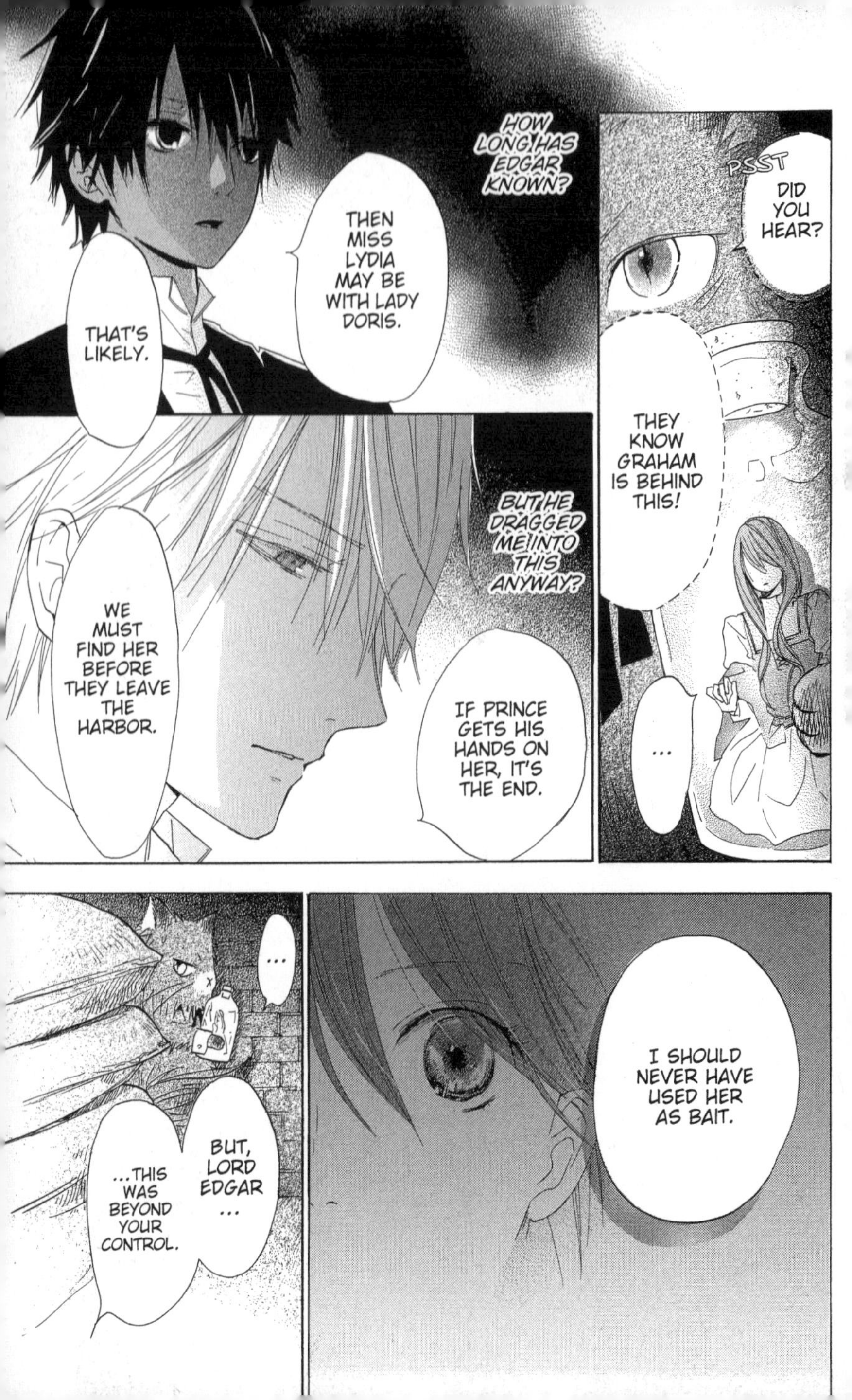
PSSST
DID YOU HEAR?
THEY KNOW GRAHAM IS BEHIND THIS!
...
HOW LONG HAS EDGAR KNOWN?
THEN MISS LYDIA MAY BE WITH LADY DORIS.
THAT'S LIKELY.
BUT HE DRAGGED ME INTO THIS ANYWAY?
IF PRINCE GETS HIS HANDS ON HER, IT'S THE END.
WE MUST FIND HER BEFORE THEY LEAVE THE HARBOR.
I SHOULD NEVER HAVE USED HER AS BAIT.
...
BUT, LORD EDGAR ...
...THIS WAS BEYOND YOUR CONTROL.

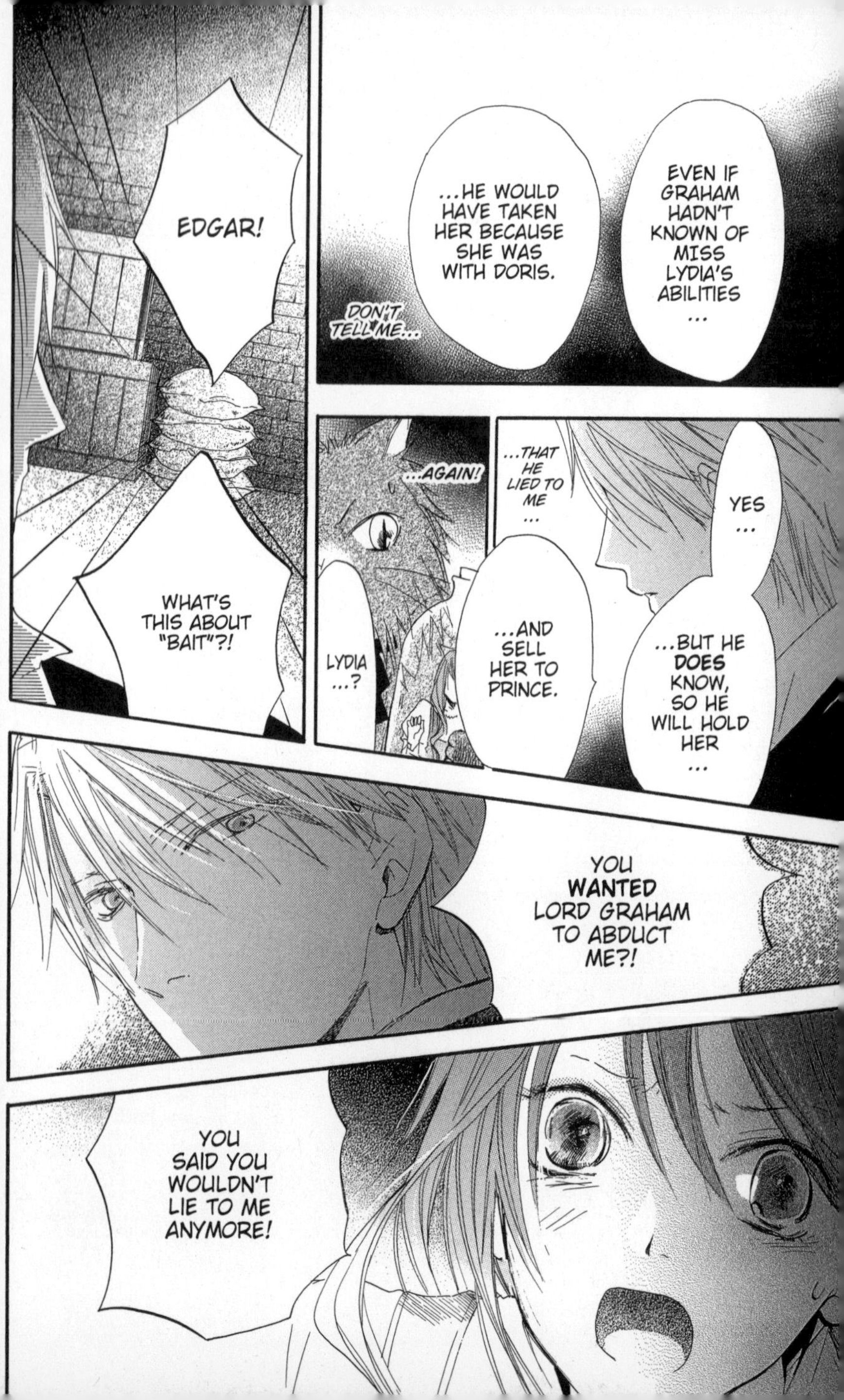
EVEN IF GRAHAM HADN'T KNOWN OF MISS LYDIA'S ABILITIES...
...HE WOULD HAVE TAKEN HER BECAUSE SHE WAS WITH DORIS.
DON'T TELL ME...
YES...
...BUT HE **DOES** KNOW, SO HE WILL HOLD HER...
...AND SELL HER TO PRINCE.
...THAT HE LIED TO ME...
...AGAIN!
LYDIA...?
EDGAR!
WHAT'S THIS ABOUT "BAIT"?!
YOU **WANTED** LORD GRAHAM TO ABDUCT ME?!
YOU SAID YOU WOULDN'T LIE TO ME ANYMORE!

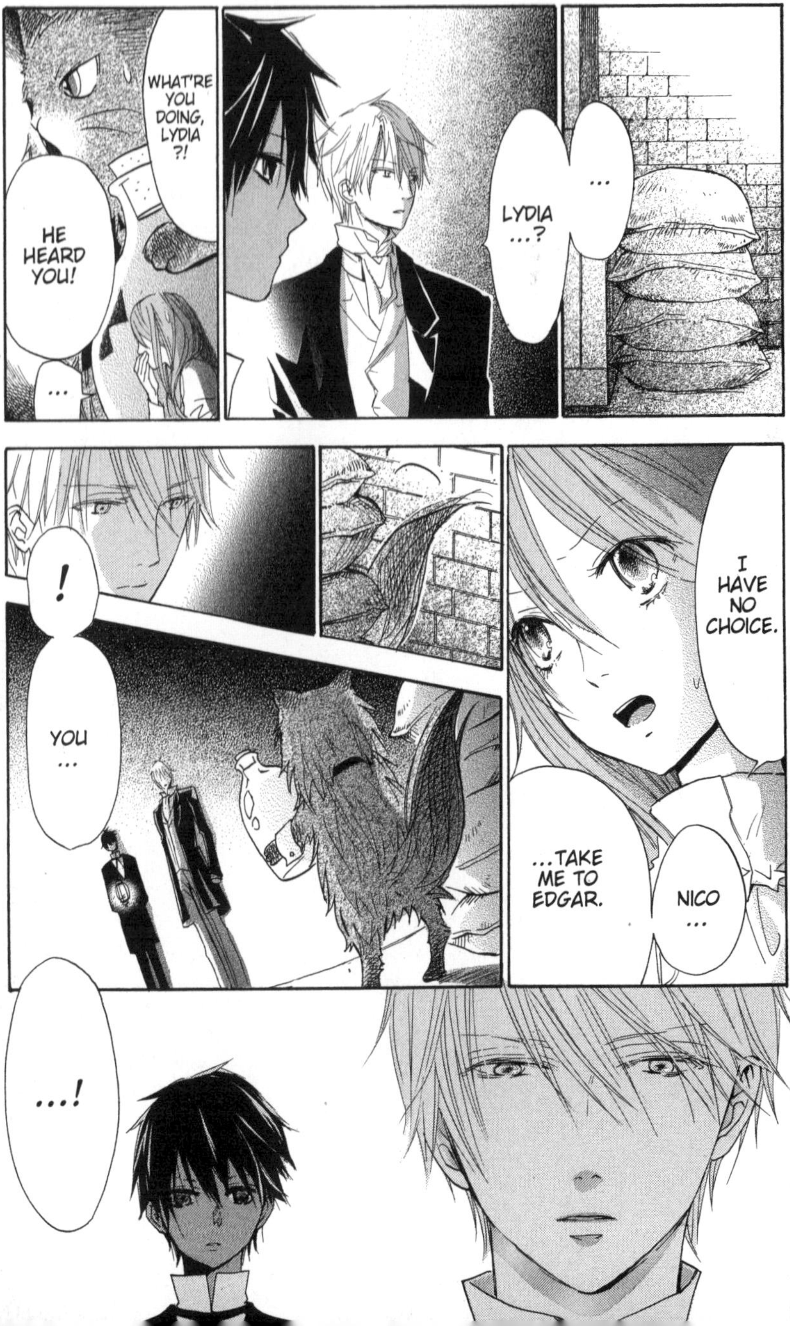
...
LYDIA ...?
WHAT'RE YOU DOING, LYDIA ?!
HE HEARD YOU!
...
I HAVE NO CHOICE.
NICO ...
...TAKE ME TO EDGAR.
!
YOU ...
...!

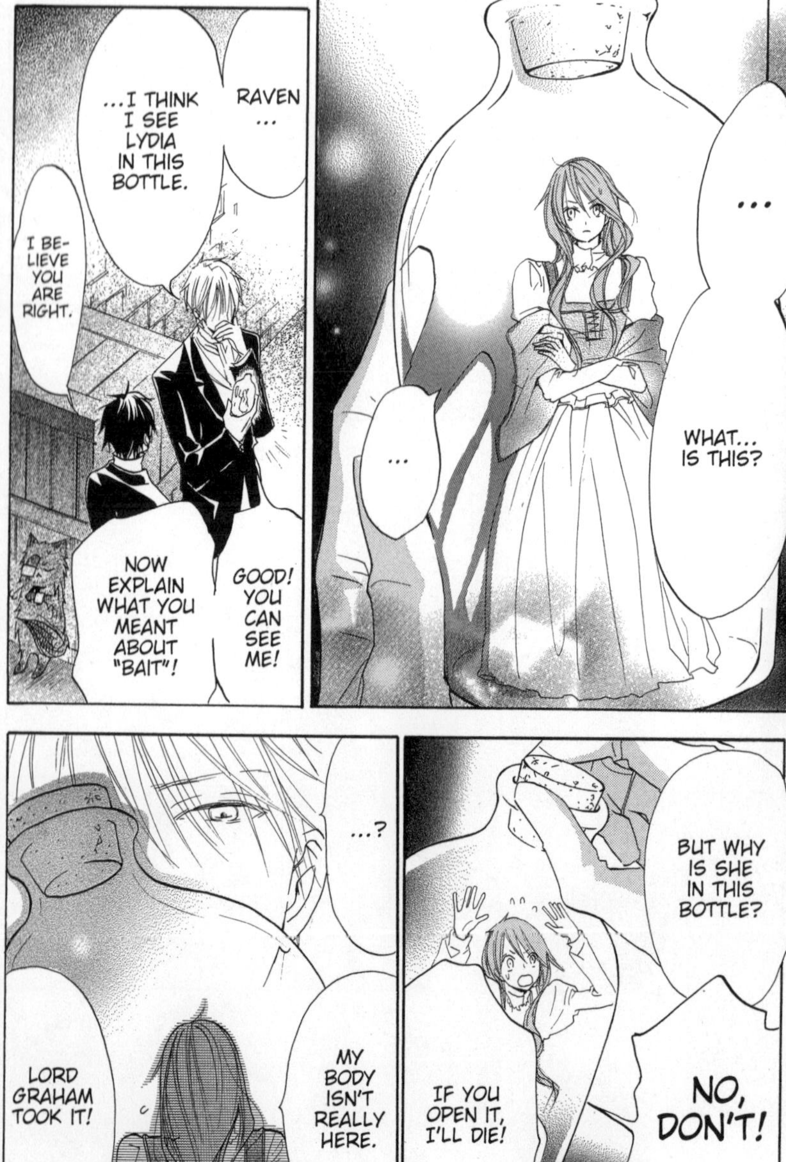
...
WHAT... IS THIS?
...
RAVEN ...
...I THINK I SEE LYDIA IN THIS BOTTLE.
I BE-LIEVE YOU ARE RIGHT.
GOOD! YOU CAN SEE ME!
NOW EXPLAIN WHAT YOU MEANT ABOUT "BAIT"!
BUT WHY IS SHE IN THIS BOTTLE?
NO, DON'T!
IF YOU OPEN IT, I'LL DIE!
...?
MY BODY ISN'T REALLY HERE.
LORD GRAHAM TOOK IT!

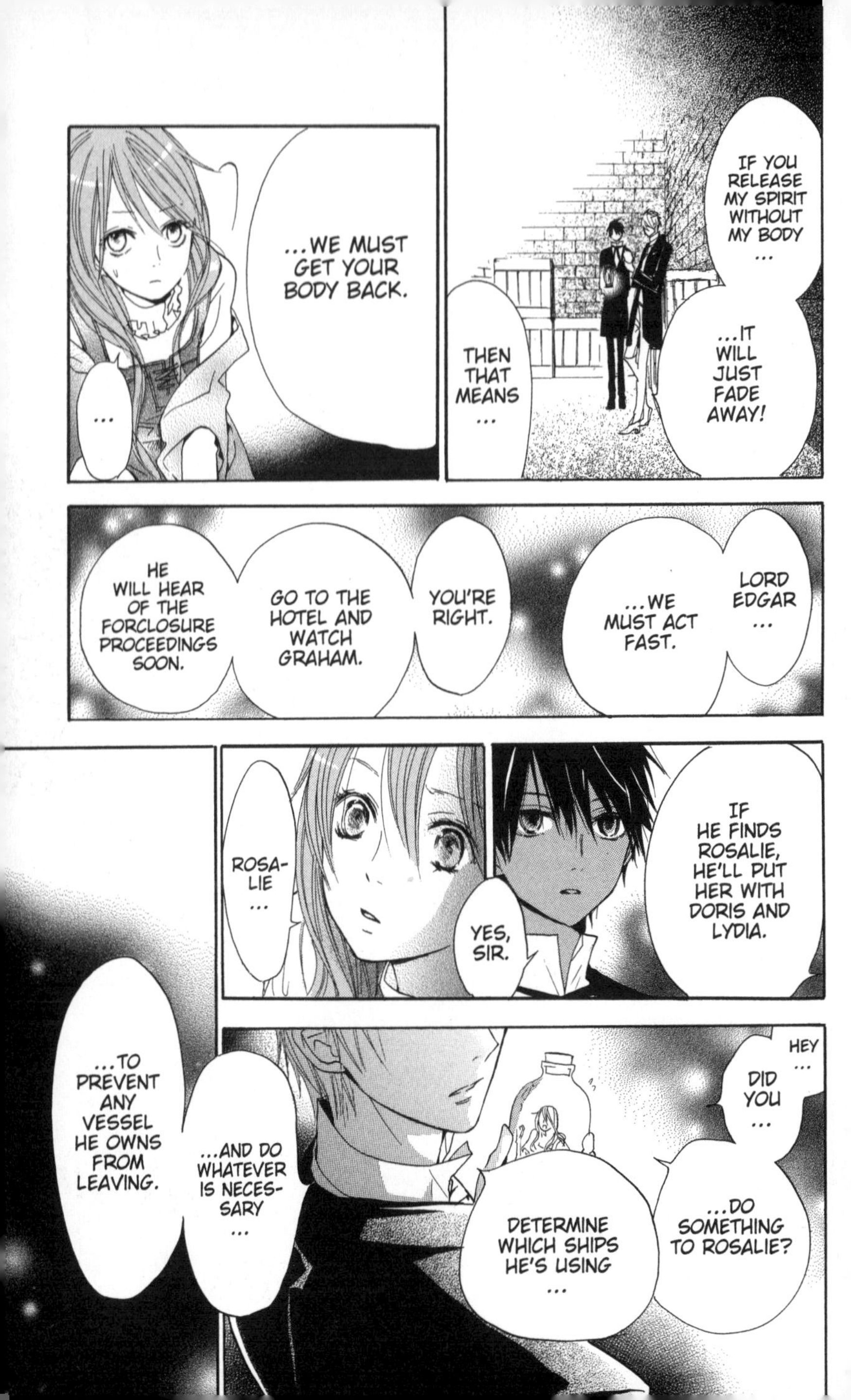
IF YOU RELEASE MY SPIRIT WITHOUT MY BODY ...
...IT WILL JUST FADE AWAY!
THEN THAT MEANS ...
...WE MUST GET YOUR BODY BACK.
...
LORD EDGAR ...
...WE MUST ACT FAST.
YOU'RE RIGHT.
GO TO THE HOTEL AND WATCH GRAHAM.
HE WILL HEAR OF THE FORCLOSURE PROCEEDINGS SOON.
IF HE FINDS ROSALIE, HE'LL PUT HER WITH DORIS AND LYDIA.
YES, SIR.
ROSA-LIE ...
HEY ...
DID YOU ...
...DO SOMETHING TO ROSALIE?
DETERMINE WHICH SHIPS HE'S USING ...
...AND DO WHATEVER IS NECES-SARY ...
...TO PREVENT ANY VESSEL HE OWNS FROM LEAVING.

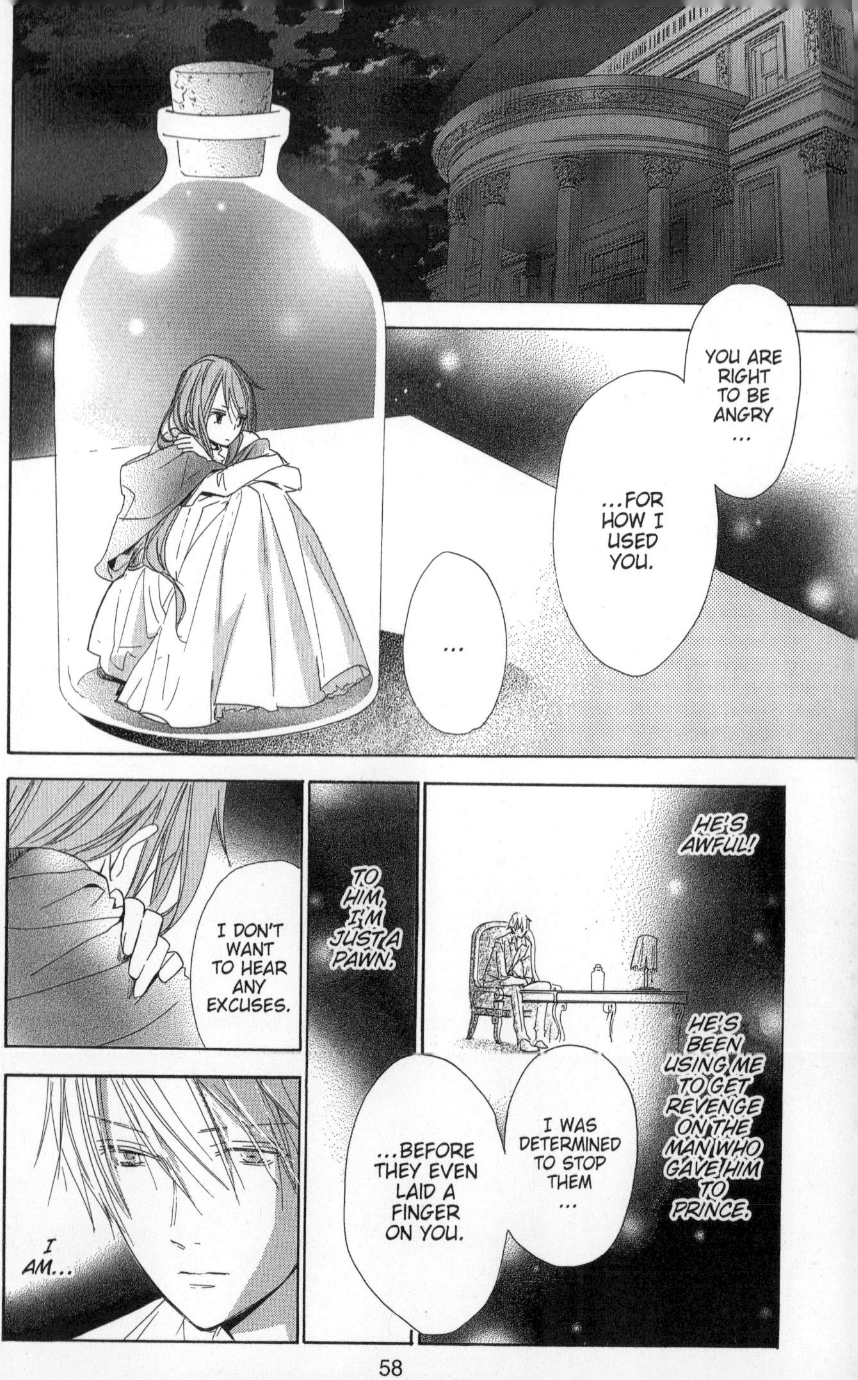
YOU ARE RIGHT TO BE ANGRY ...
...FOR HOW I USED YOU.
...
HE'S AWFUL!
HE'S BEEN USING ME TO GET REVENGE ON THE MAN WHO GAVE HIM TO PRINCE.
I WAS DETERMINED TO STOP THEM ...
...BEFORE THEY EVEN LAID A FINGER ON YOU.
TO HIM, I'M JUST A PAWN.
I DON'T WANT TO HEAR ANY EXCUSES.
I AM...

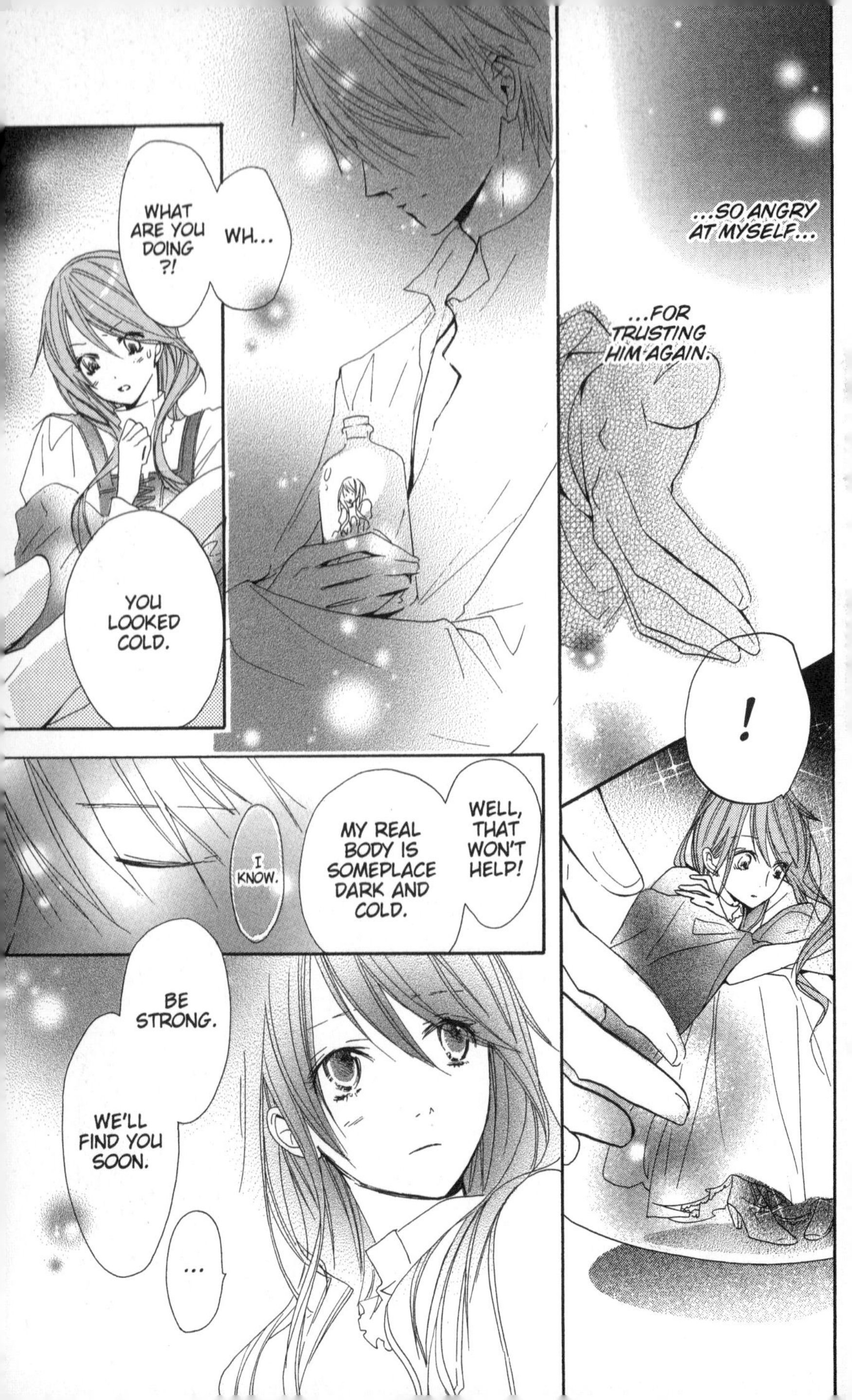
...SO ANGRY AT MYSELF...
...FOR TRUSTING HIM AGAIN.
!
WH...
WHAT ARE YOU DOING ?!
YOU LOOKED COLD.
WELL, THAT WON'T HELP!
MY REAL BODY IS SOMEPLACE DARK AND COLD.
I KNOW.
BE STRONG.
WE'LL FIND YOU SOON.
...

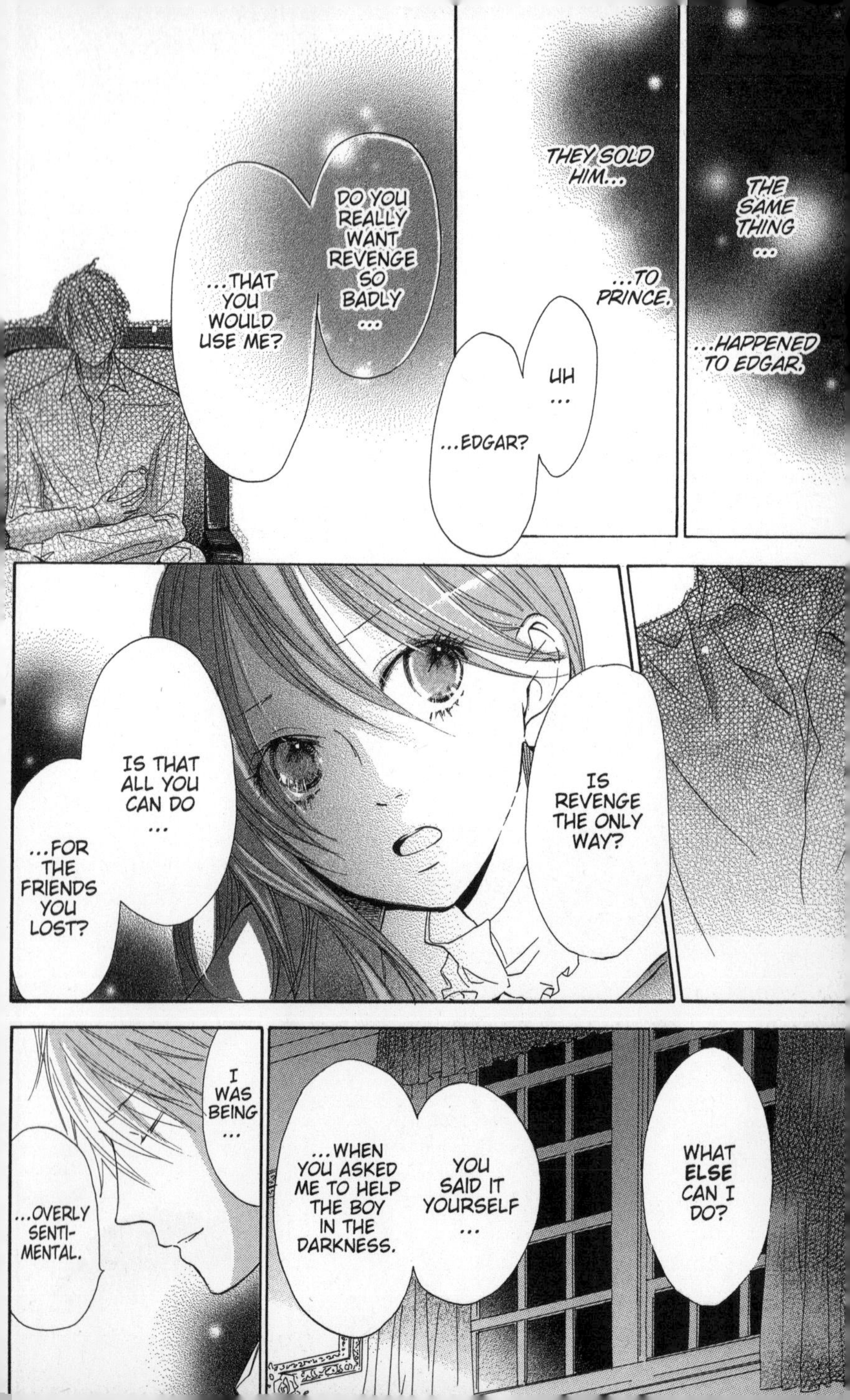
THE SAME THING...
...HAPPENED TO EDGAR.
THEY SOLD HIM...
...TO PRINCE.
UH...
...EDGAR?
DO YOU REALLY WANT REVENGE SO BADLY...
...THAT YOU WOULD USE ME?
IS REVENGE THE ONLY WAY?
IS THAT ALL YOU CAN DO...
...FOR THE FRIENDS YOU LOST?
WHAT ELSE CAN I DO?
YOU SAID IT YOURSELF...
...WHEN YOU ASKED ME TO HELP THE BOY IN THE DARKNESS.
I WAS BEING...
...OVERLY SENTI-MENTAL.

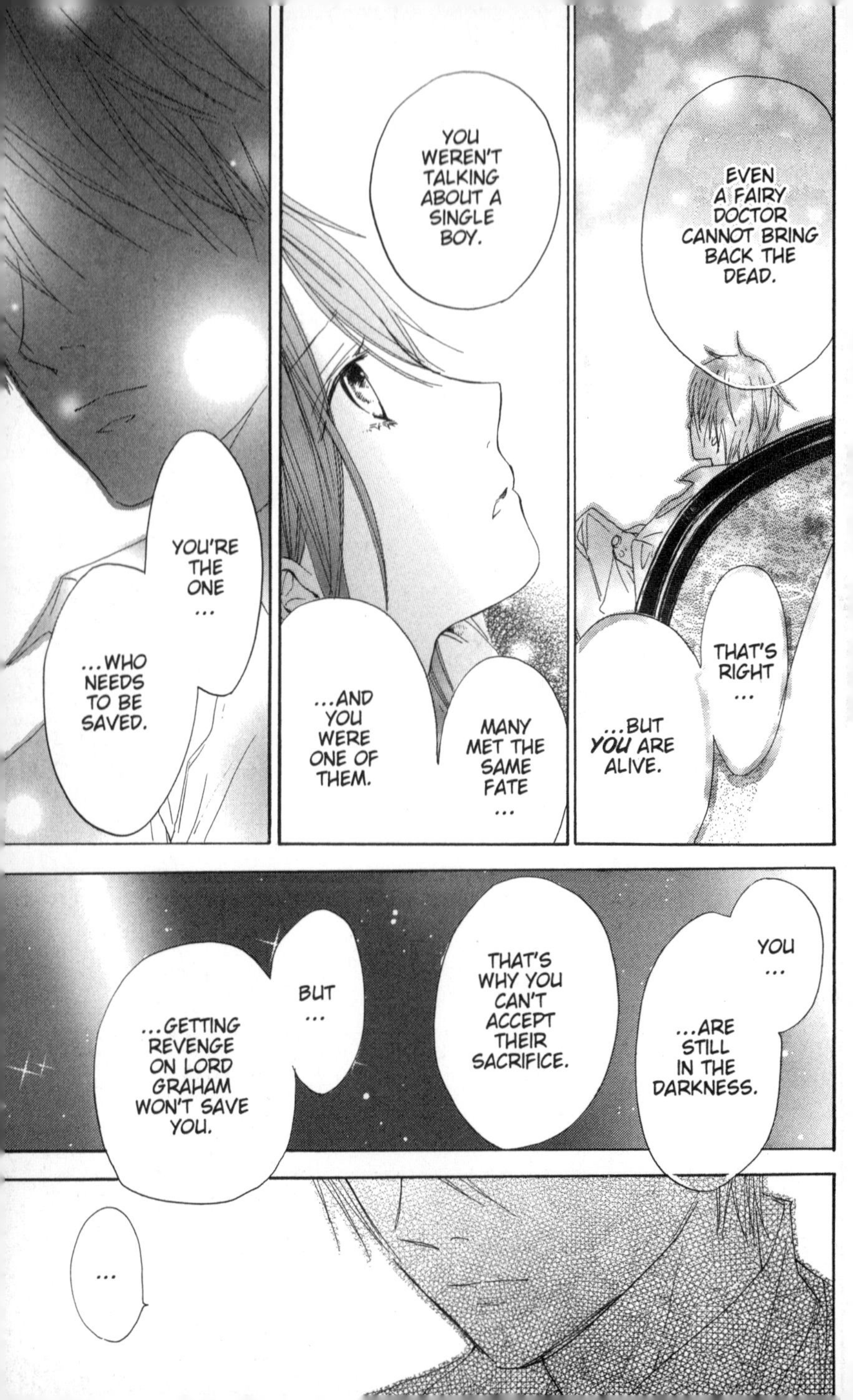
EVEN A FAIRY DOCTOR CANNOT BRING BACK THE DEAD.
THAT'S RIGHT ...
...BUT *YOU* ARE ALIVE.
YOU WEREN'T TALKING ABOUT A SINGLE BOY.
MANY MET THE SAME FATE ...
...AND YOU WERE ONE OF THEM.
YOU'RE THE ONE ...
...WHO NEEDS TO BE SAVED.
YOU ...
...ARE STILL IN THE DARKNESS.
THAT'S WHY YOU CAN'T ACCEPT THEIR SACRIFICE.
BUT ...
...GETTING REVENGE ON LORD GRAHAM WON'T SAVE YOU.
...

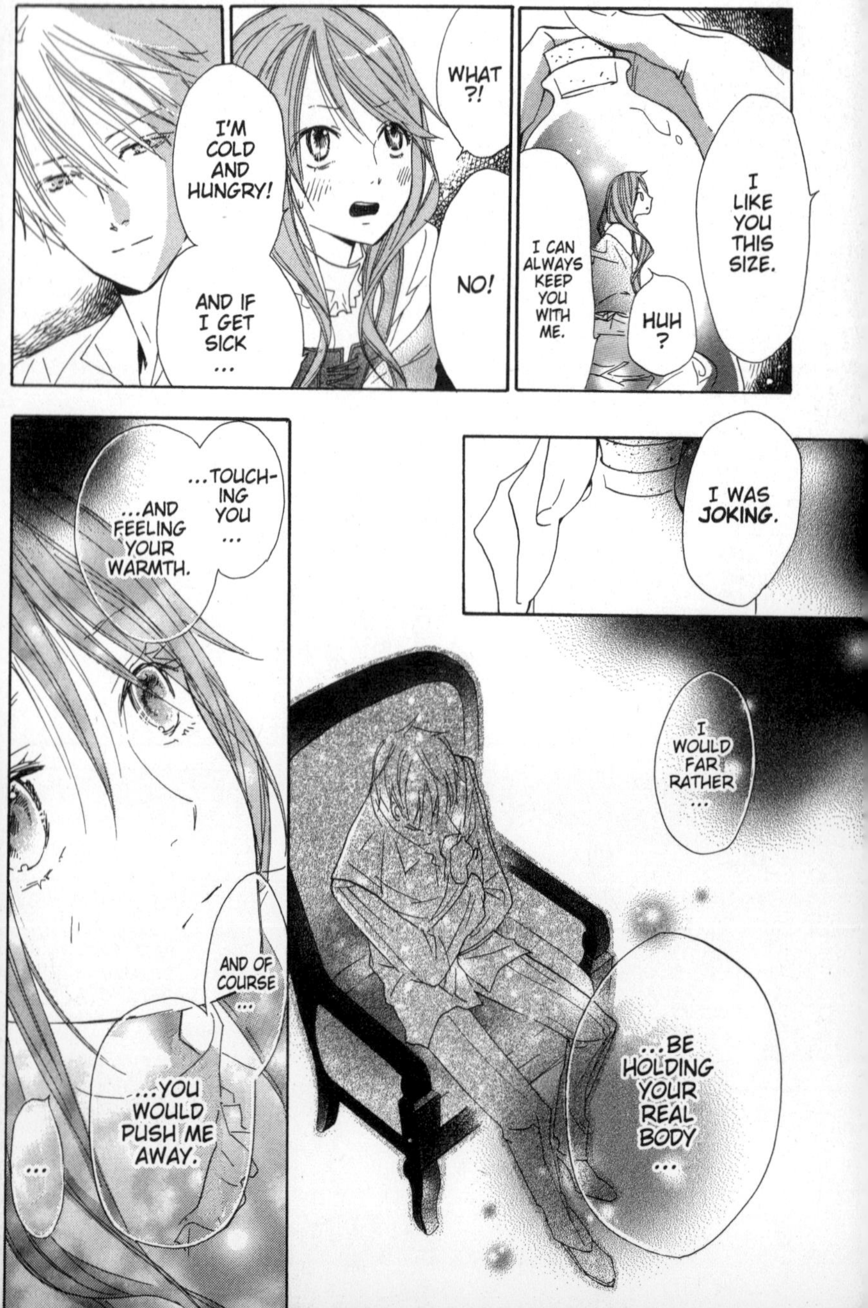
I LIKE YOU THIS SIZE.
HUH?
I CAN ALWAYS KEEP YOU WITH ME.
WHAT?!
NO!
I'M COLD AND HUNGRY!
AND IF I GET SICK ...
I WAS JOKING.
I WOULD FAR RATHER ...
...BE HOLDING YOUR REAL BODY ...
...TOUCHING-ING YOU ...
...AND FEELING YOUR WARMTH.
AND OF COURSE ...
...YOU WOULD PUSH ME AWAY.
...

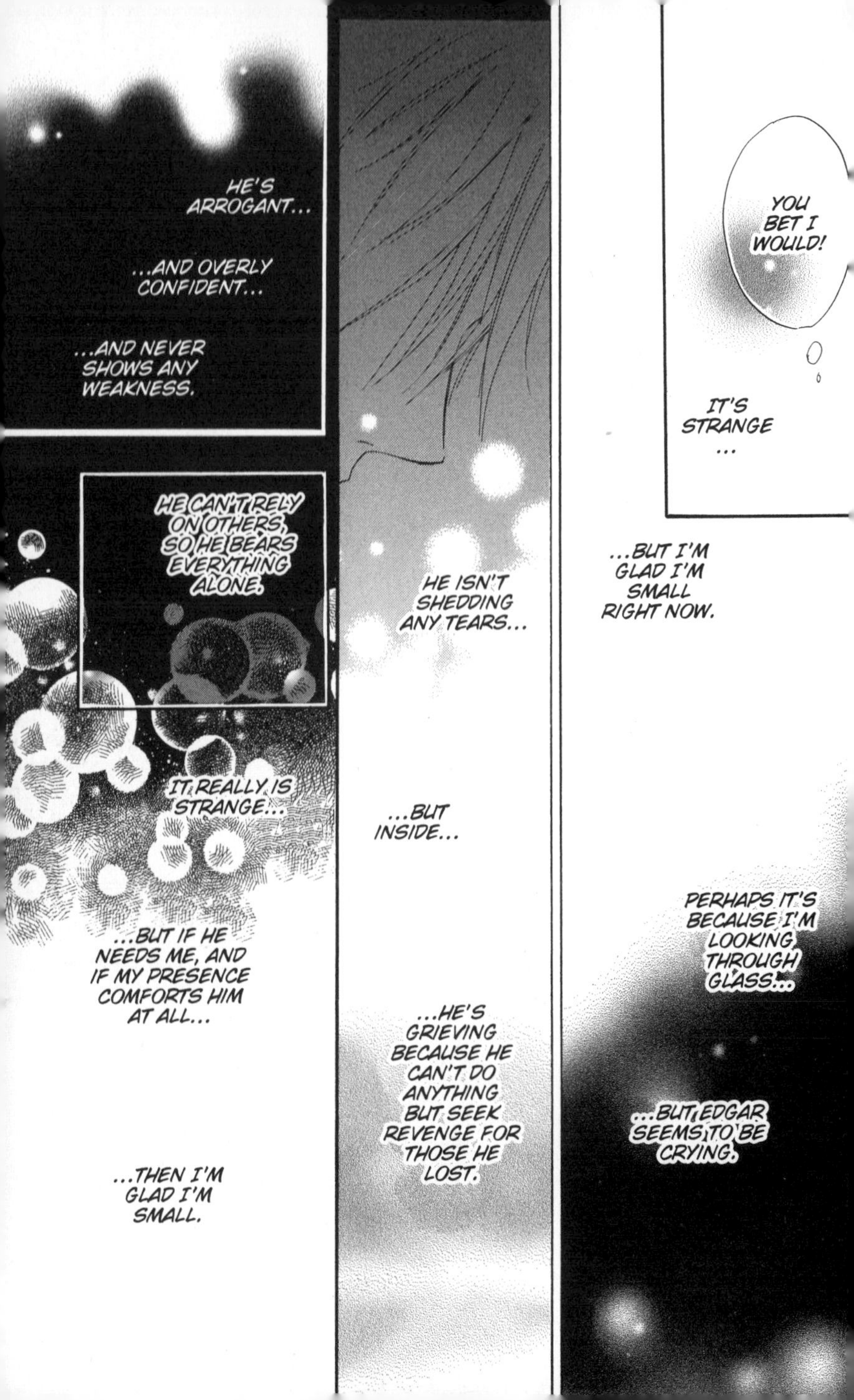
YOU BET I WOULD!
IT'S STRANGE...
...BUT I'M GLAD I'M SMALL RIGHT NOW.
PERHAPS IT'S BECAUSE I'M LOOKING THROUGH GLASS...
...BUT EDGAR SEEMS TO BE CRYING.
HE ISN'T SHEDDING ANY TEARS...
...BUT INSIDE...
...HE'S GRIEVING BECAUSE HE CAN'T DO ANYTHING BUT SEEK REVENGE FOR THOSE HE LOST.
HE'S ARROGANT...
...AND OVERLY CONFIDENT...
...AND NEVER SHOWS ANY WEAKNESS.
HE CAN'T RELY ON OTHERS, SO HE BEARS EVERYTHING ALONE.
IT REALLY IS STRANGE...
...BUT IF HE NEEDS ME, AND IF MY PRESENCE COMFORTS HIM AT ALL...
...THEN I'M GLAD I'M SMALL.

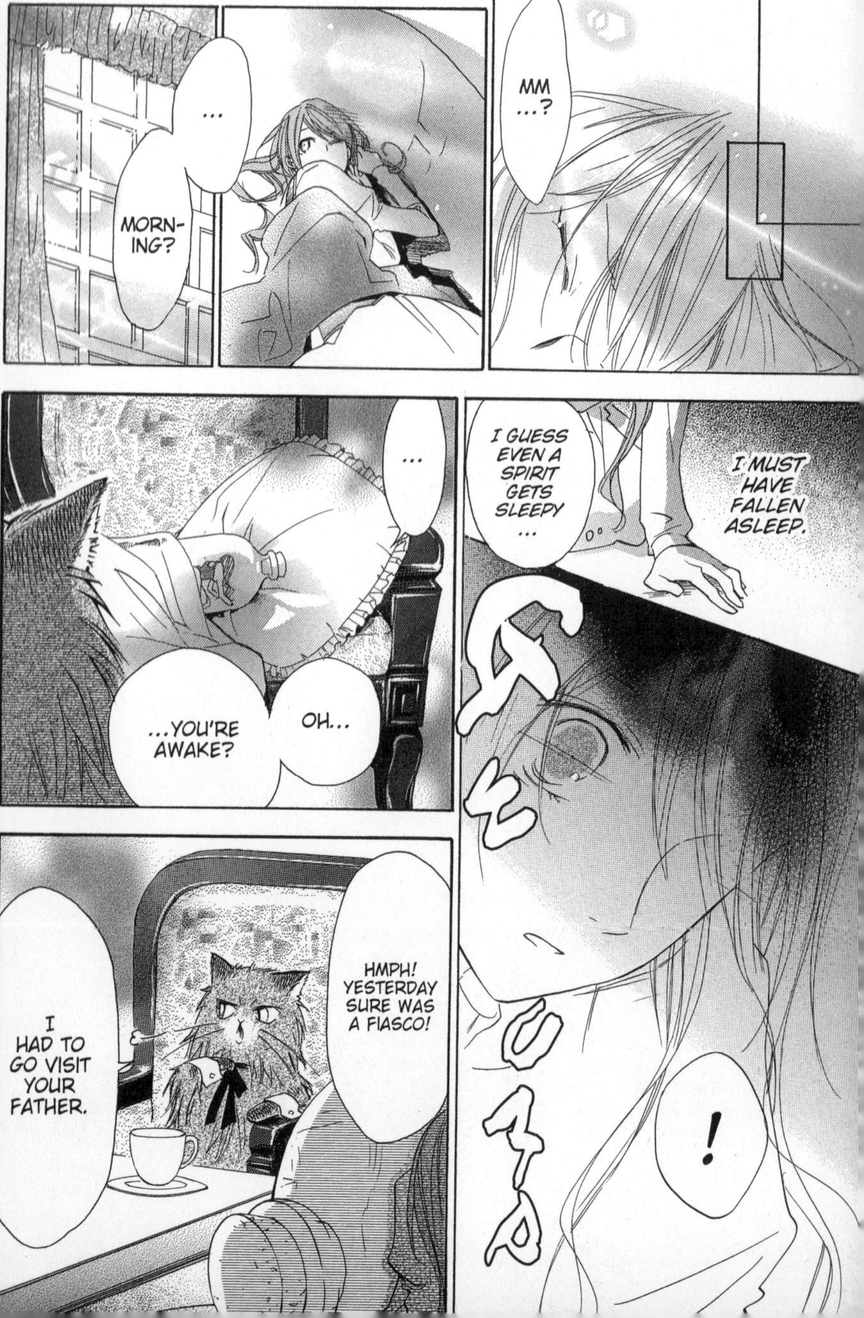
MM ...?
...
MORN-ING?
I MUST HAVE FALLEN ASLEEP.
I GUESS EVEN A SPIRIT GETS SLEEPY ...
!
...
OH...
...YOU'RE AWAKE?
HMPH! YESTERDAY SURE WAS A FIASCO!
I HAD TO GO VISIT YOUR FATHER.

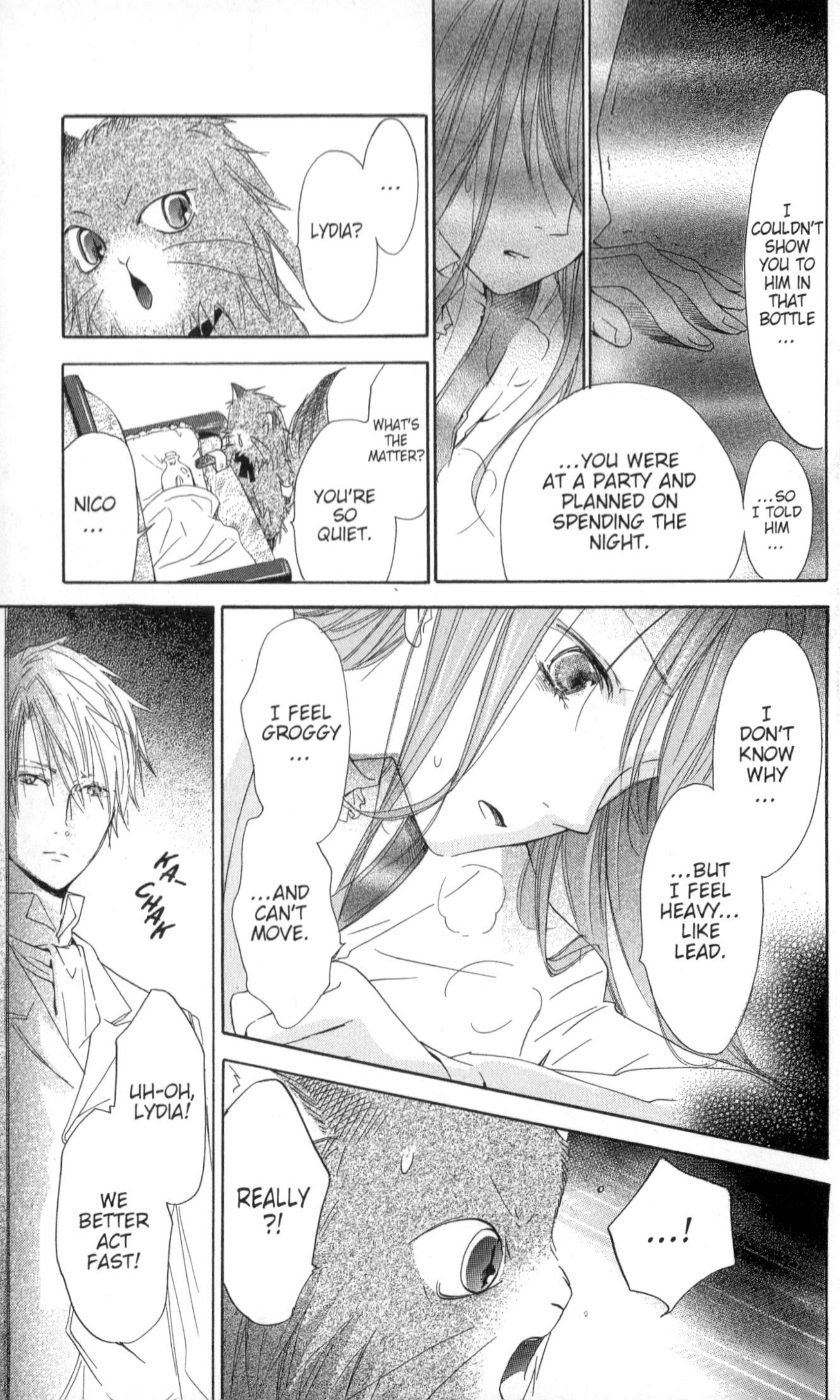
I COULDN'T SHOW YOU TO HIM IN THAT BOTTLE ...
...SO I TOLD HIM ...
...YOU WERE AT A PARTY AND PLANNED ON SPENDING THE NIGHT.
... LYDIA?
WHAT'S THE MATTER? YOU'RE SO QUIET.
NICO ...
I DON'T KNOW WHY ...
...BUT I FEEL HEAVY... LIKE LEAD.
I FEEL GROGGY ...
...AND CAN'T MOVE.
...!
REALLY ?!
KA-CHAK
UH-OH, LYDIA!
WE BETTER ACT FAST!

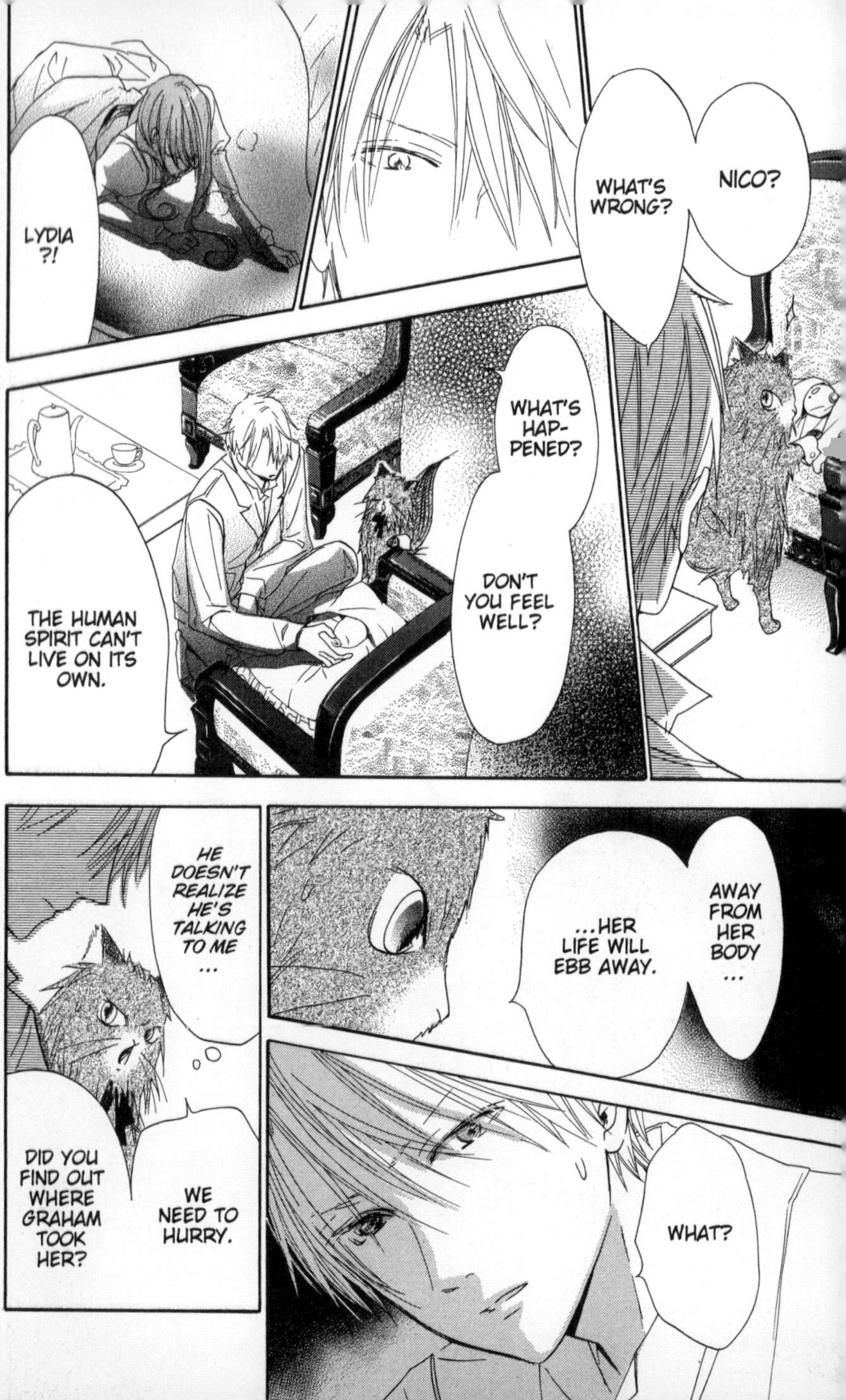
NICO?
WHAT'S WRONG?
LYDIA ?!
WHAT'S HAP-PENED?
DON'T YOU FEEL WELL?
THE HUMAN SPIRIT CAN'T LIVE ON ITS OWN.
AWAY FROM HER BODY ...
...HER LIFE WILL EBB AWAY.
WHAT?
HE DOESN'T REALIZE HE'S TALKING TO ME ...
WE NEED TO HURRY.
DID YOU FIND OUT WHERE GRAHAM TOOK HER?

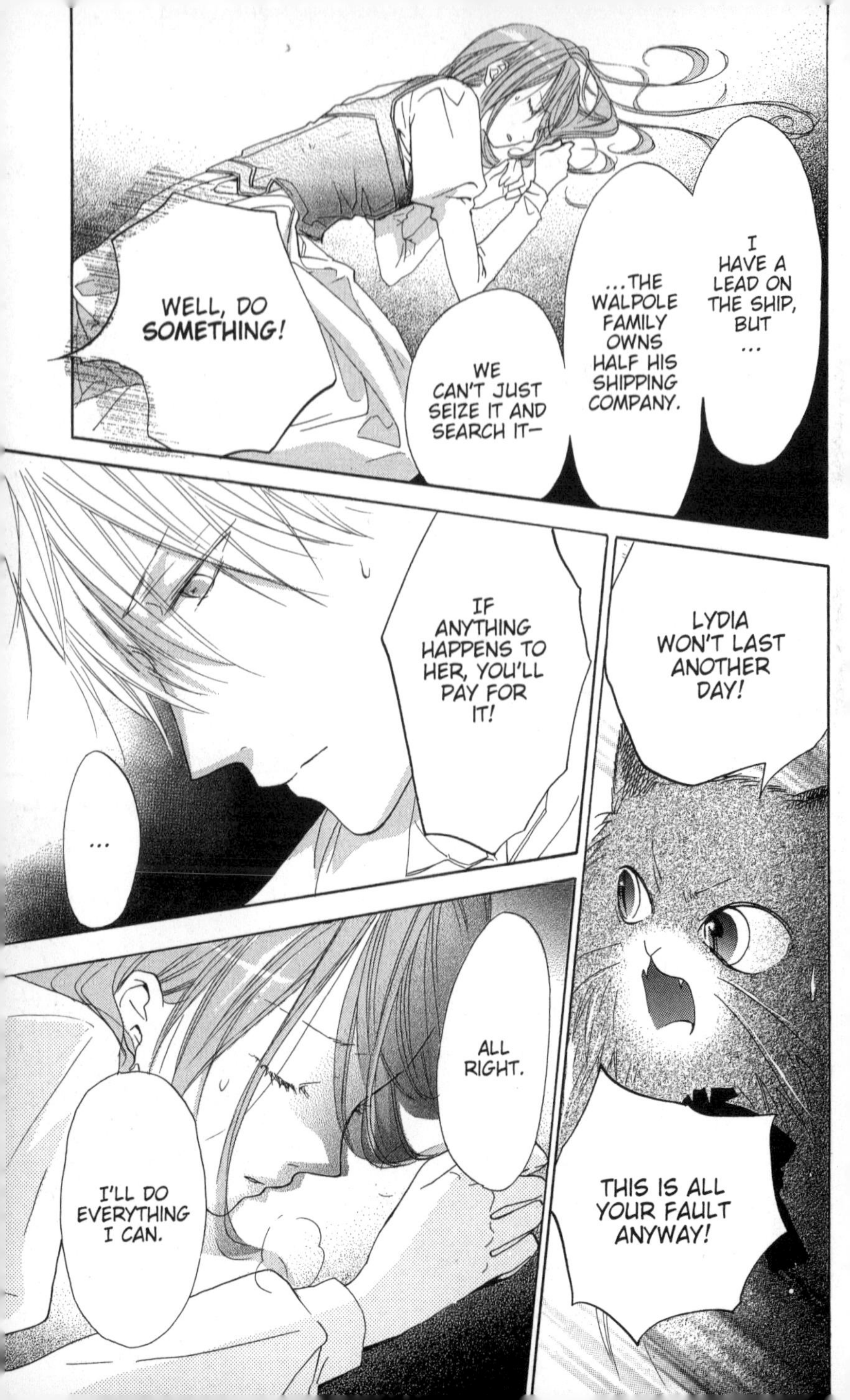

I HAVE A LEAD ON THE SHIP, BUT ...
...THE WALPOLE FAMILY OWNS HALF HIS SHIPPING COMPANY.
WE CAN'T JUST SEIZE IT AND SEARCH IT—
WELL, DO SOMETHING!
LYDIA WON'T LAST ANOTHER DAY!
THIS IS ALL YOUR FAULT ANYWAY!
IF ANYTHING HAPPENS TO HER, YOU'LL PAY FOR IT!
...
ALL RIGHT.
I'LL DO EVERYTHING I CAN.

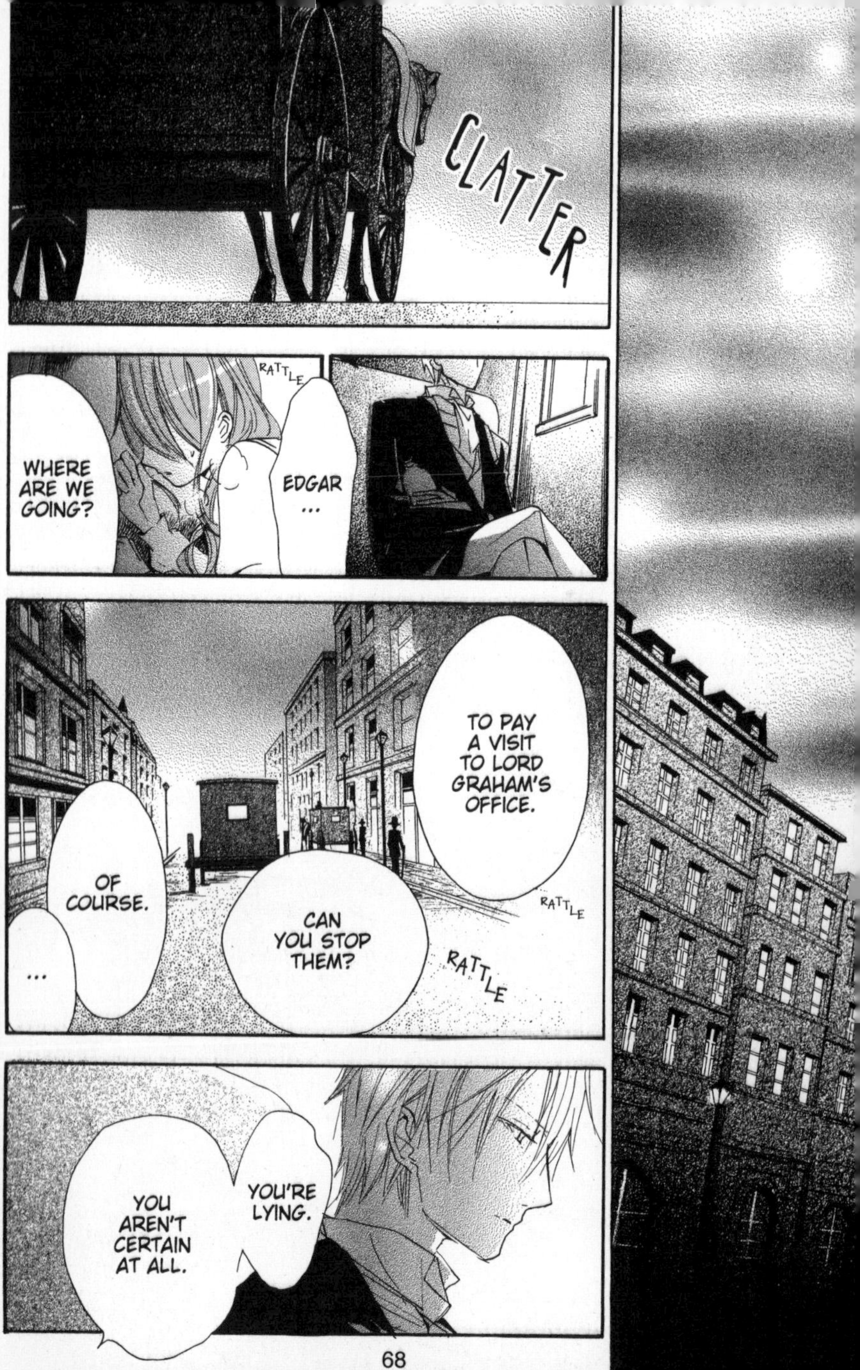
CLATTER
RATTLE
EDGAR ...
WHERE ARE WE GOING?
TO PAY A VISIT TO LORD GRAHAM'S OFFICE.
RATTLE
CAN YOU STOP THEM?
RATTLE
OF COURSE.
...
YOU'RE LYING.
YOU AREN'T CERTAIN AT ALL.

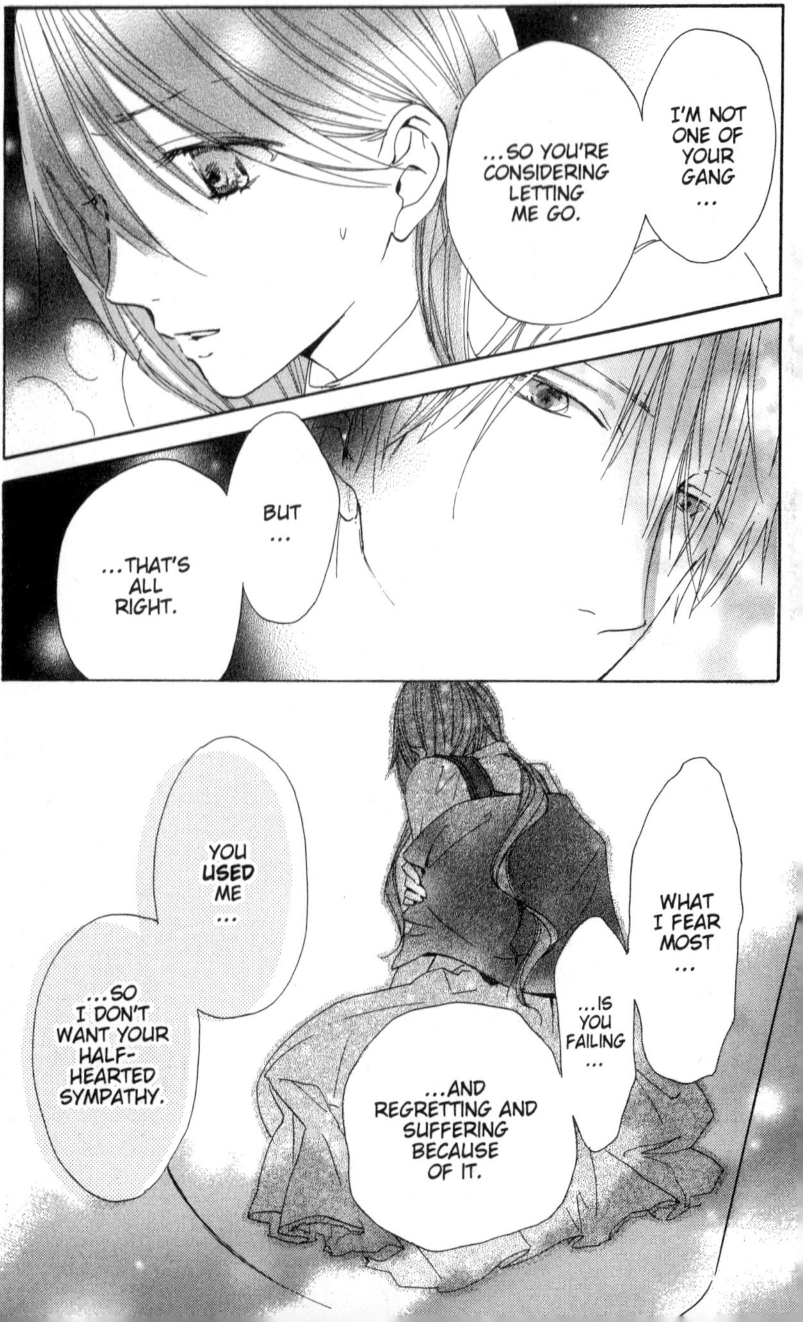
I'M NOT ONE OF YOUR GANG ...
...SO YOU'RE CONSIDERING LETTING ME GO.
BUT ...
...THAT'S ALL RIGHT.
YOU USED ME ...
...SO I DON'T WANT YOUR HALF-HEARTED SYMPATHY.
WHAT I FEAR MOST ...
...IS YOU FAILING ...
...AND REGRETTING AND SUFFERING BECAUSE OF IT.

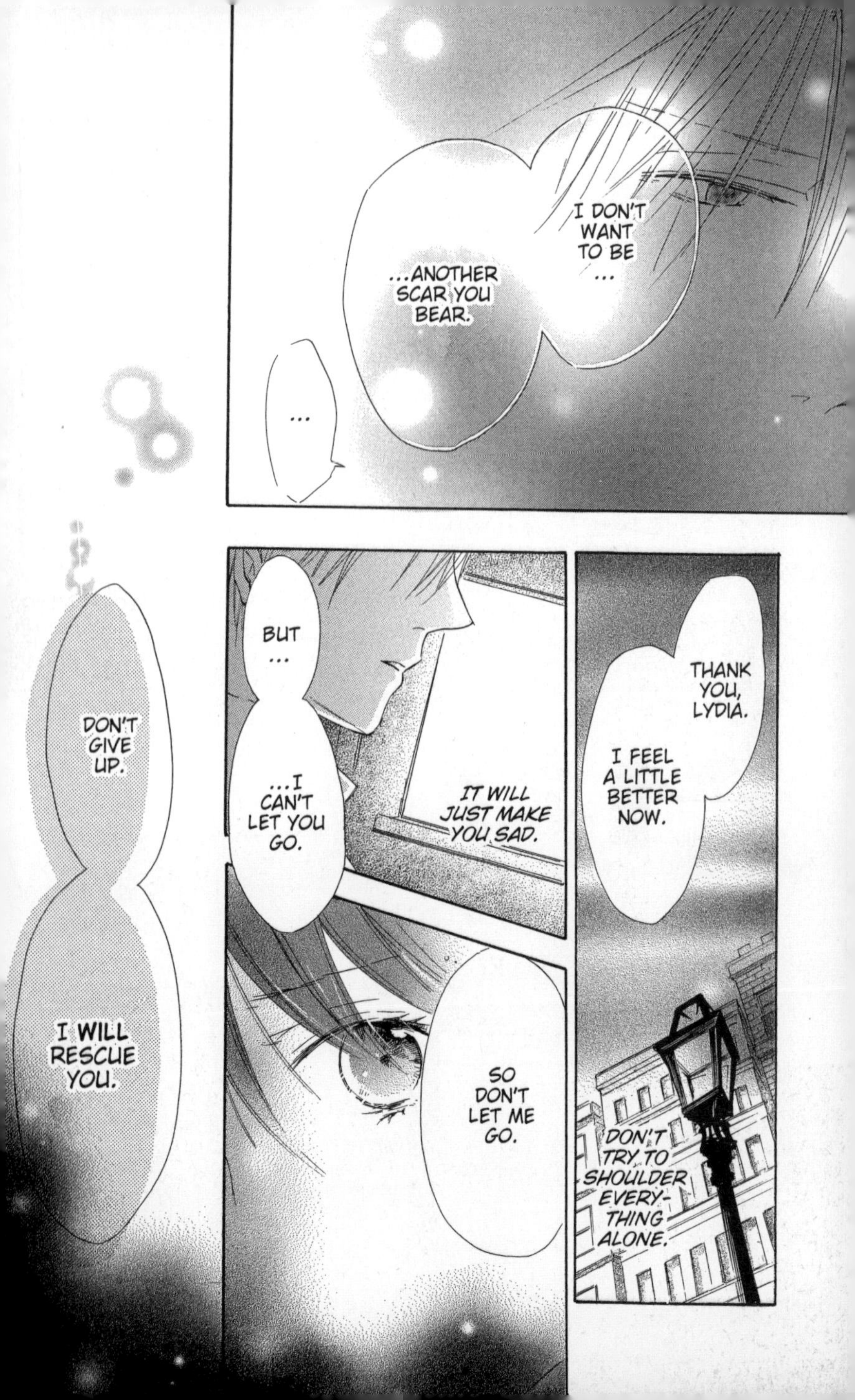
I DON'T WANT TO BE ...
...ANOTHER SCAR YOU BEAR.
...
THANK YOU, LYDIA.
I FEEL A LITTLE BETTER NOW.
DON'T TRY TO SHOULDER EVERY-THING ALONE.
IT WILL JUST MAKE YOU SAD.
BUT ...
...I CAN'T LET YOU GO.
SO DON'T LET ME GO.
DON'T GIVE UP.
I WILL RESCUE YOU.

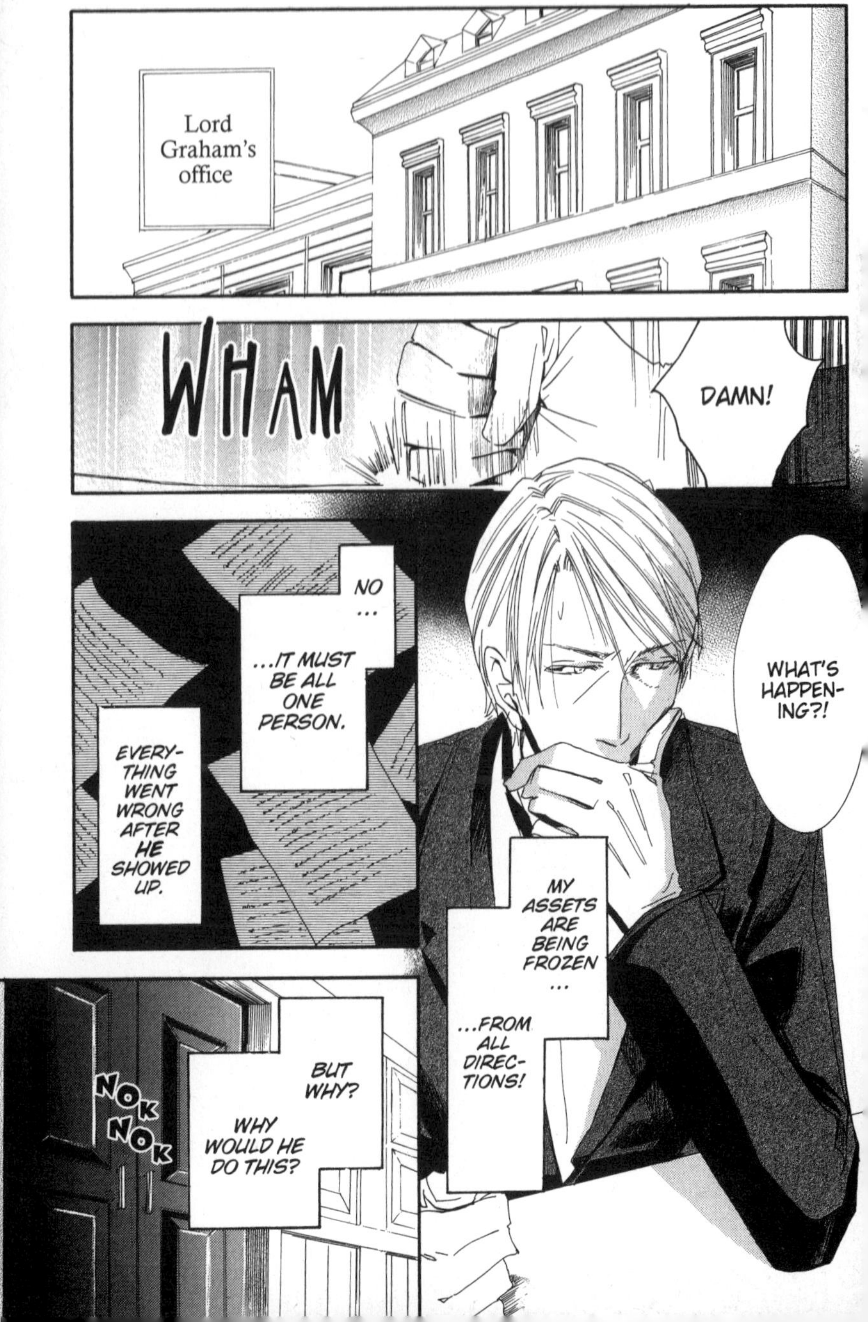
Lord Graham's office
DAMN!
WHAM
WHAT'S HAPPENING?!
MY ASSETS ARE BEING FROZEN...
...FROM ALL DIRECTIONS!
NO...
...IT MUST BE ALL ONE PERSON.
EVERYTHING WENT WRONG AFTER HE SHOWED UP.
BUT WHY?
WHY WOULD HE DO THIS?
NOK NOK

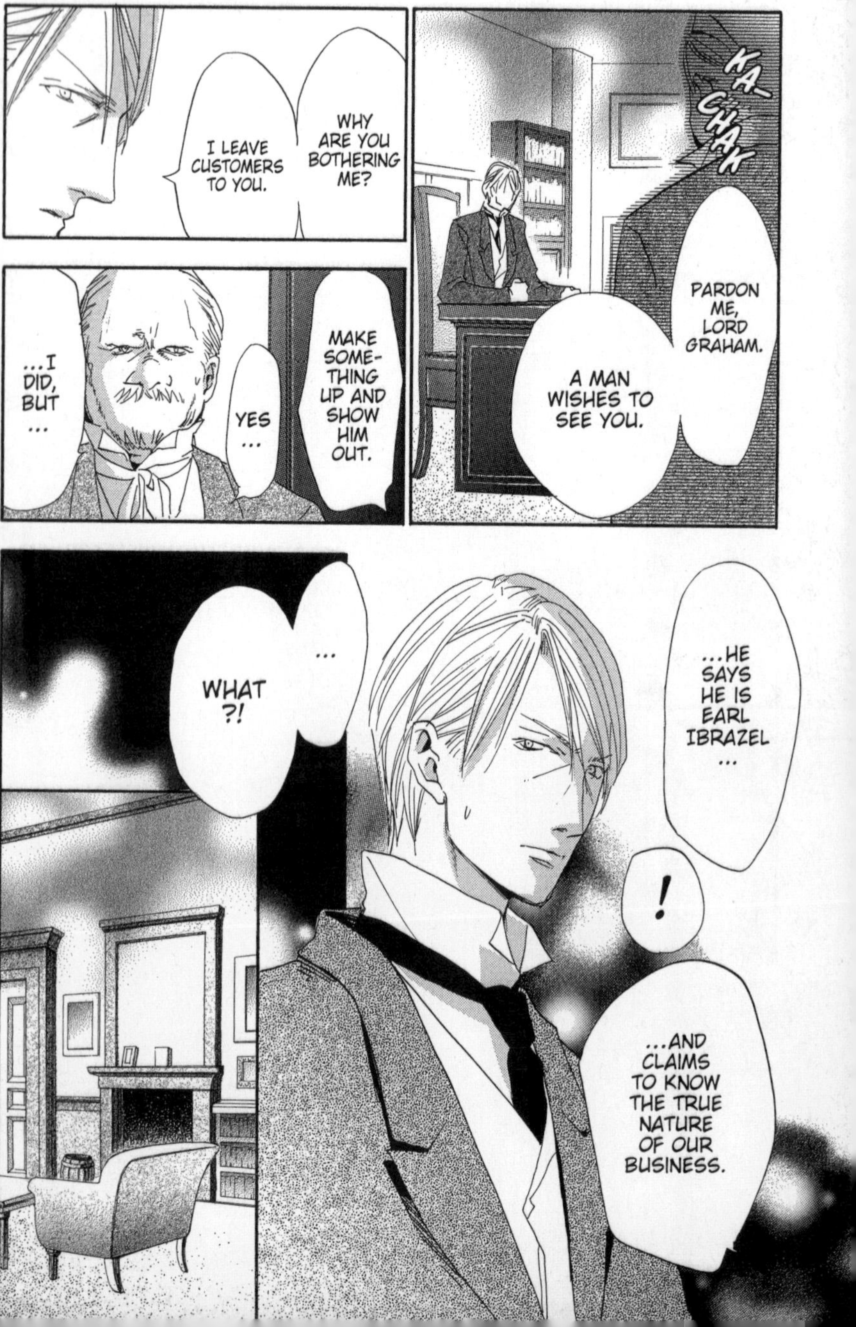
KA-CHAK
PARDON ME, LORD GRAHAM.
A MAN WISHES TO SEE YOU.
WHY ARE YOU BOTHERING ME?
I LEAVE CUSTOMERS TO YOU.
MAKE SOME-THING UP AND SHOW HIM OUT.
YES ...
...I DID, BUT ...
...HE SAYS HE IS EARL IBRAZEL ...
!
...AND CLAIMS TO KNOW THE TRUE NATURE OF OUR BUSINESS.
...
WHAT ?!

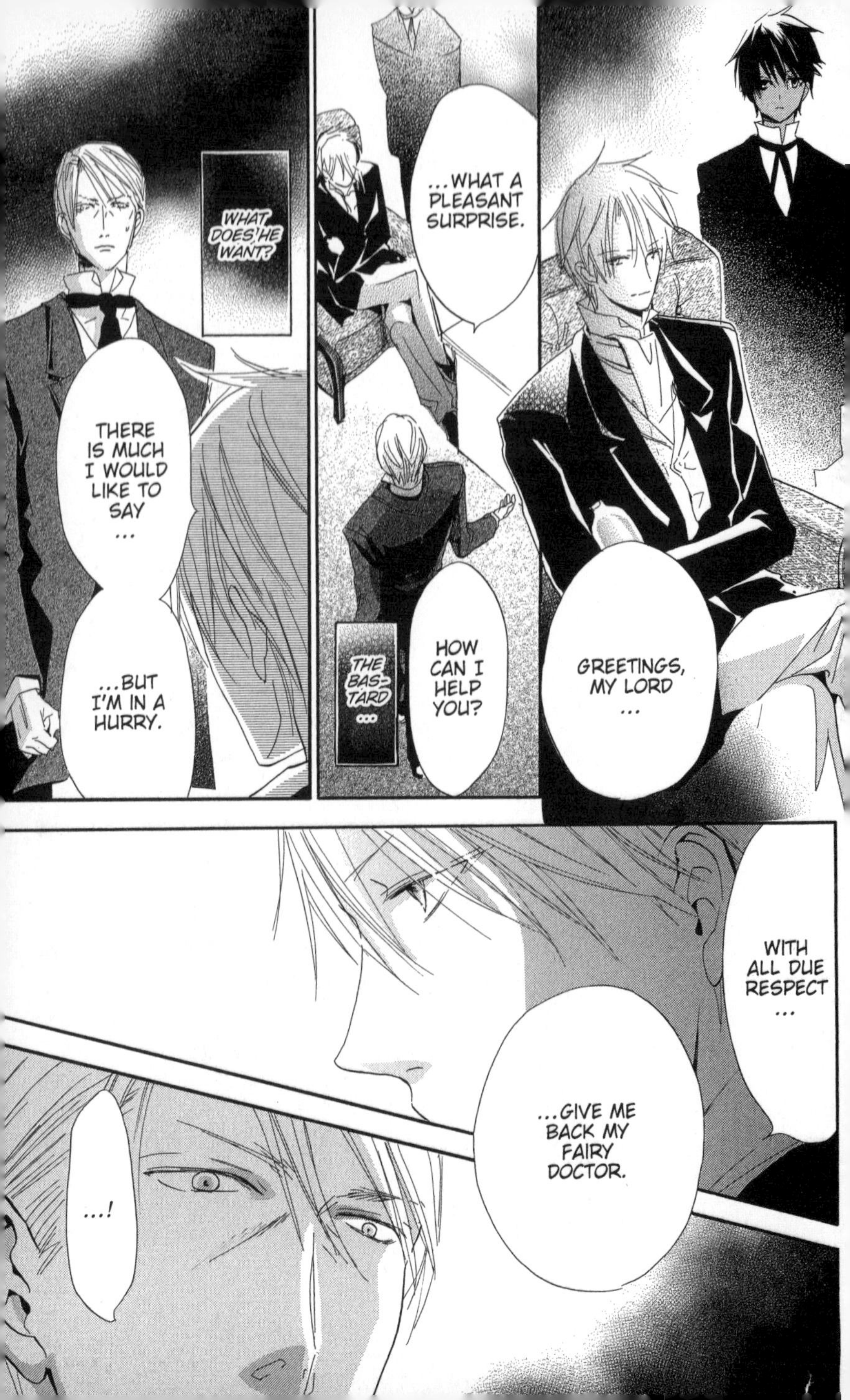
GREETINGS, MY LORD ...
...WHAT A PLEASANT SURPRISE.
HOW CAN I HELP YOU?
THE BAS- TARD ...
WHAT DOES HE WANT?
THERE IS MUCH I WOULD LIKE TO SAY ...
...BUT I'M IN A HURRY.
WITH ALL DUE RESPECT ...
...GIVE ME BACK MY FAIRY DOCTOR.
...!

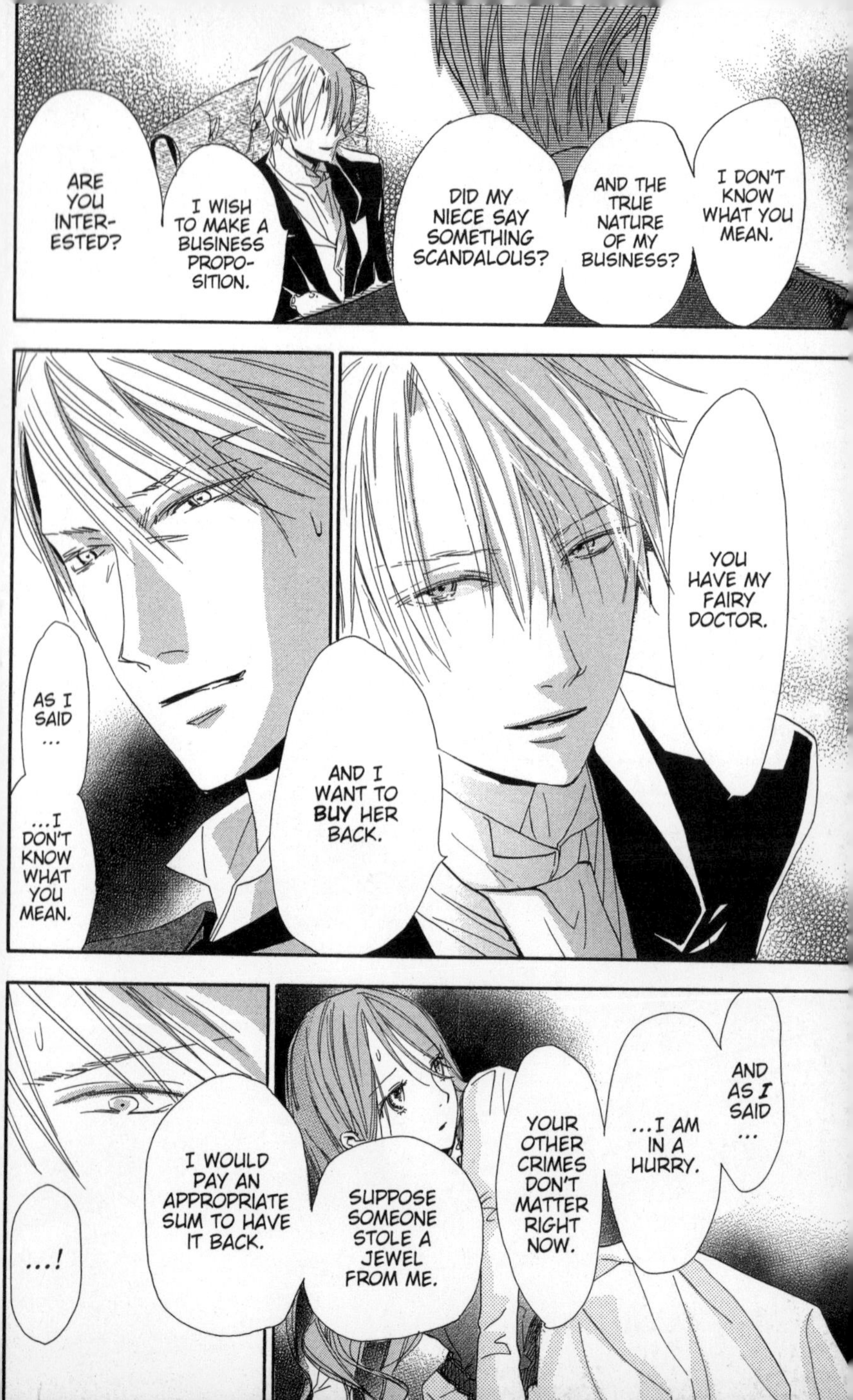
I DON'T KNOW WHAT YOU MEAN.
AND THE TRUE NATURE OF MY BUSINESS?
DID MY NIECE SAY SOMETHING SCANDALOUS?
I WISH TO MAKE A BUSINESS PROPOSITION.
ARE YOU INTERESTED?
YOU HAVE MY FAIRY DOCTOR.
AND I WANT TO **BUY** HER BACK.
AS I SAID ...
...I DON'T KNOW WHAT YOU MEAN.
AND AS *I* SAID ...
...I AM IN A HURRY.
YOUR OTHER CRIMES DON'T MATTER RIGHT NOW.
SUPPOSE SOMEONE STOLE A JEWEL FROM ME.
I WOULD PAY AN APPROPRIATE SUM TO HAVE IT BACK.
...!

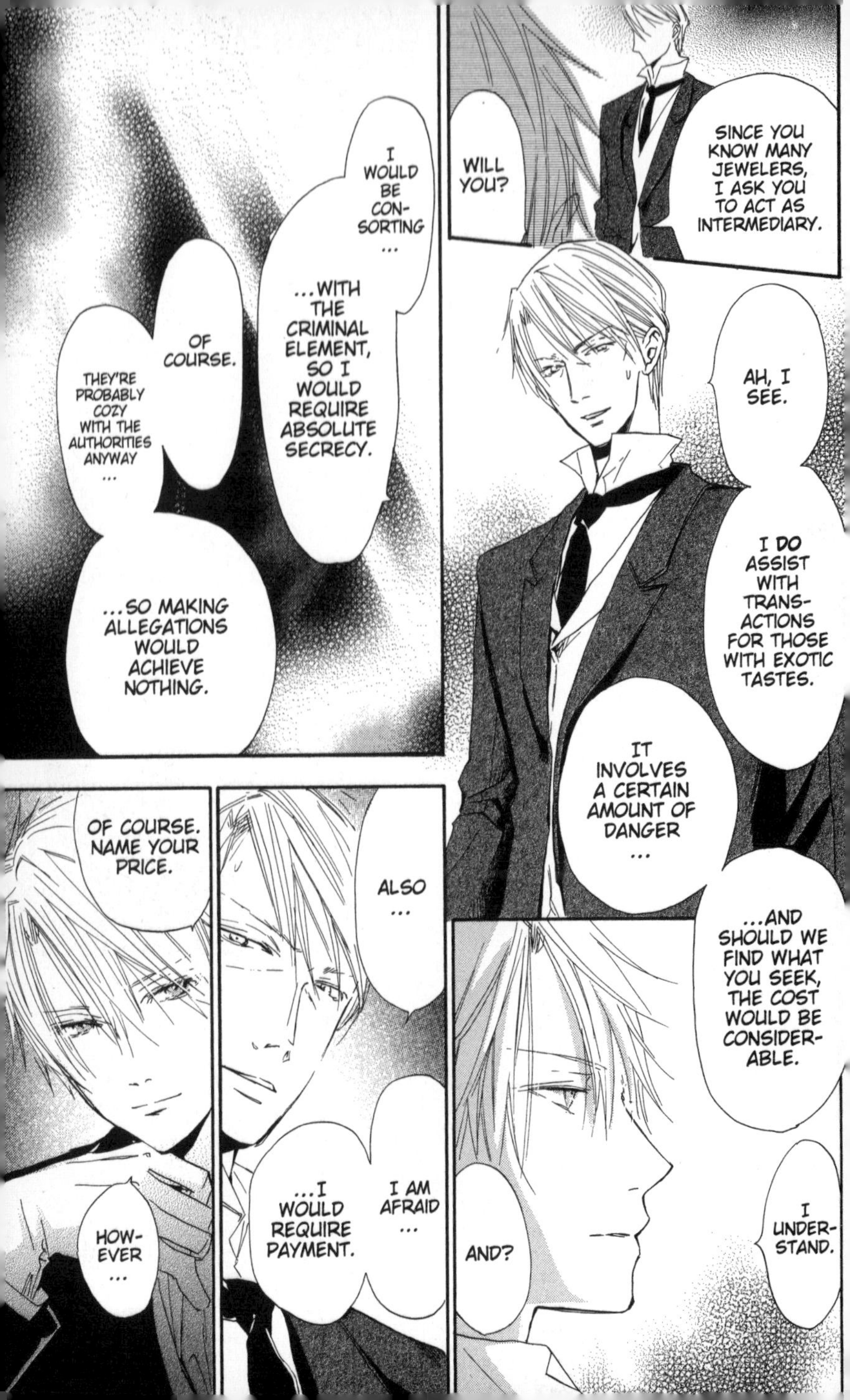
SINCE YOU KNOW MANY JEWELERS, I ASK YOU TO ACT AS INTERMEDIARY.
WILL YOU?
AH, I SEE.
I DO ASSIST WITH TRANS-ACTIONS FOR THOSE WITH EXOTIC TASTES.
IT INVOLVES A CERTAIN AMOUNT OF DANGER ...
...AND SHOULD WE FIND WHAT YOU SEEK, THE COST WOULD BE CONSIDER-ABLE.
I UNDER-STAND.
AND?
I WOULD BE CON-SORTING ...
...WITH THE CRIMINAL ELEMENT, SO I WOULD REQUIRE ABSOLUTE SECRECY.
OF COURSE.
THEY'RE PROBABLY COZY WITH THE AUTHORITIES ANYWAY ...
...SO MAKING ALLEGATIONS WOULD ACHIEVE NOTHING.
ALSO ...
I AM AFRAID ...
...I WOULD REQUIRE PAYMENT.
OF COURSE. NAME YOUR PRICE.
HOW-EVER ...

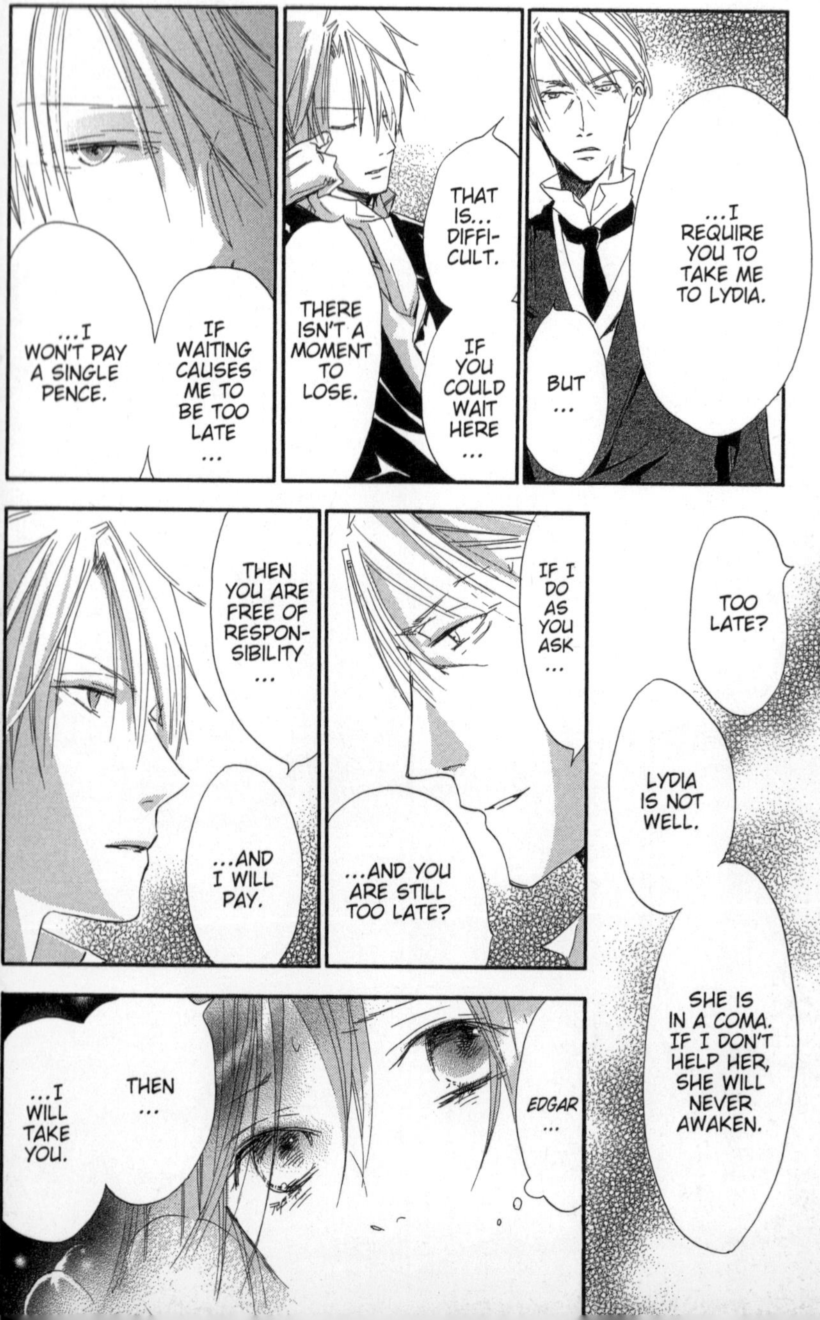
...I REQUIRE YOU TO TAKE ME TO LYDIA.
BUT...
THAT IS... DIFFICULT.
IF YOU COULD WAIT HERE...
THERE ISN'T A MOMENT TO LOSE.
IF WAITING CAUSES ME TO BE TOO LATE...
...I WON'T PAY A SINGLE PENCE.
TOO LATE?
LYDIA IS NOT WELL.
SHE IS IN A COMA. IF I DON'T HELP HER, SHE WILL NEVER AWAKEN.
IF I DO AS YOU ASK...
...AND YOU ARE STILL TOO LATE?
THEN YOU ARE FREE OF RESPONSIBILITY...
...AND I WILL PAY.
EDGAR...
THEN...
...I WILL TAKE YOU.

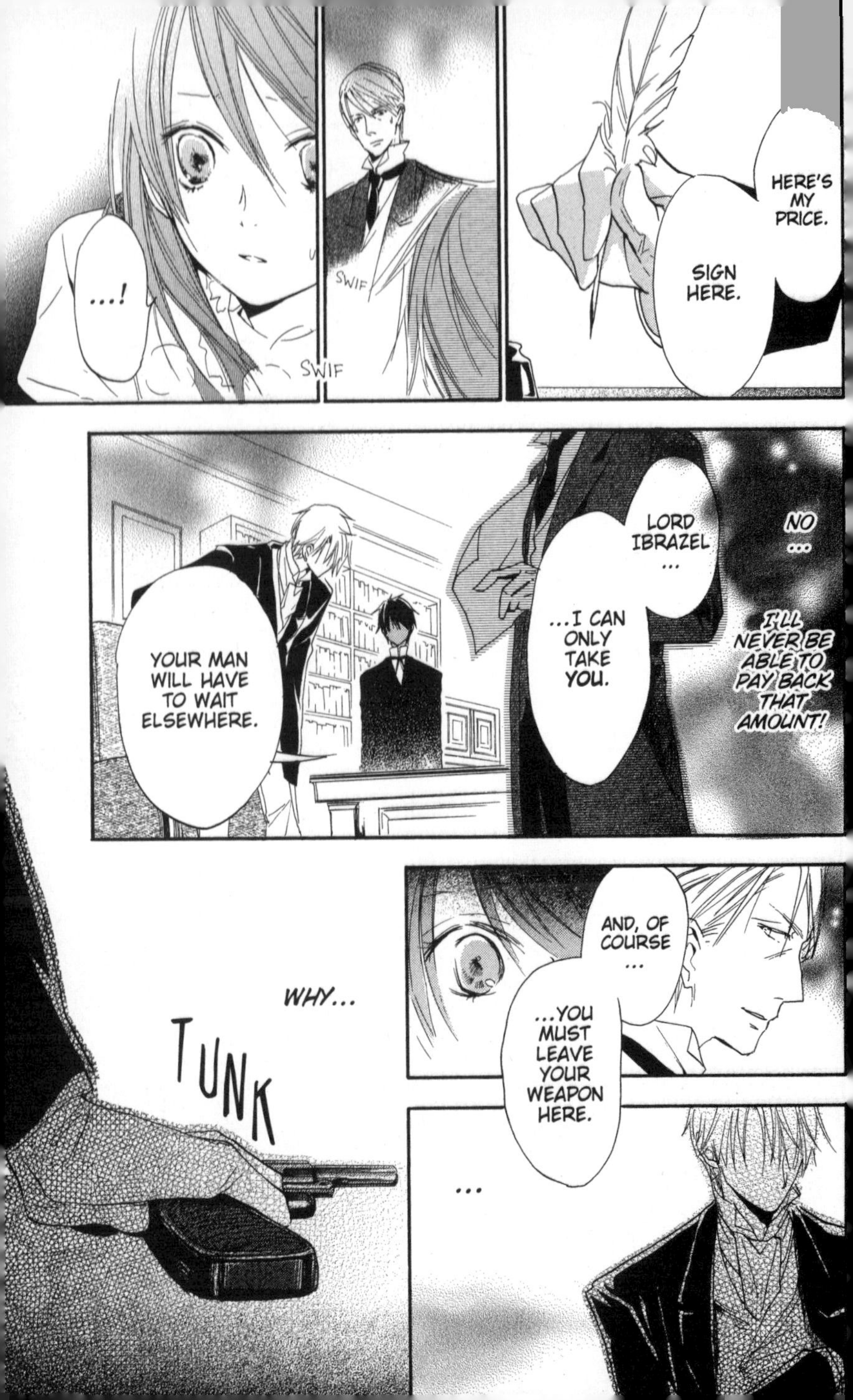
HERE'S MY PRICE.
SIGN HERE.
SWIF
SWIF
...!
NO... I'LL NEVER BE ABLE TO PAY BACK THAT AMOUNT!
LORD IBRAZEL...
...I CAN ONLY TAKE YOU.
YOUR MAN WILL HAVE TO WAIT ELSEWHERE.
AND, OF COURSE...
...YOU MUST LEAVE YOUR WEAPON HERE.
...
WHY...
TUNK

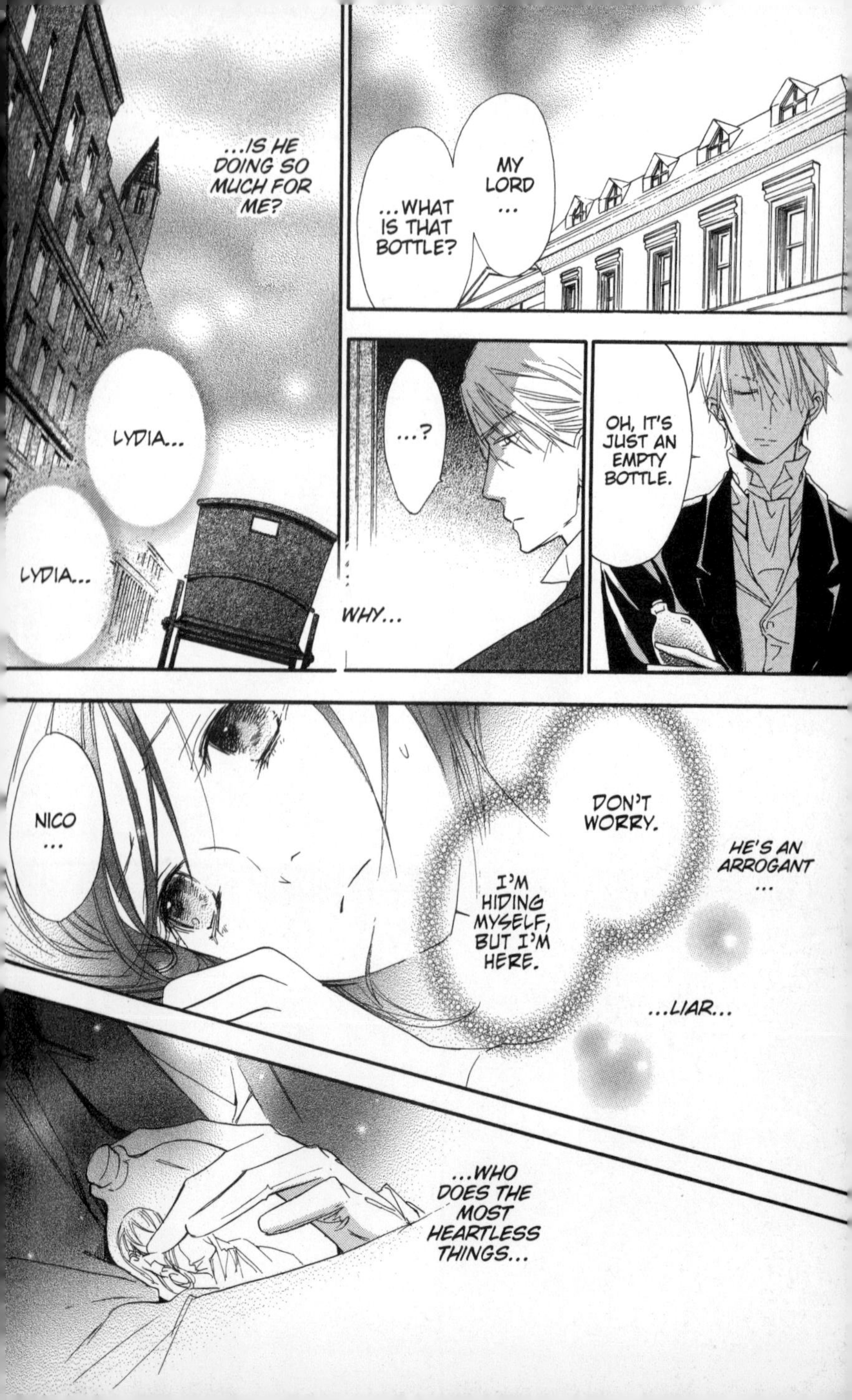
MY LORD...
...WHAT IS THAT BOTTLE?
OH, IT'S JUST AN EMPTY BOTTLE.
...?
WHY...
...IS HE DOING SO MUCH FOR ME?
LYDIA...
LYDIA...
DON'T WORRY.
I'M HIDING MYSELF, BUT I'M HERE.
NICO...
HE'S AN ARROGANT...
...LIAR...
...WHO DOES THE MOST HEARTLESS THINGS...

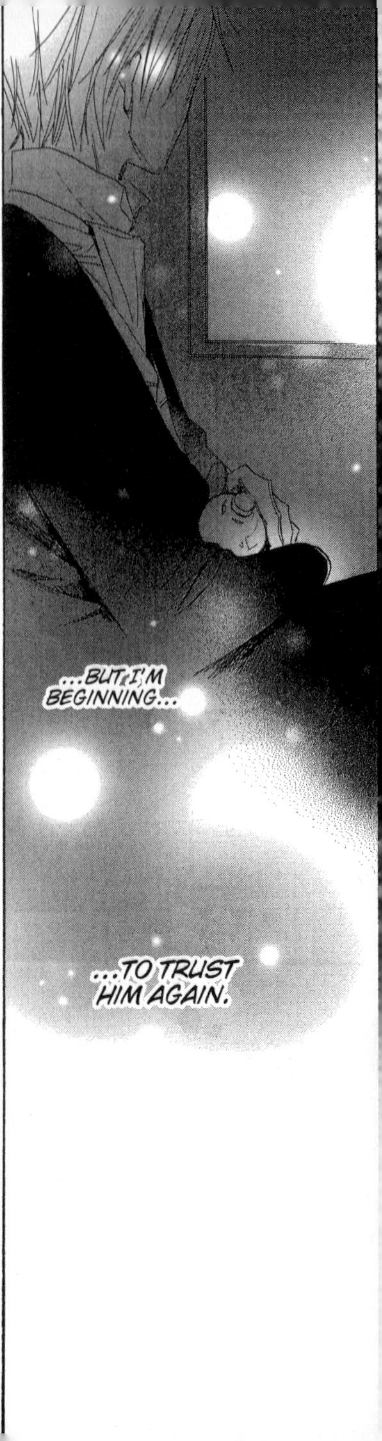
...BUT I'M BEGINNING...
...TO TRUST HIM AGAIN.
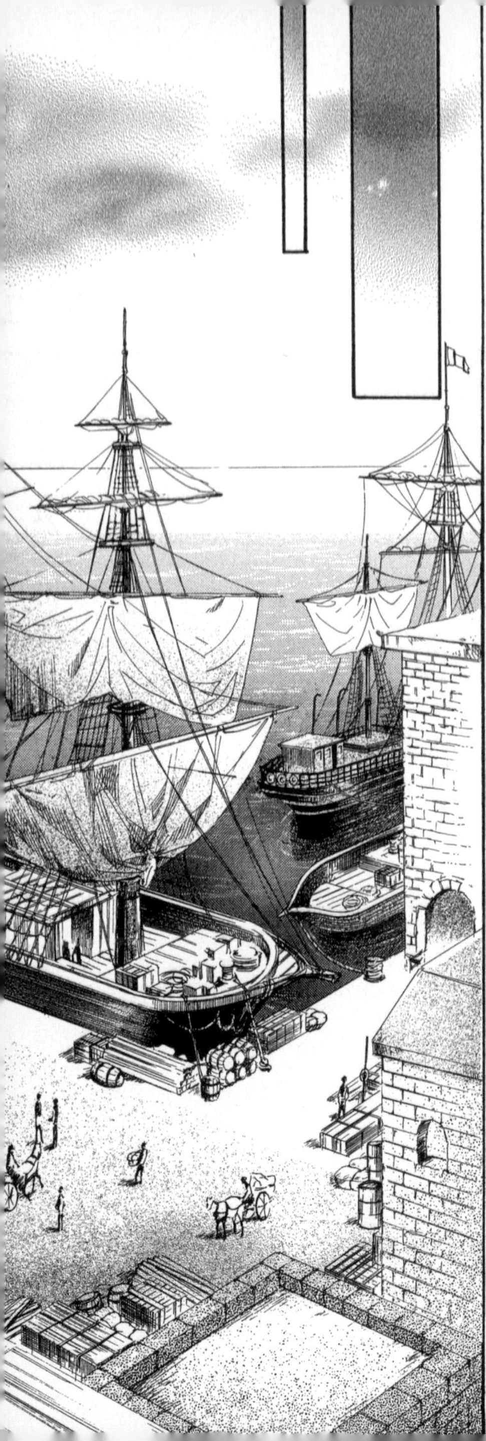

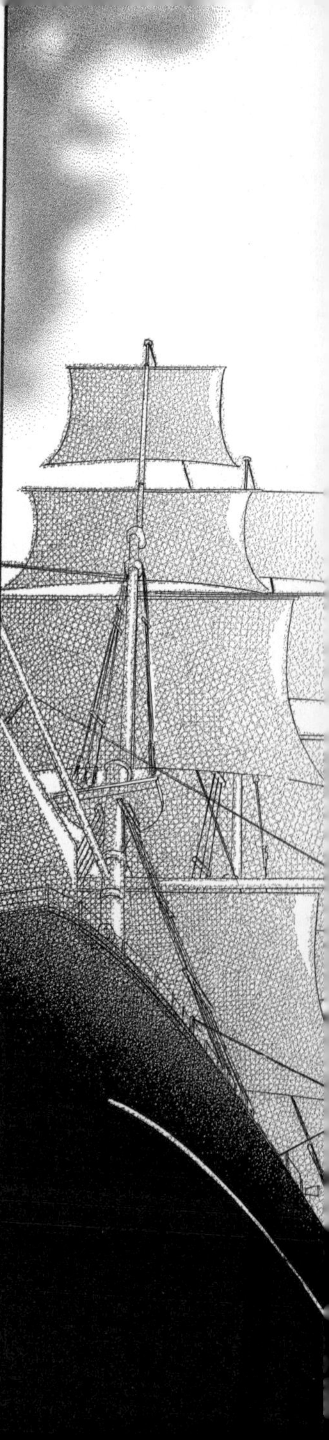

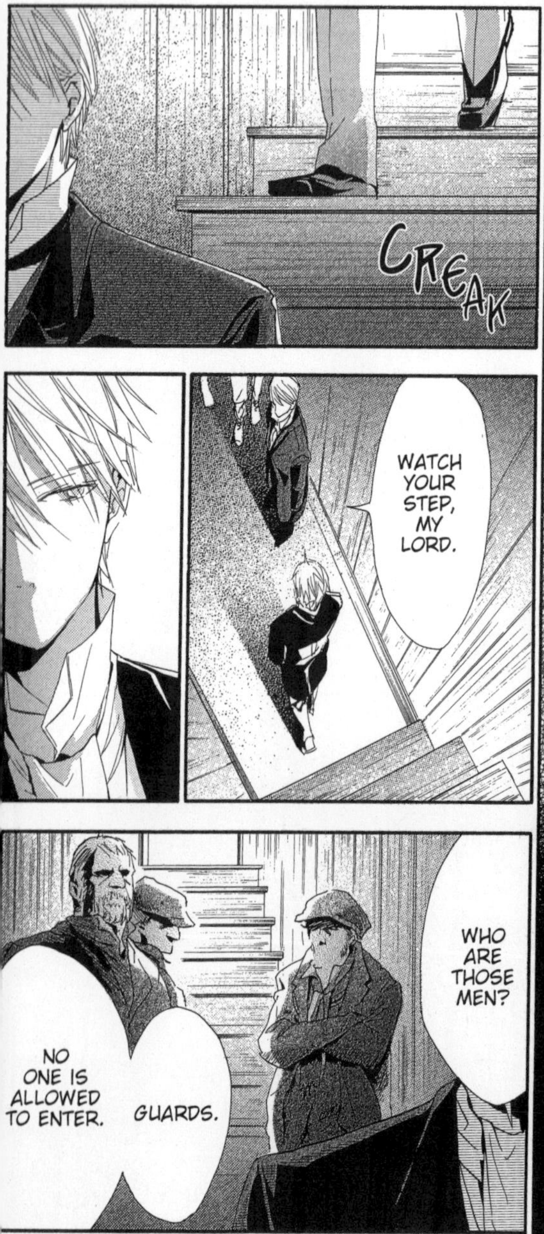
CREAK
WATCH YOUR STEP, MY LORD.
WHO ARE THOSE MEN?
GUARDS.
NO ONE IS ALLOWED TO ENTER.

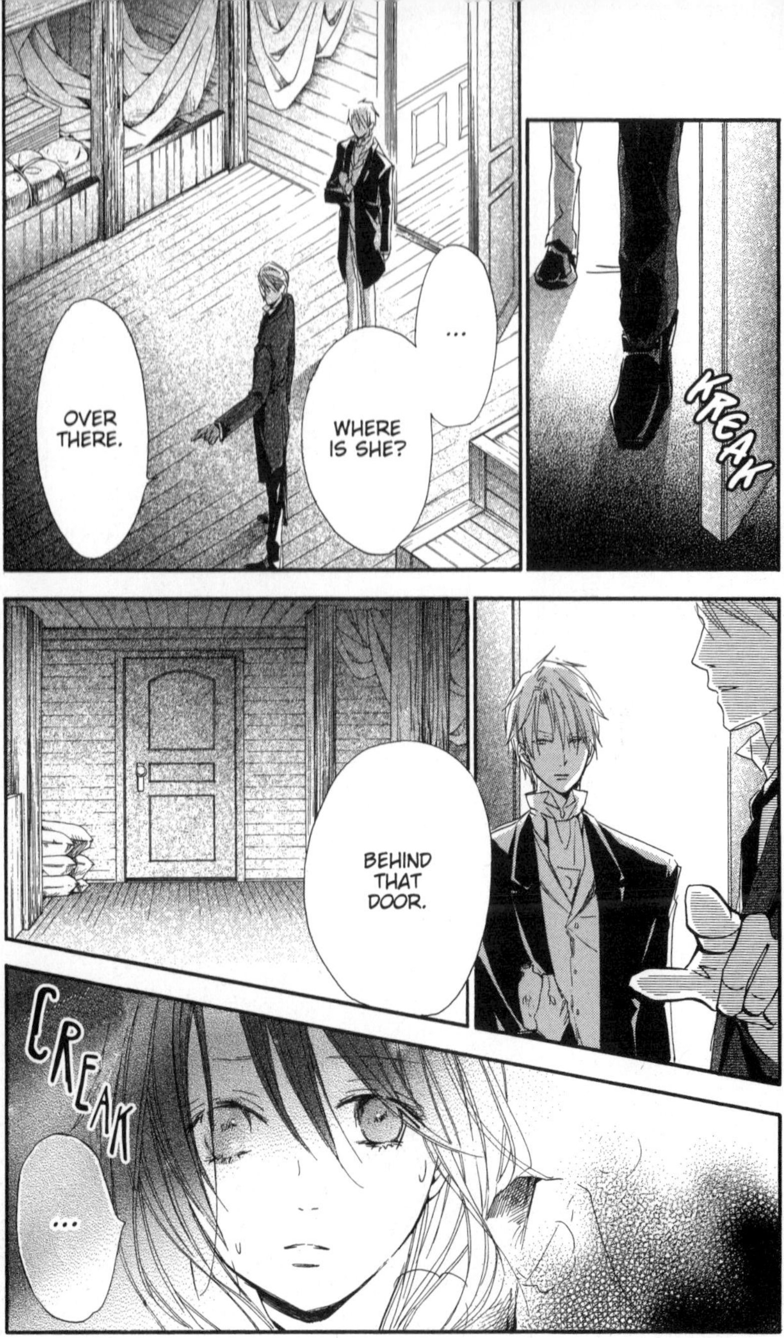
KREAK
...
WHERE IS SHE?
OVER THERE.
BEHIND THAT DOOR.
CREAK
...

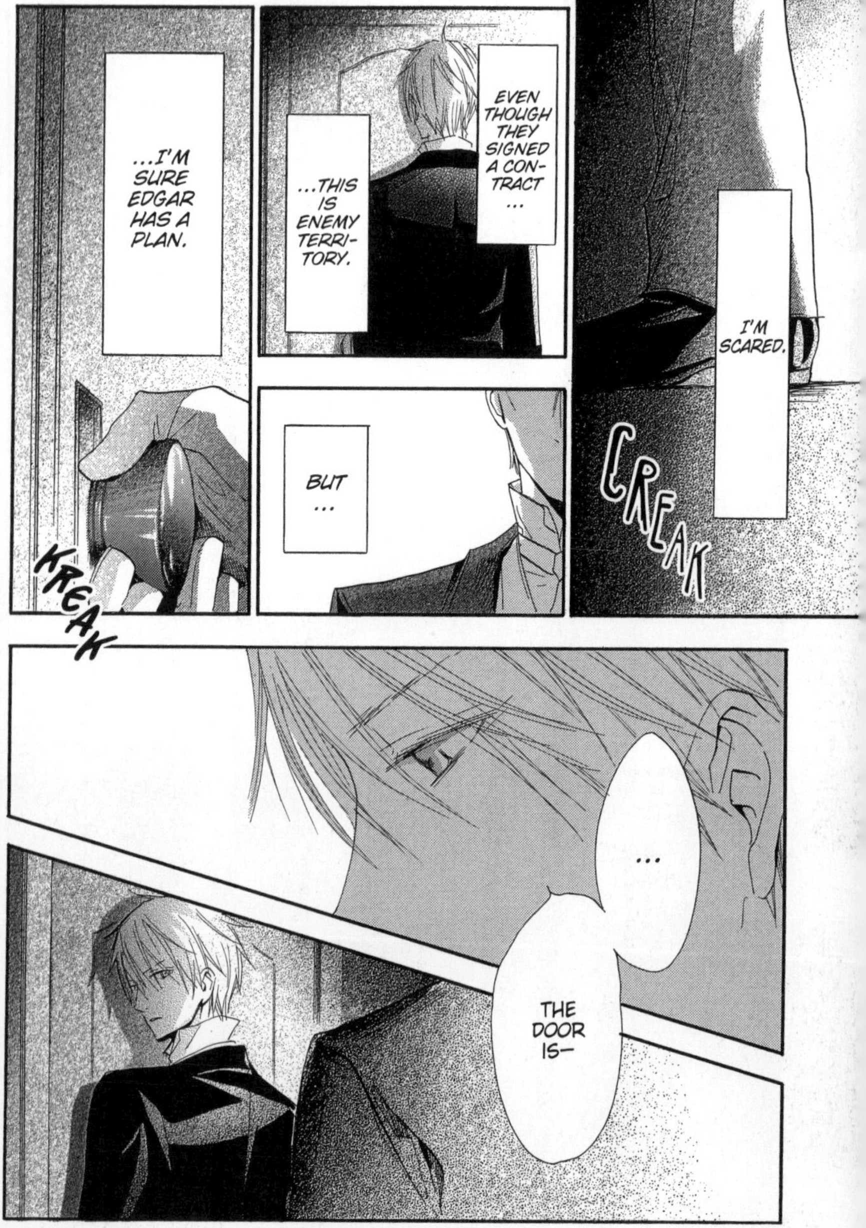
I'M SCARED.
CREAK
EVEN THOUGH THEY SIGNED A CONTRACT...
...THIS IS ENEMY TERRITORY.
BUT...
...I'M SURE EDGAR HAS A PLAN.
KREAK
...
THE DOOR IS—

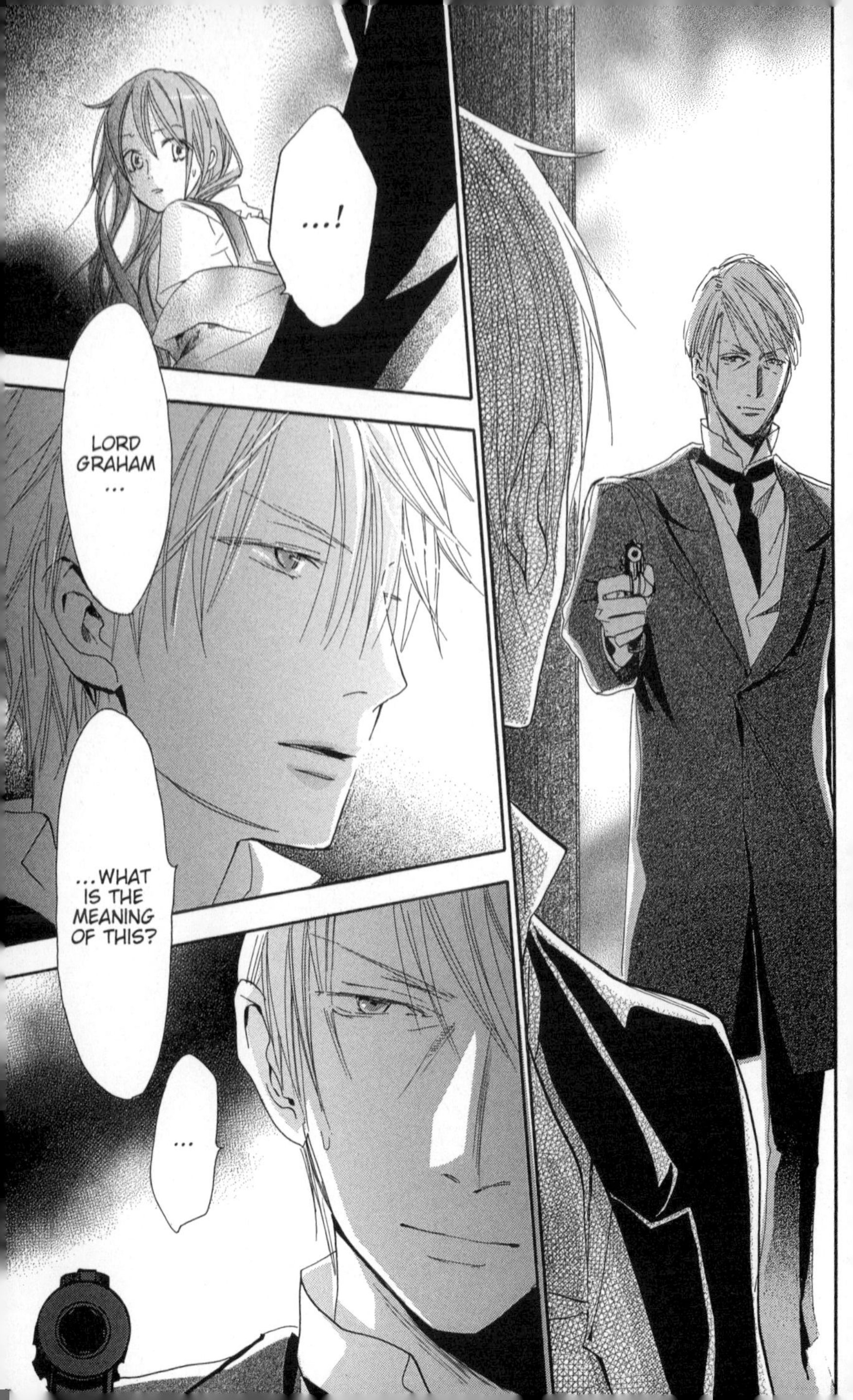
...!
LORD GRAHAM ...
...WHAT IS THE MEANING OF THIS?
...

The Earl & the Fairy

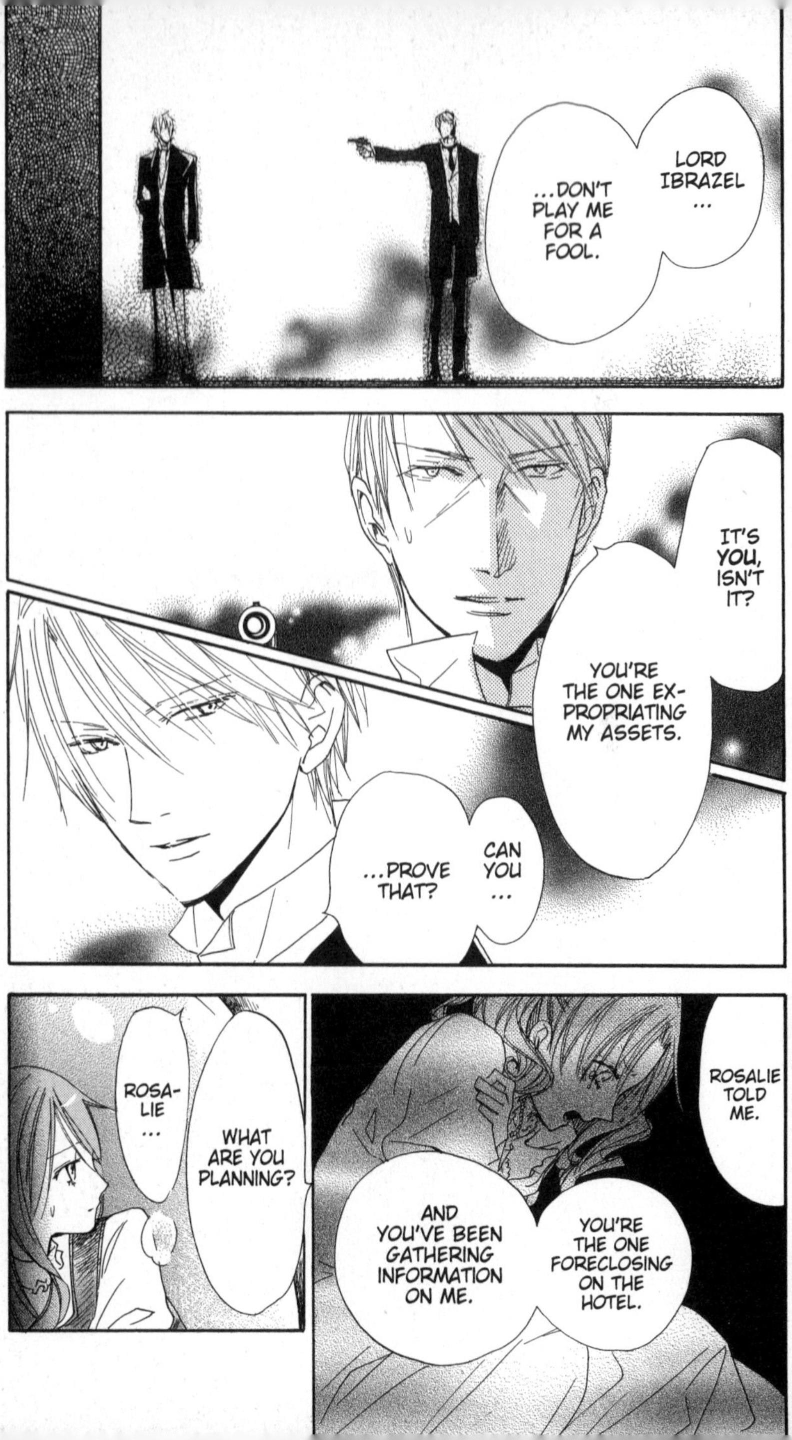
LORD IBRAZEL...
...DON'T PLAY ME FOR A FOOL.
IT'S YOU, ISN'T IT?
YOU'RE THE ONE EX-PROPRIATING MY ASSETS.
CAN YOU...
...PROVE THAT?
ROSALIE TOLD ME.
YOU'RE THE ONE FORECLOSING ON THE HOTEL.
AND YOU'VE BEEN GATHERING INFORMATION ON ME.
WHAT ARE YOU PLANNING?
ROSA-LIE...

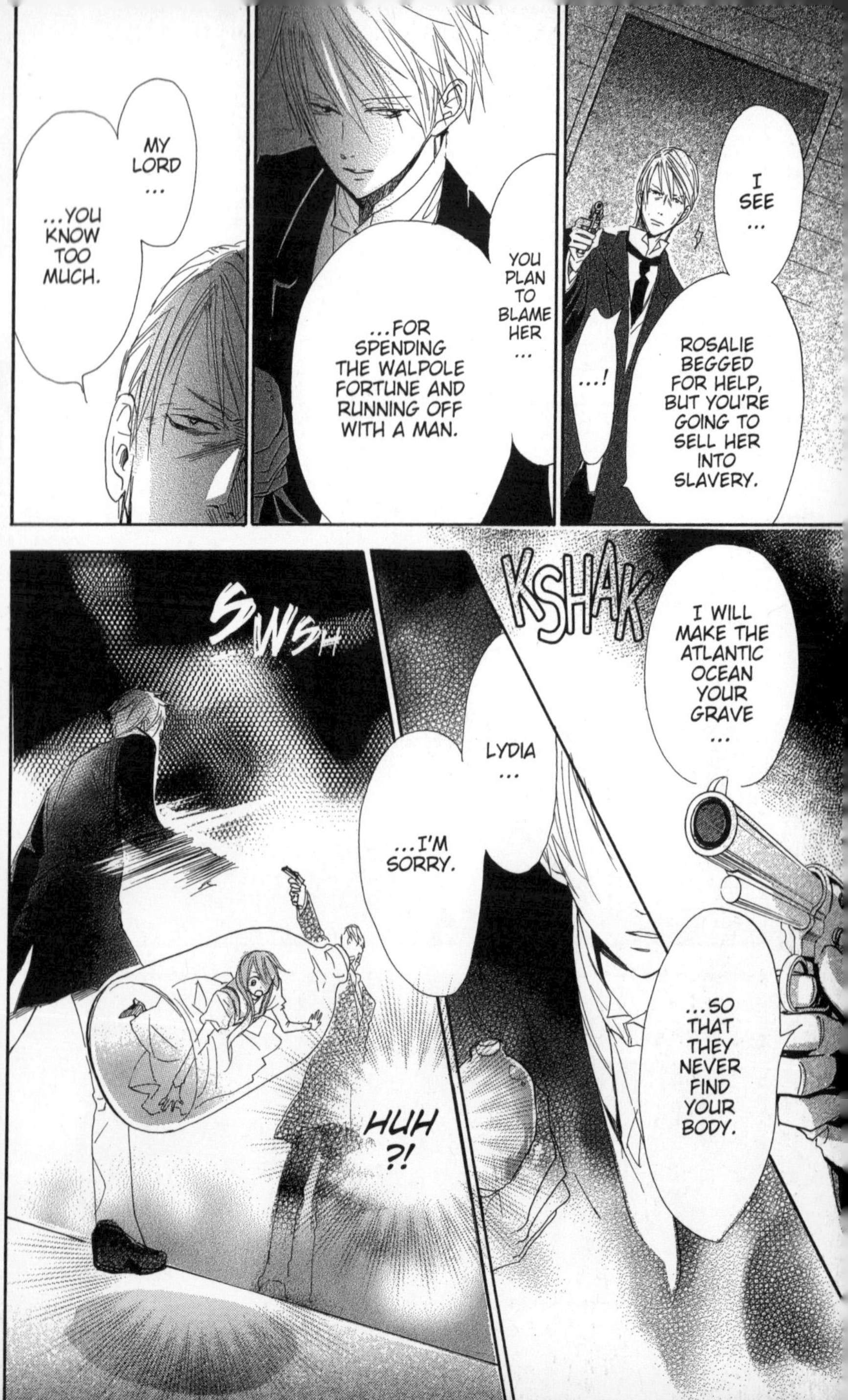
I SEE ...
ROSALIE BEGGED FOR HELP, BUT YOU'RE GOING TO SELL HER INTO SLAVERY.
...!
YOU PLAN TO BLAME HER ...
...FOR SPENDING THE WALPOLE FORTUNE AND RUNNING OFF WITH A MAN.
MY LORD ...
...YOU KNOW TOO MUCH.
KSHAK
I WILL MAKE THE ATLANTIC OCEAN YOUR GRAVE ...
...SO THAT THEY NEVER FIND YOUR BODY.
LYDIA ...
...I'M SORRY.
SWSH
HUH ?!

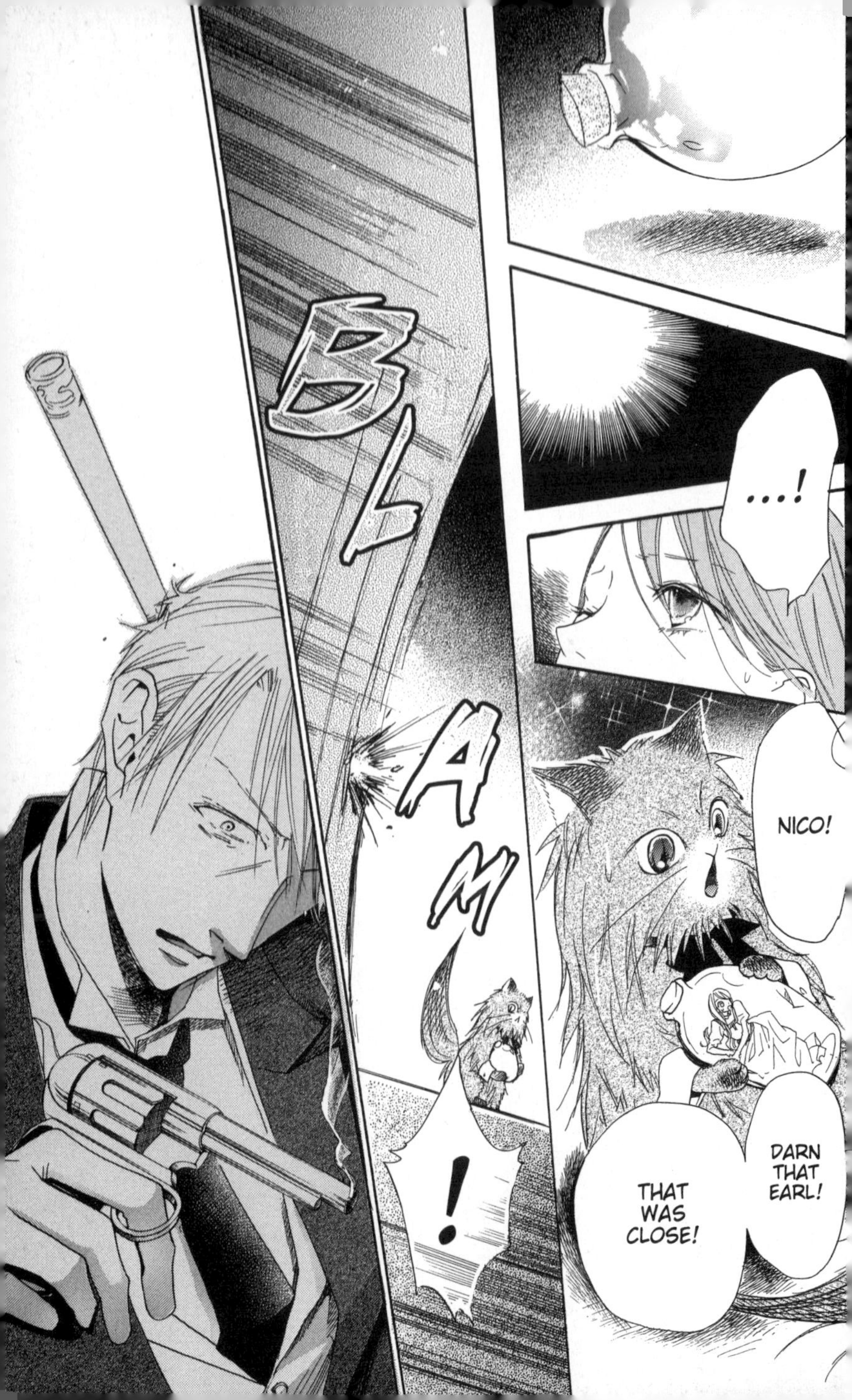
...!
NICO!
DARN THAT EARL!
THAT WAS CLOSE!
!
BLAM

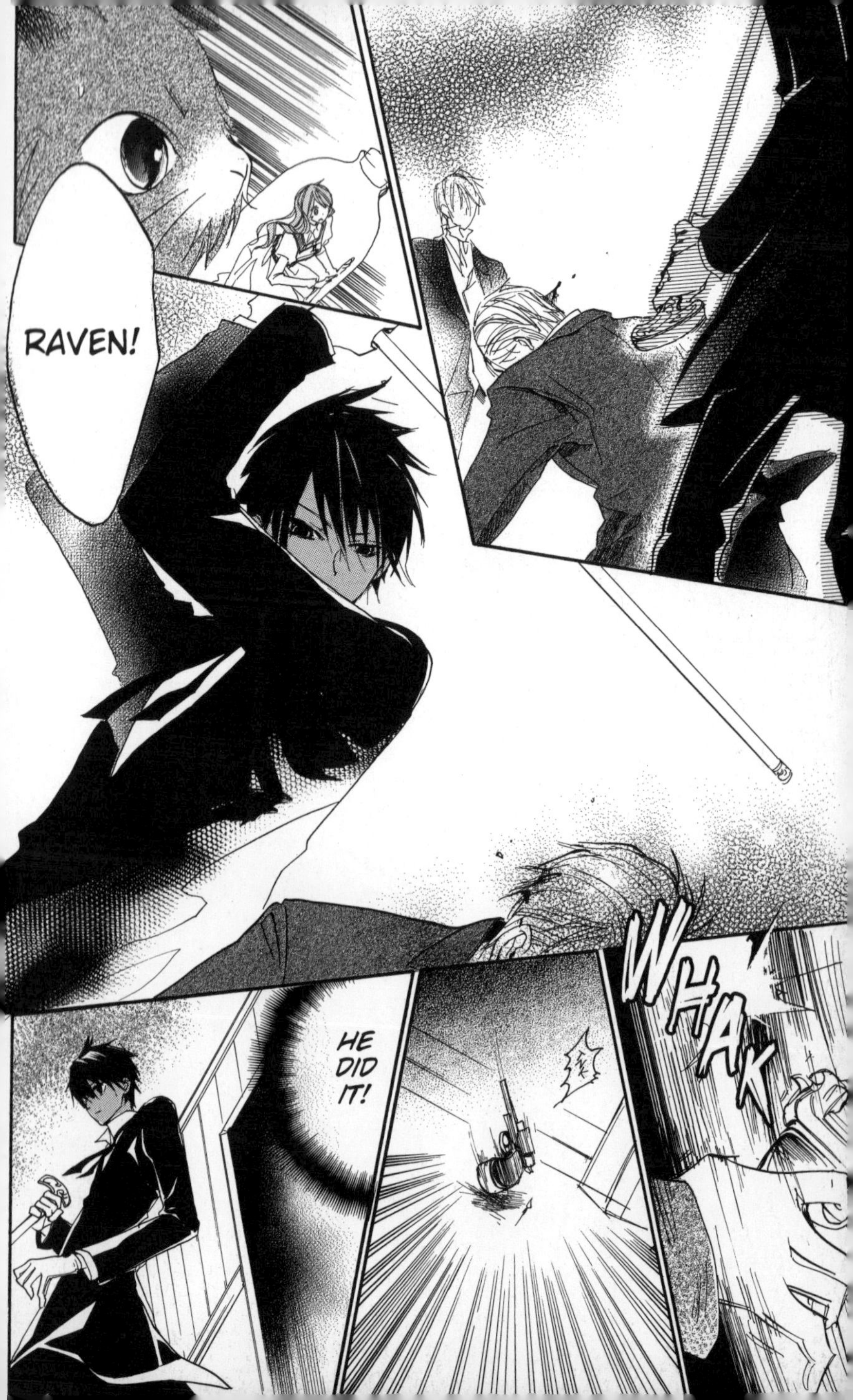
RAVEN!
WHAK
HE DID IT!

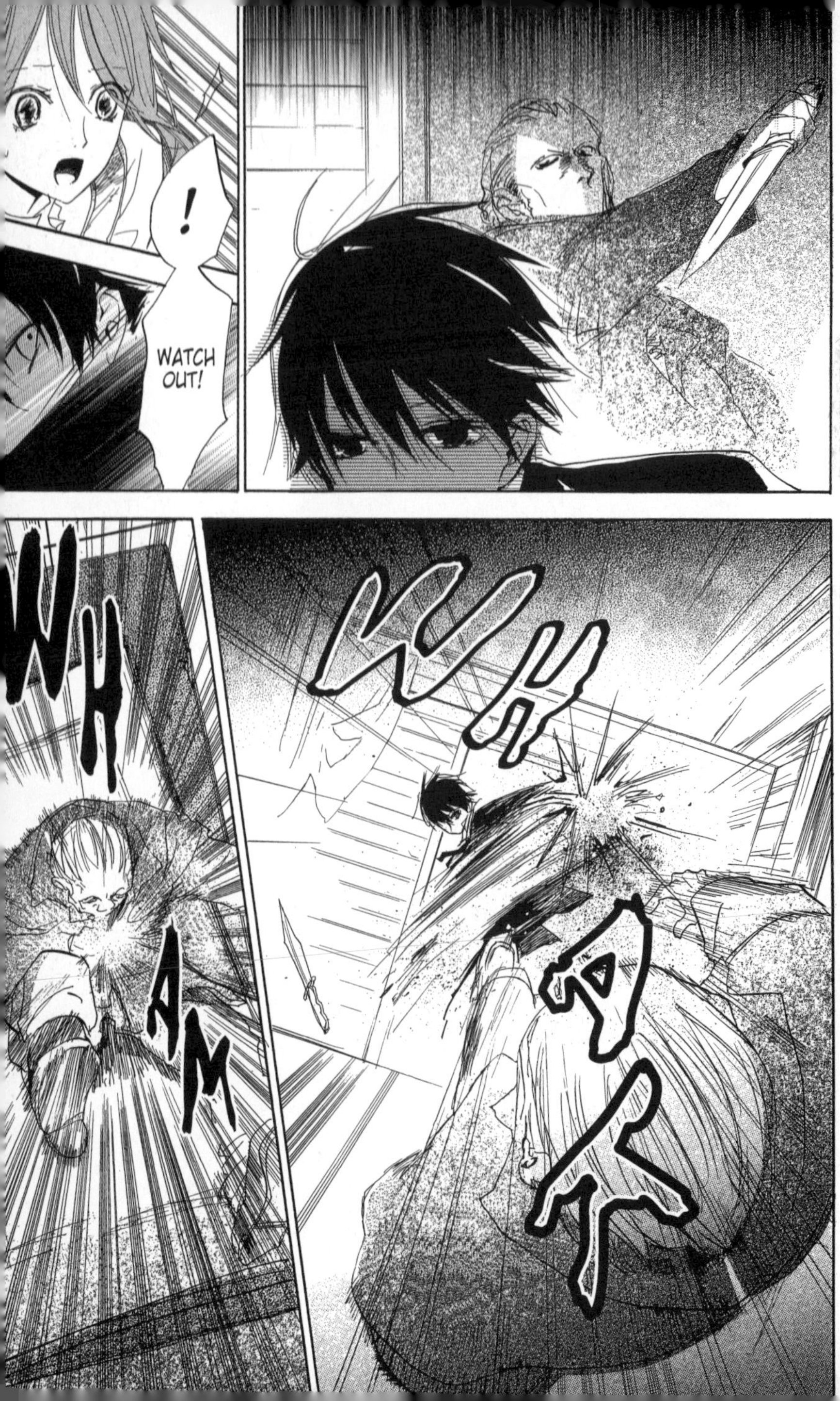
!
WATCH OUT!
WHAM

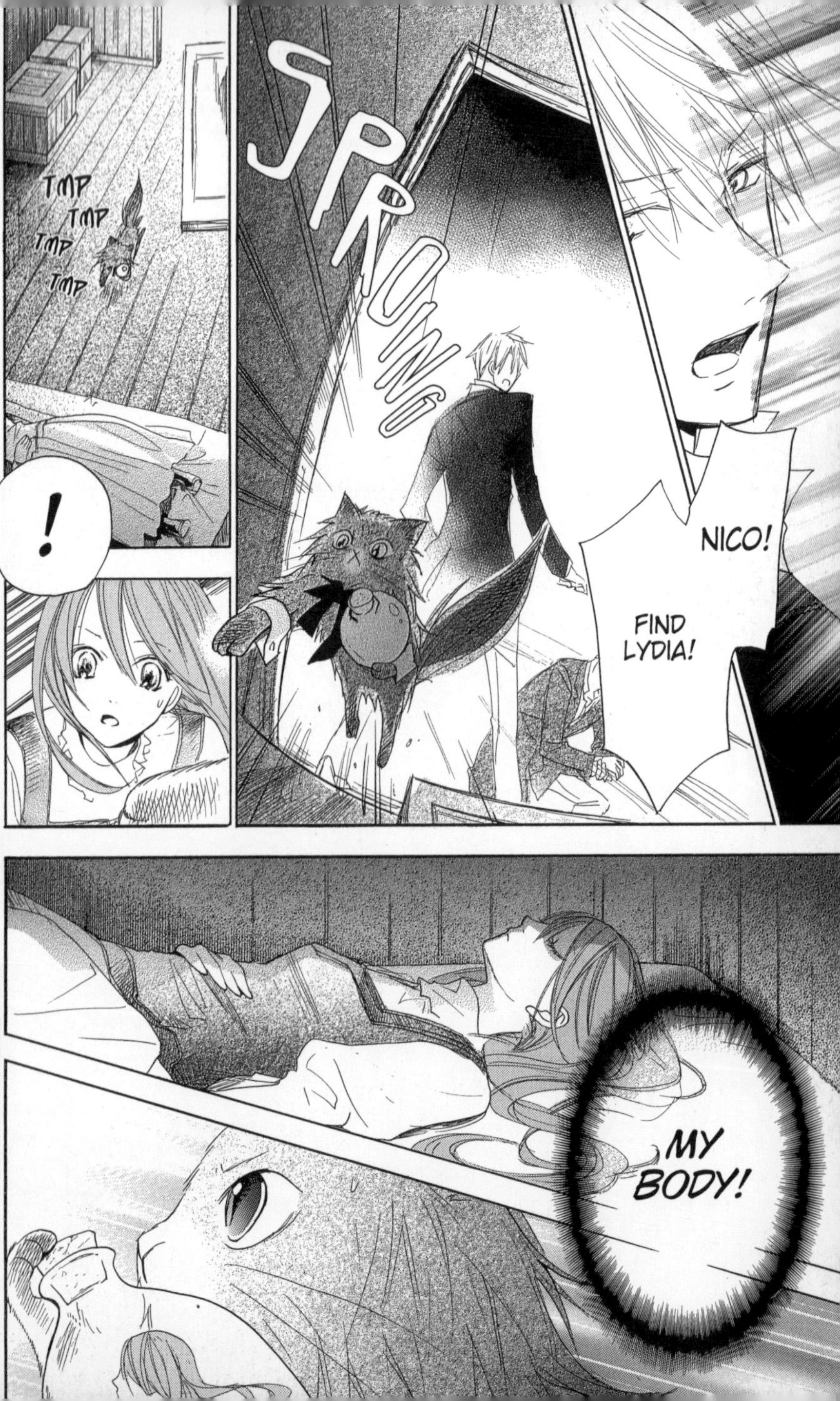
NICO!
FIND LYDIA!
SPROING
TMP TMP TMP TMP
!
MY BODY!

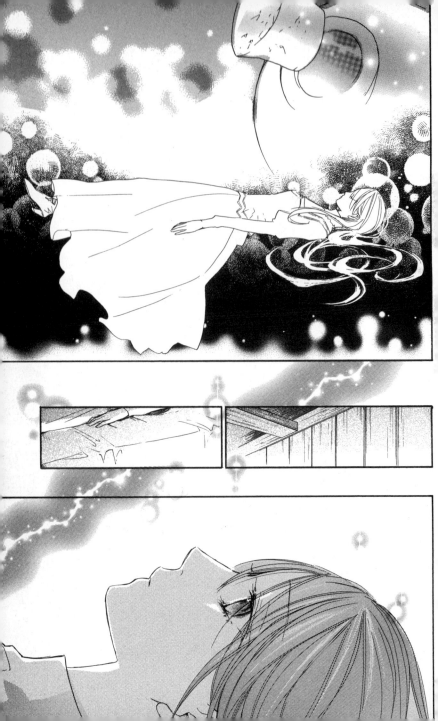

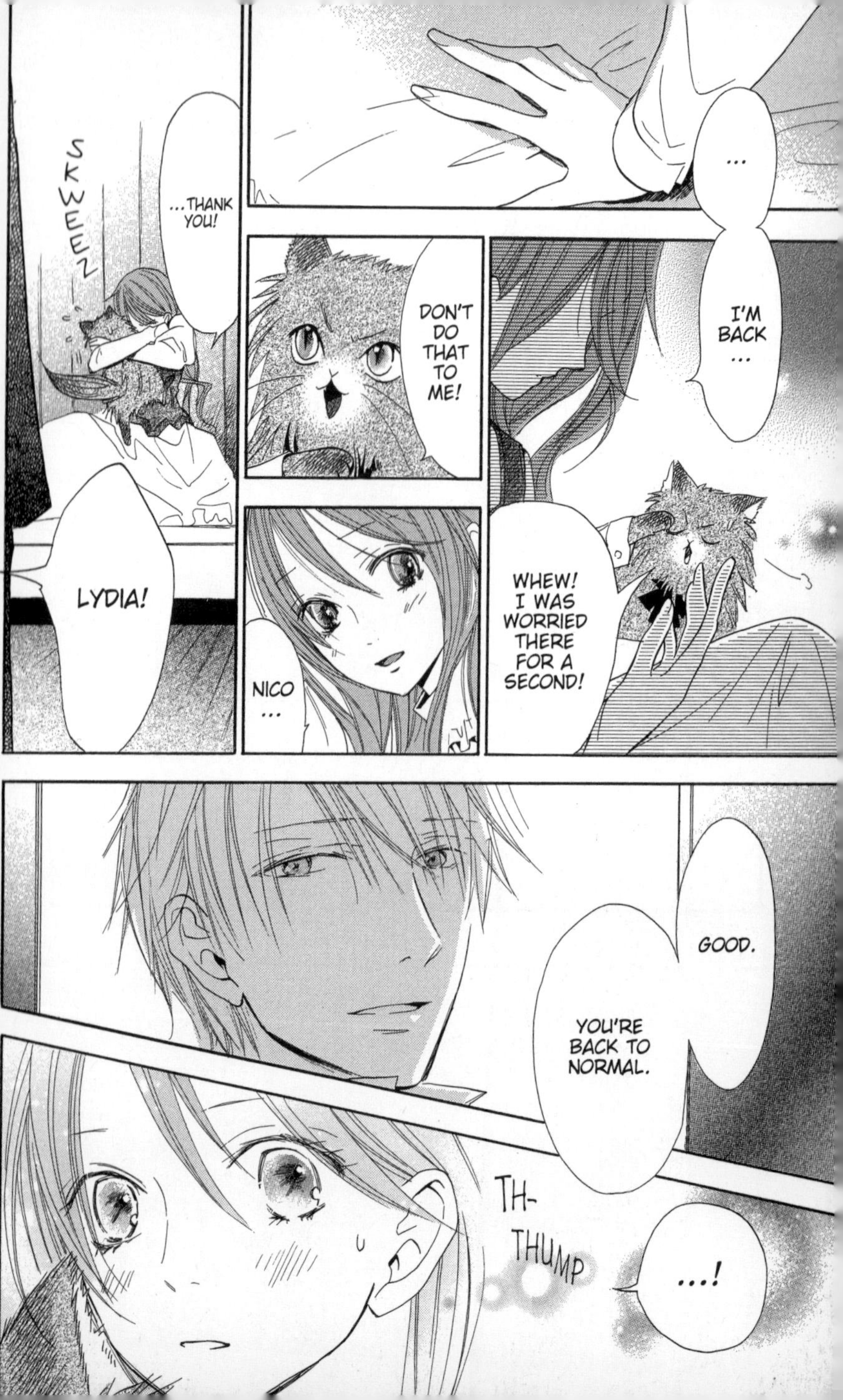
...
I'M BACK...
WHEW! I WAS WORRIED THERE FOR A SECOND!
DON'T DO THAT TO ME!
NICO...
...THANK YOU!
SKWEEZ
LYDIA!
GOOD.
YOU'RE BACK TO NORMAL.
TH-THUMP
...!

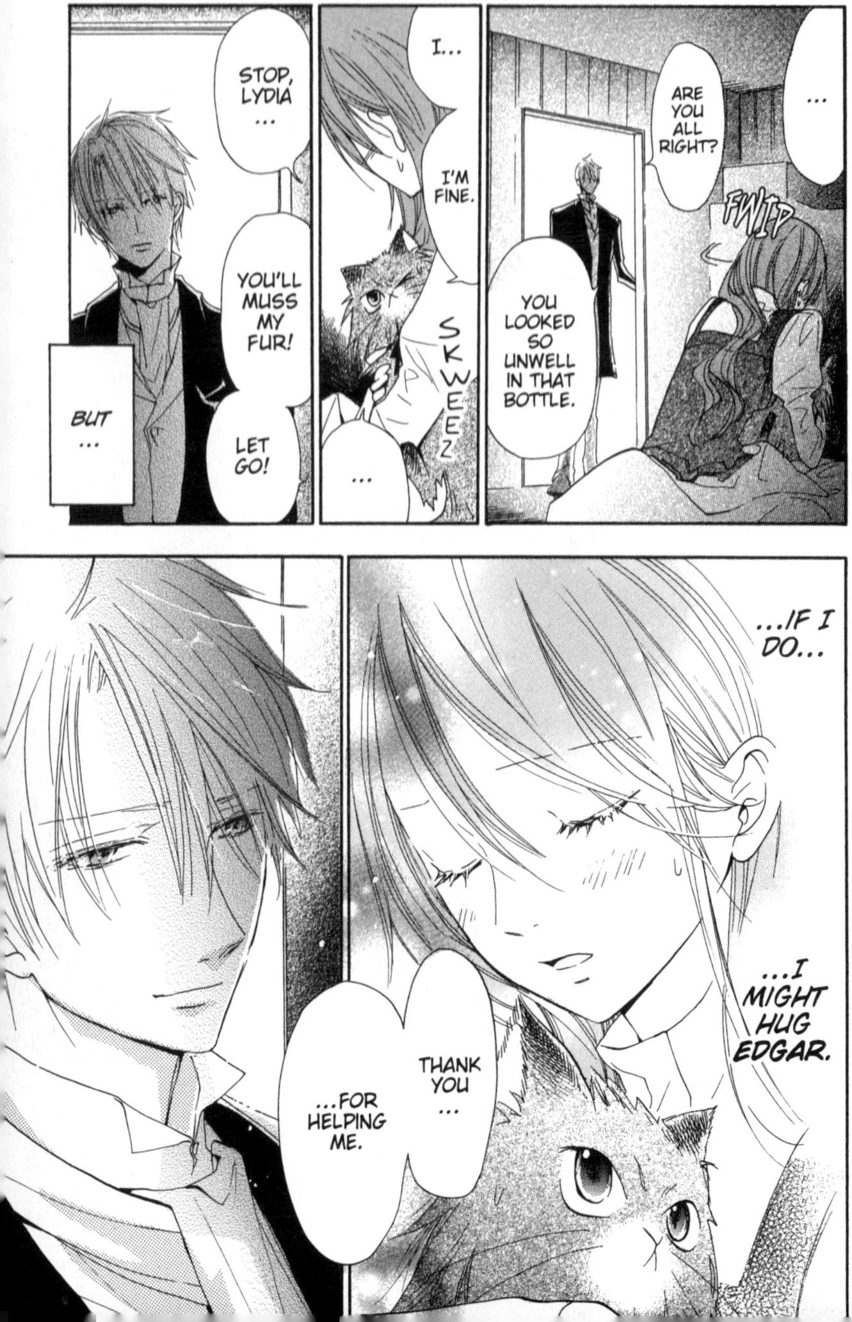
...
ARE YOU ALL RIGHT?
FWIP
YOU LOOKED SO UNWELL IN THAT BOTTLE.
I...
I'M FINE.
SKWEEZ
...
STOP, LYDIA ...
YOU'LL MUSS MY FUR!
LET GO!
BUT ...
...IF I DO...
...I MIGHT HUG EDGAR.
THANK YOU ...
...FOR HELPING ME.

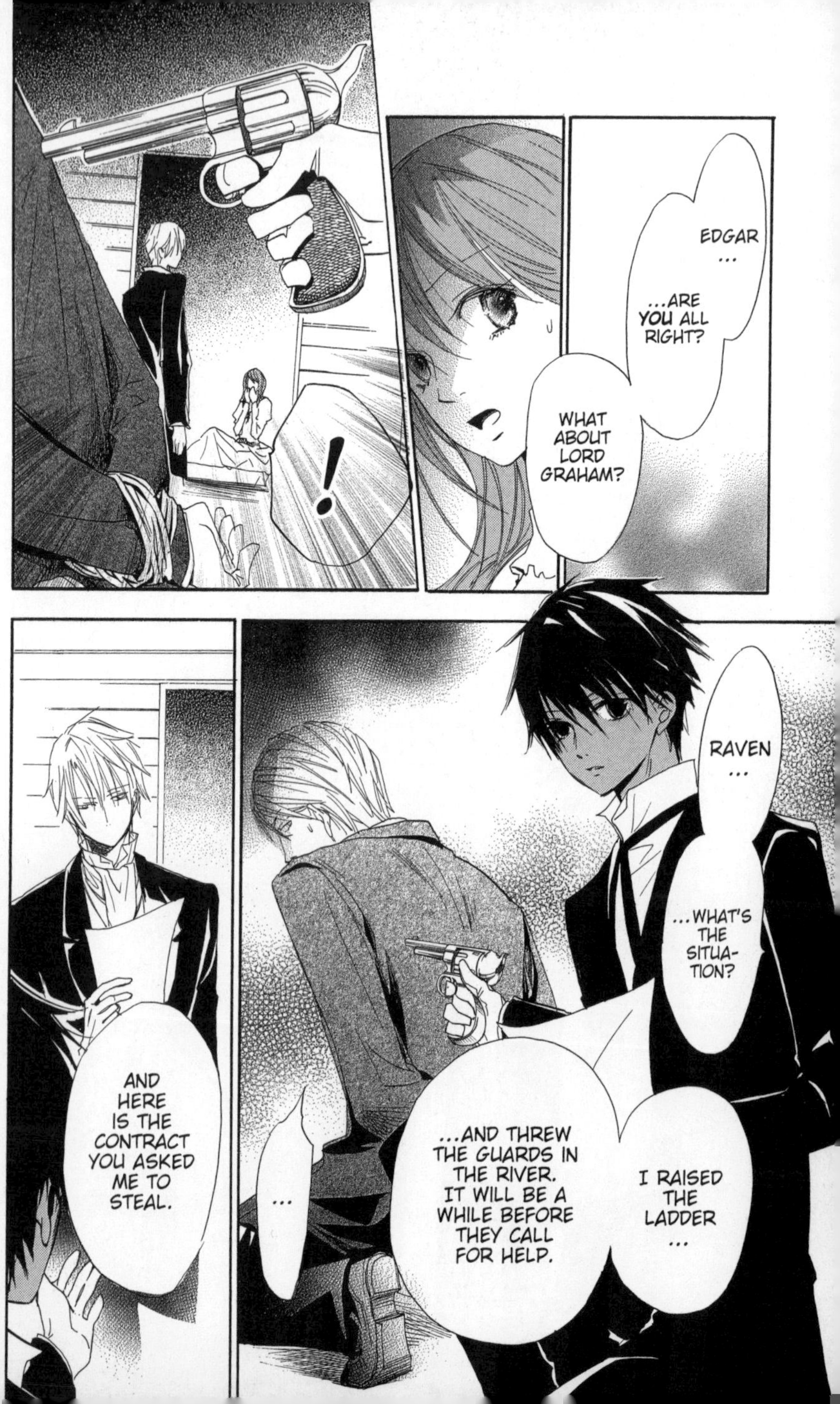
EDGAR ...
...ARE YOU ALL RIGHT?
WHAT ABOUT LORD GRAHAM?
!
RAVEN ...
...WHAT'S THE SITUA-TION?
I RAISED THE LADDER ...
...AND THREW THE GUARDS IN THE RIVER. IT WILL BE A WHILE BEFORE THEY CALL FOR HELP.
...
AND HERE IS THE CONTRACT YOU ASKED ME TO STEAL.

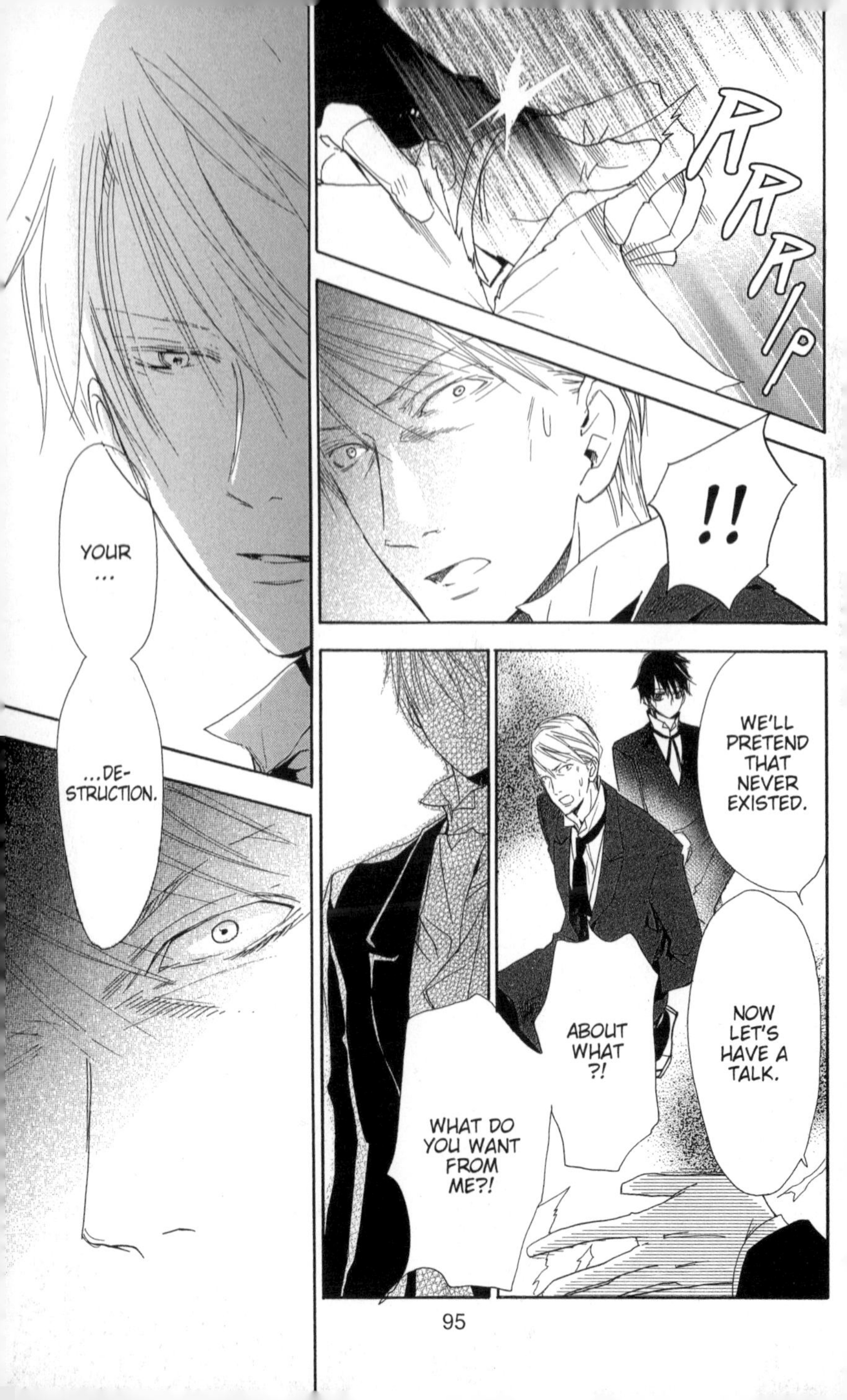
RRRIP
!!
WE'LL PRETEND THAT NEVER EXISTED.
NOW LET'S HAVE A TALK.
ABOUT WHAT?!
WHAT DO YOU WANT FROM ME?!
YOUR...
...DE-STRUCTION.

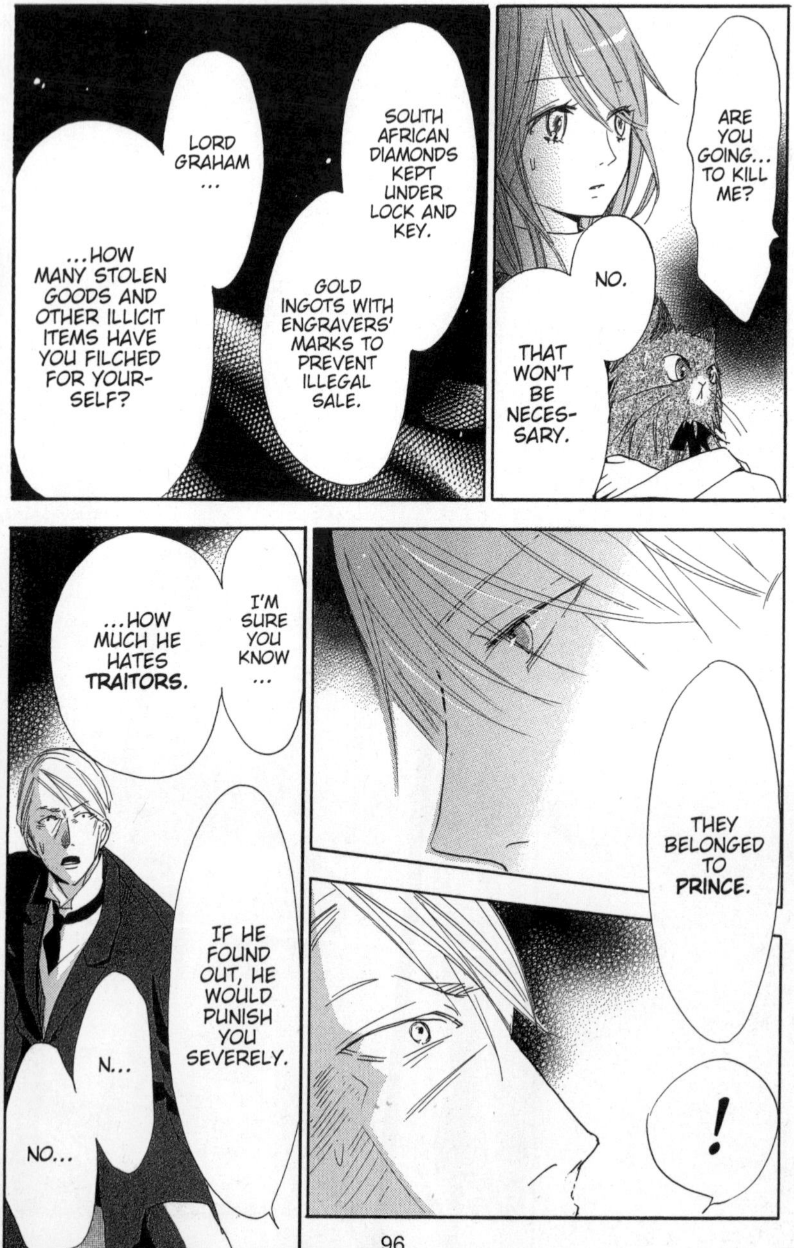
ARE YOU GOING... TO KILL ME?
NO.
THAT WON'T BE NECES-SARY.
SOUTH AFRICAN DIAMONDS KEPT UNDER LOCK AND KEY.
GOLD INGOTS WITH ENGRAVERS' MARKS TO PREVENT ILLEGAL SALE.
LORD GRAHAM...
...HOW MANY STOLEN GOODS AND OTHER ILLICIT ITEMS HAVE YOU FILCHED FOR YOUR-SELF?
THEY BELONGED TO **PRINCE.**
!
I'M SURE YOU KNOW...
...HOW MUCH HE HATES **TRAITORS.**
IF HE FOUND OUT, HE WOULD PUNISH YOU SEVERELY.
N...
NO...

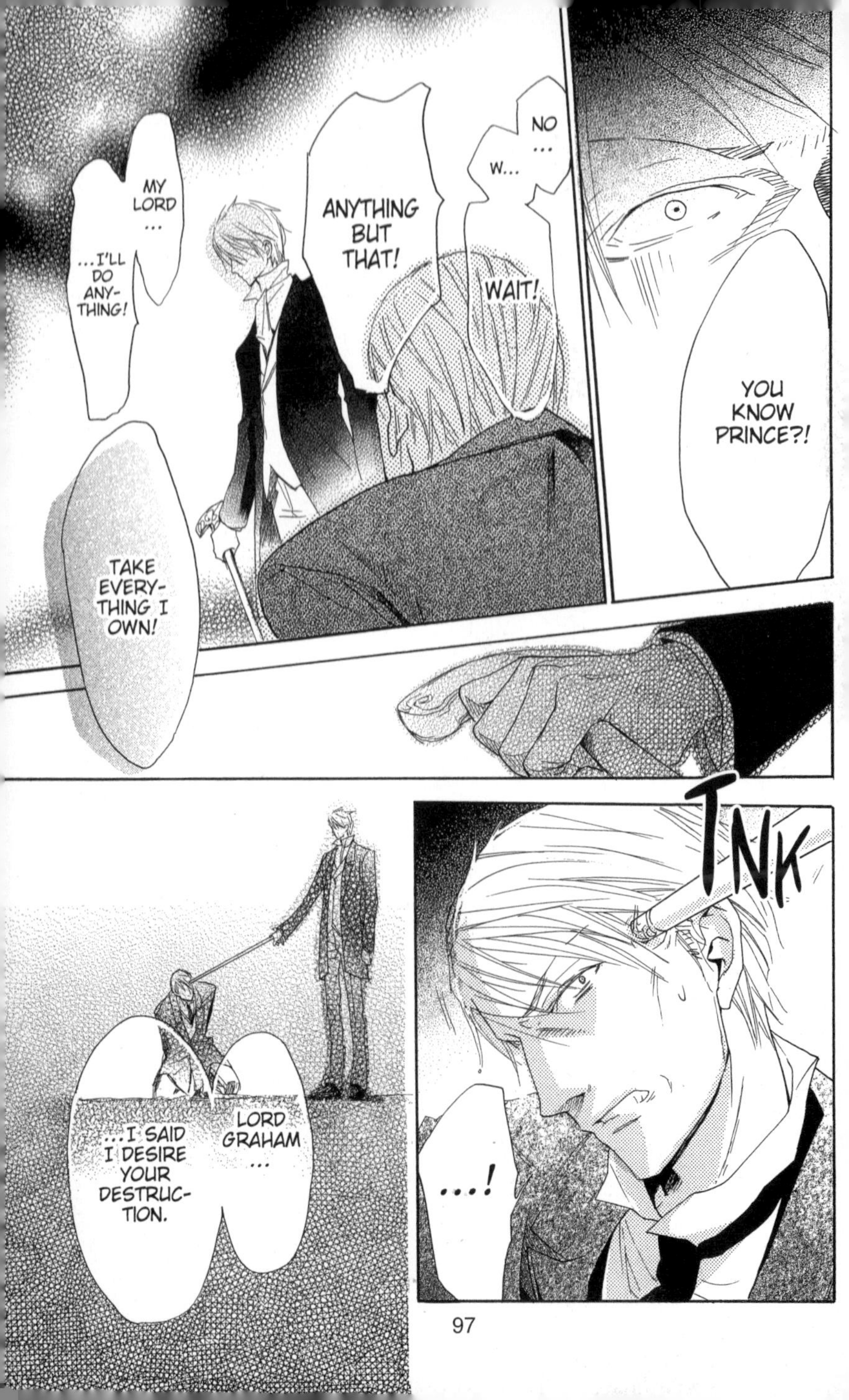
YOU KNOW PRINCE?!
NO... W...
WAIT!
ANYTHING BUT THAT!
MY LORD... ...I'LL DO ANYTHING!
TAKE EVERYTHING I OWN!
TNK
...!
LORD GRAHAM...
...I SAID I DESIRE YOUR DESTRUCTION.

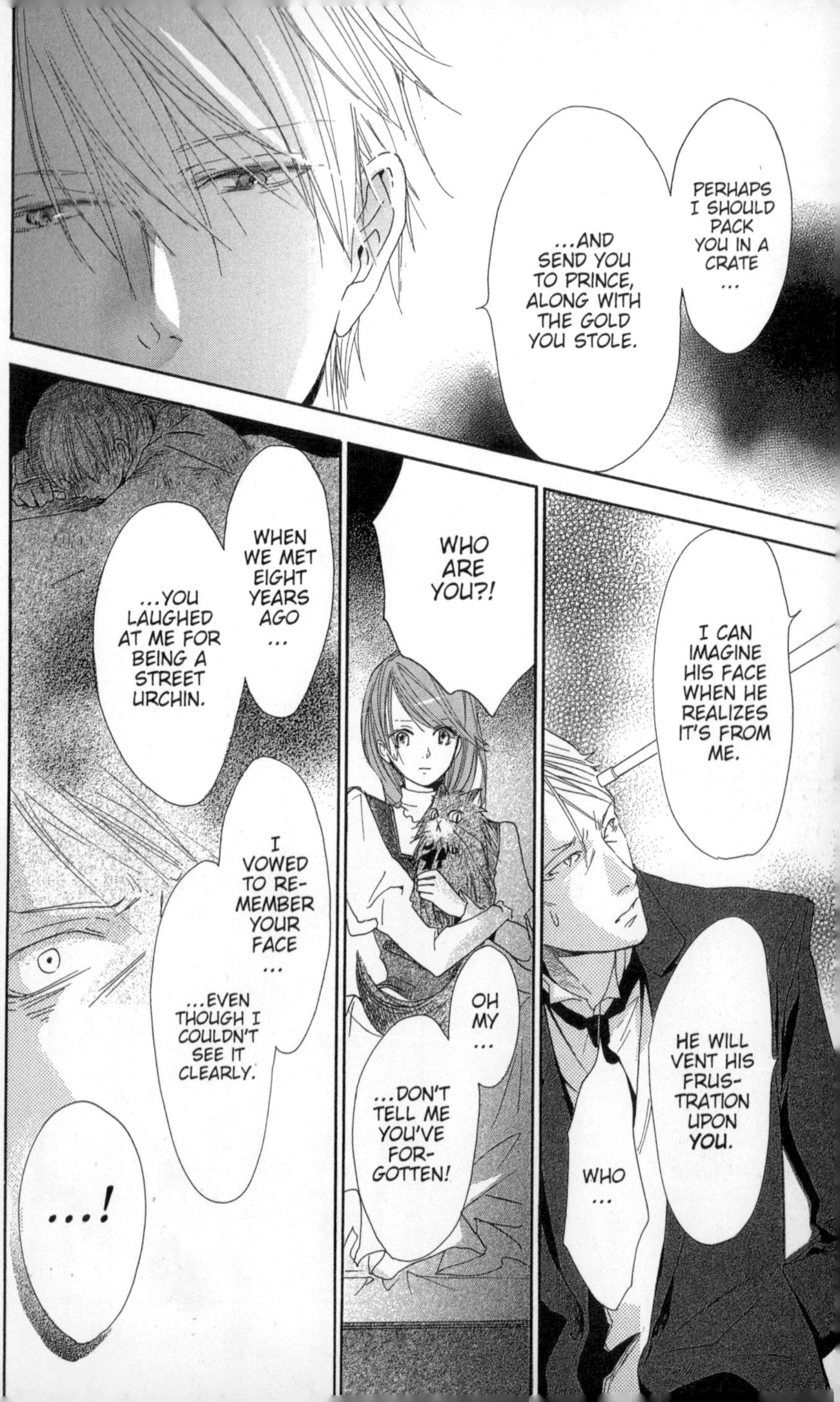
PERHAPS I SHOULD PACK YOU IN A CRATE...
...AND SEND YOU TO PRINCE, ALONG WITH THE GOLD YOU STOLE.
I CAN IMAGINE HIS FACE WHEN HE REALIZES IT'S FROM ME.
HE WILL VENT HIS FRUSTRATION UPON YOU.
WHO...
WHO ARE YOU?!
OH MY...
...DON'T TELL ME YOU'VE FORGOTTEN!
WHEN WE MET EIGHT YEARS AGO...
...YOU LAUGHED AT ME FOR BEING A STREET URCHIN.
I VOWED TO REMEMBER YOUR FACE...
...EVEN THOUGH I COULDN'T SEE IT CLEARLY.
...!

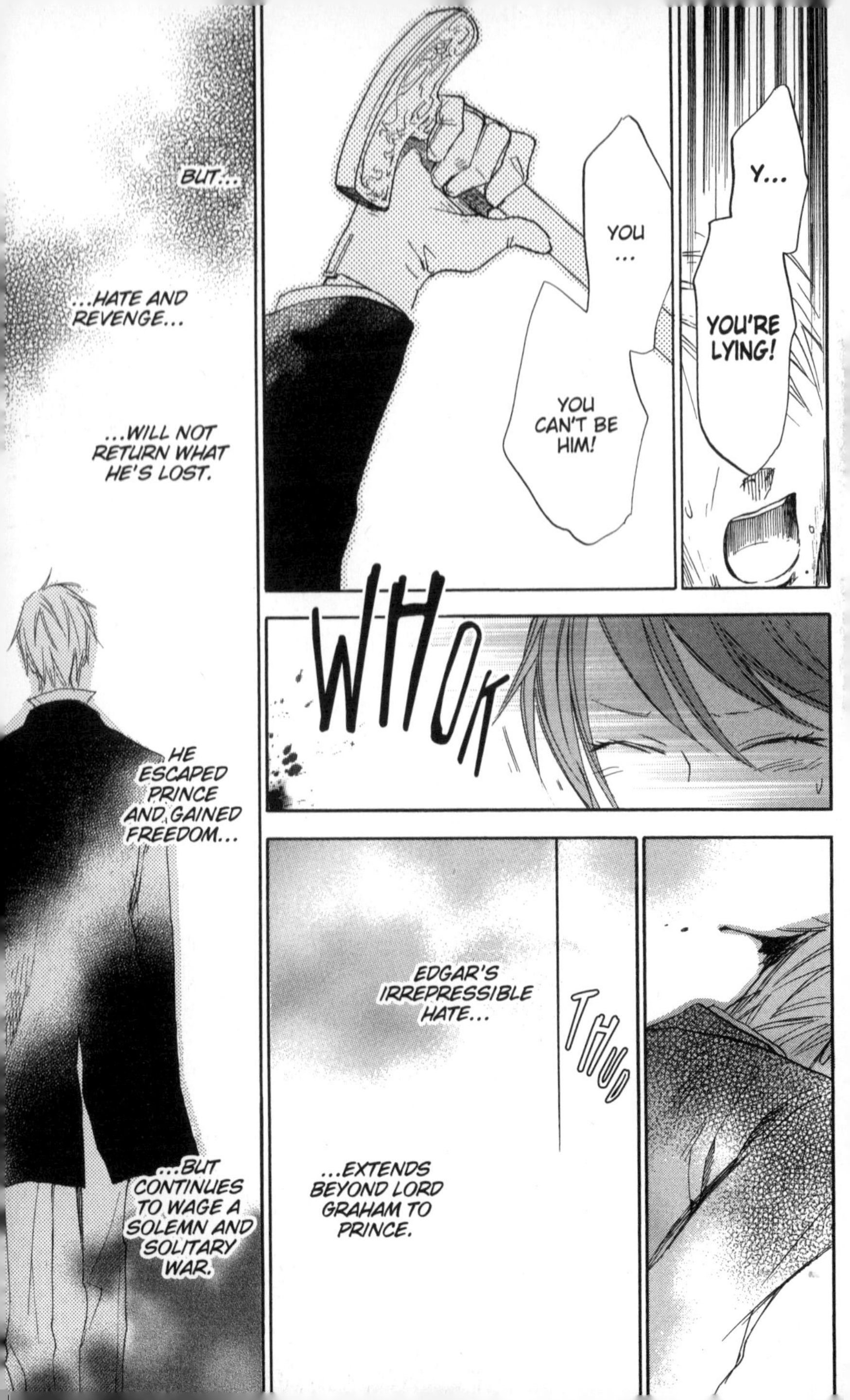
Y...
YOU'RE LYING!
YOU ...
YOU CAN'T BE HIM!
WHOK
THUD
EDGAR'S IRREPRESSIBLE HATE...
...EXTENDS BEYOND LORD GRAHAM TO PRINCE.
BUT...
...HATE AND REVENGE...
...WILL NOT RETURN WHAT HE'S LOST.
HE ESCAPED PRINCE AND GAINED FREEDOM...
...BUT CONTINUES TO WAGE A SOLEMN AND SOLITARY WAR.

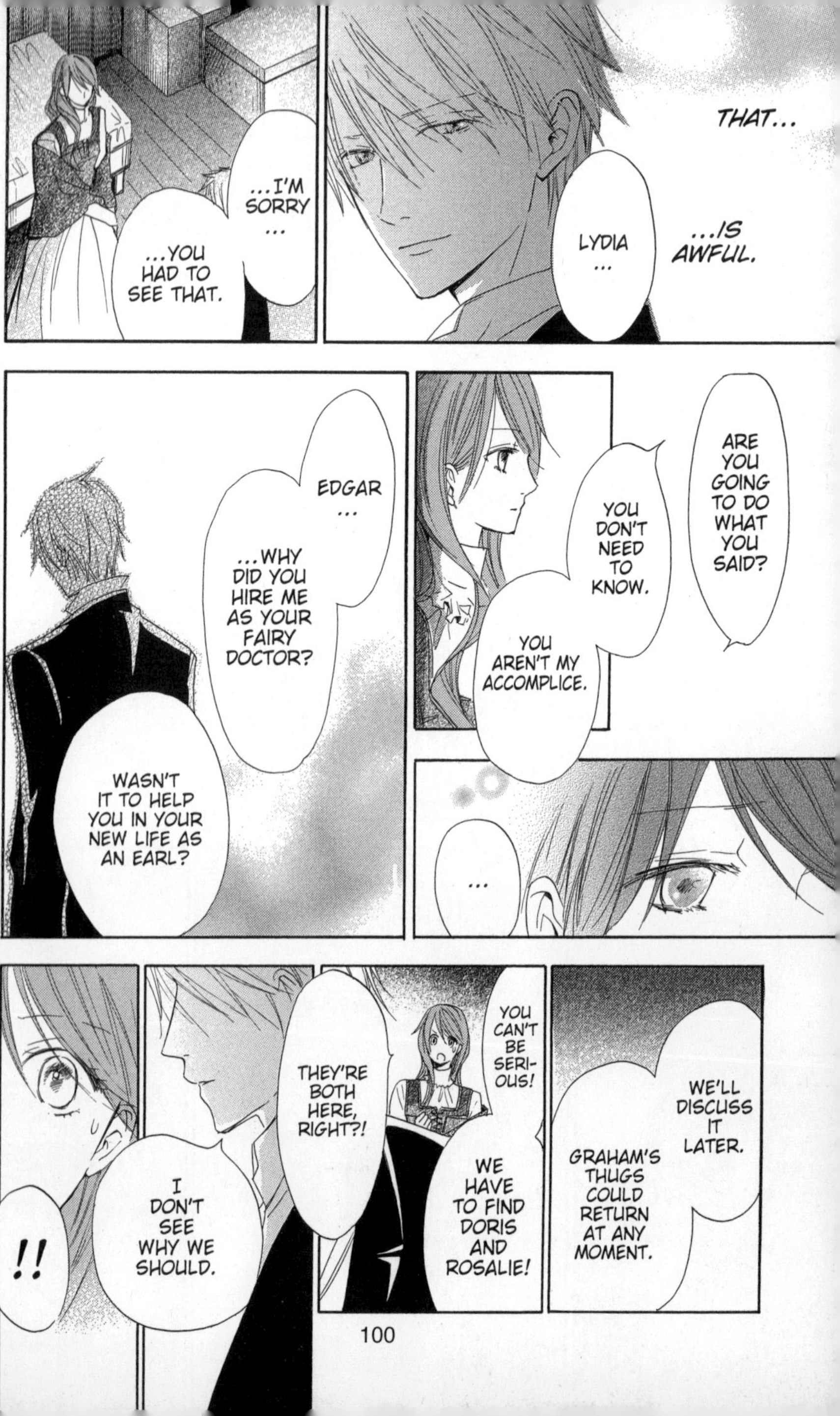
THAT...
...IS AWFUL.
LYDIA...
...I'M SORRY...
...YOU HAD TO SEE THAT.
ARE YOU GOING TO DO WHAT YOU SAID?
YOU DON'T NEED TO KNOW.
YOU AREN'T MY ACCOMPLICE.
...
EDGAR...
...WHY DID YOU HIRE ME AS YOUR FAIRY DOCTOR?
WASN'T IT TO HELP YOU IN YOUR NEW LIFE AS AN EARL?
WE'LL DISCUSS IT LATER.
GRAHAM'S THUGS COULD RETURN AT ANY MOMENT.
YOU CAN'T BE SERI-OUS!
THEY'RE BOTH HERE, RIGHT?!
WE HAVE TO FIND DORIS AND ROSALIE!
I DON'T SEE WHY WE SHOULD.
!!

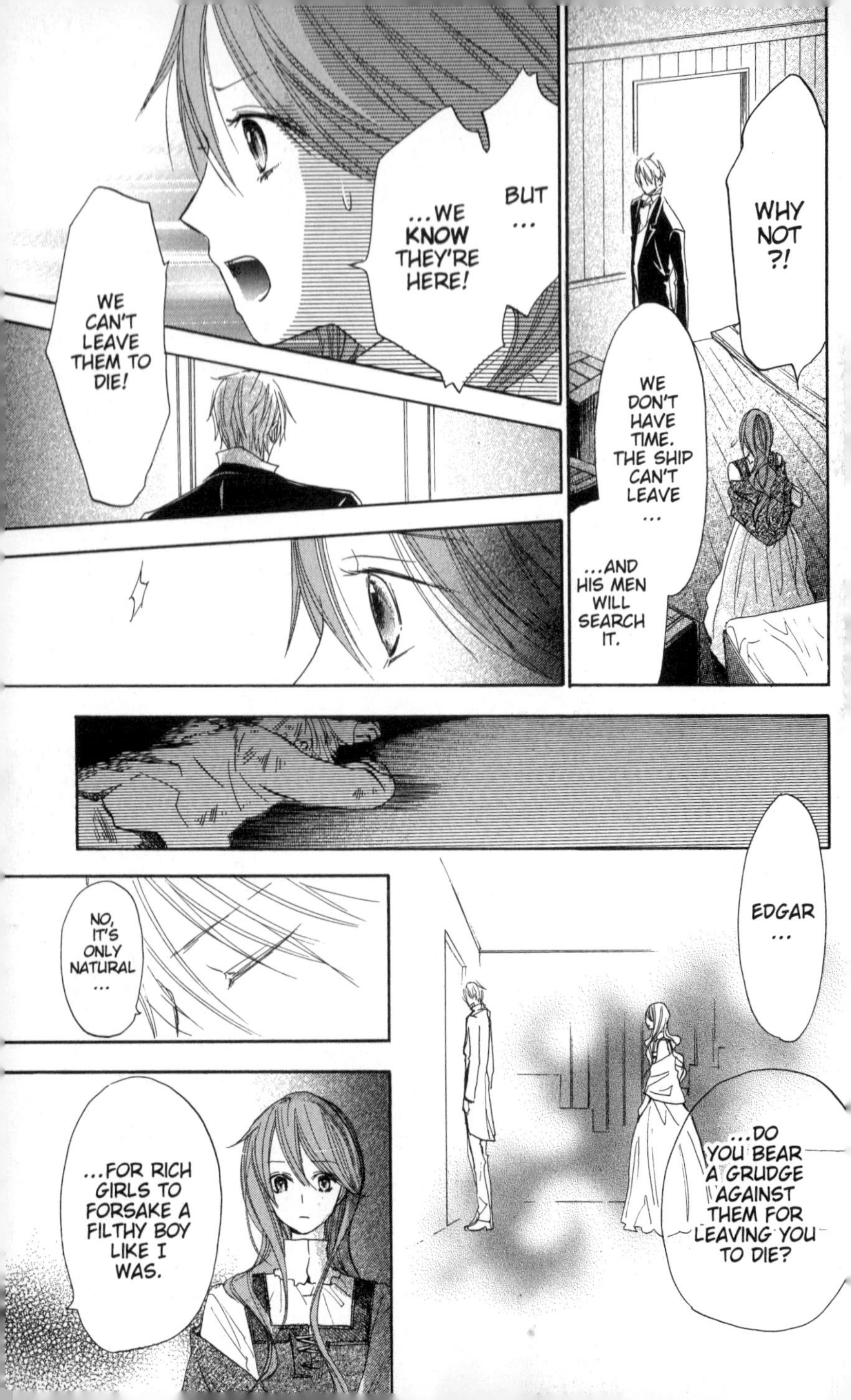
WHY NOT ?!
WE DON'T HAVE TIME. THE SHIP CAN'T LEAVE ...
...AND HIS MEN WILL SEARCH IT.
BUT ...
...WE KNOW THEY'RE HERE!
WE CAN'T LEAVE THEM TO DIE!
EDGAR ...
...DO YOU BEAR A GRUDGE AGAINST THEM FOR LEAVING YOU TO DIE?
NO, IT'S ONLY NATURAL ...
...FOR RICH GIRLS TO FORSAKE A FILTHY BOY LIKE I WAS.

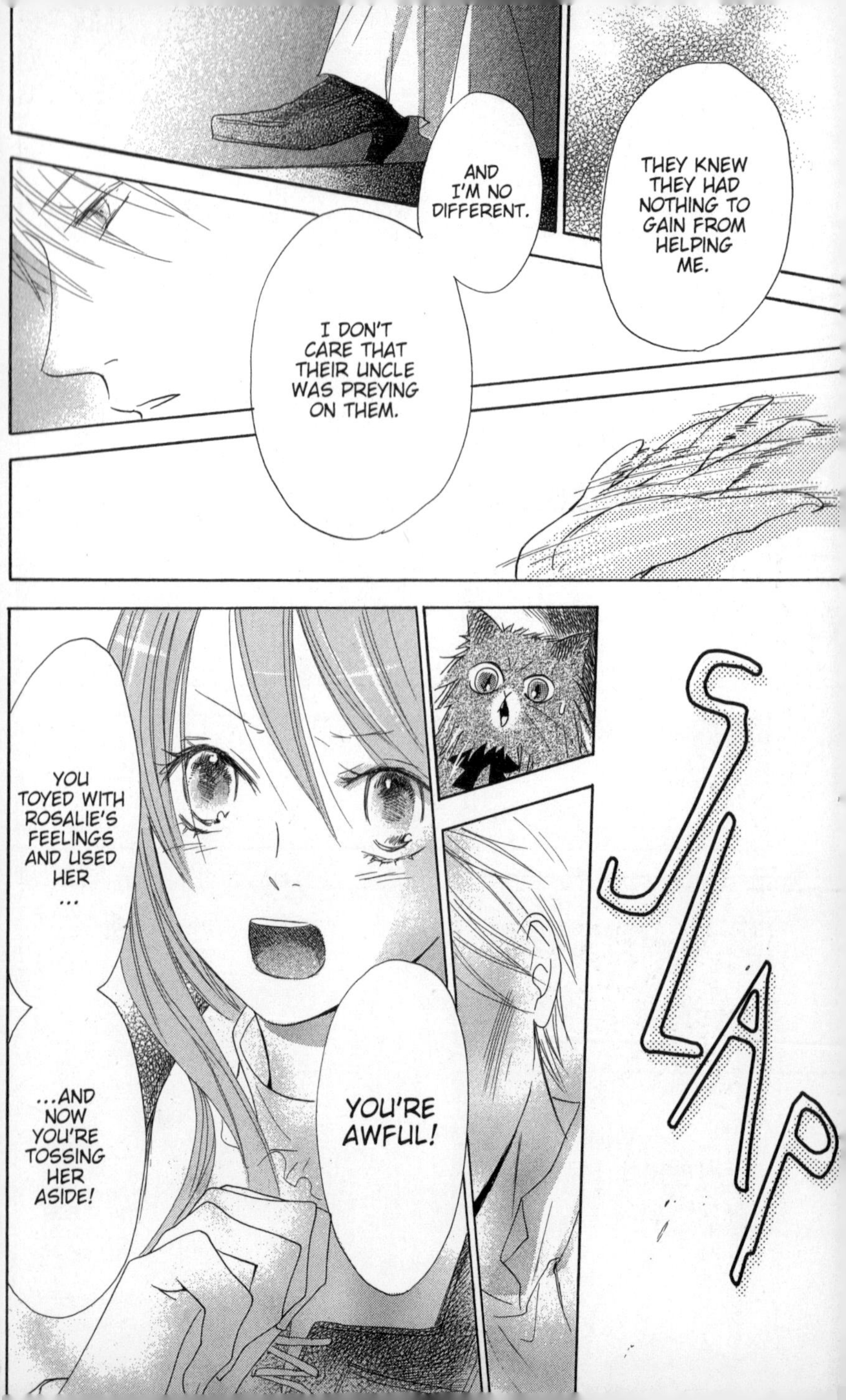
THEY KNEW THEY HAD NOTHING TO GAIN FROM HELPING ME.
AND I'M NO DIFFERENT.
I DON'T CARE THAT THEIR UNCLE WAS PREYING ON THEM.
SLAP
YOU'RE AWFUL!
YOU TOYED WITH ROSALIE'S FEELINGS AND USED HER...
...AND NOW YOU'RE TOSSING HER ASIDE!

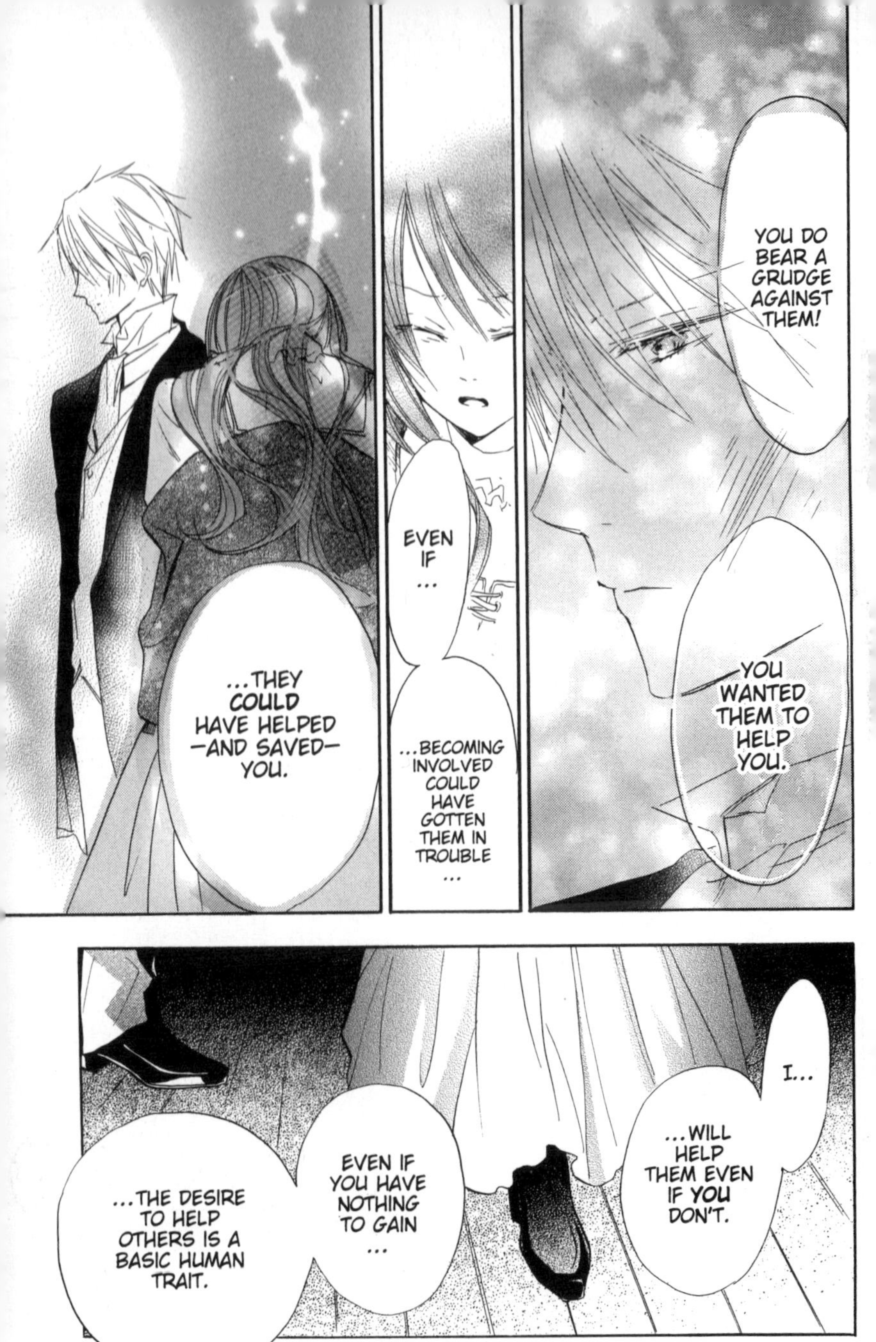
YOU DO BEAR A GRUDGE AGAINST THEM!
YOU WANTED THEM TO HELP YOU.
EVEN IF ...
...BECOMING INVOLVED COULD HAVE GOTTEN THEM IN TROUBLE ...
...THEY COULD HAVE HELPED —AND SAVED— YOU.
I...
...WILL HELP THEM EVEN IF YOU DON'T.
EVEN IF YOU HAVE NOTHING TO GAIN ...
...THE DESIRE TO HELP OTHERS IS A BASIC HUMAN TRAIT.

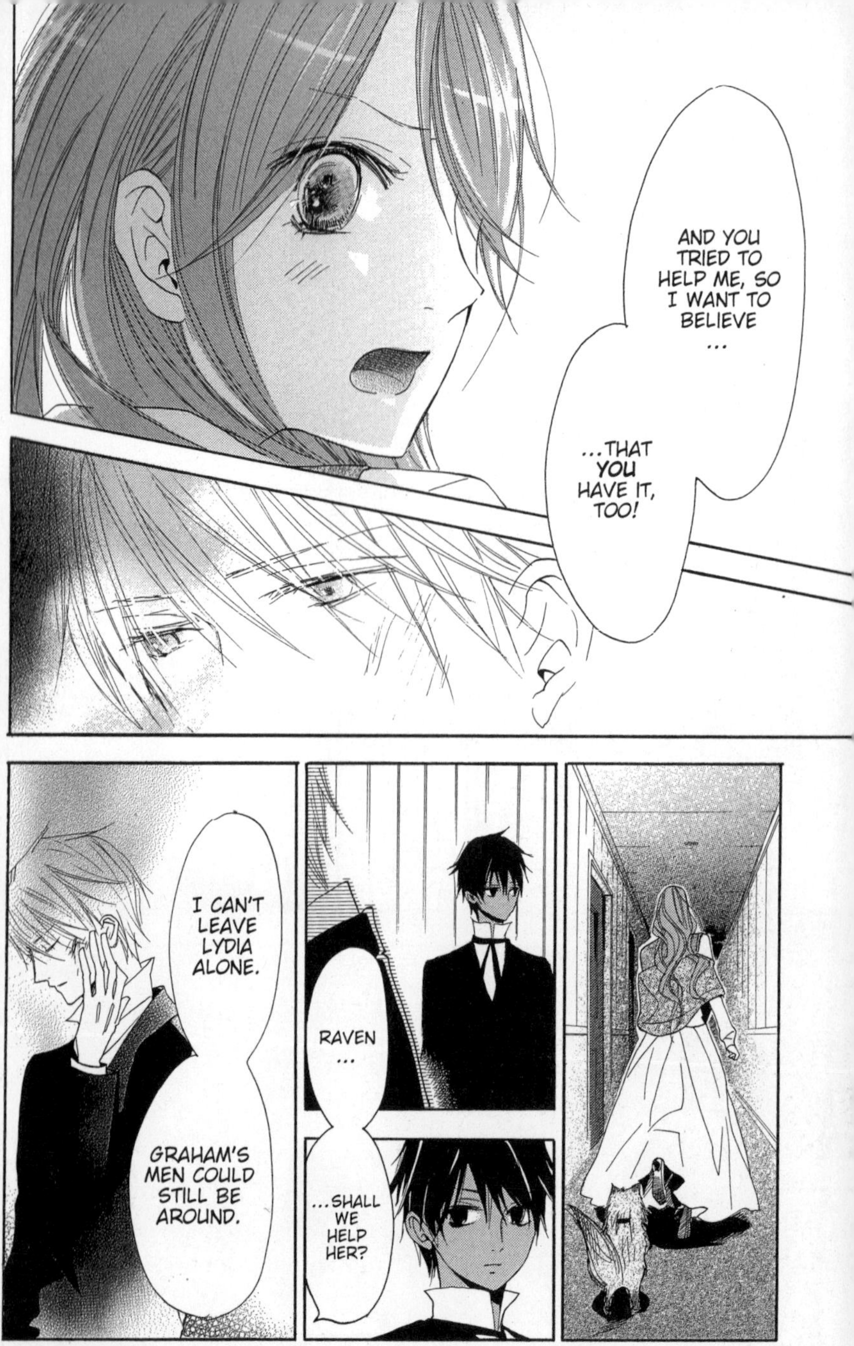
AND YOU TRIED TO HELP ME, SO I WANT TO BELIEVE ...
...THAT **YOU** HAVE IT, TOO!
RAVEN ...
...SHALL WE HELP HER?
I CAN'T LEAVE LYDIA ALONE.
GRAHAM'S MEN COULD STILL BE AROUND.

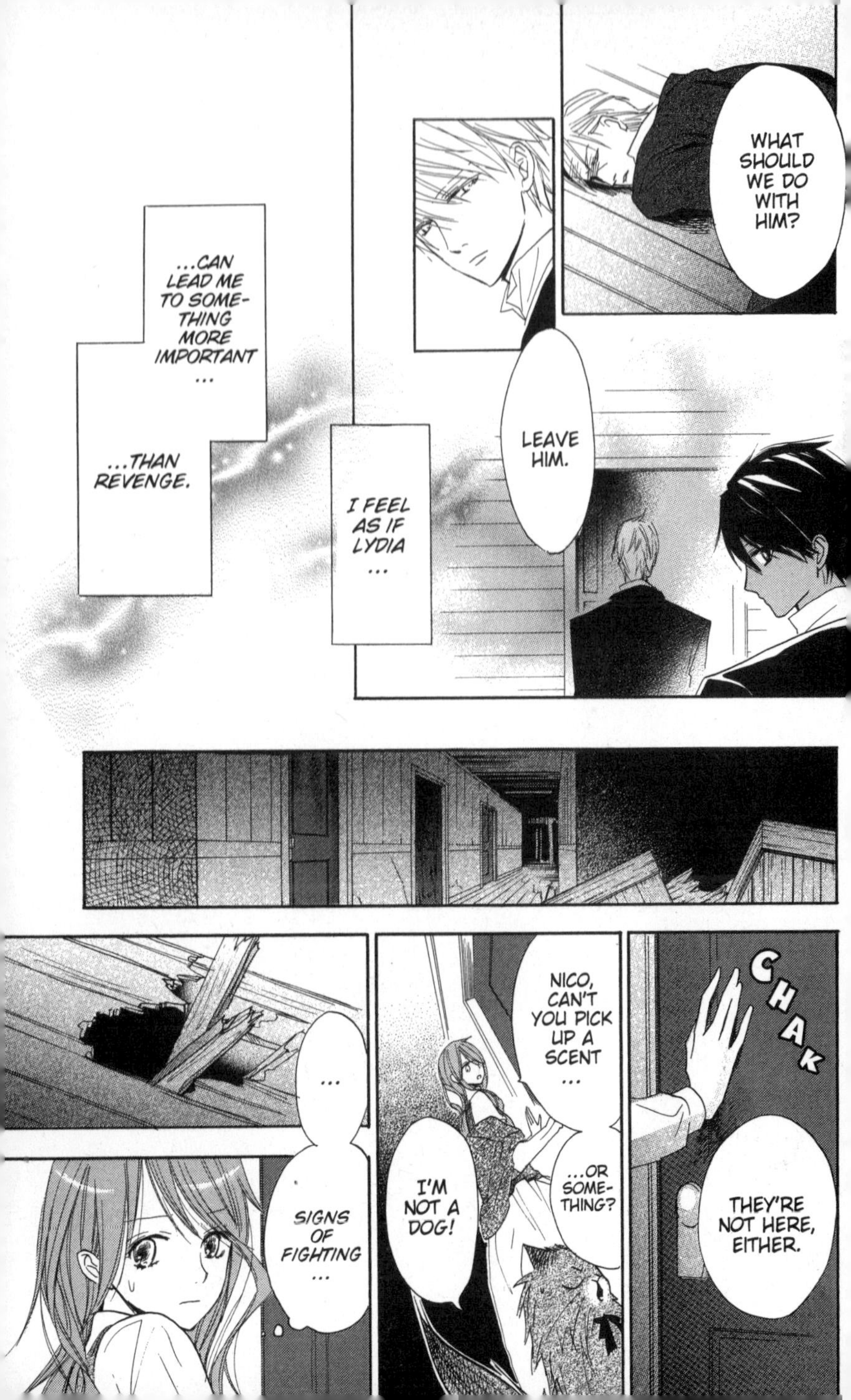
WHAT SHOULD WE DO WITH HIM?
LEAVE HIM.
I FEEL AS IF LYDIA ...
...CAN LEAD ME TO SOME-THING MORE IMPORTANT ...
...THAN REVENGE.
CHAK
THEY'RE NOT HERE, EITHER.
NICO, CAN'T YOU PICK UP A SCENT ...
...OR SOME-THING?
I'M NOT A DOG!
...
SIGNS OF FIGHTING ...

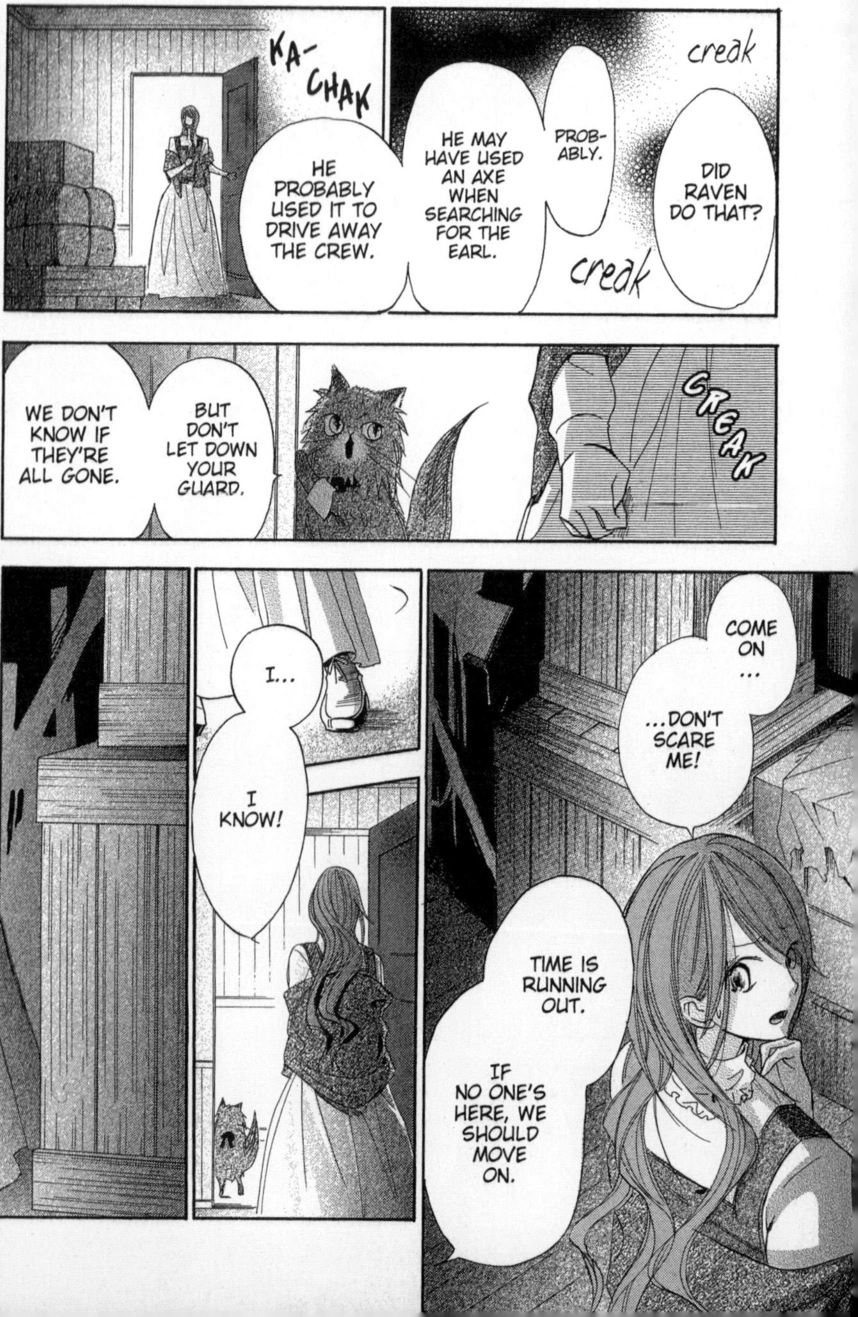
creak
DID RAVEN DO THAT?
PROB-ABLY.
creak
HE MAY HAVE USED AN AXE WHEN SEARCHING FOR THE EARL.
HE PROBABLY USED IT TO DRIVE AWAY THE CREW.
KA-CHAK
CREAK
BUT DON'T LET DOWN YOUR GUARD.
WE DON'T KNOW IF THEY'RE ALL GONE.
COME ON ...
...DON'T SCARE ME!
TIME IS RUNNING OUT.
IF NO ONE'S HERE, WE SHOULD MOVE ON.
I...
I KNOW!

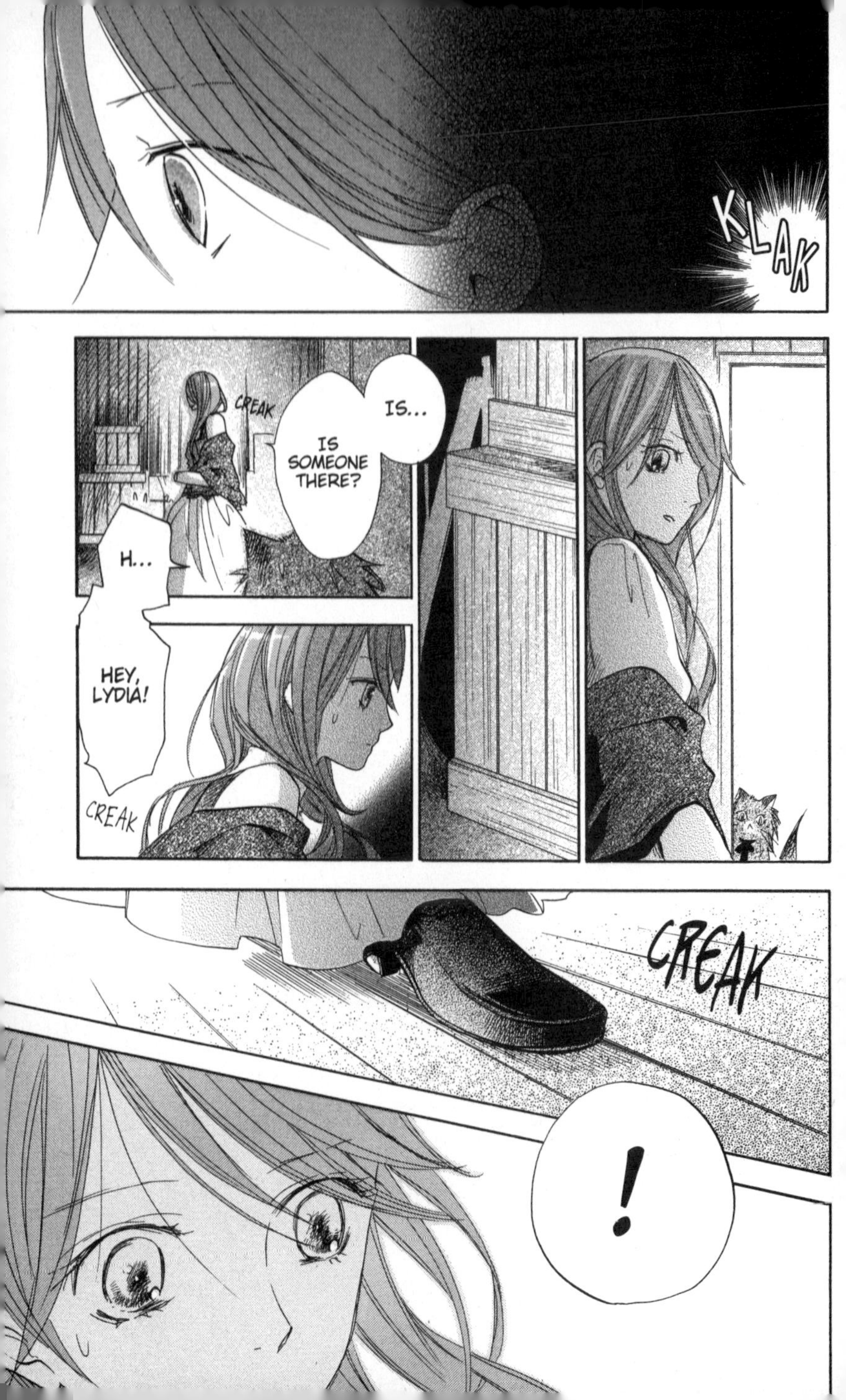
KLAK
IS...
IS SOMEONE THERE?
CREAK
H...
HEY, LYDIA!
CREAK
CREAK
!

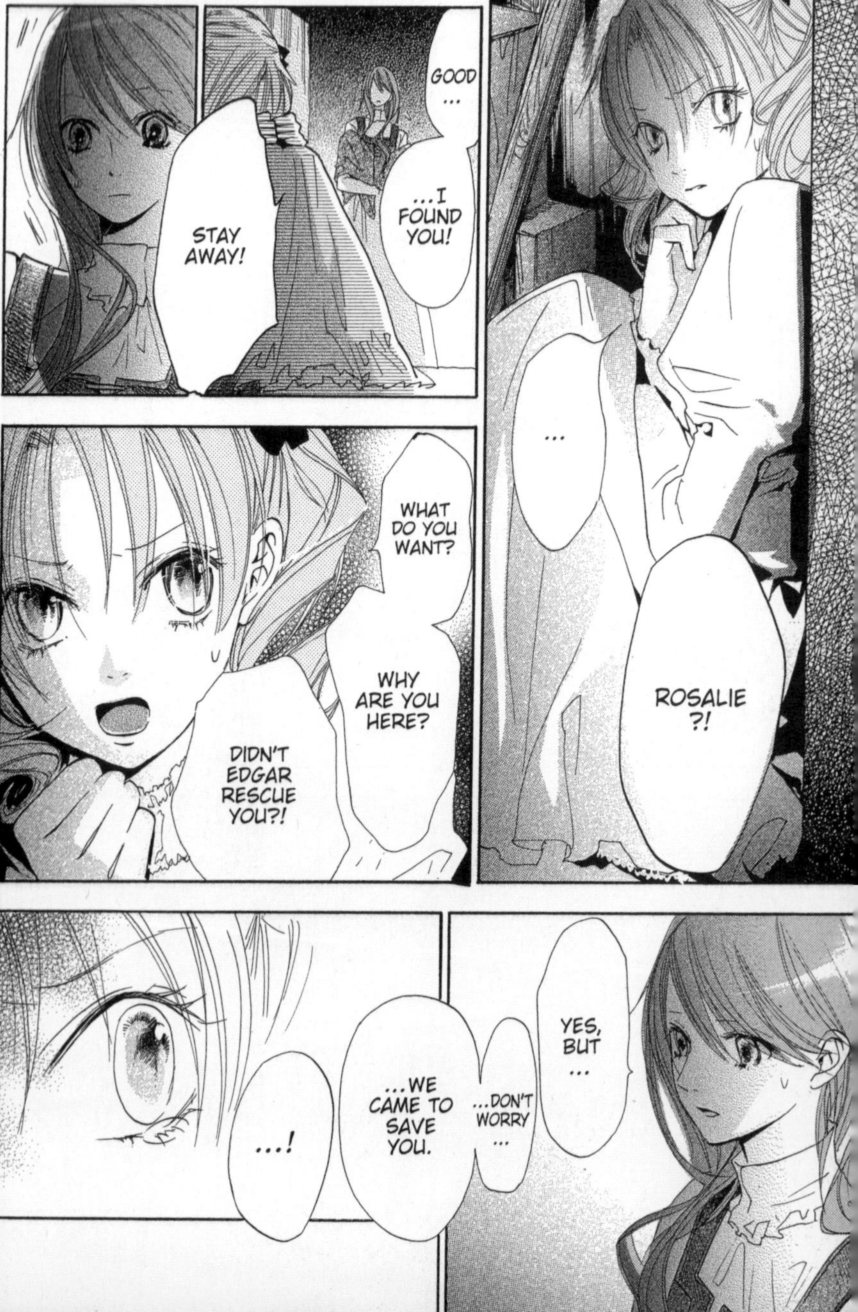
...
ROSALIE ?!
GOOD ...
...I FOUND YOU!
STAY AWAY!
WHAT DO YOU WANT?
WHY ARE YOU HERE?
DIDN'T EDGAR RESCUE YOU?!
YES, BUT ...
...DON'T WORRY ...
...WE CAME TO SAVE YOU.
...!

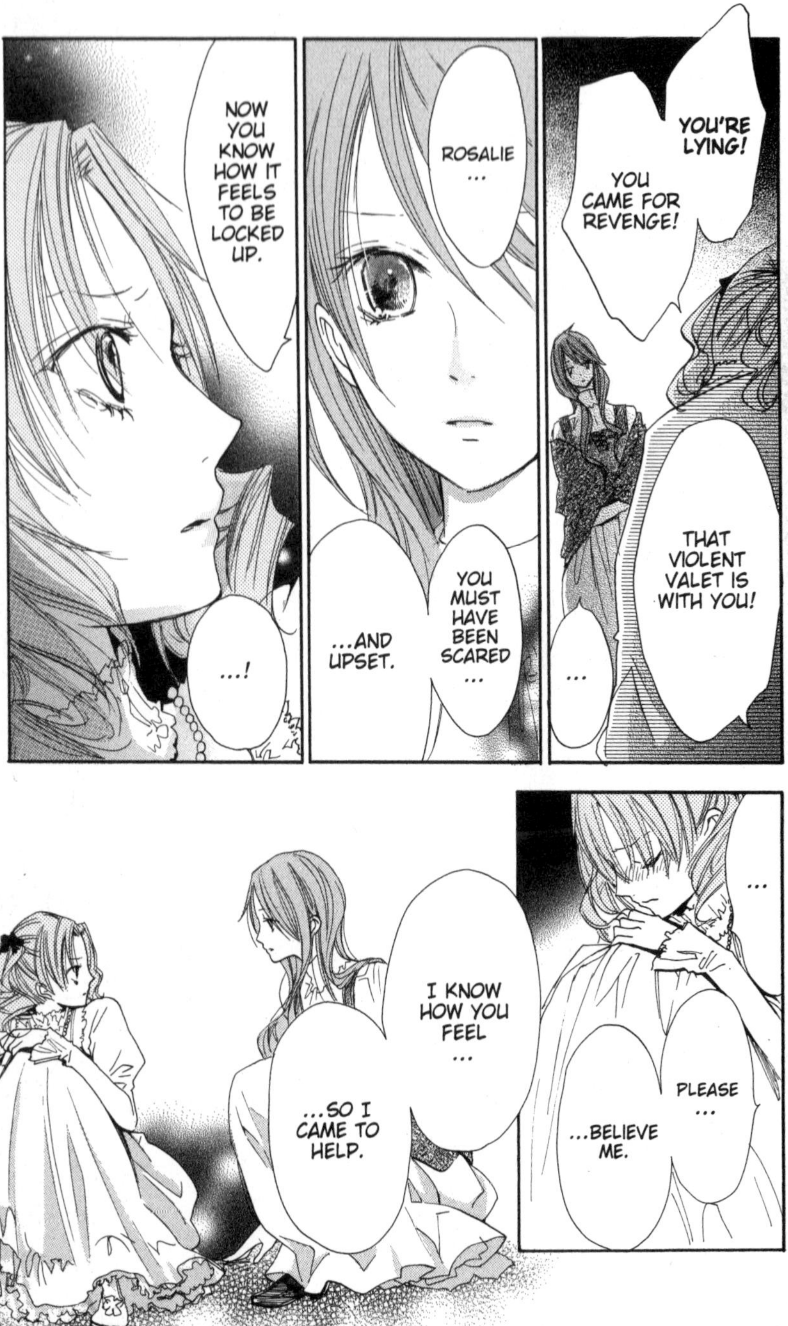

YOU'RE LYING!
YOU CAME FOR REVENGE!
THAT VIOLENT VALET IS WITH YOU!
...
ROSALIE ...
YOU MUST HAVE BEEN SCARED ...
...AND UPSET.
NOW YOU KNOW HOW IT FEELS TO BE LOCKED UP.
...!
...
PLEASE ...
...BELIEVE ME.
I KNOW HOW YOU FEEL ...
...SO I CAME TO HELP.

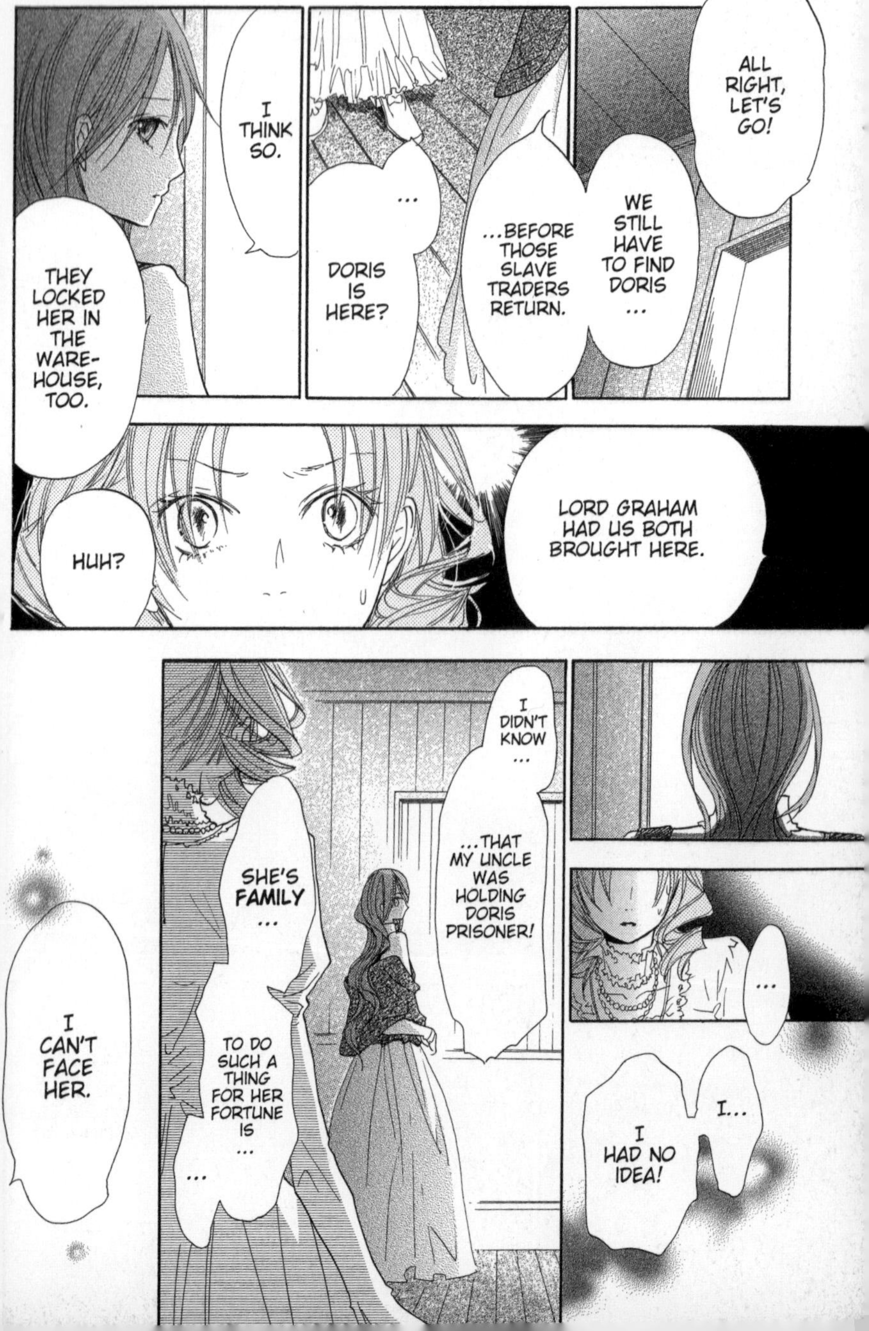
ALL RIGHT, LET'S GO!
WE STILL HAVE TO FIND DORIS...
...BEFORE THOSE SLAVE TRADERS RETURN.
...
DORIS IS HERE?
I THINK SO.
THEY LOCKED HER IN THE WAREHOUSE, TOO.
LORD GRAHAM HAD US BOTH BROUGHT HERE.
HUH?
...
I...
I HAD NO IDEA!
I DIDN'T KNOW...
...THAT MY UNCLE WAS HOLDING DORIS PRISONER!
SHE'S **FAMILY**...
TO DO SUCH A THING FOR HER FORTUNE IS...
...
I CAN'T FACE HER.

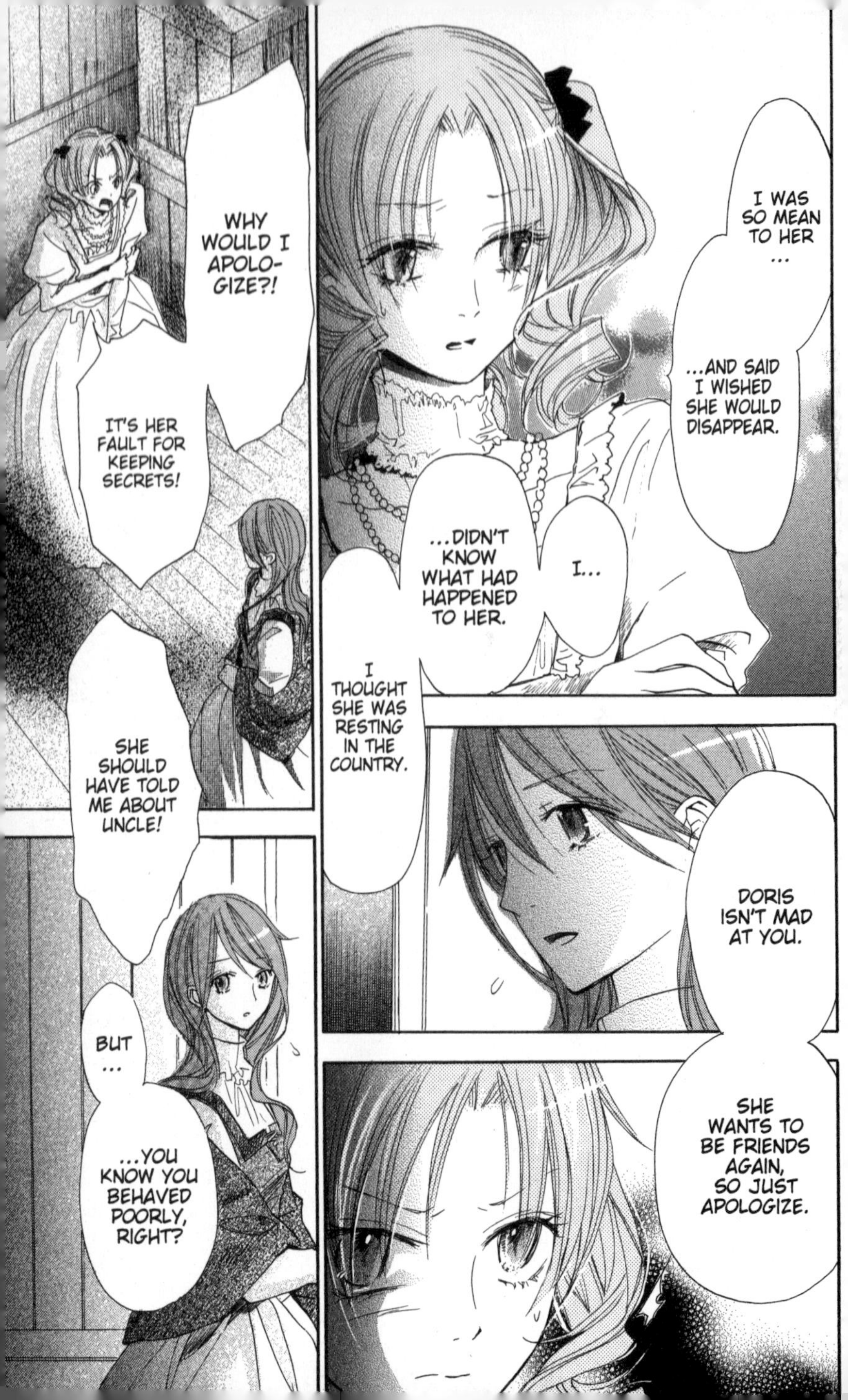
I WAS SO MEAN TO HER ...
...AND SAID I WISHED SHE WOULD DISAPPEAR.
I...
...DIDN'T KNOW WHAT HAD HAPPENED TO HER.
I THOUGHT SHE WAS RESTING IN THE COUNTRY.
DORIS ISN'T MAD AT YOU.
SHE WANTS TO BE FRIENDS AGAIN, SO JUST APOLOGIZE.
WHY WOULD I APOLOGIZE?!
IT'S HER FAULT FOR KEEPING SECRETS!
SHE SHOULD HAVE TOLD ME ABOUT UNCLE!
BUT ...
...YOU KNOW YOU BEHAVED POORLY, RIGHT?

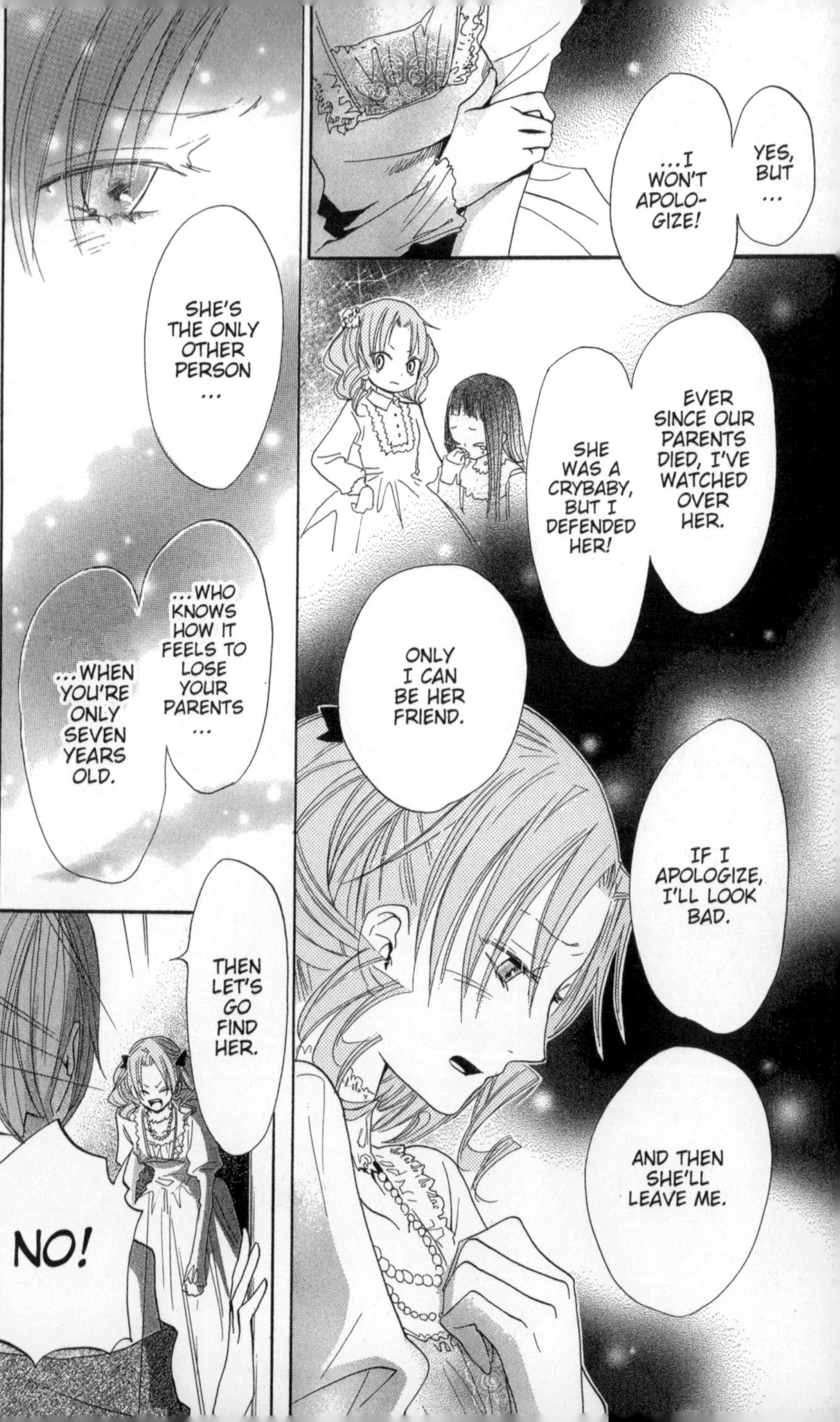
YES, BUT ...
...I WON'T APOLOGIZE!
EVER SINCE OUR PARENTS DIED, I'VE WATCHED OVER HER.
SHE WAS A CRYBABY, BUT I DEFENDED HER!
ONLY I CAN BE HER FRIEND.
IF I APOLOGIZE, I'LL LOOK BAD.
AND THEN SHE'LL LEAVE ME.
SHE'S THE ONLY OTHER PERSON ...
...WHO KNOWS HOW IT FEELS TO LOSE YOUR PARENTS ...
...WHEN YOU'RE ONLY SEVEN YEARS OLD.
THEN LET'S GO FIND HER.
NO!

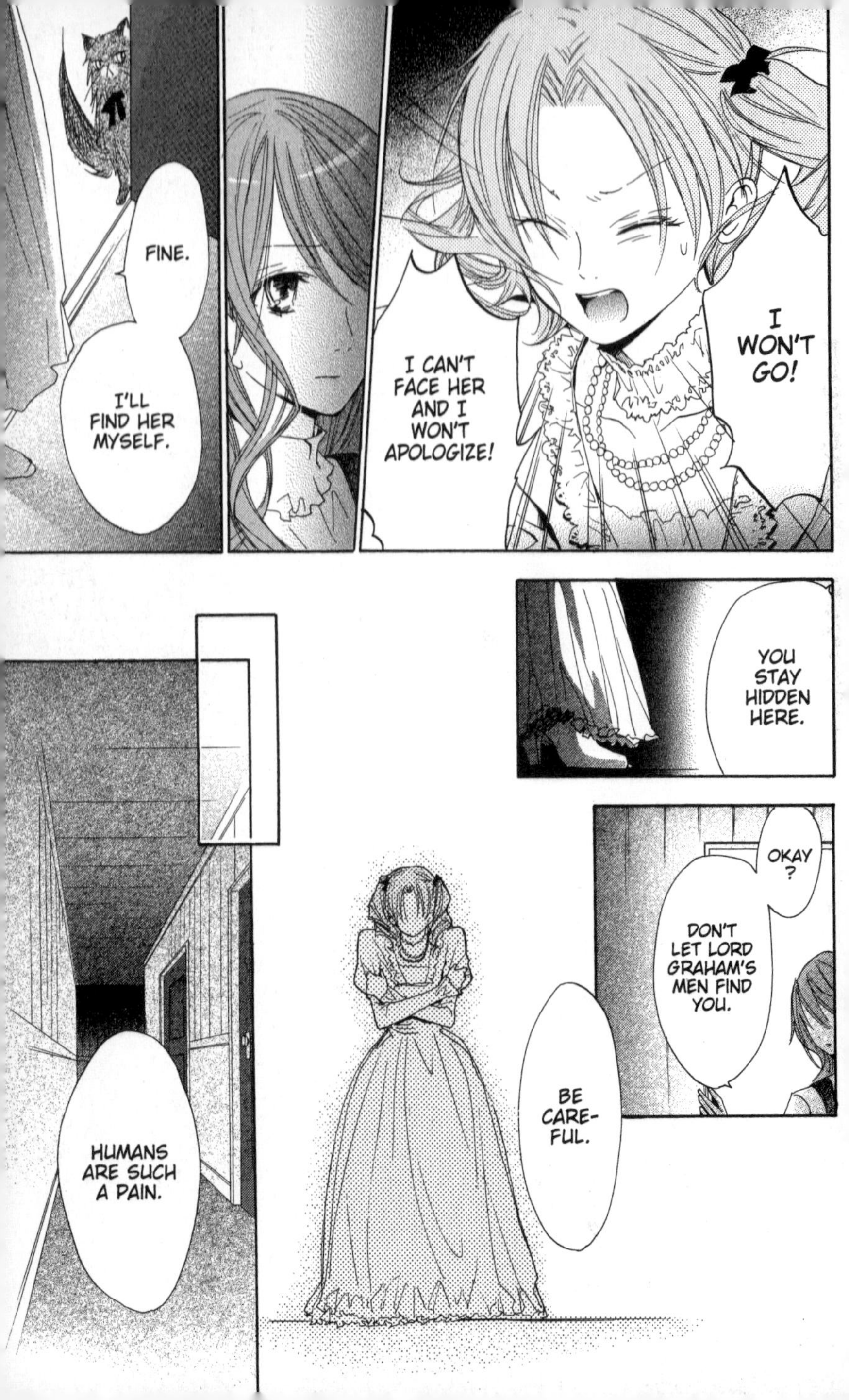
I WON'T GO!
I CAN'T FACE HER AND I WON'T APOLOGIZE!
FINE.
I'LL FIND HER MYSELF.
YOU STAY HIDDEN HERE.
OKAY?
DON'T LET LORD GRAHAM'S MEN FIND YOU.
BE CARE-FUL.
HUMANS ARE SUCH A PAIN.

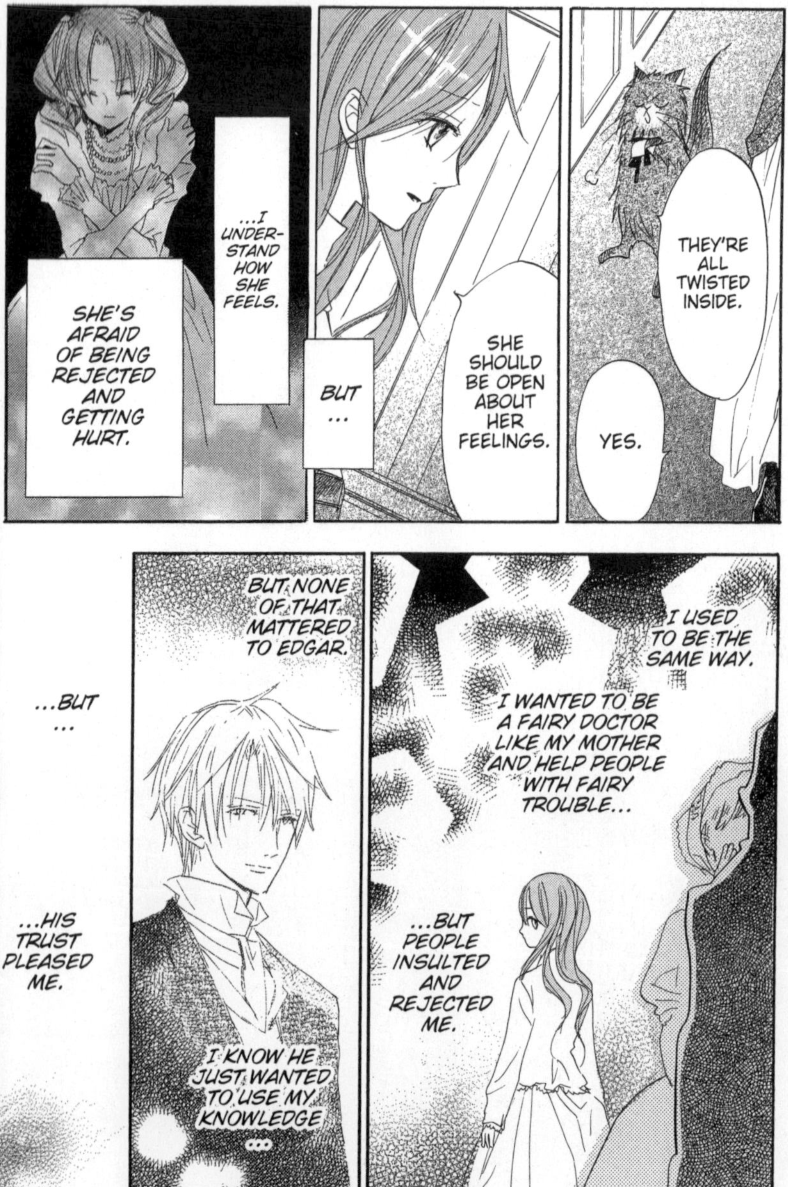
THEY'RE ALL TWISTED INSIDE.
YES.
SHE SHOULD BE OPEN ABOUT HER FEELINGS.
BUT ...
...I UNDER-STAND HOW SHE FEELS.
SHE'S AFRAID OF BEING REJECTED AND GETTING HURT.
I USED TO BE THE SAME WAY.
I WANTED TO BE A FAIRY DOCTOR LIKE MY MOTHER AND HELP PEOPLE WITH FAIRY TROUBLE...
...BUT PEOPLE INSULTED AND REJECTED ME.
BUT NONE OF THAT MATTERED TO EDGAR.
...BUT ...
...HIS TRUST PLEASED ME.
I KNOW HE JUST WANTED TO USE MY KNOWLEDGE ...

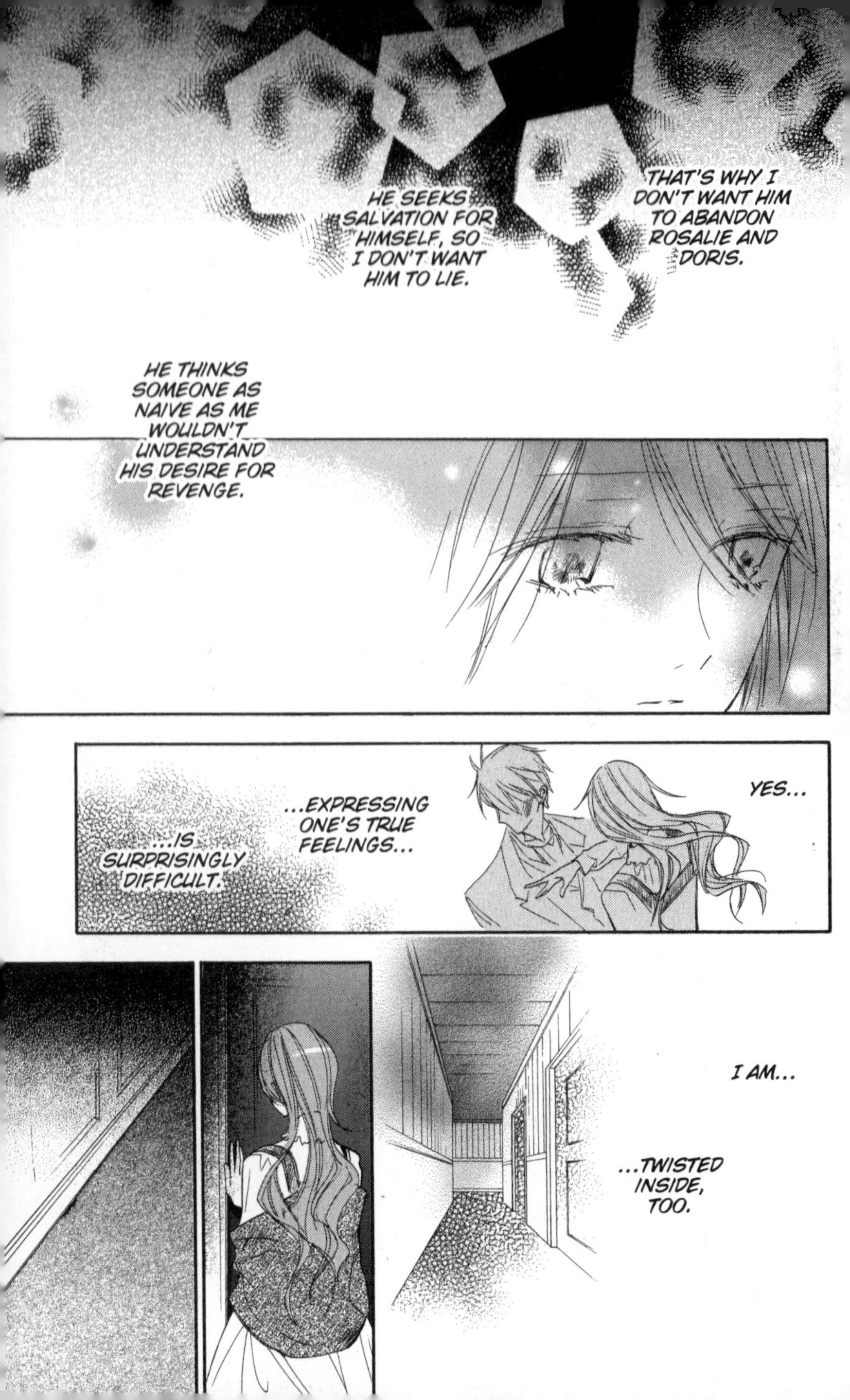
THAT'S WHY I DON'T WANT HIM TO ABANDON ROSALIE AND DORIS.
HE SEEKS SALVATION FOR HIMSELF, SO I DON'T WANT HIM TO LIE.
HE THINKS SOMEONE AS NAIVE AS ME WOULDN'T UNDERSTAND HIS DESIRE FOR REVENGE.
YES...
...EXPRESSING ONE'S TRUE FEELINGS...
...IS SURPRISINGLY DIFFICULT.
I AM...
...TWISTED INSIDE, TOO.

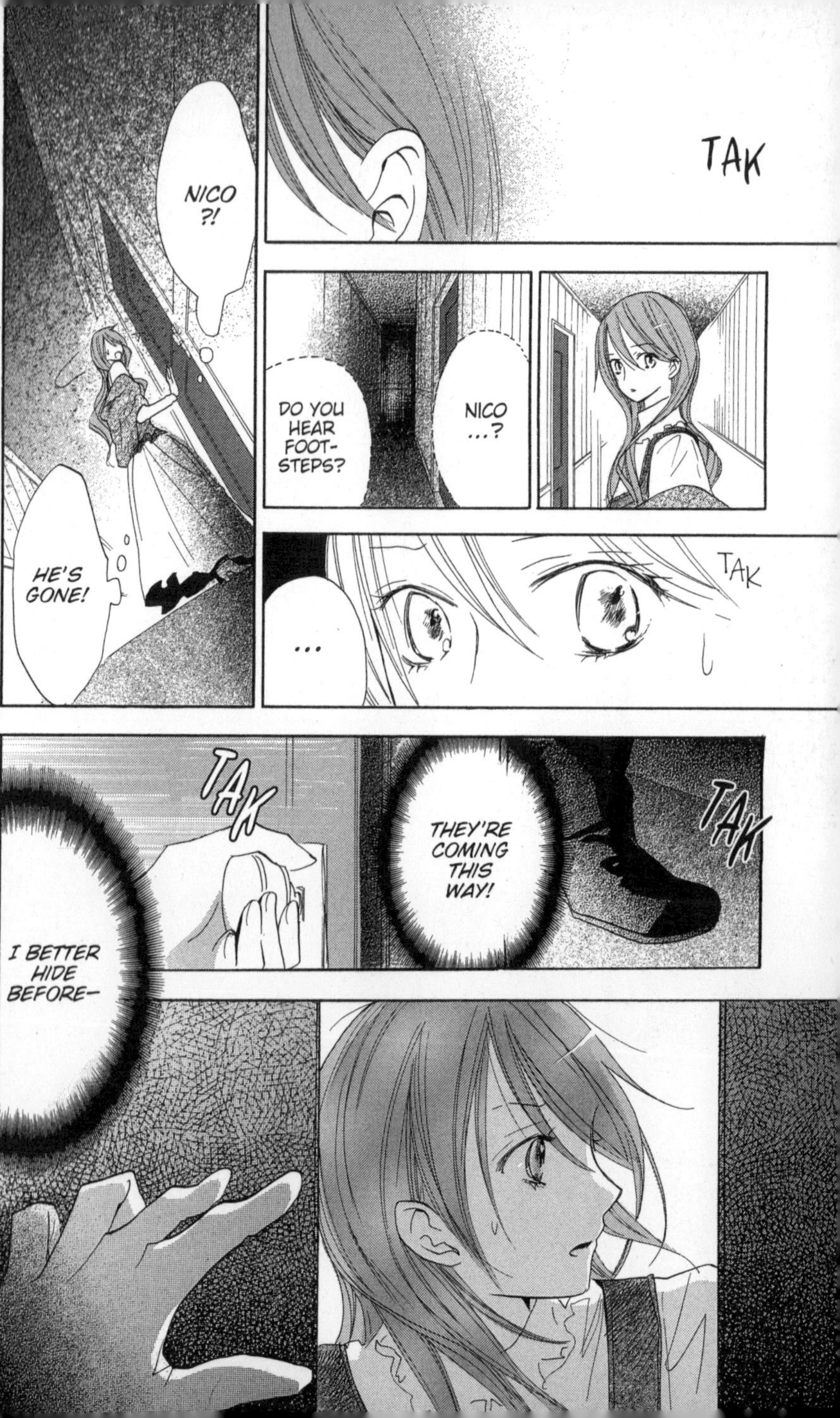
TAK
NICO ...?
DO YOU HEAR FOOT-STEPS?
TAK
...
NICO ?!
HE'S GONE!
TAK
THEY'RE COMING THIS WAY!
TAK
I BETTER HIDE BEFORE—

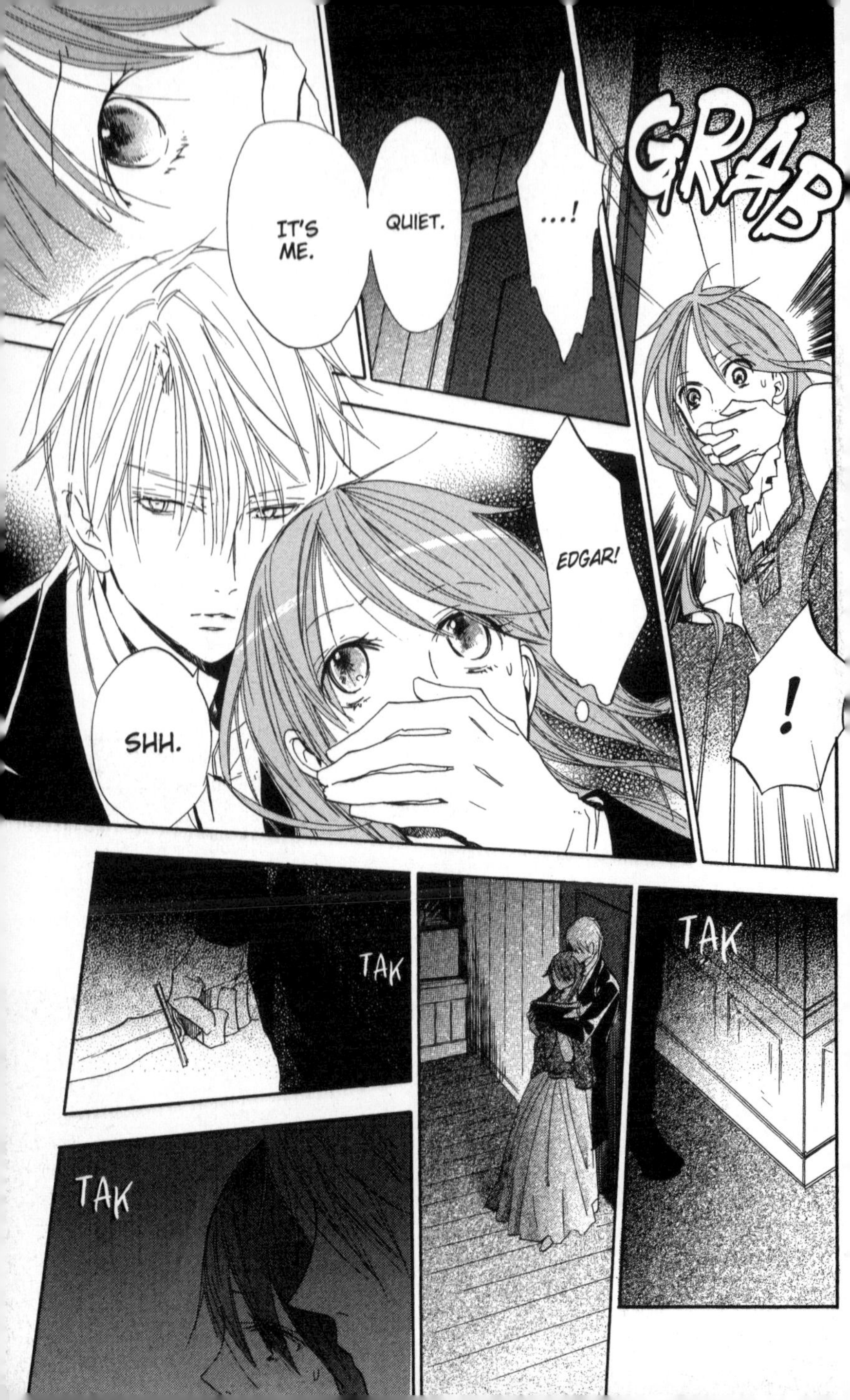
GRAB
!
...!
QUIET.
IT'S ME.
EDGAR!
SHH.
TAK
TAK
TAK

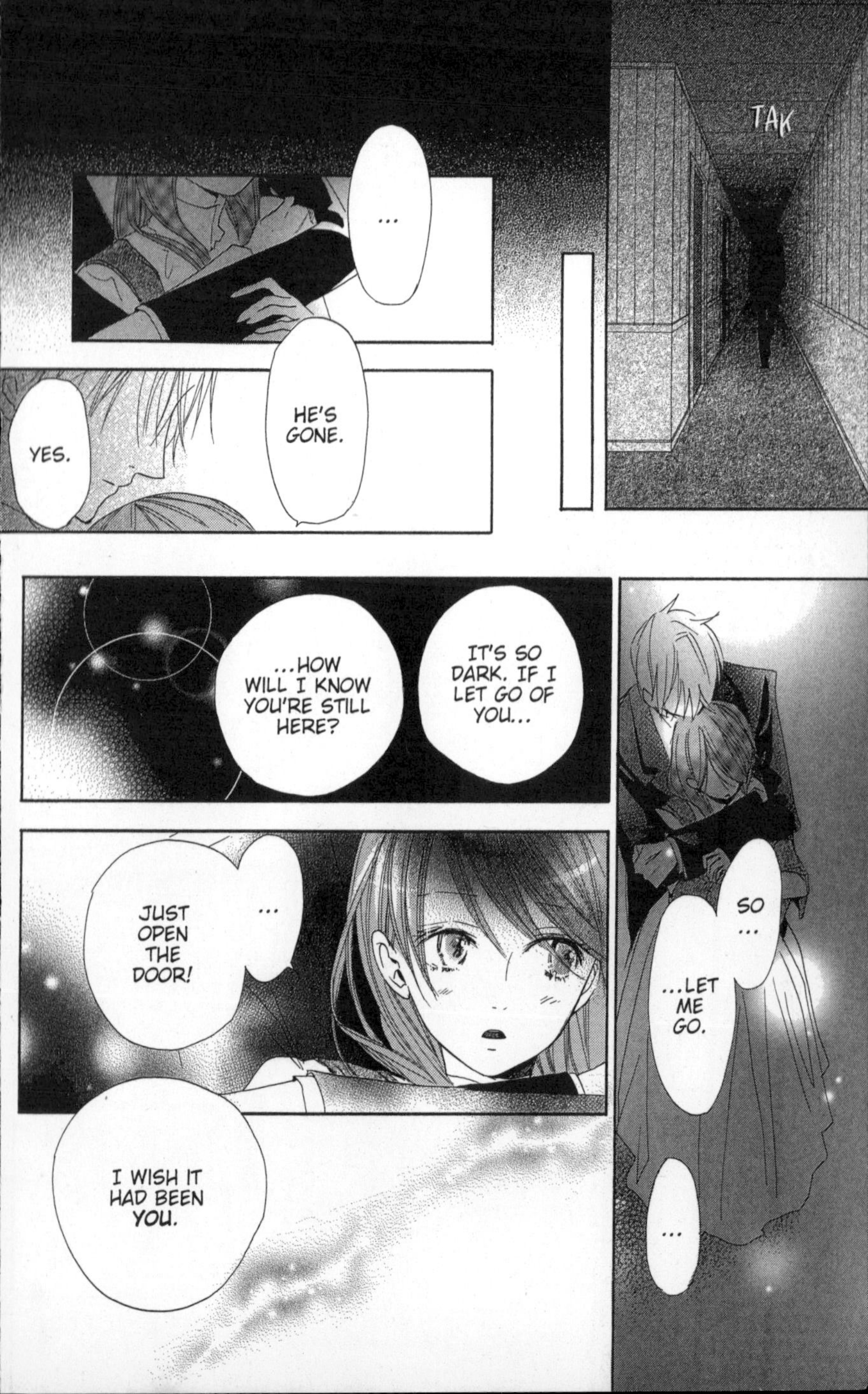
TAK
...
HE'S GONE.
YES.
SO ...
...LET ME GO.
...
IT'S SO DARK. IF I LET GO OF YOU...
...HOW WILL I KNOW YOU'RE STILL HERE?
...
JUST OPEN THE DOOR!
I WISH IT HAD BEEN YOU.

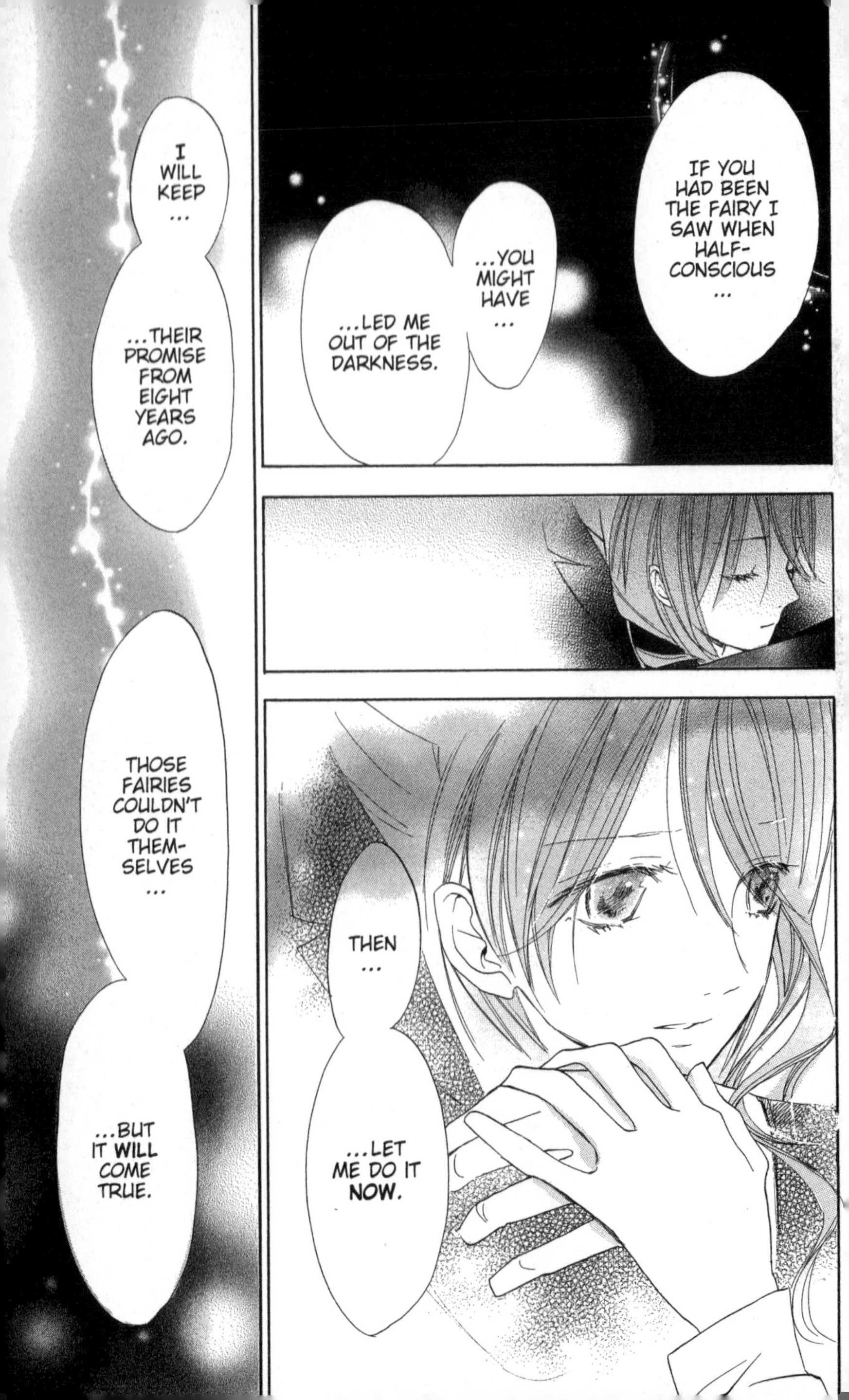
IF YOU HAD BEEN THE FAIRY I SAW WHEN HALF-CONSCIOUS...
...YOU MIGHT HAVE...
...LED ME OUT OF THE DARKNESS.
THEN...
...LET ME DO IT NOW.
I WILL KEEP...
...THEIR PROMISE FROM EIGHT YEARS AGO.
THOSE FAIRIES COULDN'T DO IT THEMSELVES...
...BUT IT WILL COME TRUE.

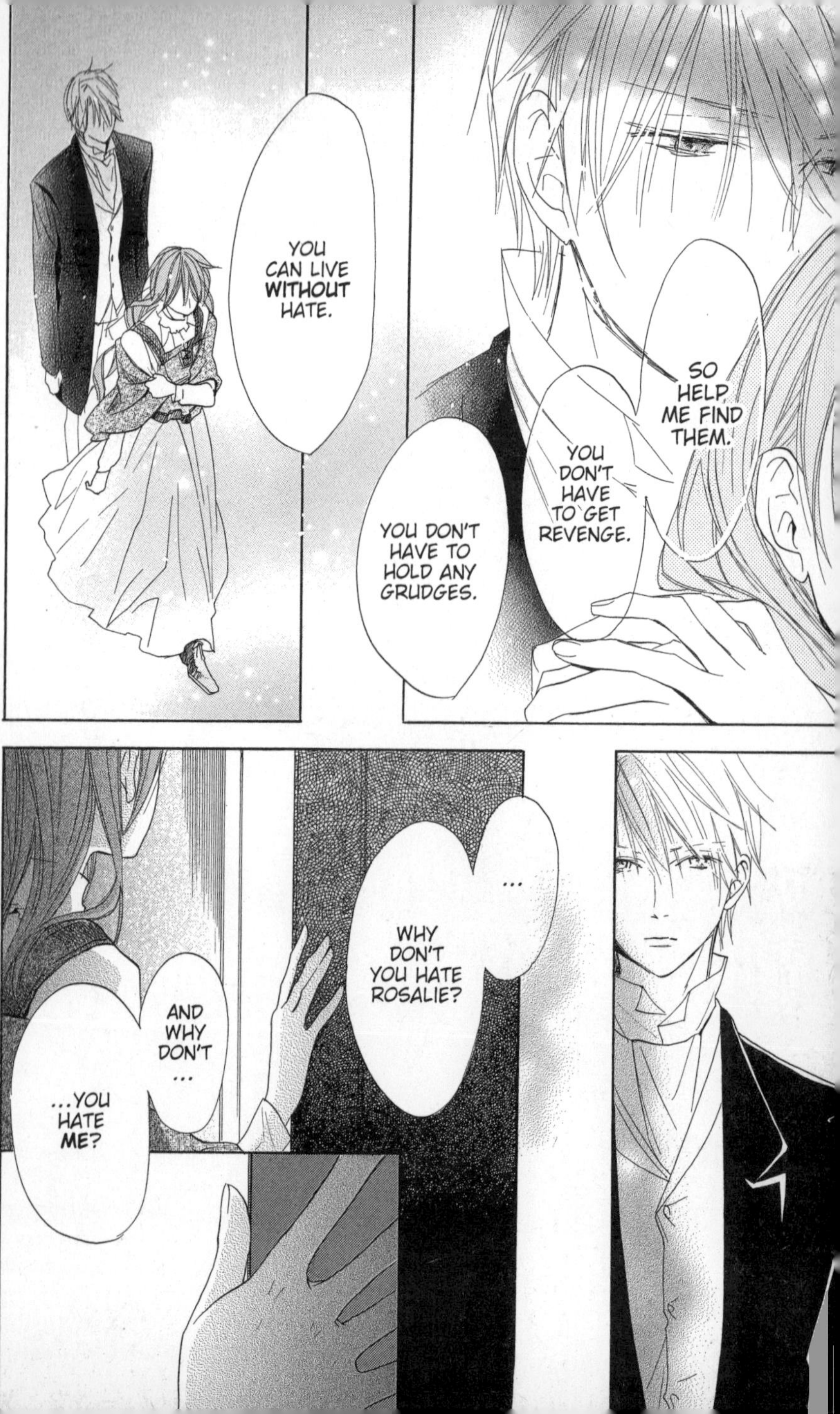
SO HELP ME FIND THEM.
YOU DON'T HAVE TO GET REVENGE.
YOU DON'T HAVE TO HOLD ANY GRUDGES.
YOU CAN LIVE WITHOUT HATE.
...
WHY DON'T YOU HATE ROSALIE?
AND WHY DON'T ...
...YOU HATE ME?

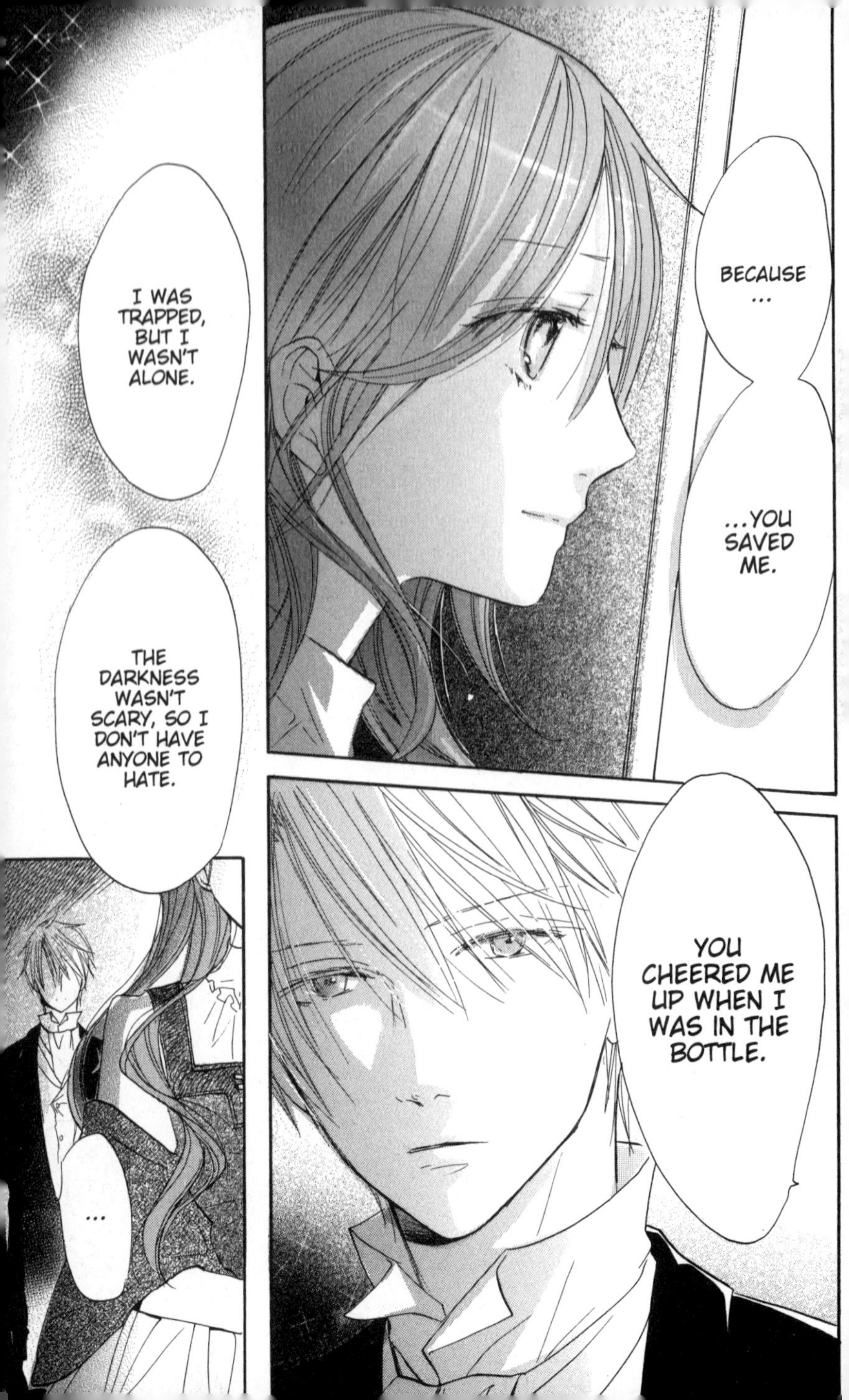
BECAUSE ...
...YOU SAVED ME.
I WAS TRAPPED, BUT I WASN'T ALONE.
THE DARKNESS WASN'T SCARY, SO I DON'T HAVE ANYONE TO HATE.
YOU CHEERED ME UP WHEN I WAS IN THE BOTTLE.
...

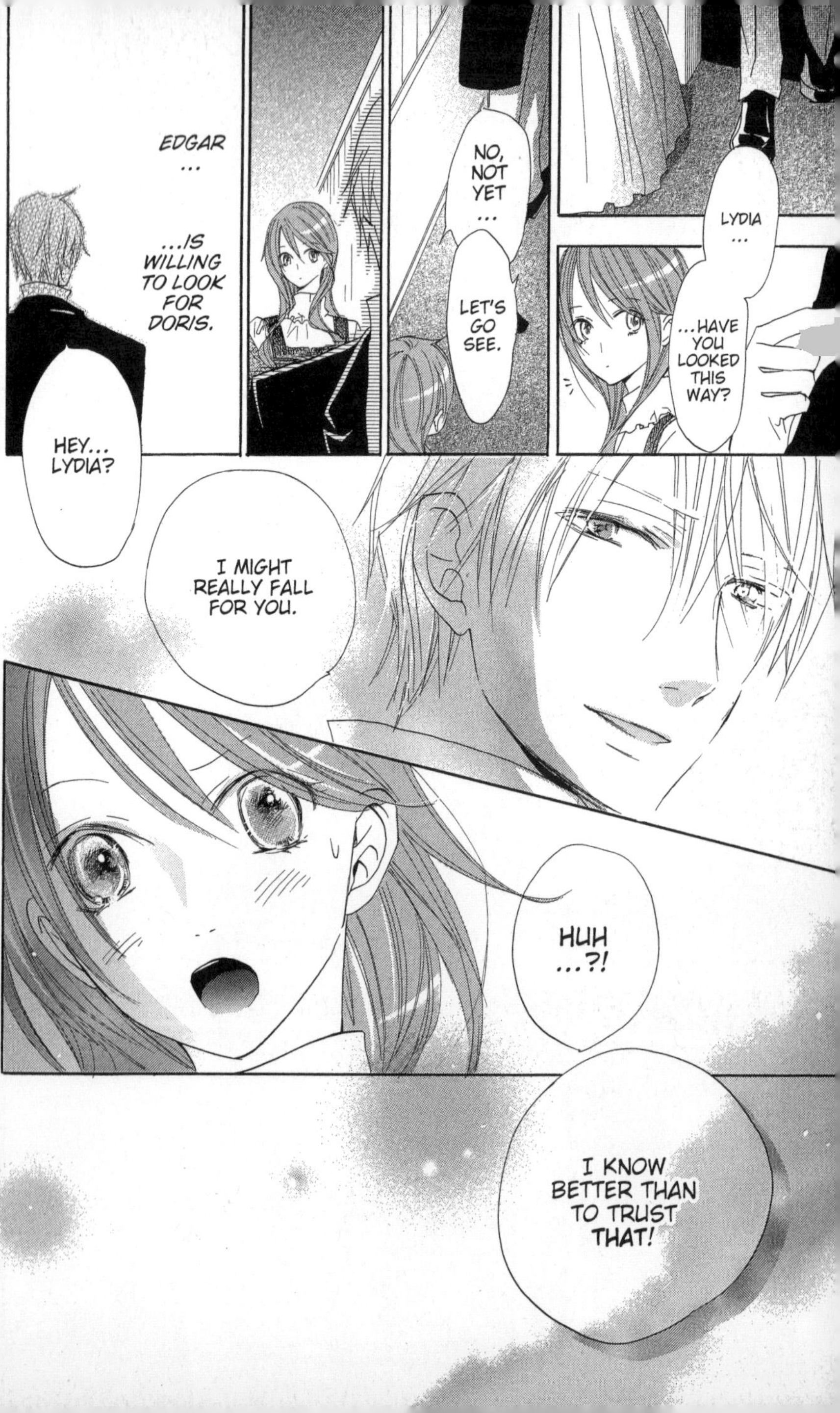
LYDIA...
...HAVE YOU LOOKED THIS WAY?
NO, NOT YET...
LET'S GO SEE.
EDGAR...
...IS WILLING TO LOOK FOR DORIS.
HEY... LYDIA?
I MIGHT REALLY FALL FOR YOU.
HUH...?!
I KNOW BETTER THAN TO TRUST THAT!

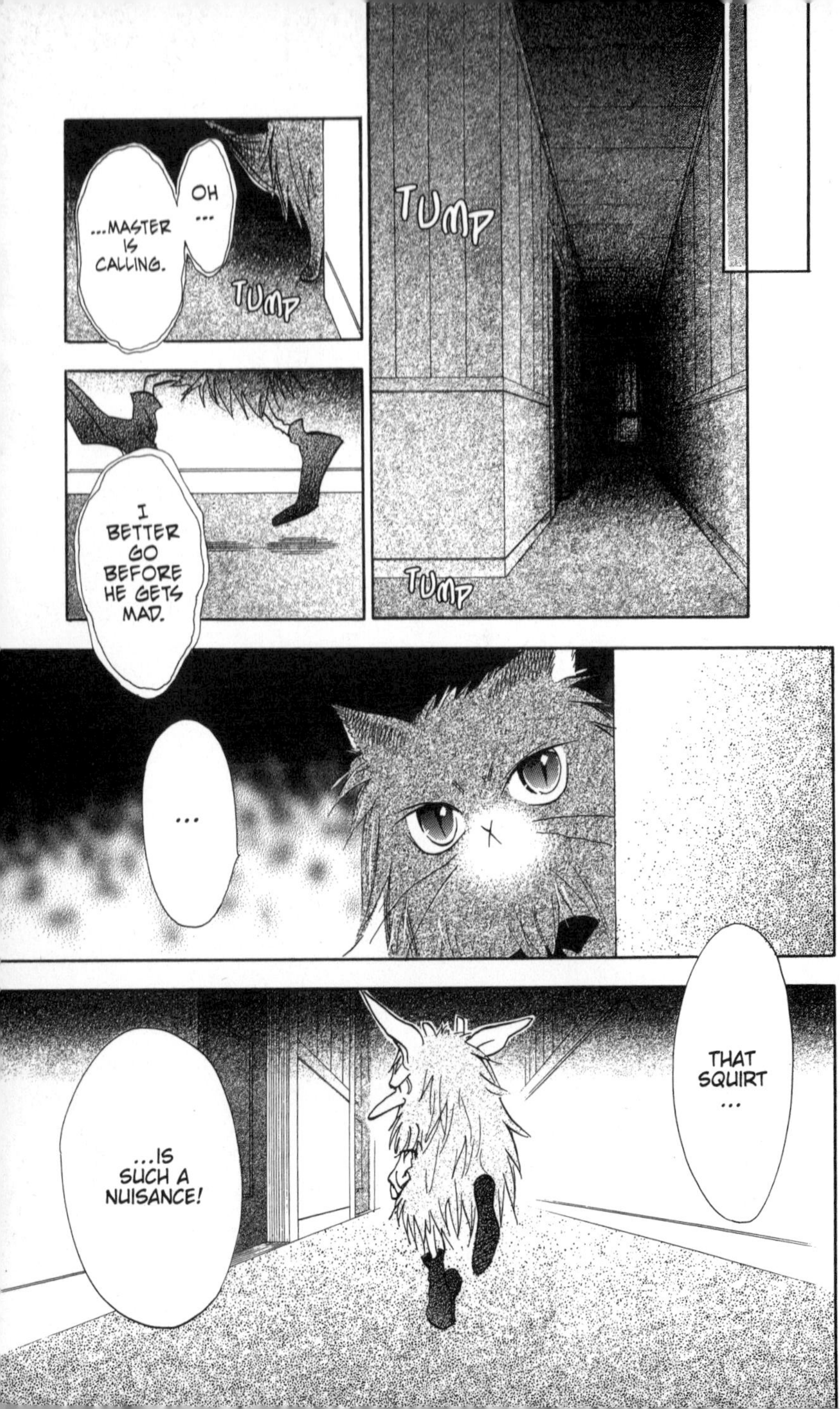
TUMP
TUMP
OH ...
...MASTER IS CALLING.
TUMP
I BETTER GO BEFORE HE GETS MAD.
...
THAT SQUIRT ...
...IS SUCH A NUISANCE!

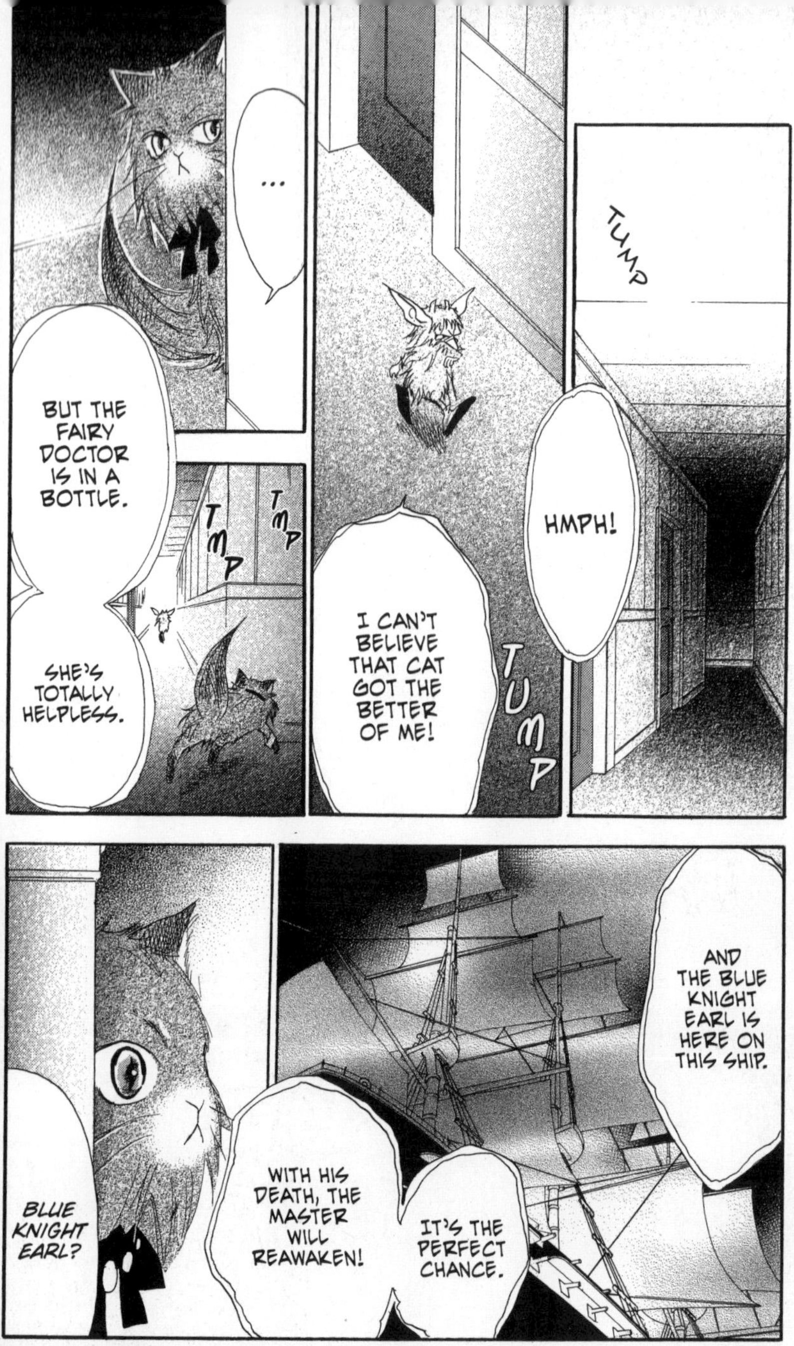
TUMP
HMPH!
TUMP
I CAN'T BELIEVE THAT CAT GOT THE BETTER OF ME!
...
BUT THE FAIRY DOCTOR IS IN A BOTTLE.
TMP
TMP
SHE'S TOTALLY HELPLESS.
AND THE BLUE KNIGHT EARL IS HERE ON THIS SHIP.
IT'S THE PERFECT CHANCE.
WITH HIS DEATH, THE MASTER WILL REAWAKEN!
BLUE KNIGHT EARL?

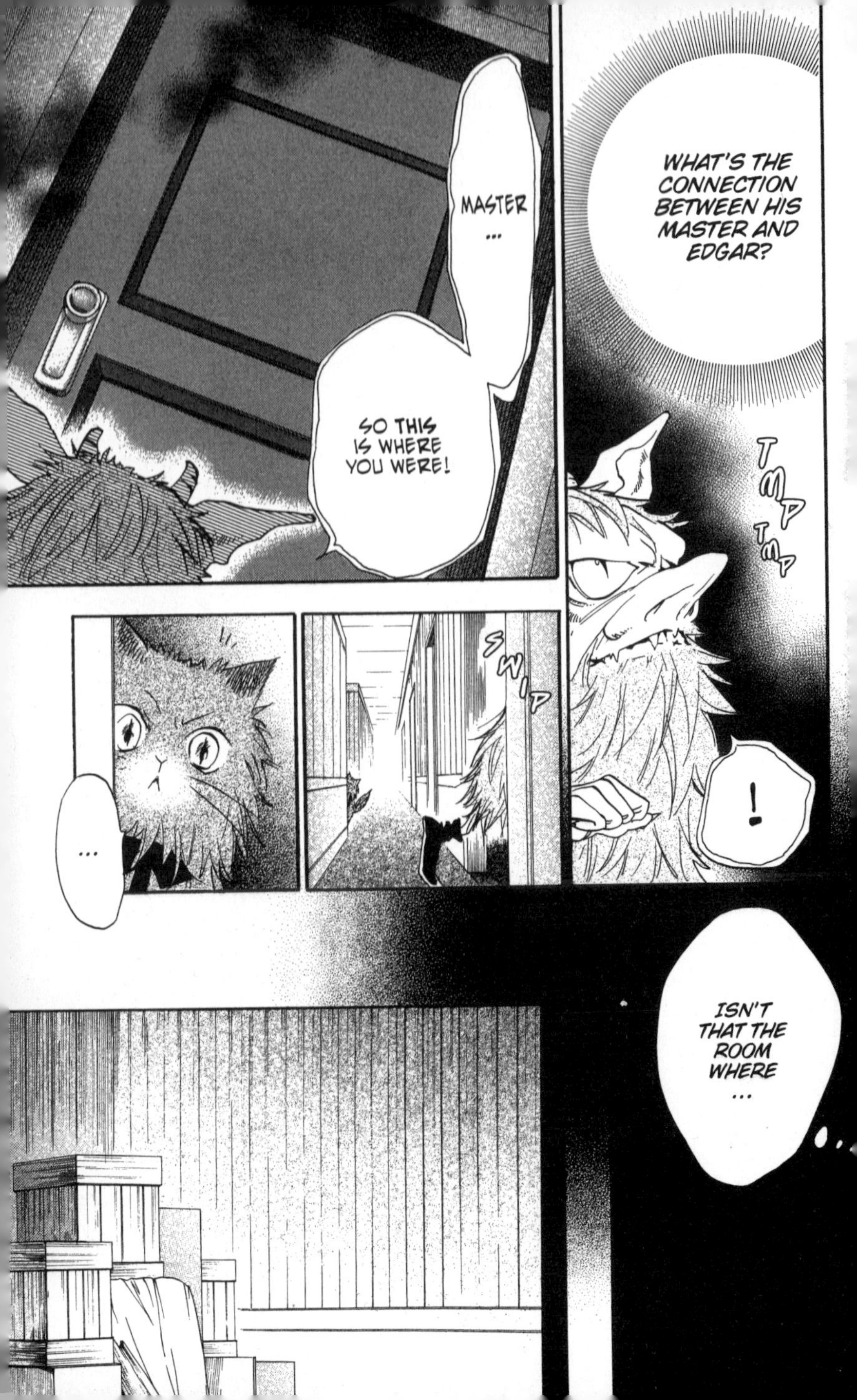
WHAT'S THE CONNECTION BETWEEN HIS MASTER AND EDGAR?
TMP TMP
!
MASTER ...
SO THIS IS WHERE YOU WERE!
SWIP
...
ISN'T THAT THE ROOM WHERE ...

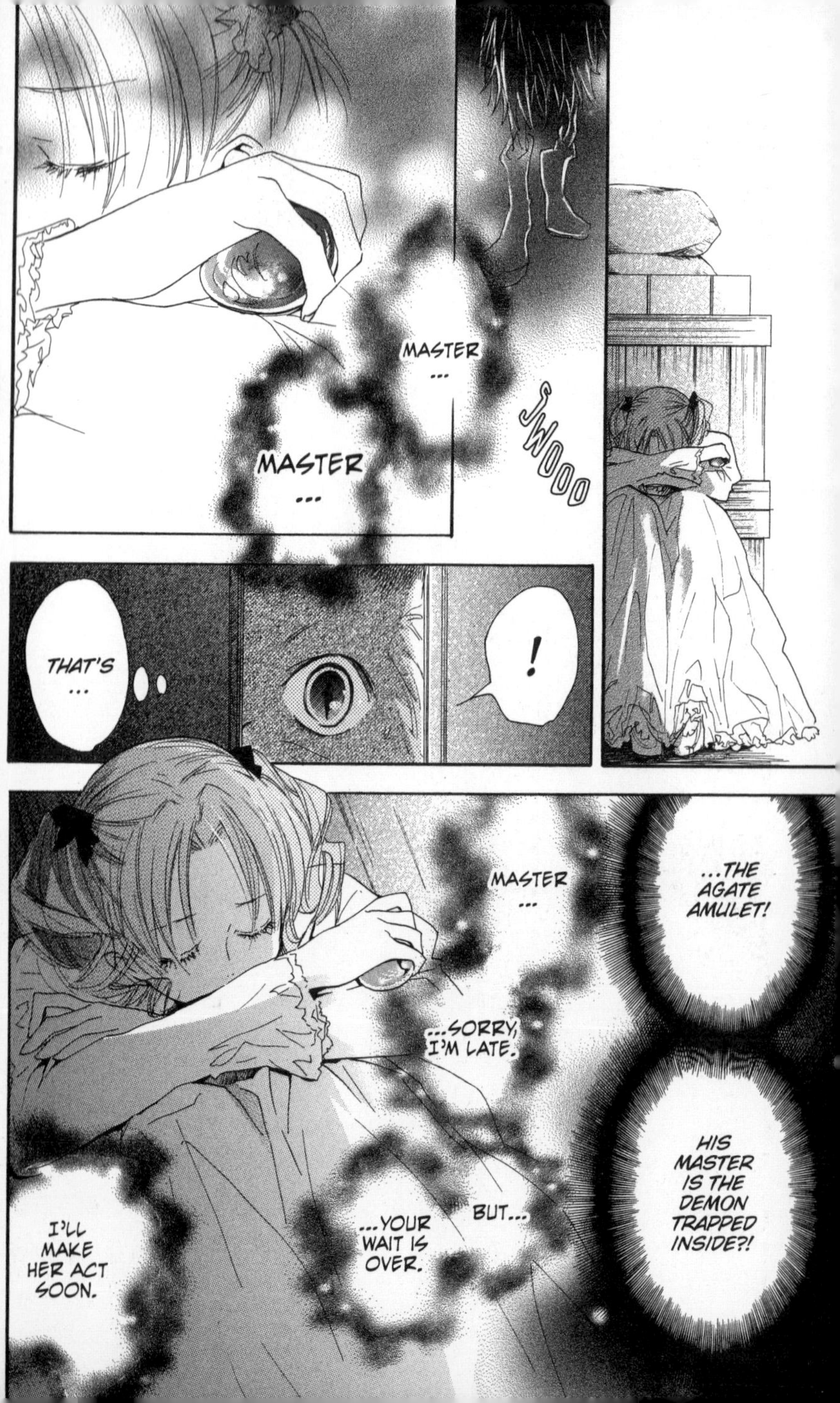
SWOOO
MASTER ...
MASTER ...
!
THAT'S ...
...THE AGATE AMULET!
HIS MASTER IS THE DEMON TRAPPED INSIDE?!
MASTER ...
...SORRY, I'M LATE.
BUT...
...YOUR WAIT IS OVER.
I'LL MAKE HER ACT SOON.

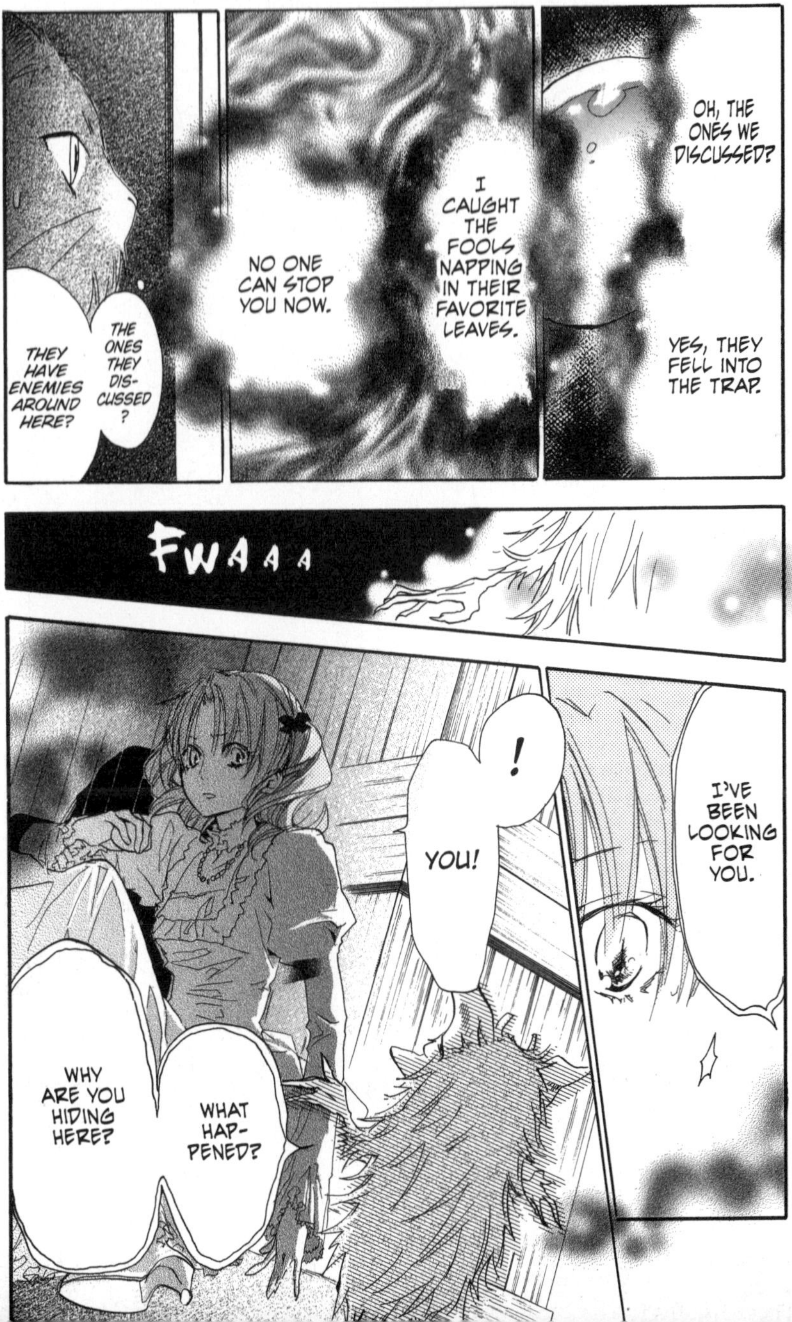
OH, THE ONES WE DISCUSSED?
YES, THEY FELL INTO THE TRAP.
I CAUGHT THE FOOLS NAPPING IN THEIR FAVORITE LEAVES.
NO ONE CAN STOP YOU NOW.
THE ONES THEY DIS-CUSSED?
THEY HAVE ENEMIES AROUND HERE?
FWAAA
I'VE BEEN LOOKING FOR YOU.
!
YOU!
WHAT HAP-PENED?
WHY ARE YOU HIDING HERE?

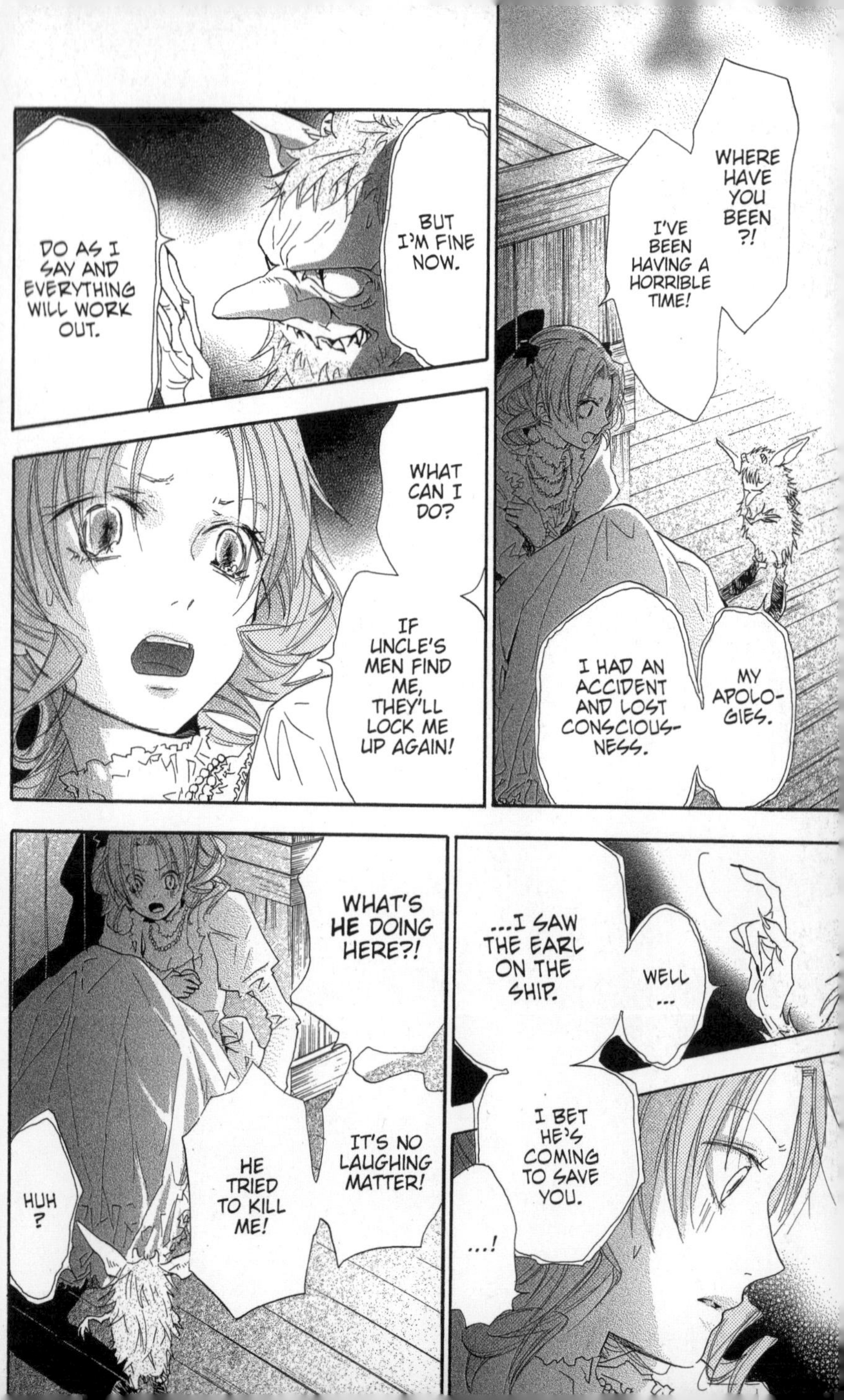
WHERE HAVE YOU BEEN?!
I'VE BEEN HAVING A HORRIBLE TIME!
MY APOLOGIES.
I HAD AN ACCIDENT AND LOST CONSCIOUS-NESS.
BUT I'M FINE NOW.
DO AS I SAY AND EVERYTHING WILL WORK OUT.
WHAT CAN I DO?
IF UNCLE'S MEN FIND ME, THEY'LL LOCK ME UP AGAIN!
WELL ...
...I SAW THE EARL ON THE SHIP.
I BET HE'S COMING TO SAVE YOU.
...!
WHAT'S HE DOING HERE?!
IT'S NO LAUGHING MATTER!
HE TRIED TO KILL ME!
HUH ?

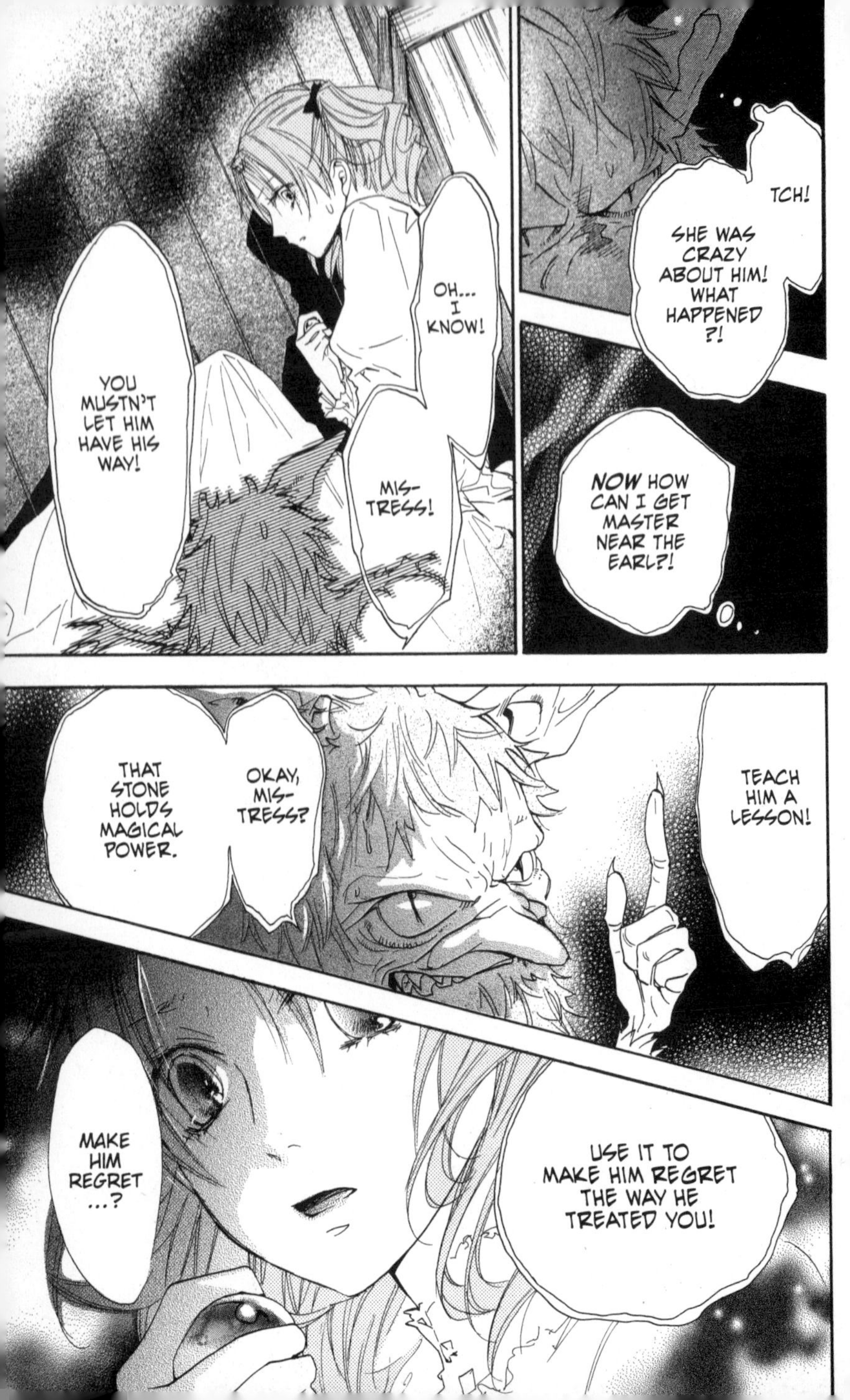
TCH!
SHE WAS CRAZY ABOUT HIM! WHAT HAPPENED ?!
NOW HOW CAN I GET MASTER NEAR THE EARL?!
OH... I KNOW!
MIS-TRESS!
YOU MUSTN'T LET HIM HAVE HIS WAY!
TEACH HIM A LESSON!
OKAY, MIS-TRESS?
THAT STONE HOLDS MAGICAL POWER.
USE IT TO MAKE HIM REGRET THE WAY HE TREATED YOU!
MAKE HIM REGRET ...?

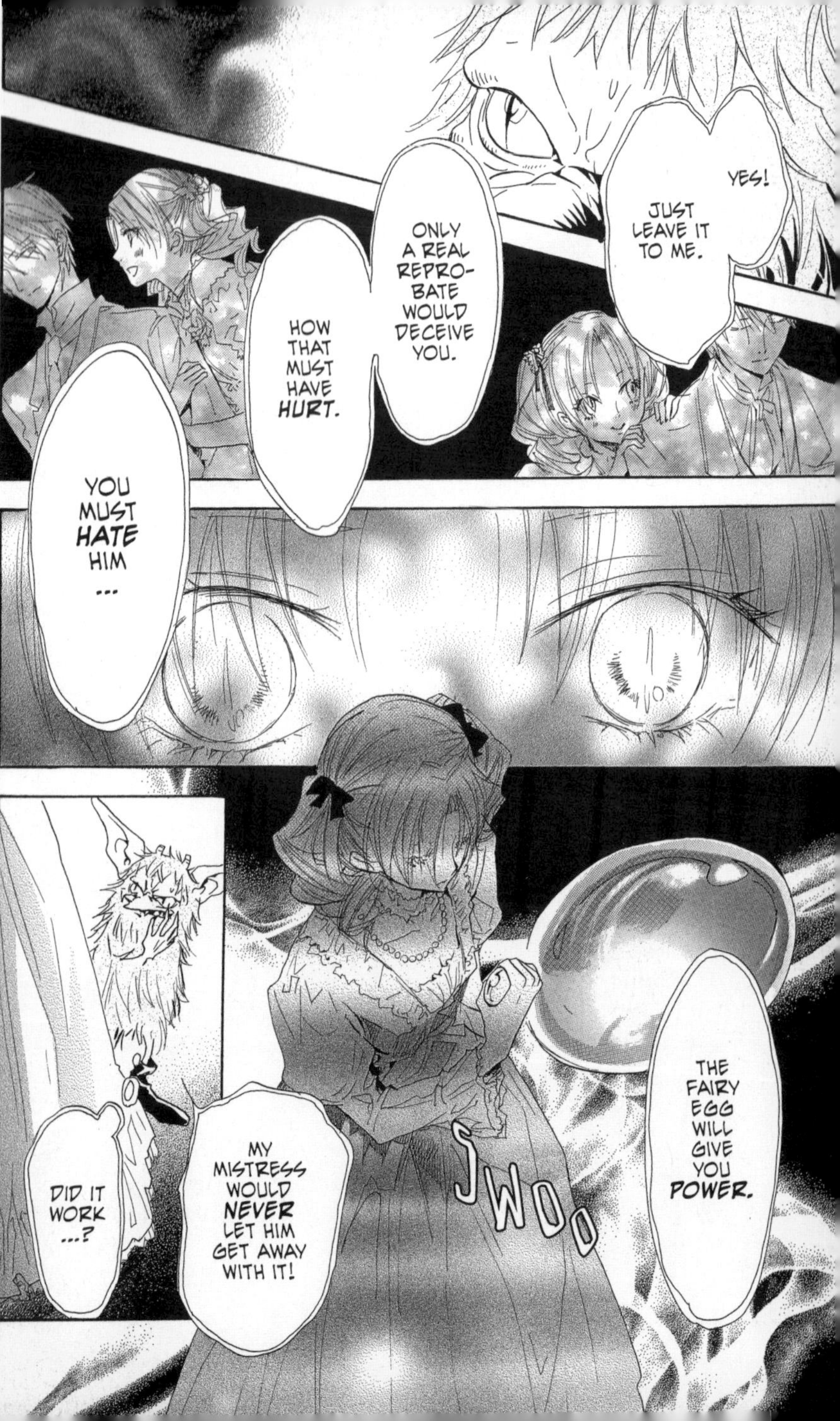
YES! JUST LEAVE IT TO ME.
ONLY A REAL REPRO- BATE WOULD DECEIVE YOU.
HOW THAT MUST HAVE HURT.
YOU MUST HATE HIM ...
THE FAIRY EGG WILL GIVE YOU POWER.
SWOO
MY MISTRESS WOULD NEVER LET HIM GET AWAY WITH IT!
DID IT WORK ...?

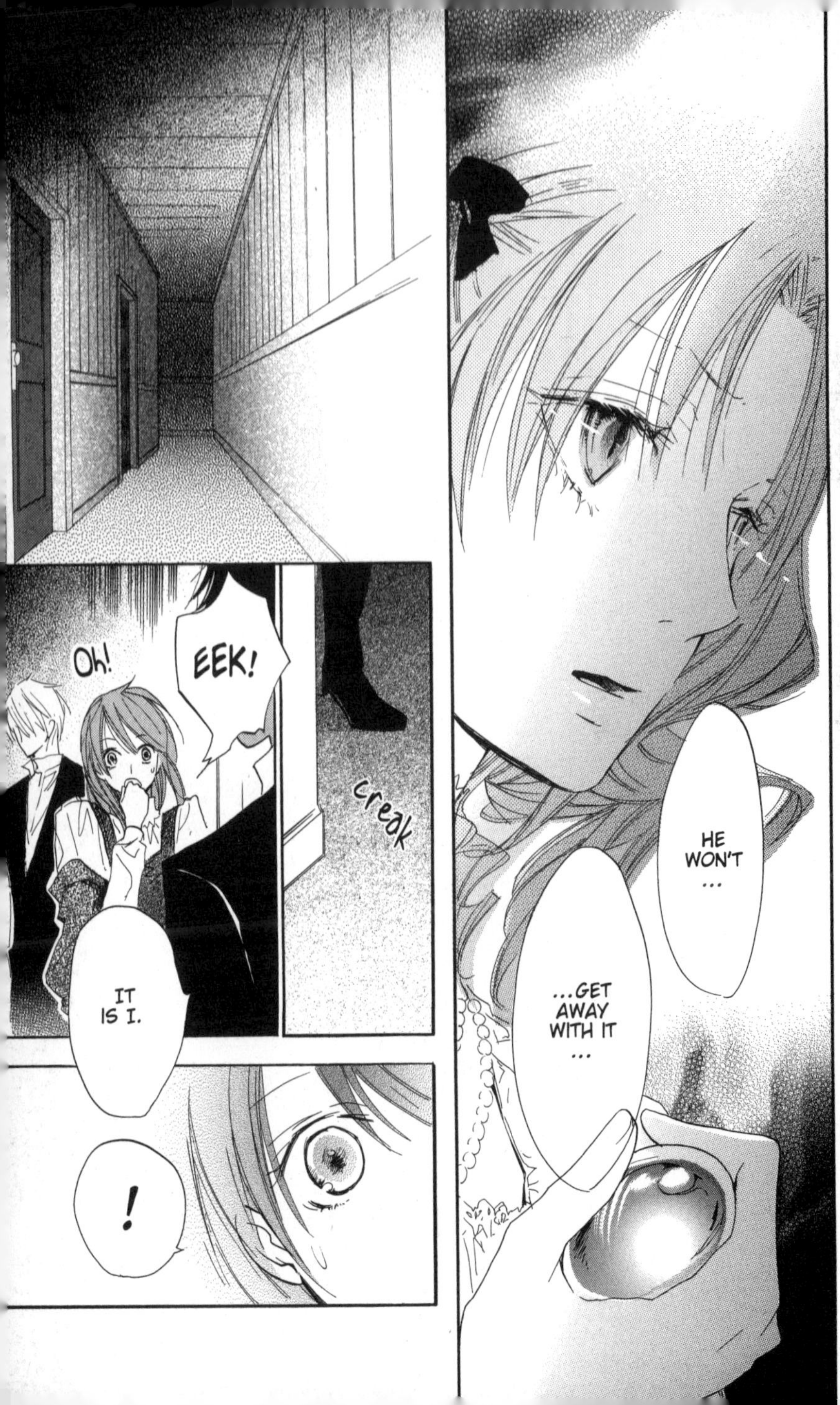
HE WON'T ...
...GET AWAY WITH IT ...
creak
EEK!
Oh!
IT IS I.
!

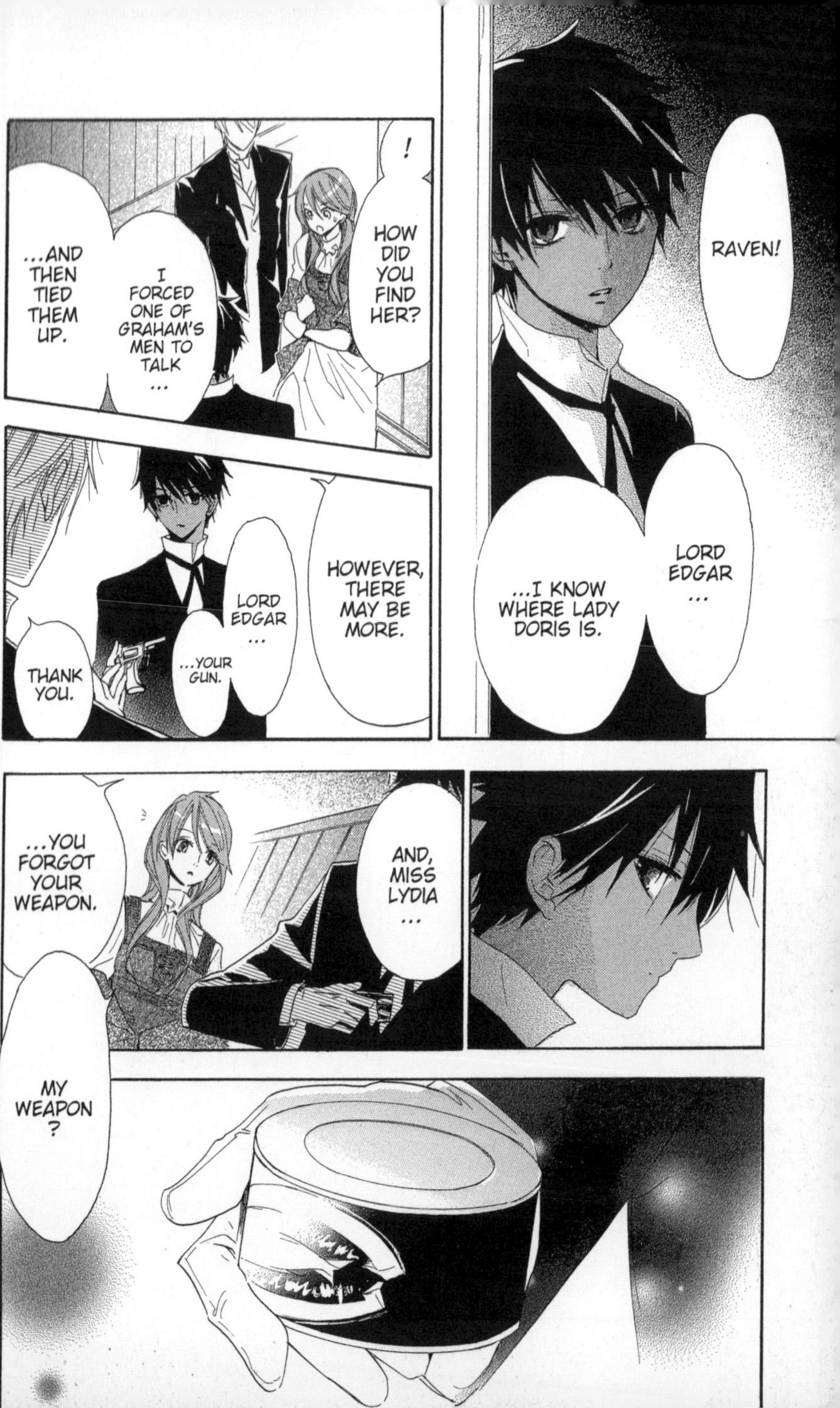
RAVEN!
LORD EDGAR ...
...I KNOW WHERE LADY DORIS IS.
!
HOW DID YOU FIND HER?
I FORCED ONE OF GRAHAM'S MEN TO TALK ...
...AND THEN TIED THEM UP.
HOWEVER, THERE MAY BE MORE.
LORD EDGAR ...
...YOUR GUN.
THANK YOU.
AND, MISS LYDIA ...
...YOU FORGOT YOUR WEAPON.
MY WEAPON ?

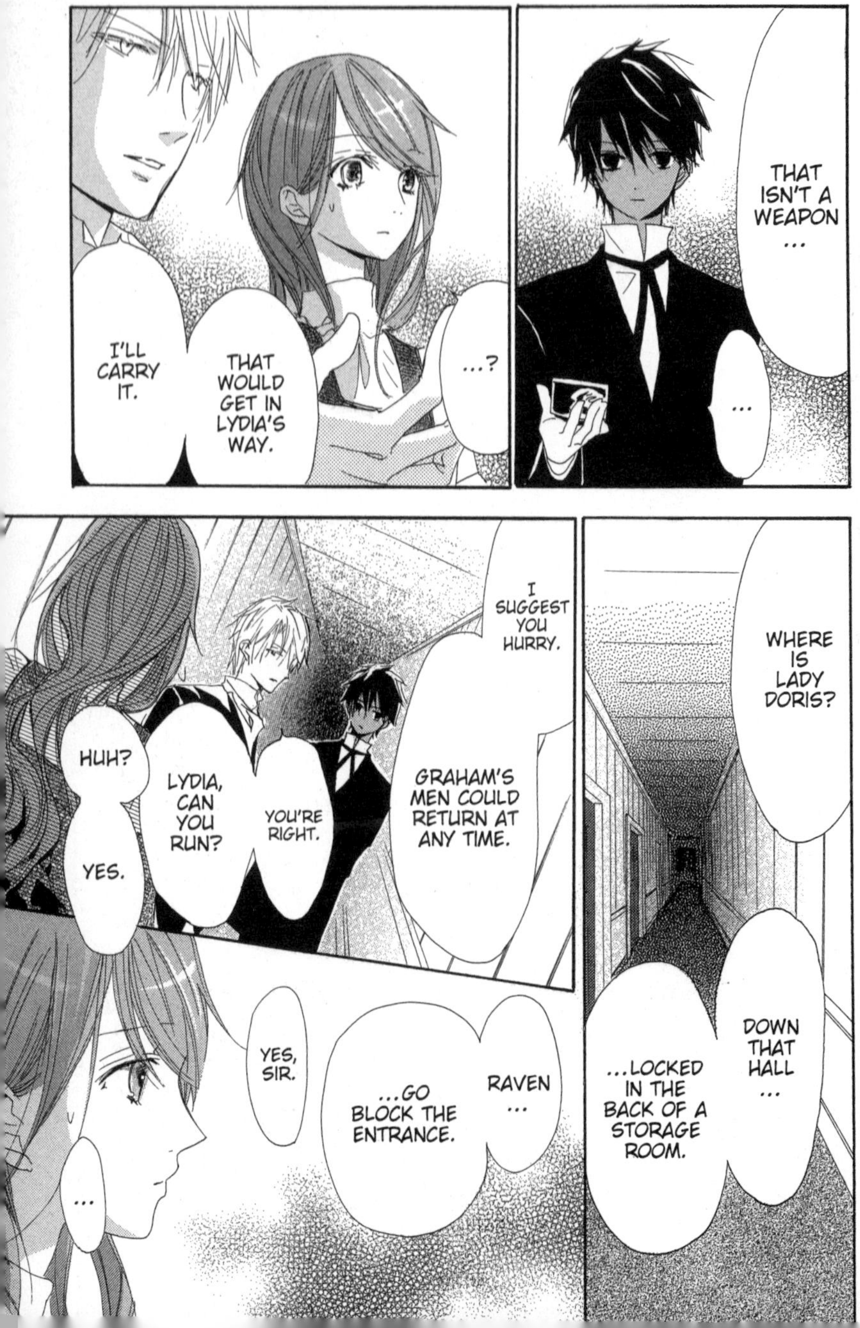
THAT ISN'T A WEAPON ...
...
...?
THAT WOULD GET IN LYDIA'S WAY.
I'LL CARRY IT.
WHERE IS LADY DORIS?
DOWN THAT HALL ...
...LOCKED IN THE BACK OF A STORAGE ROOM.
I SUGGEST YOU HURRY.
GRAHAM'S MEN COULD RETURN AT ANY TIME.
YOU'RE RIGHT.
LYDIA, CAN YOU RUN?
HUH?
YES.
RAVEN ...
...GO BLOCK THE ENTRANCE.
YES, SIR.
...

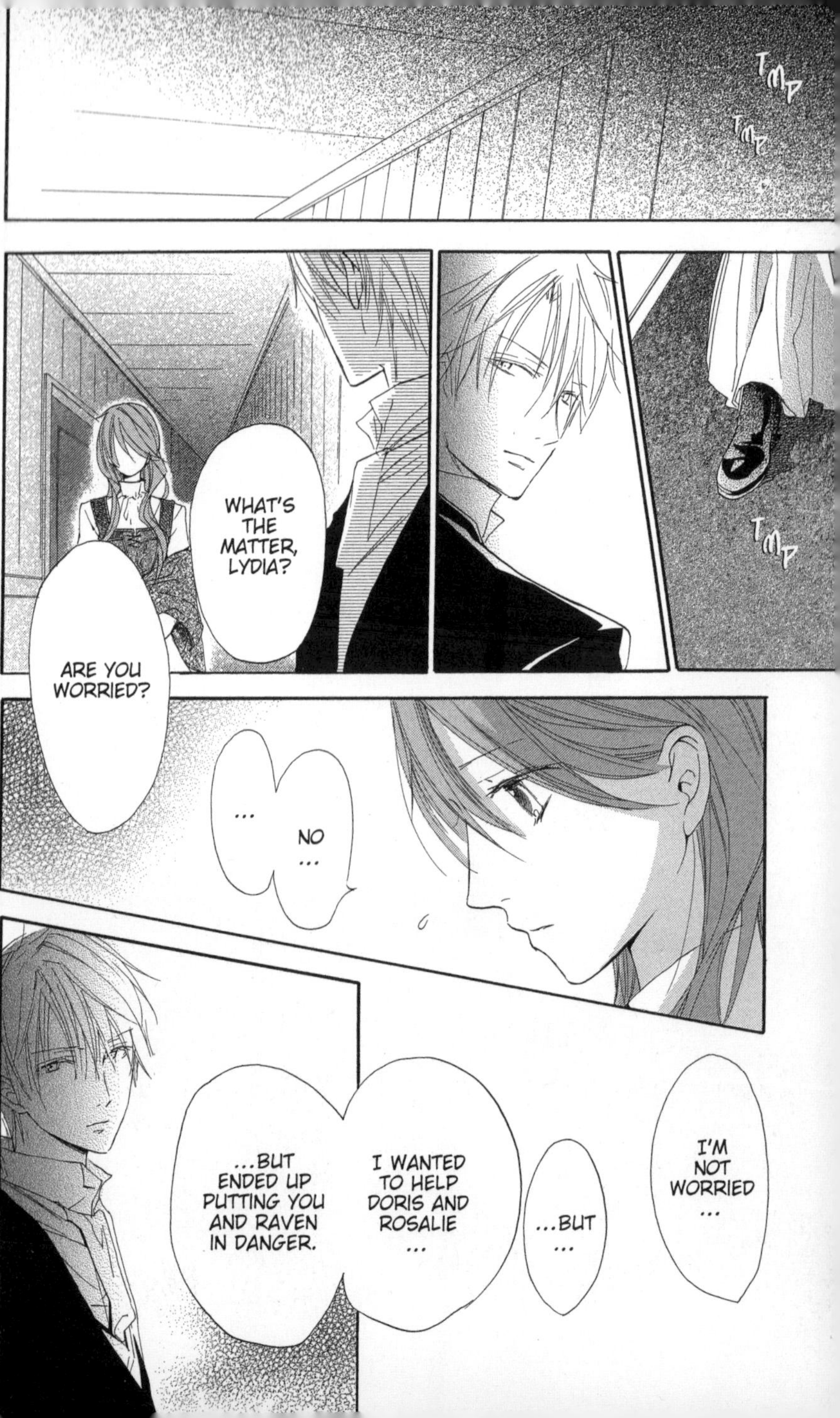
TMP
TMP
TMP
WHAT'S THE MATTER, LYDIA?
ARE YOU WORRIED?
... NO ...
I'M NOT WORRIED ...
...BUT ...
I WANTED TO HELP DORIS AND ROSALIE ...
...BUT ENDED UP PUTTING YOU AND RAVEN IN DANGER.

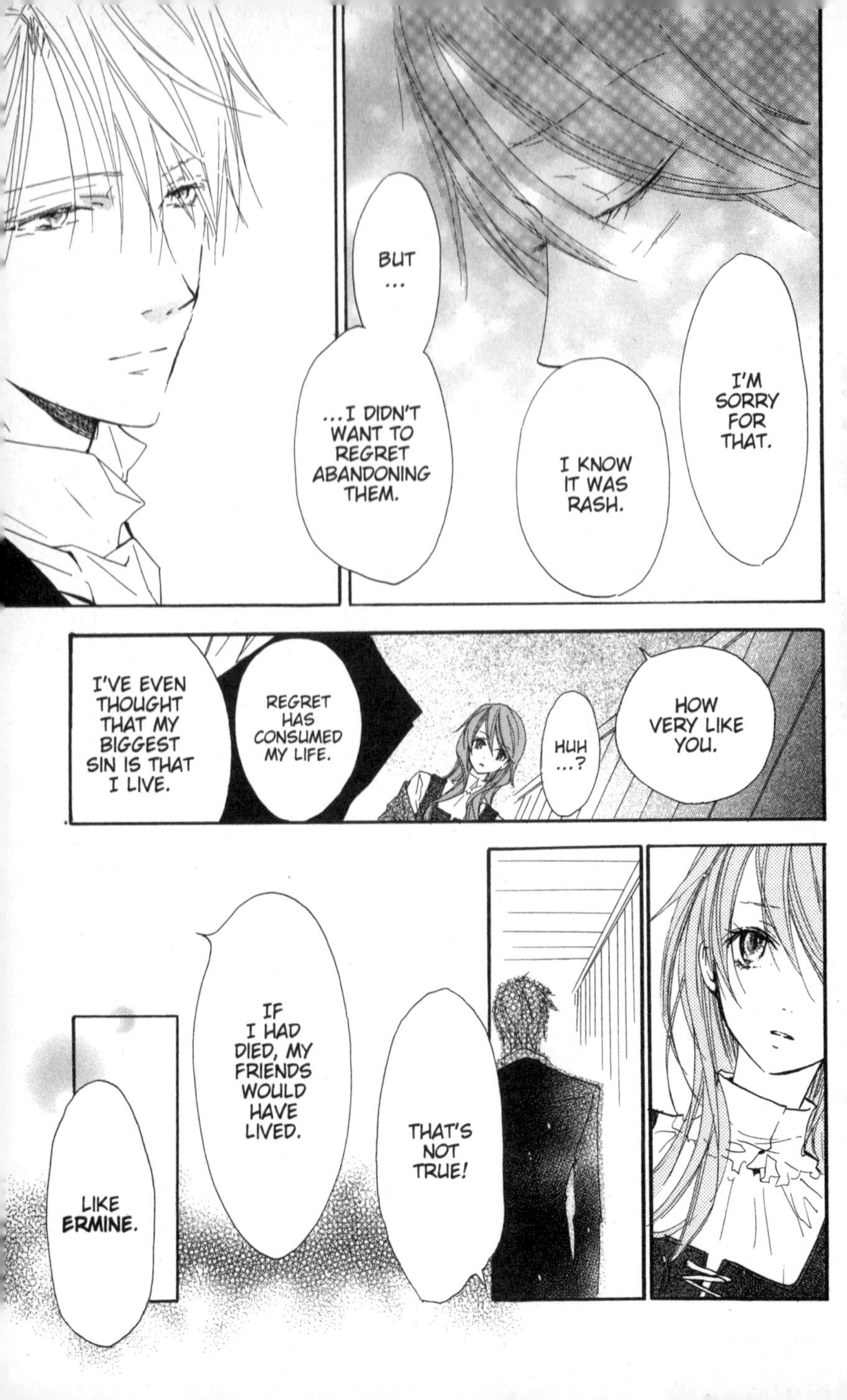
I'M SORRY FOR THAT.
I KNOW IT WAS RASH.
BUT...
...I DIDN'T WANT TO REGRET ABANDONING THEM.
HOW VERY LIKE YOU.
HUH...?
REGRET HAS CONSUMED MY LIFE.
I'VE EVEN THOUGHT THAT MY BIGGEST SIN IS THAT I LIVE.
THAT'S NOT TRUE!
IF I HAD DIED, MY FRIENDS WOULD HAVE LIVED.
LIKE ERMINE.

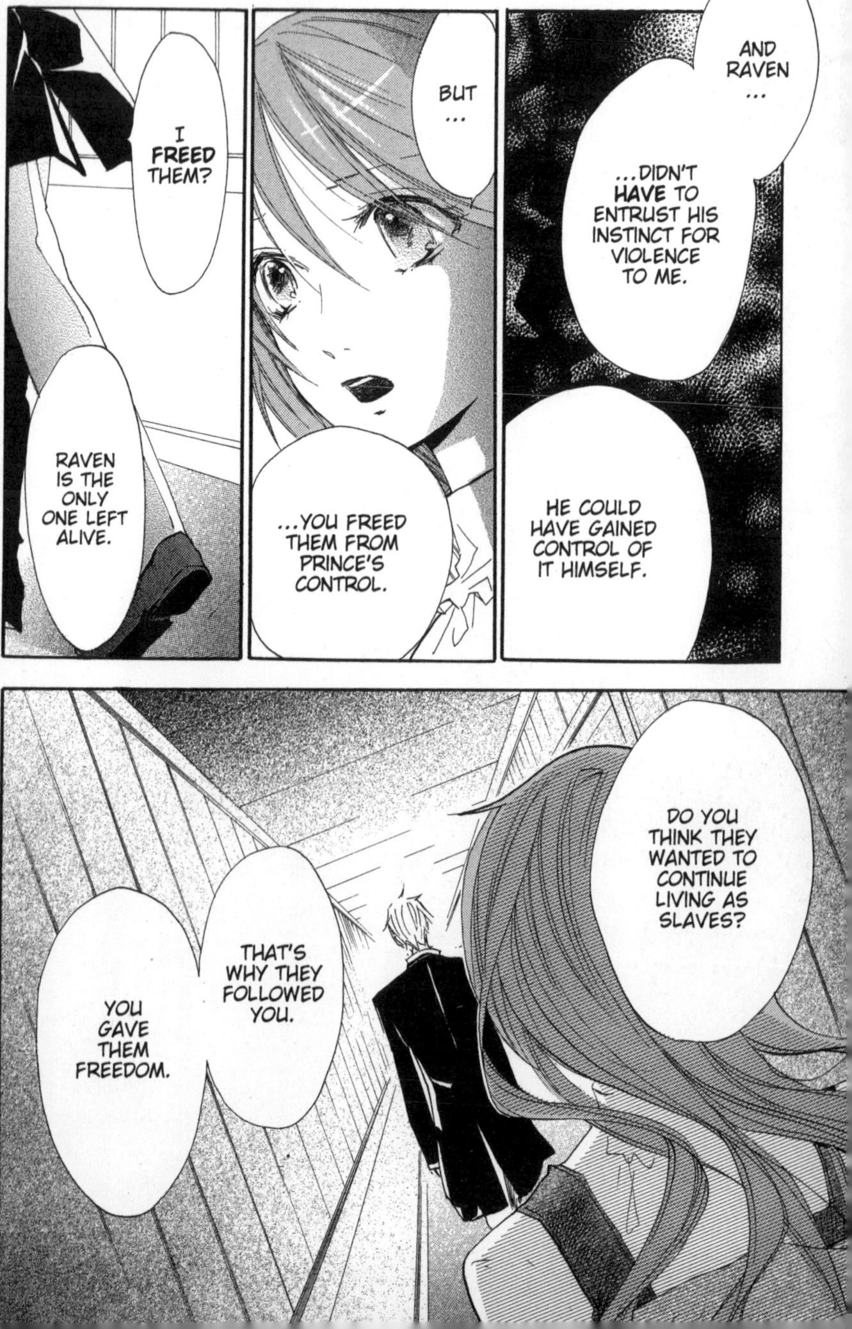
AND RAVEN ...
...DIDN'T HAVE TO ENTRUST HIS INSTINCT FOR VIOLENCE TO ME.
HE COULD HAVE GAINED CONTROL OF IT HIMSELF.
BUT ...
...YOU FREED THEM FROM PRINCE'S CONTROL.
I FREED THEM?
RAVEN IS THE ONLY ONE LEFT ALIVE.
DO YOU THINK THEY WANTED TO CONTINUE LIVING AS SLAVES?
THAT'S WHY THEY FOLLOWED YOU.
YOU GAVE THEM FREEDOM.

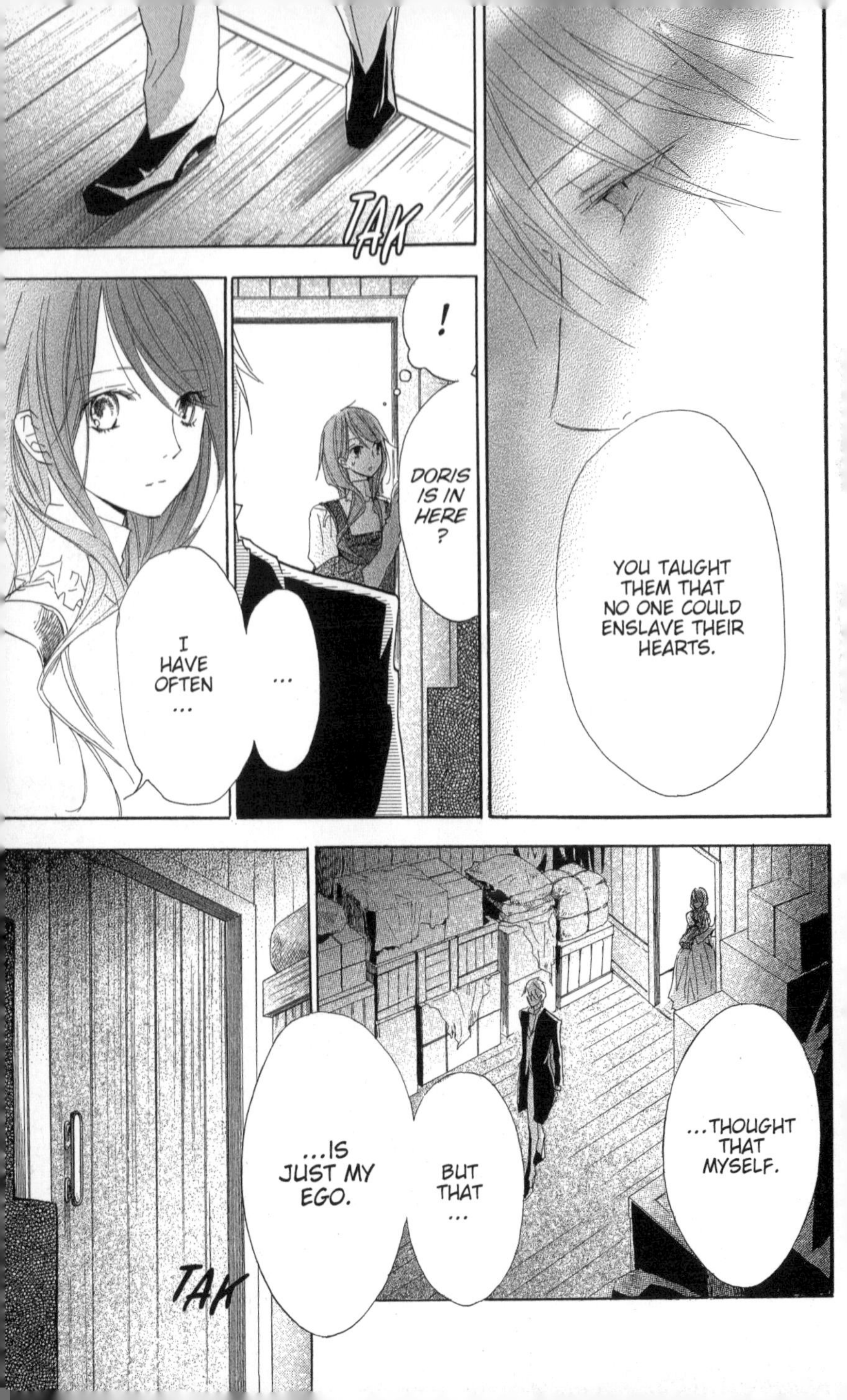
YOU TAUGHT THEM THAT NO ONE COULD ENSLAVE THEIR HEARTS.
TAK
!
DORIS IS IN HERE?
...
I HAVE OFTEN ...
...THOUGHT THAT MYSELF.
BUT THAT ...
...IS JUST MY EGO.
TAK

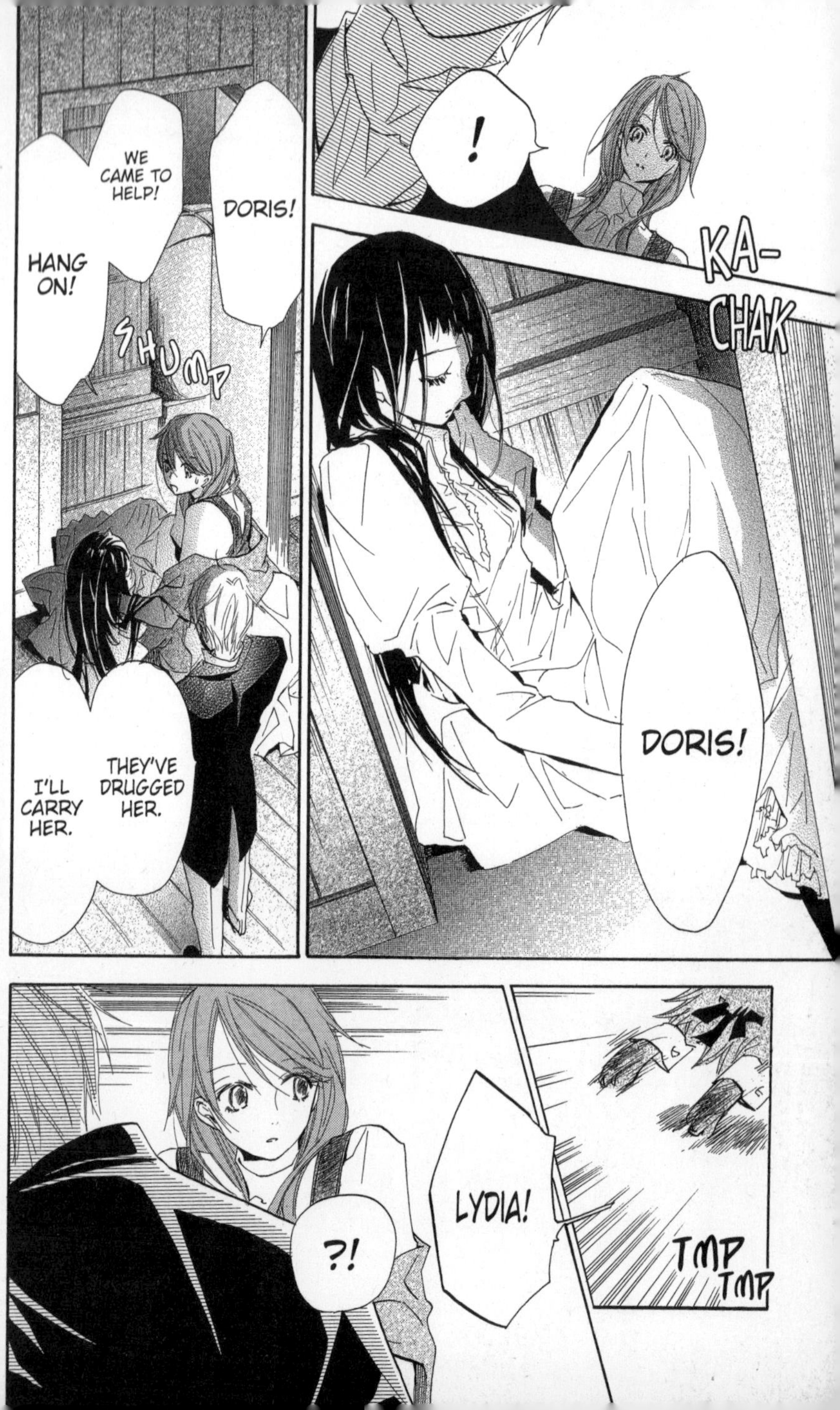
!
KA-CHAK
DORIS!
DORIS!
WE CAME TO HELP!
HANG ON!
SHUMP
THEY'VE DRUGGED HER.
I'LL CARRY HER.
LYDIA!
TMP TMP
?!

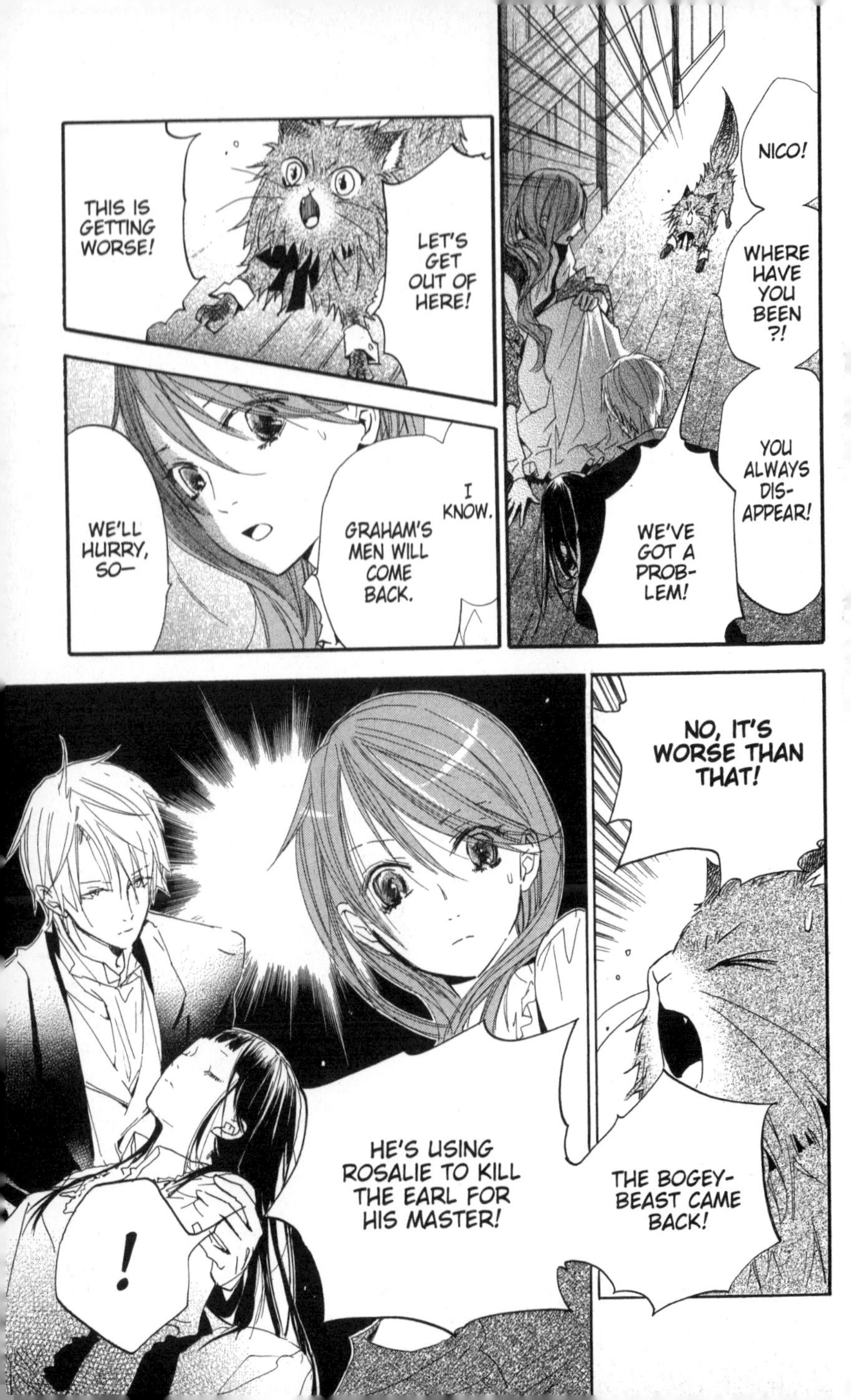
NICO!
WHERE HAVE YOU BEEN?!
YOU ALWAYS DIS-APPEAR!
WE'VE GOT A PROB-LEM!
LET'S GET OUT OF HERE!
THIS IS GETTING WORSE!
I KNOW.
GRAHAM'S MEN WILL COME BACK.
WE'LL HURRY, SO—
NO, IT'S WORSE THAN THAT!
THE BOGEY-BEAST CAME BACK!
HE'S USING ROSALIE TO KILL THE EARL FOR HIS MASTER!
!

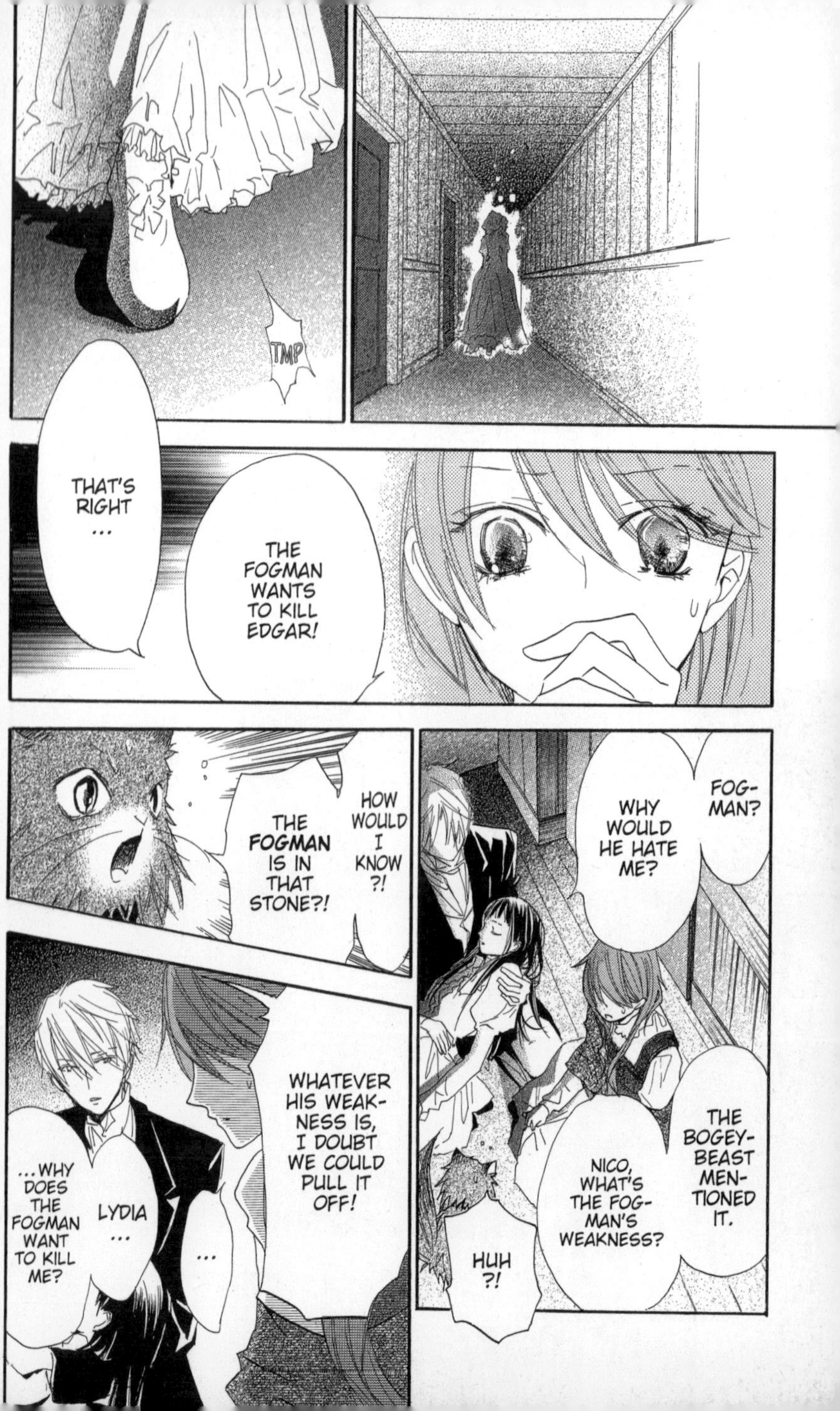
TMP
THAT'S RIGHT ...
THE FOGMAN WANTS TO KILL EDGAR!
FOG-MAN?
WHY WOULD HE HATE ME?
THE BOGEY-BEAST MENTIONED IT.
NICO, WHAT'S THE FOG-MAN'S WEAKNESS?
HUH ?!
HOW WOULD I KNOW ?!
THE FOGMAN IS IN THAT STONE?!
WHATEVER HIS WEAK-NESS IS, I DOUBT WE COULD PULL IT OFF!
...
LYDIA ...
...WHY DOES THE FOGMAN WANT TO KILL ME?

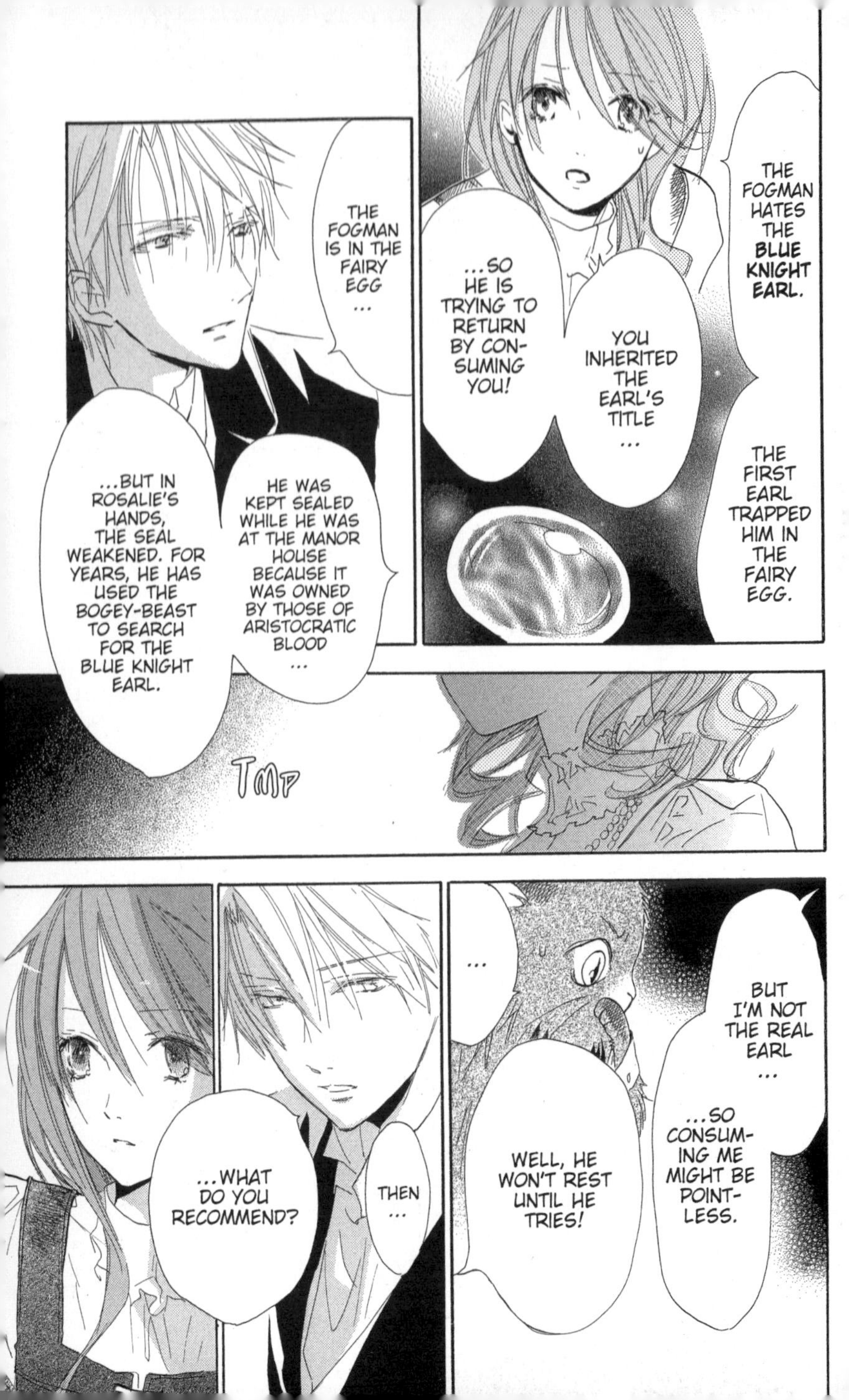
THE FOGMAN HATES THE BLUE KNIGHT EARL.
THE FIRST EARL TRAPPED HIM IN THE FAIRY EGG.
YOU INHERITED THE EARL'S TITLE ...
...SO HE IS TRYING TO RETURN BY CON-SUMING YOU!
THE FOGMAN IS IN THE FAIRY EGG ...
HE WAS KEPT SEALED WHILE HE WAS AT THE MANOR HOUSE BECAUSE IT WAS OWNED BY THOSE OF ARISTOCRATIC BLOOD ...
...BUT IN ROSALIE'S HANDS, THE SEAL WEAKENED. FOR YEARS, HE HAS USED THE BOGEY-BEAST TO SEARCH FOR THE BLUE KNIGHT EARL.
TMP
BUT I'M NOT THE REAL EARL ...
...SO CONSUM-ING ME MIGHT BE POINT-LESS.
...
WELL, HE WON'T REST UNTIL HE TRIES!
THEN ...
...WHAT DO YOU RECOMMEND?

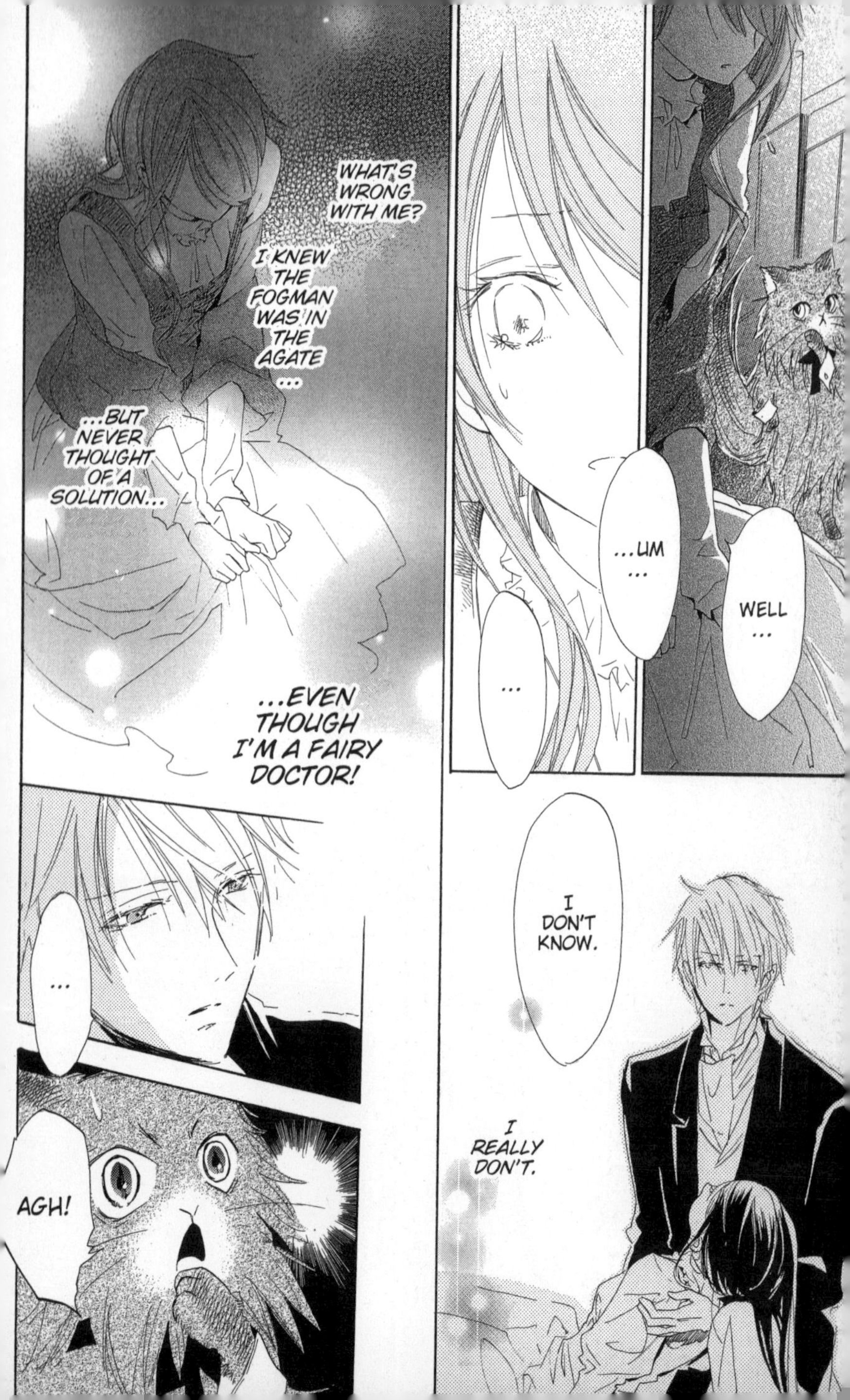
WELL...
...UM...
...
WHAT'S WRONG WITH ME?
I KNEW THE FOGMAN WAS IN THE AGATE...
...BUT NEVER THOUGHT OF A SOLUTION...
...EVEN THOUGH I'M A FAIRY DOCTOR!
I DON'T KNOW.
I REALLY DON'T.
...
AGH!

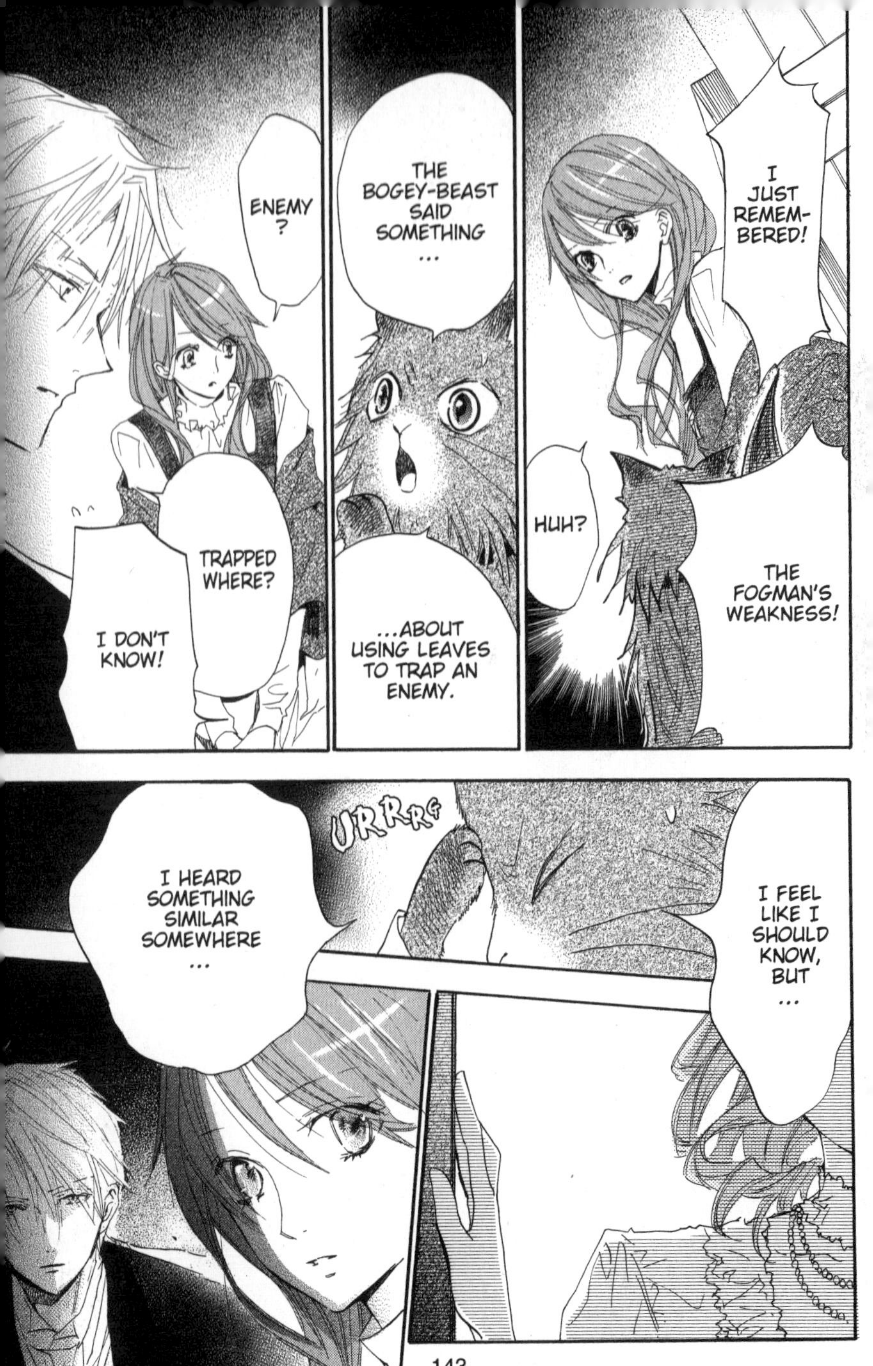
I JUST REMEMBERED!
THE FOGMAN'S WEAKNESS!
HUH?
THE BOGEY-BEAST SAID SOMETHING ...
...ABOUT USING LEAVES TO TRAP AN ENEMY.
ENEMY ?
TRAPPED WHERE?
I DON'T KNOW!
URRRRG
I FEEL LIKE I SHOULD KNOW, BUT ...
I HEARD SOMETHING SIMILAR SOMEWHERE ...

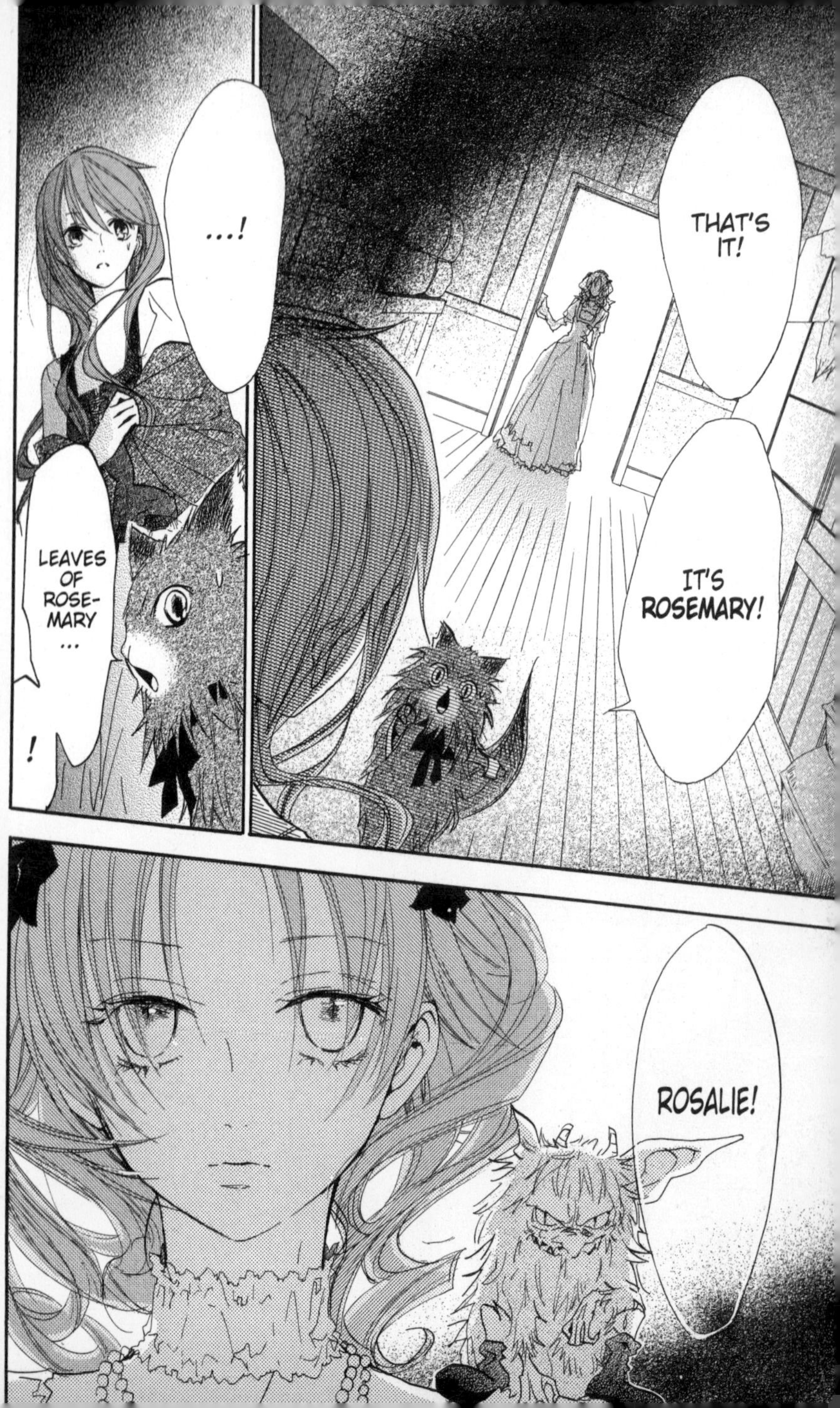
THAT'S IT!
IT'S ROSEMARY!
...!
LEAVES OF ROSE-MARY ...
!
ROSALIE!

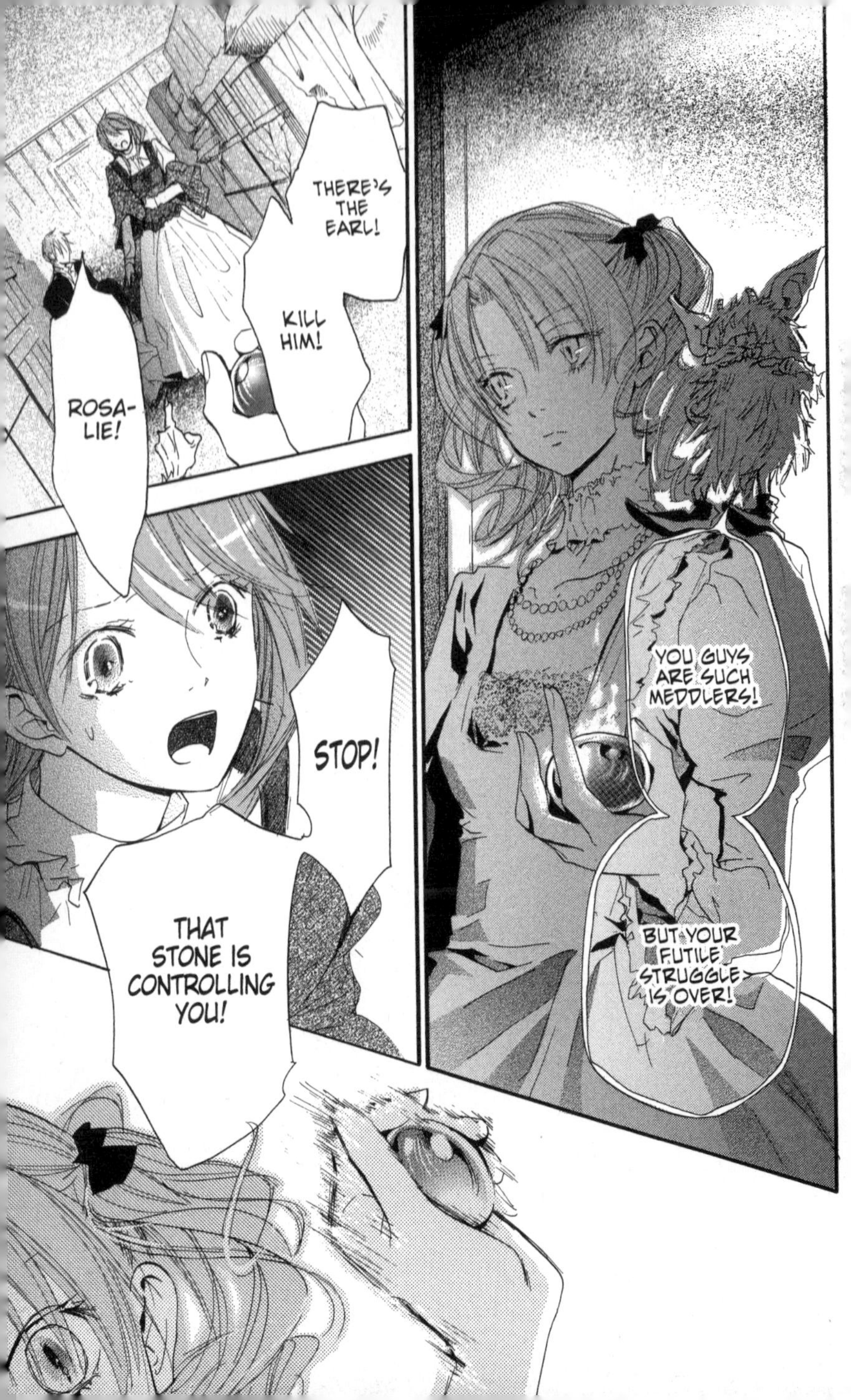
YOU GUYS ARE SUCH MEDDLERS!
BUT YOUR FUTILE STRUGGLE IS OVER!
THERE'S THE EARL!
KILL HIM!
ROSA-LIE!
STOP!
THAT STONE IS CONTROLLING YOU!

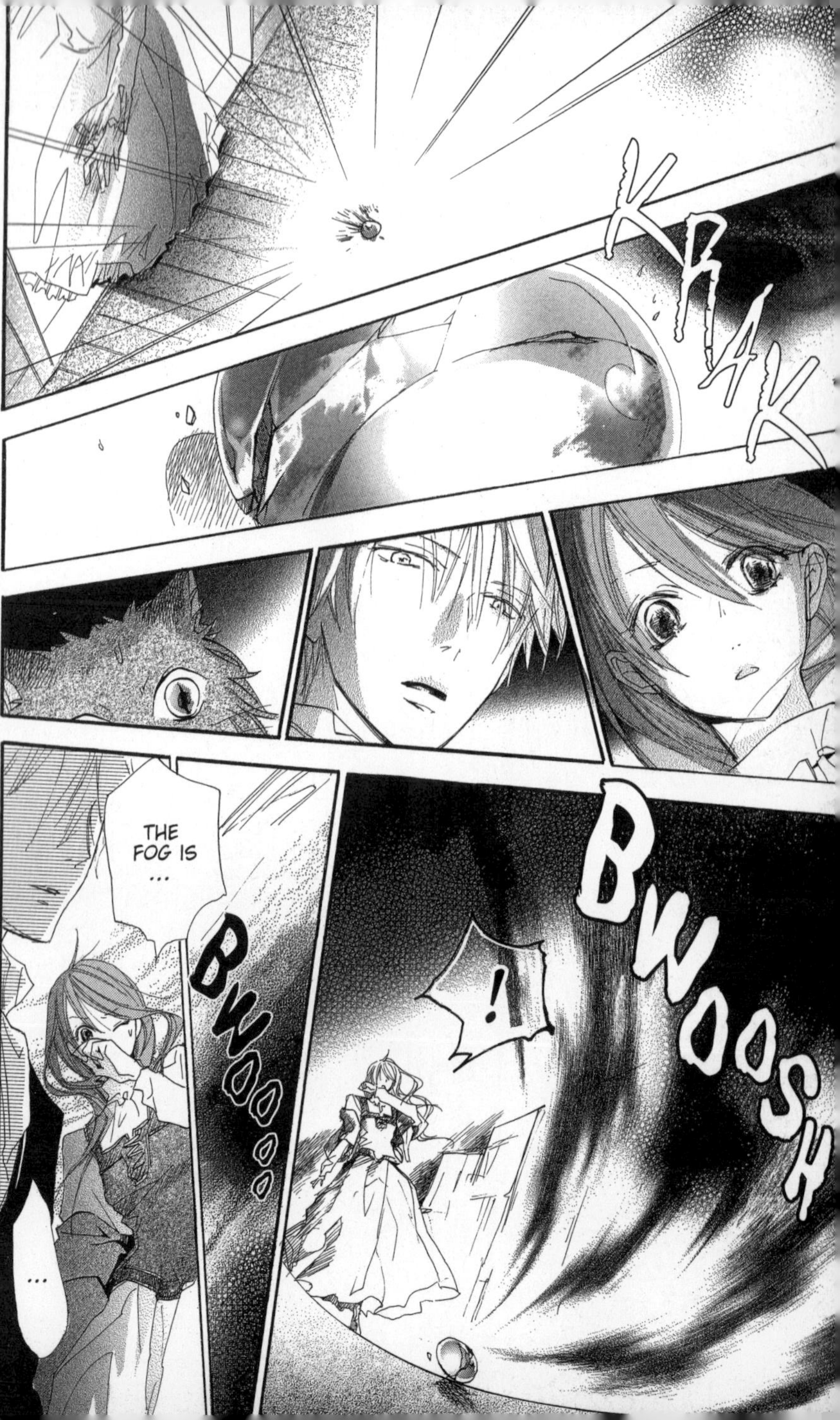
KRAK
BWOOSH
!
BWOOOOO
THE FOG IS ...
...

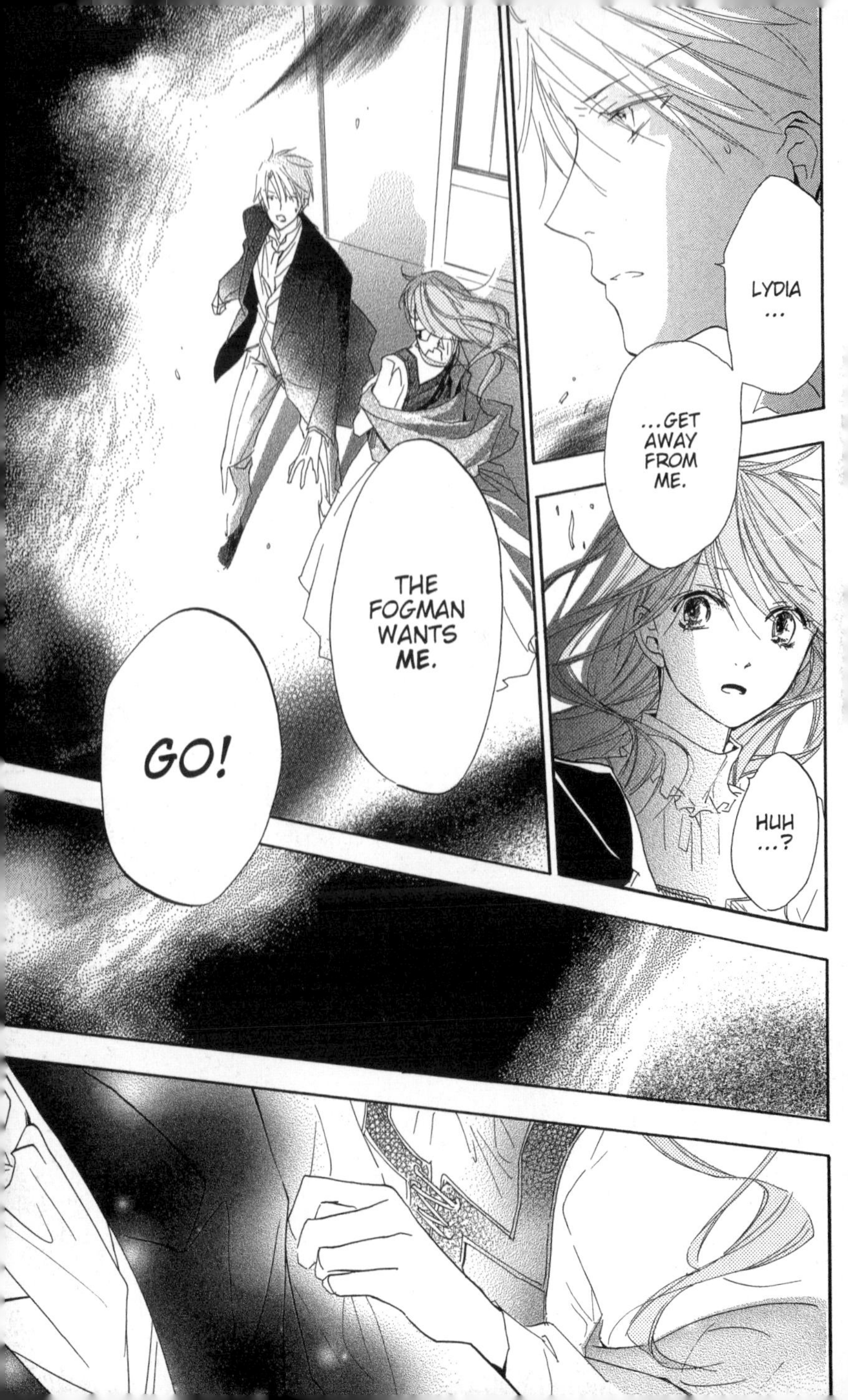
LYDIA ...
...GET AWAY FROM ME.
HUH ...?
THE FOGMAN WANTS ME.
GO!

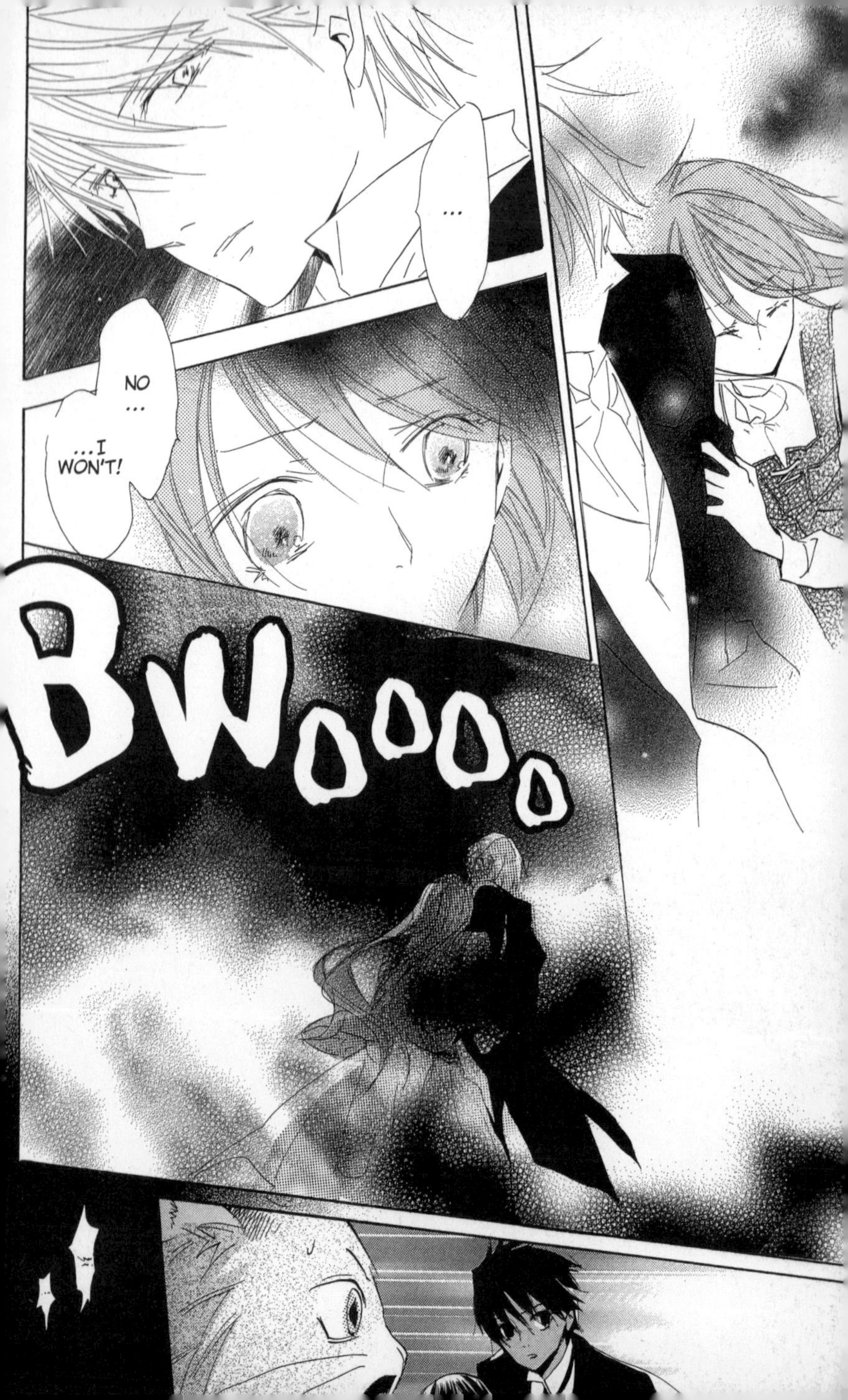
...
NO ... ...I WON'T!
BWOOOO

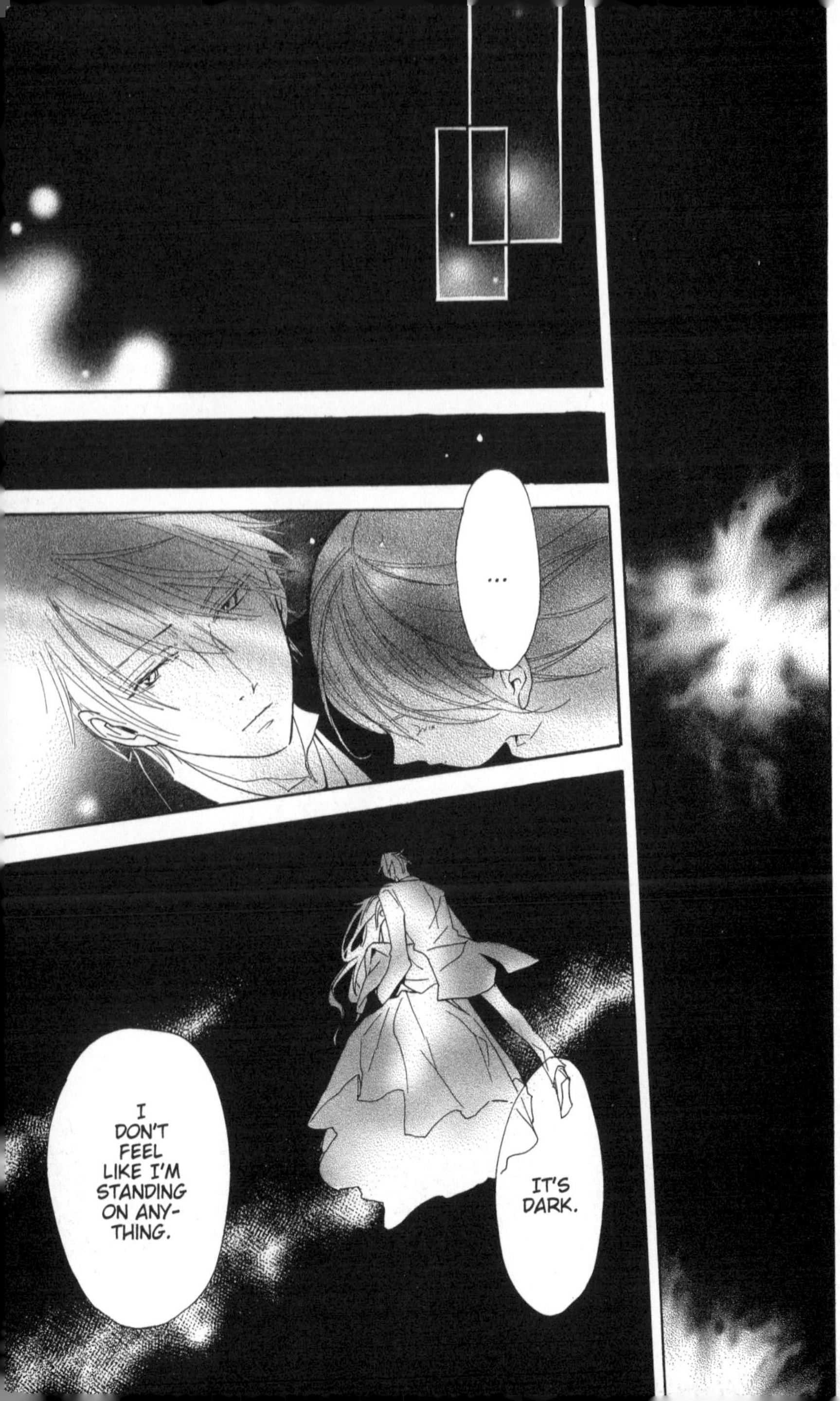
...
IT'S DARK.
I DON'T FEEL LIKE I'M STANDING ON ANY-THING.

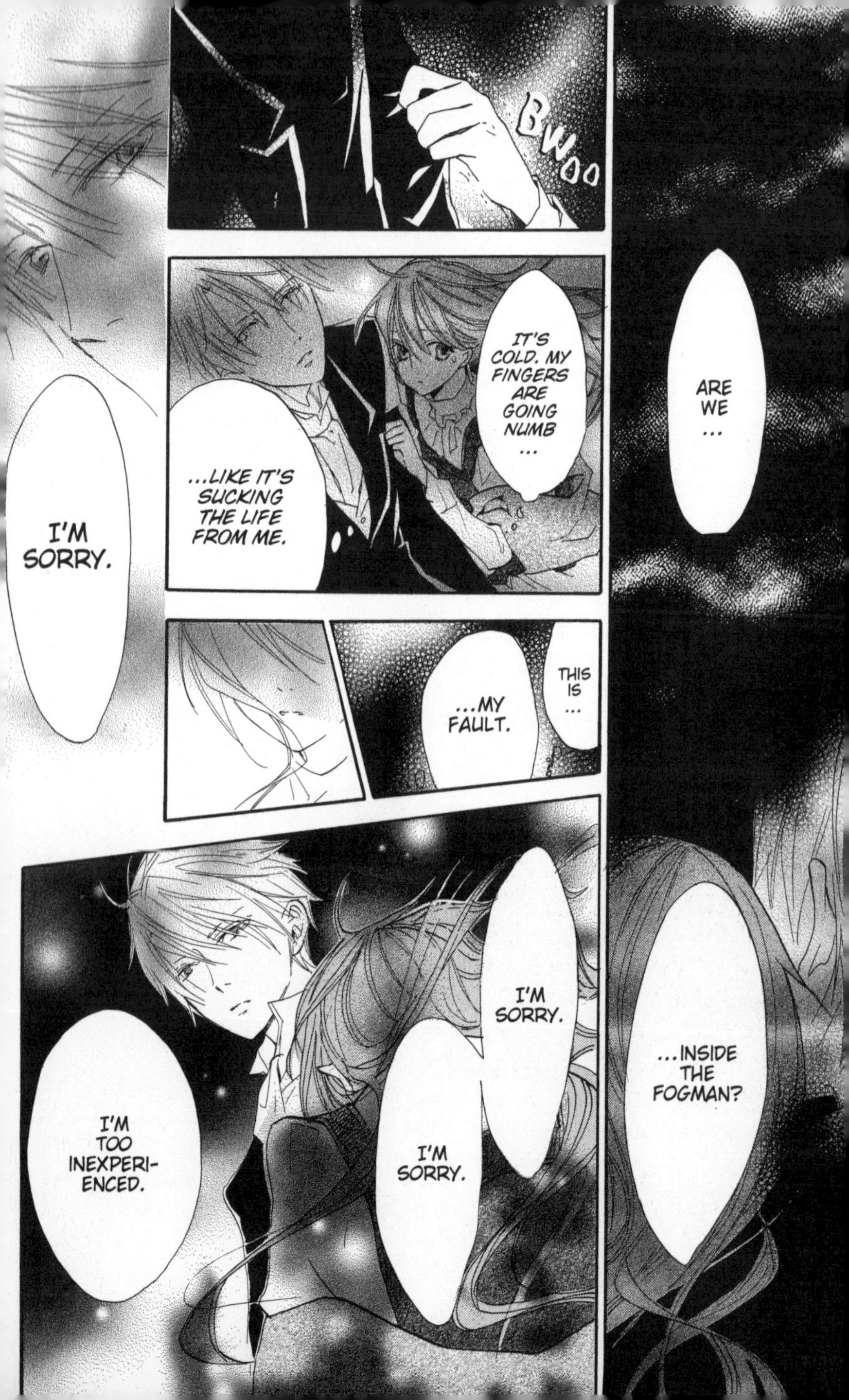
ARE WE...
...INSIDE THE FOGMAN?
BWOO
IT'S COLD. MY FINGERS ARE GOING NUMB...
...LIKE IT'S SUCKING THE LIFE FROM ME.
THIS IS...
...MY FAULT.
I'M SORRY.
I'M SORRY.
I'M SORRY.
I'M TOO INEXPERIENCED.

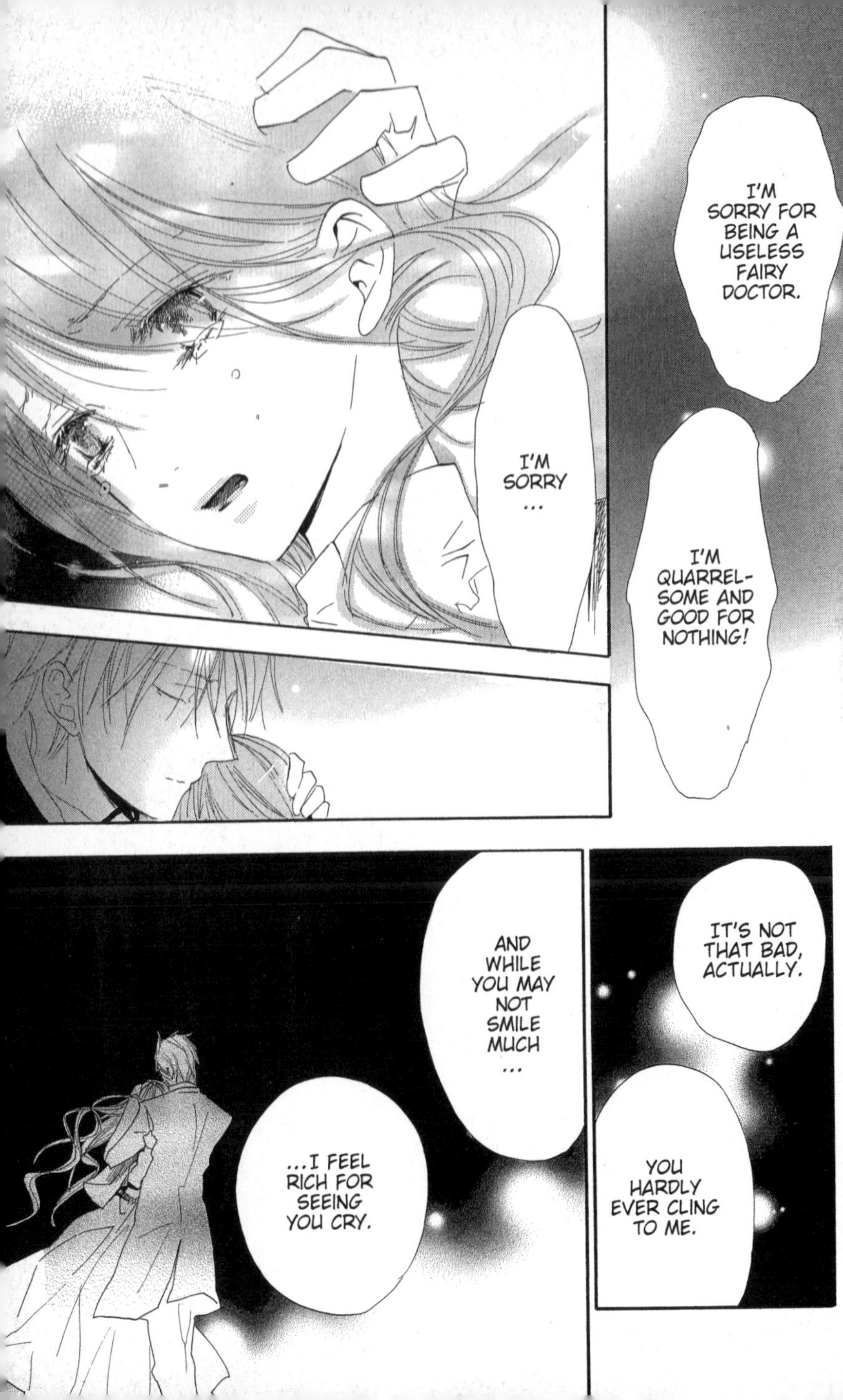
I'M SORRY FOR BEING A USELESS FAIRY DOCTOR.
I'M QUARREL-SOME AND GOOD FOR NOTHING!
I'M SORRY...
IT'S NOT THAT BAD, ACTUALLY.
YOU HARDLY EVER CLING TO ME.
AND WHILE YOU MAY NOT SMILE MUCH...
...I FEEL RICH FOR SEEING YOU CRY.

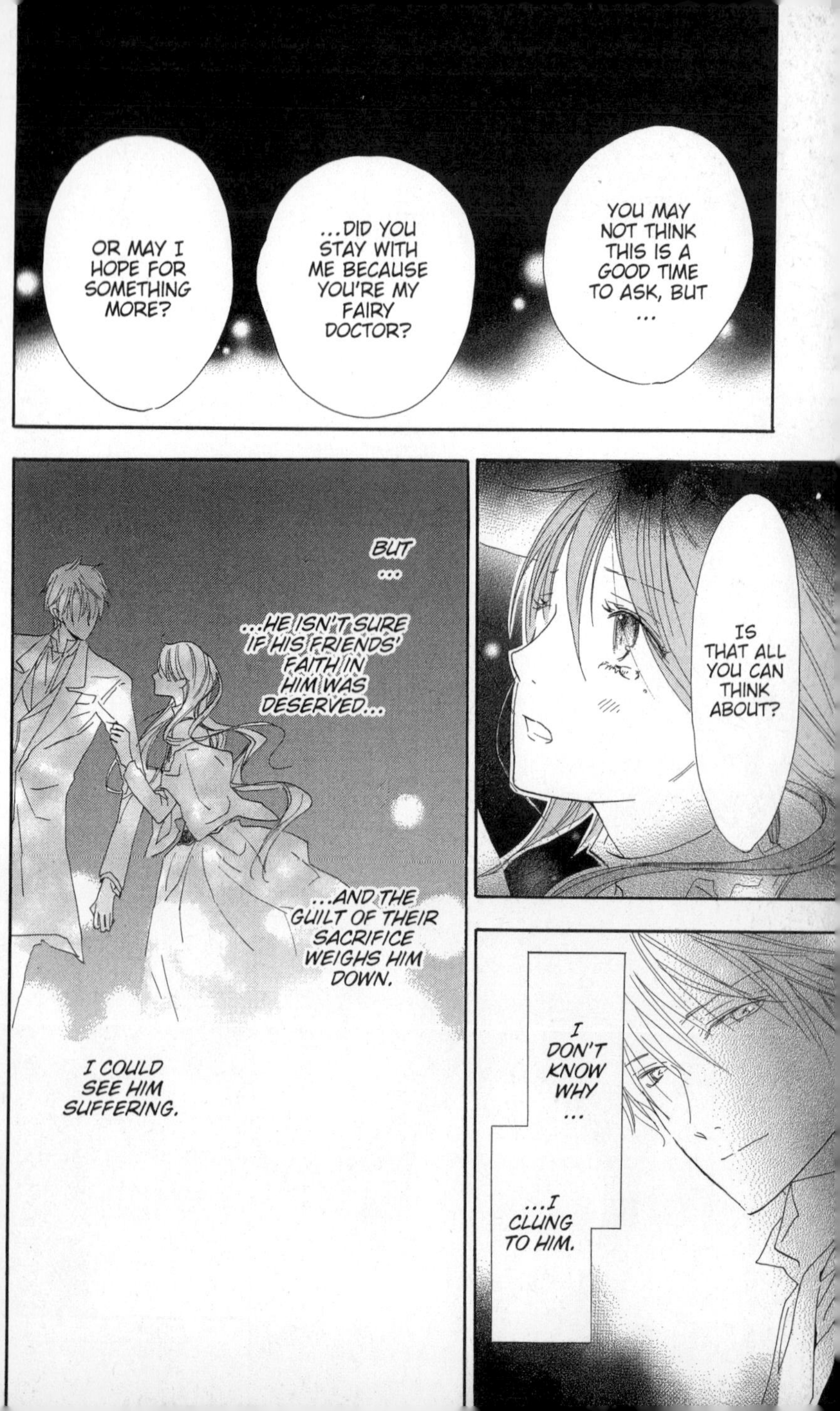
YOU MAY NOT THINK THIS IS A GOOD TIME TO ASK, BUT ...
...DID YOU STAY WITH ME BECAUSE YOU'RE MY FAIRY DOCTOR?
OR MAY I HOPE FOR SOMETHING MORE?
IS THAT ALL YOU CAN THINK ABOUT?
I DON'T KNOW WHY ...
...I CLUNG TO HIM.
BUT ...
...HE ISN'T SURE IF HIS FRIENDS' FAITH IN HIM WAS DESERVED...
...AND THE GUILT OF THEIR SACRIFICE WEIGHS HIM DOWN.
I COULD SEE HIM SUFFERING.

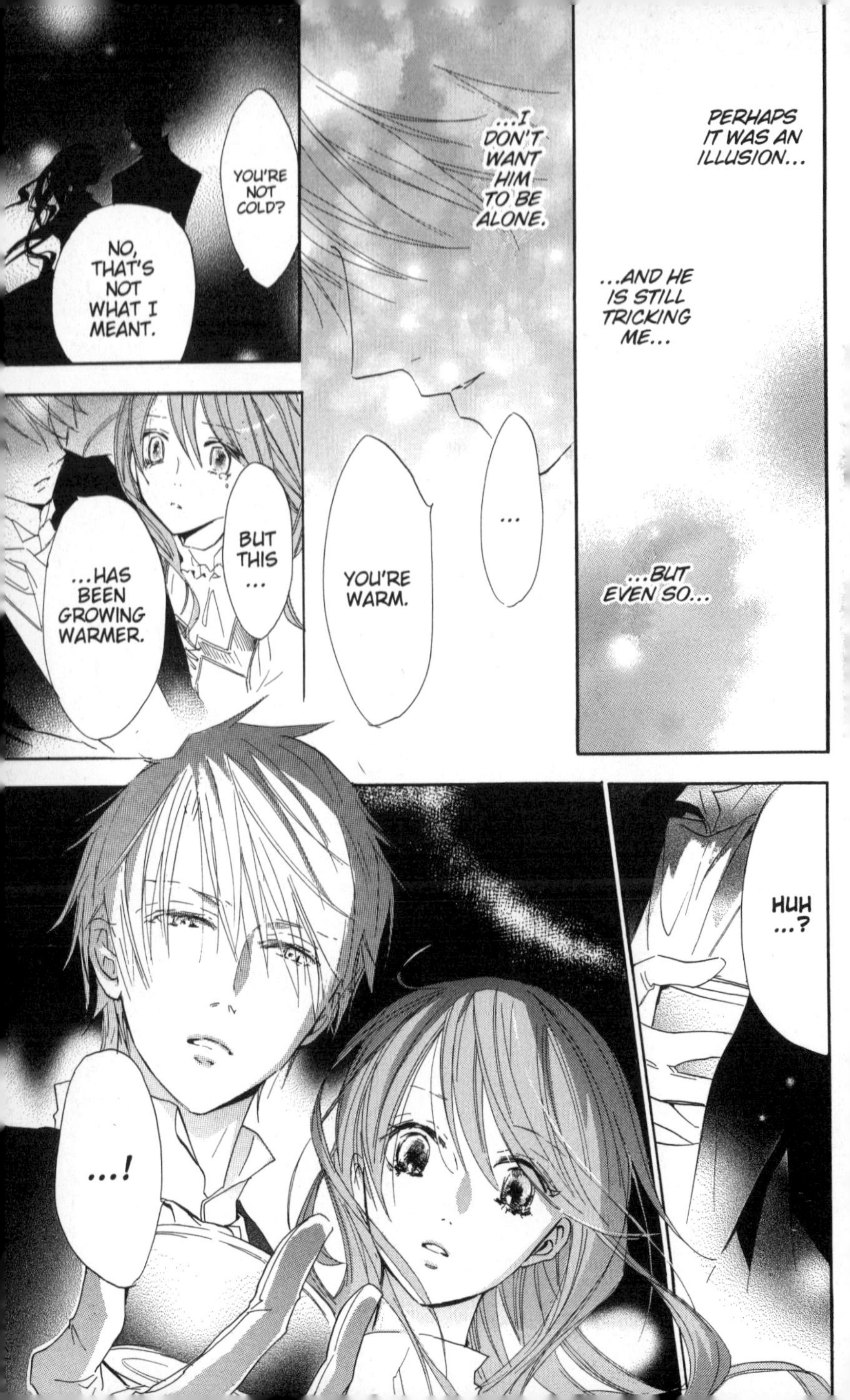
PERHAPS IT WAS AN ILLUSION...
...AND HE IS STILL TRICKING ME...
...BUT EVEN SO...
...I DON'T WANT HIM TO BE ALONE.
...
YOU'RE WARM.
YOU'RE NOT COLD?
NO, THAT'S NOT WHAT I MEANT.
BUT THIS...
...HAS BEEN GROWING WARMER.
HUH...?
...!

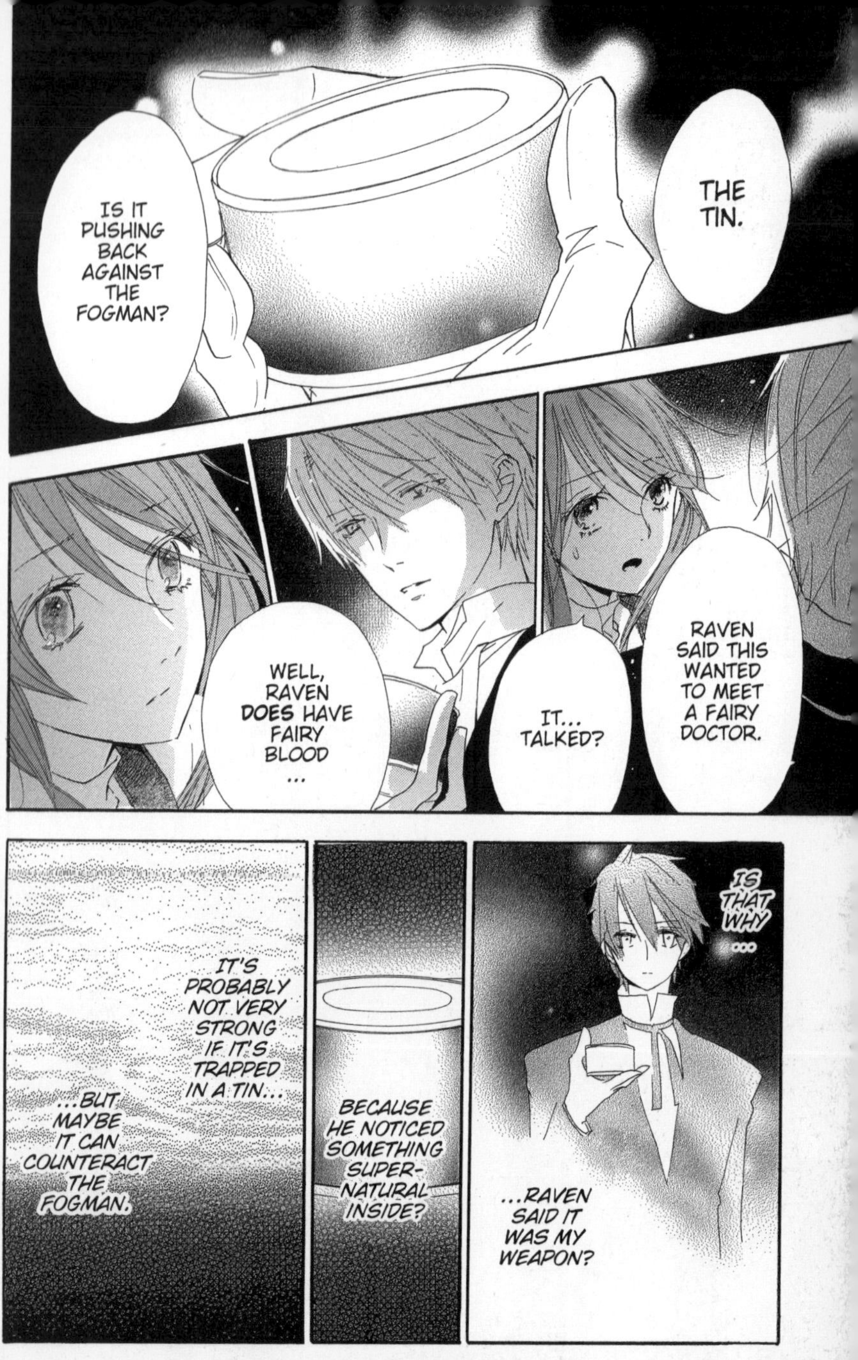
THE TIN.
IS IT PUSHING BACK AGAINST THE FOGMAN?
RAVEN SAID THIS WANTED TO MEET A FAIRY DOCTOR.
IT... TALKED?
WELL, RAVEN DOES HAVE FAIRY BLOOD ...
IS THAT WHY...
...RAVEN SAID IT WAS MY WEAPON?
BECAUSE HE NOTICED SOMETHING SUPER-NATURAL INSIDE?
IT'S PROBABLY NOT VERY STRONG IF IT'S TRAPPED IN A TIN...
...BUT MAYBE IT CAN COUNTERACT THE FOGMAN.

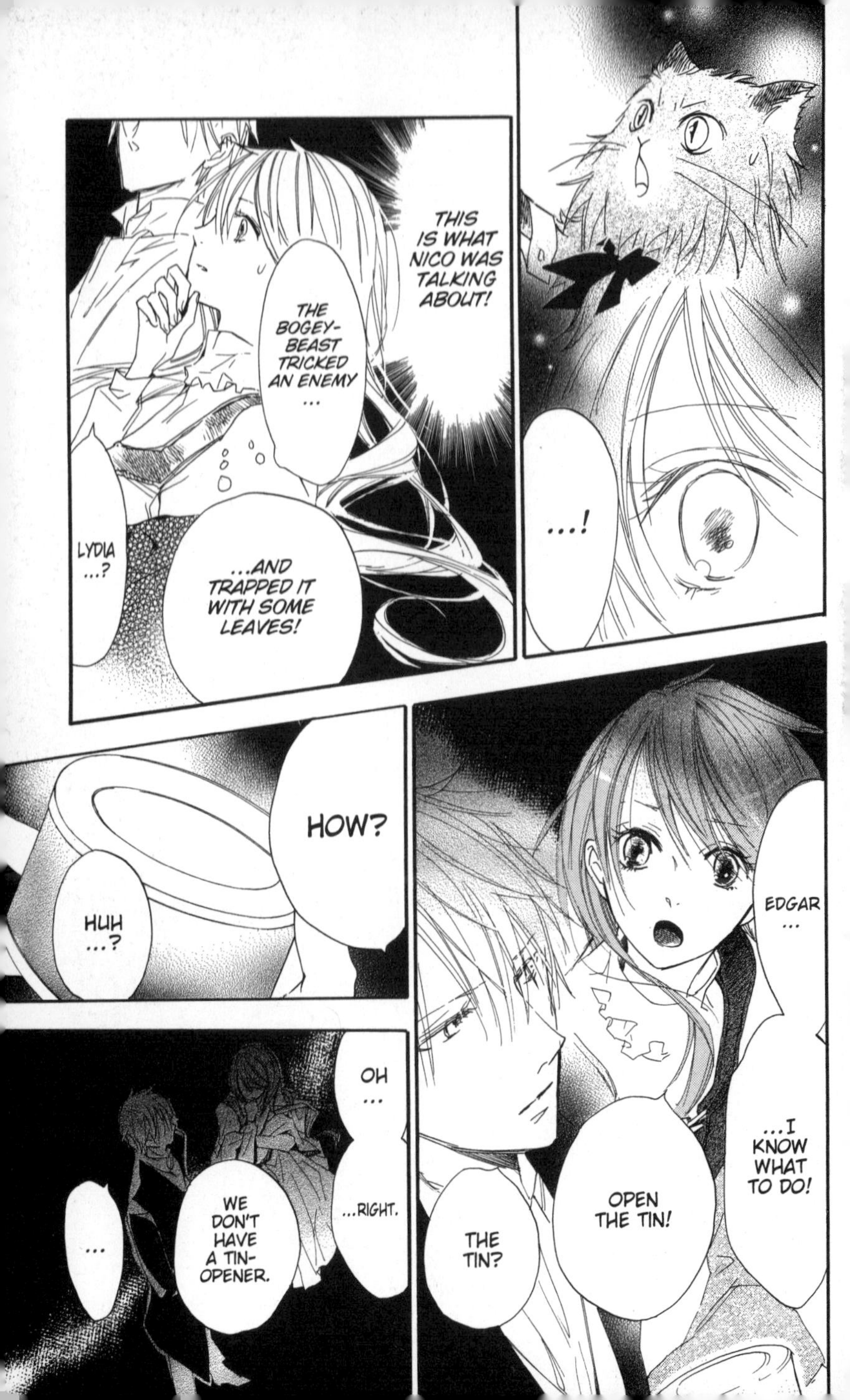
...!
THIS IS WHAT NICO WAS TALKING ABOUT!
THE BOGEY-BEAST TRICKED AN ENEMY ...
...AND TRAPPED IT WITH SOME LEAVES!
LYDIA ...?
EDGAR ...
...I KNOW WHAT TO DO!
OPEN THE TIN!
THE TIN?
HOW?
HUH ...?
OH ...
...RIGHT.
WE DON'T HAVE A TIN-OPENER.
...

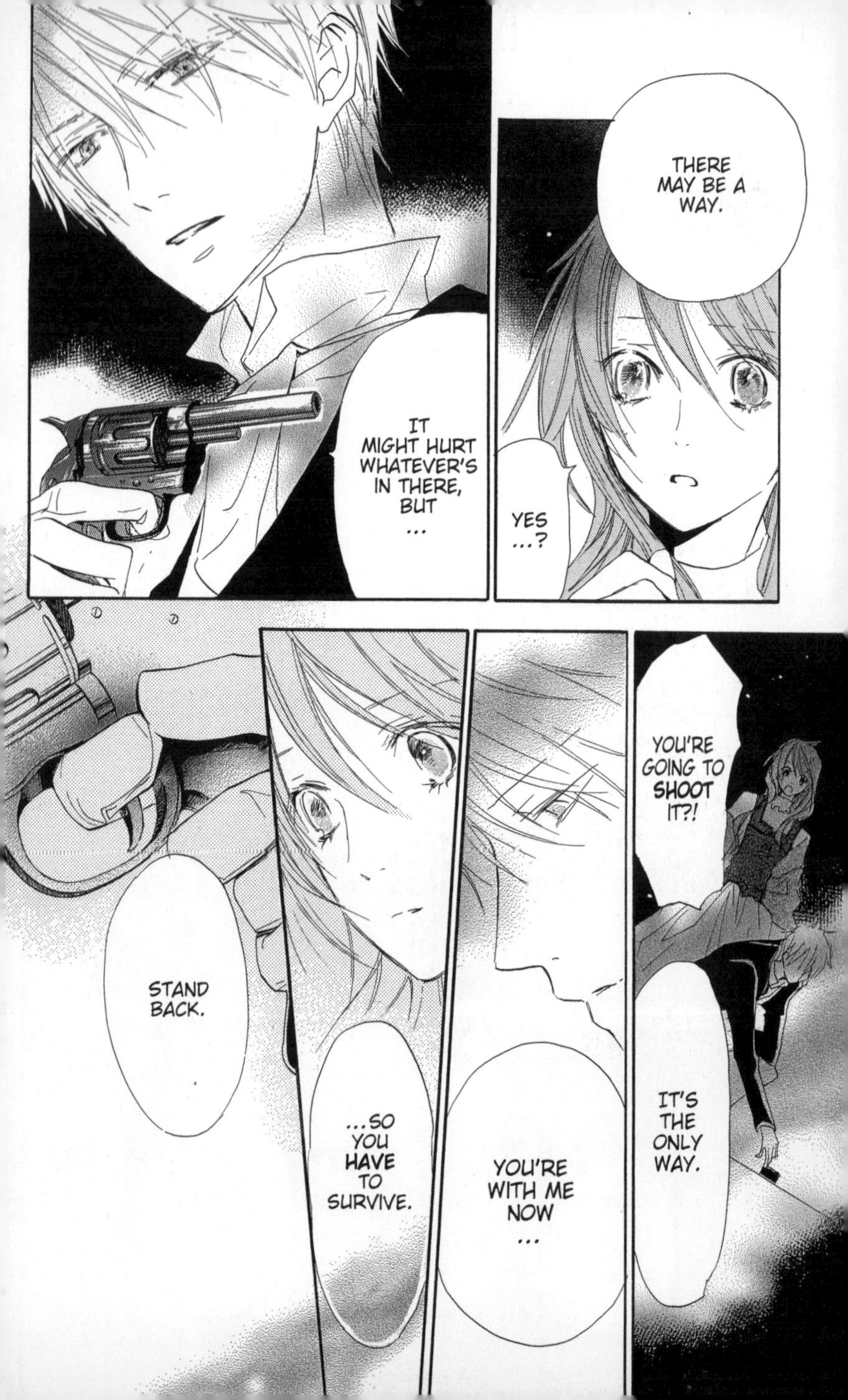
THERE MAY BE A WAY.
YES...?
IT MIGHT HURT WHATEVER'S IN THERE, BUT...
YOU'RE GOING TO SHOOT IT?!
IT'S THE ONLY WAY.
YOU'RE WITH ME NOW...
...SO YOU HAVE TO SURVIVE.
STAND BACK.

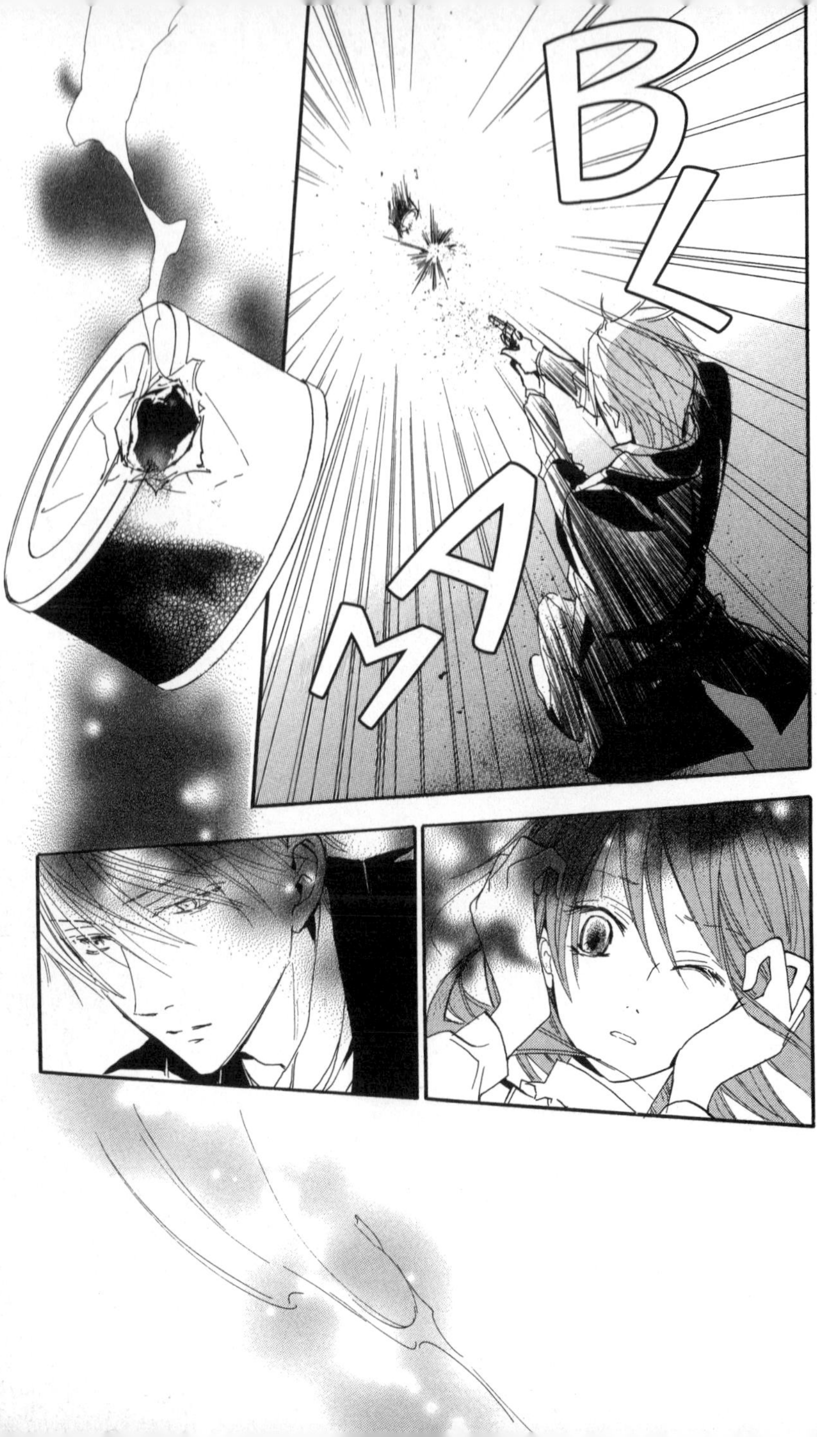
BLAM

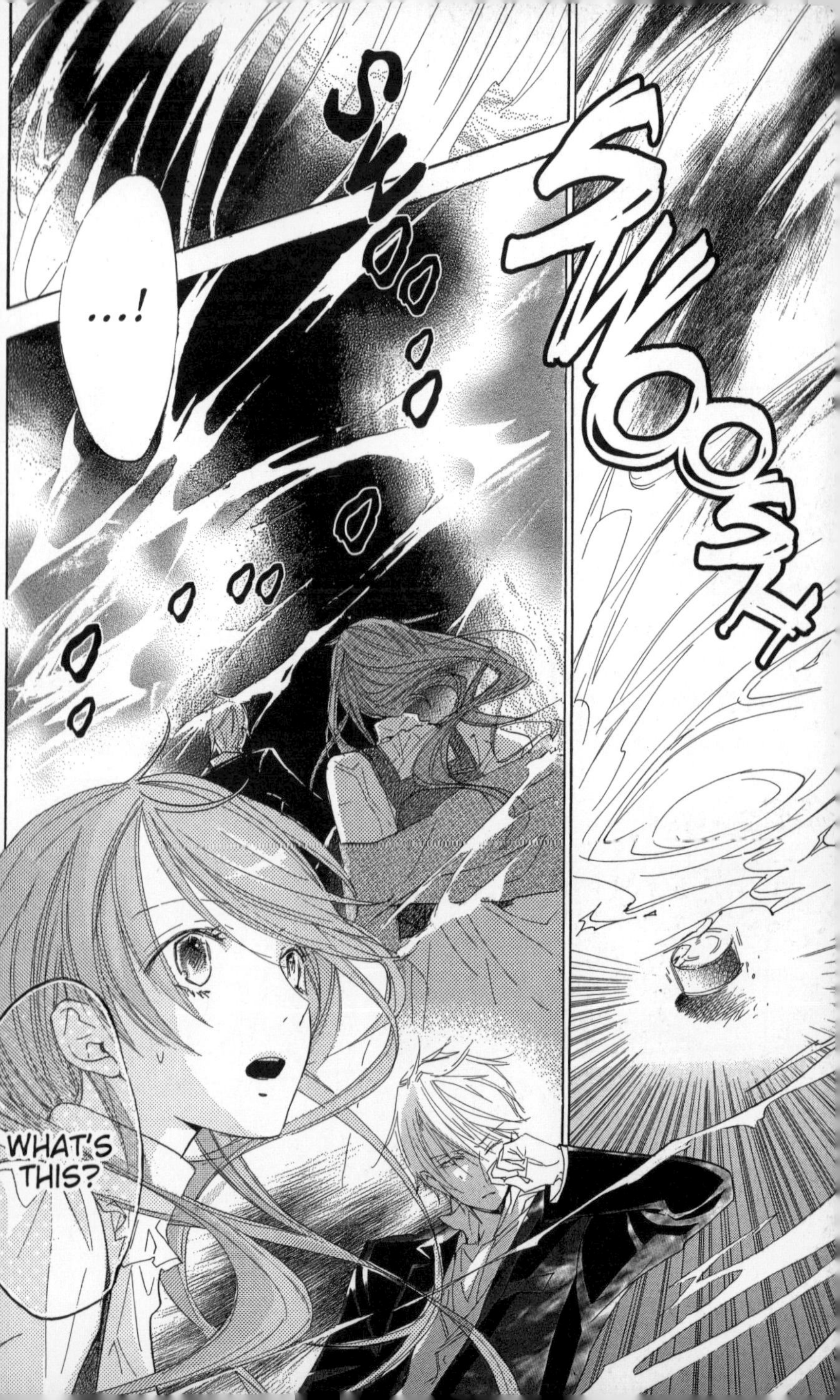
SWOOSH
SWOO...
...!
WHAT'S THIS?

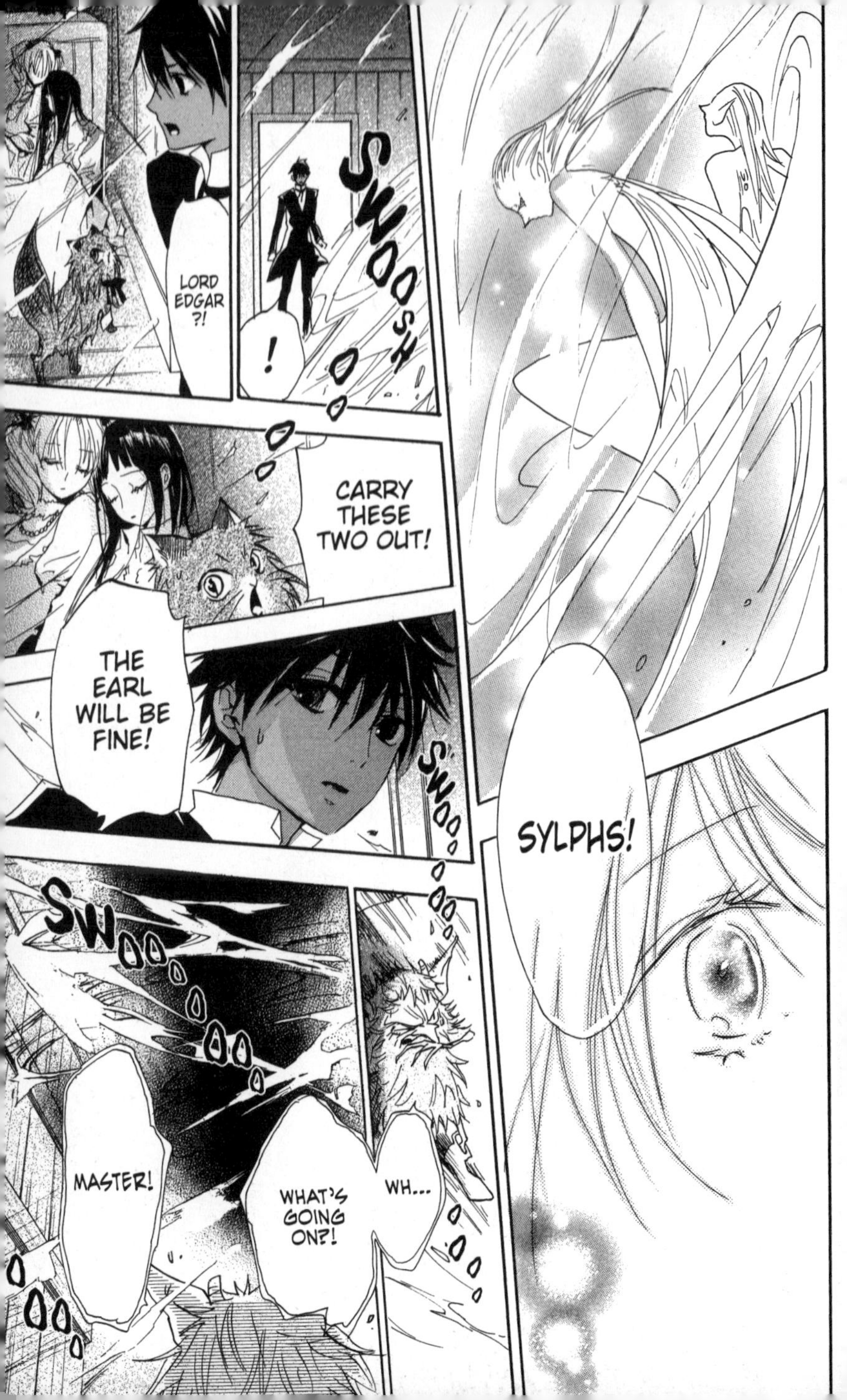
SYLPHS!
SWOOSH
!
LORD EDGAR ?!
CARRY THESE TWO OUT!
SWOO
THE EARL WILL BE FINE!
WH...
WHAT'S GOING ON?!
SWOOO
MASTER!

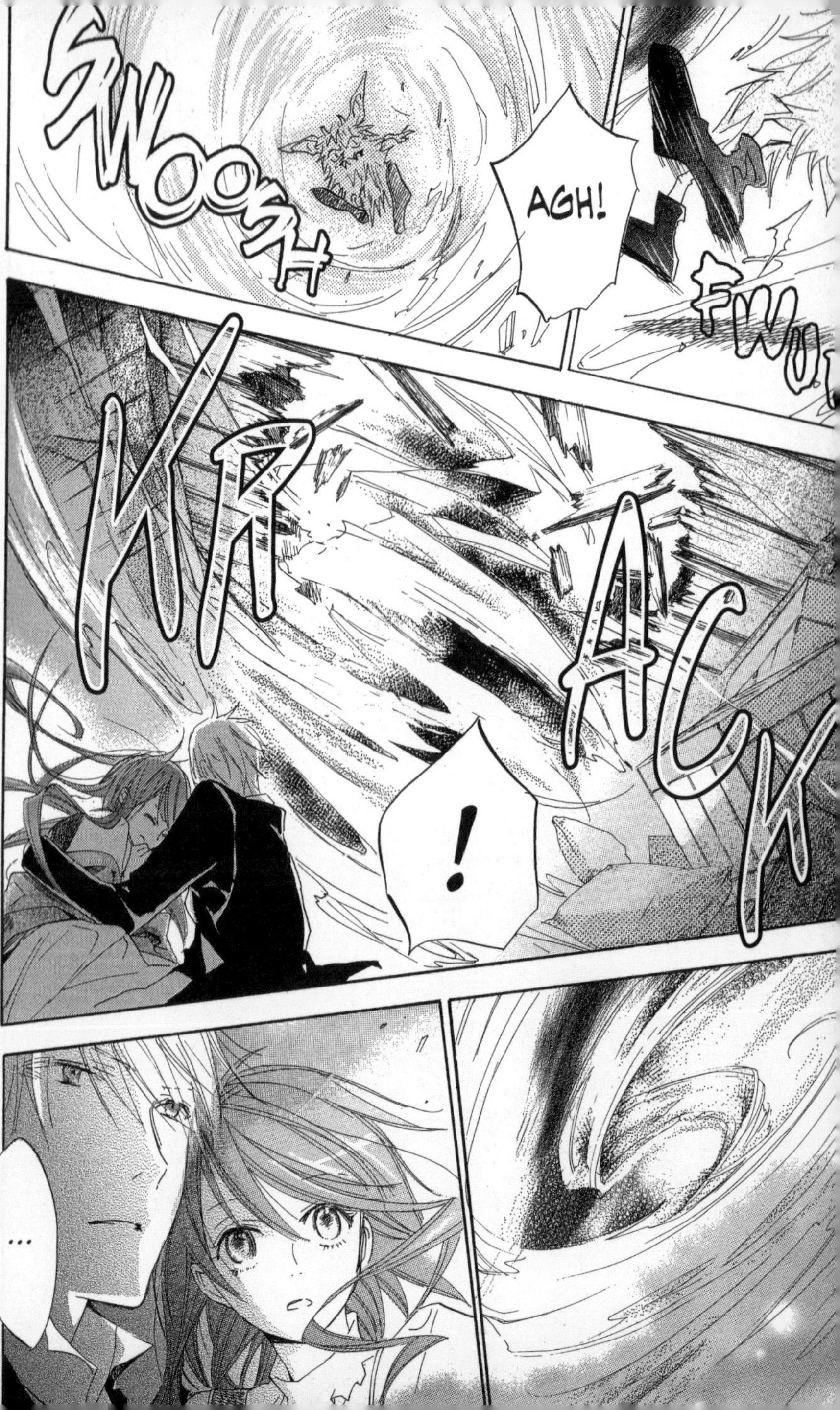
FWUP
AGH!
SWOOSH
KRACK
!
...

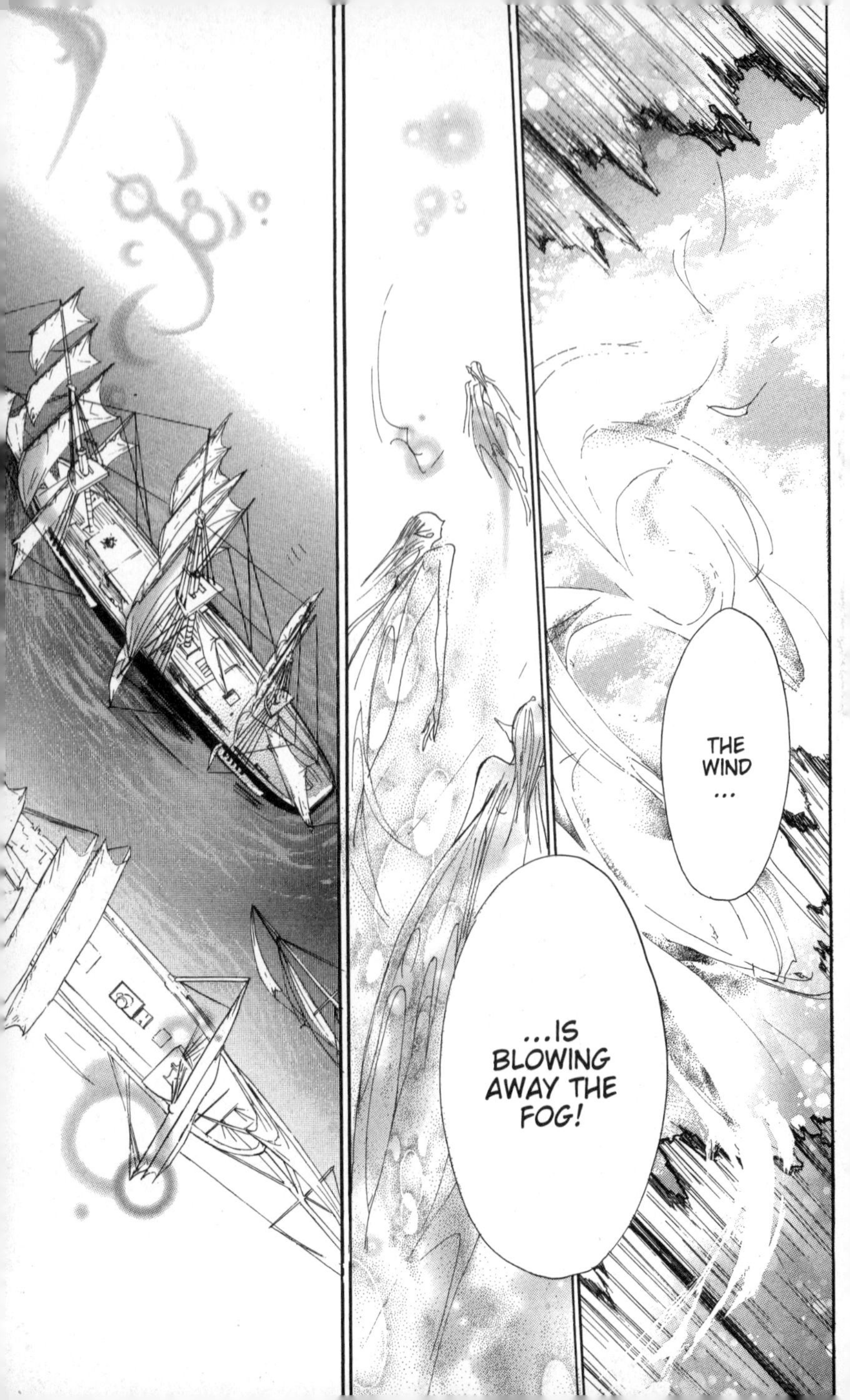
THE WIND ...
...IS BLOWING AWAY THE FOG!

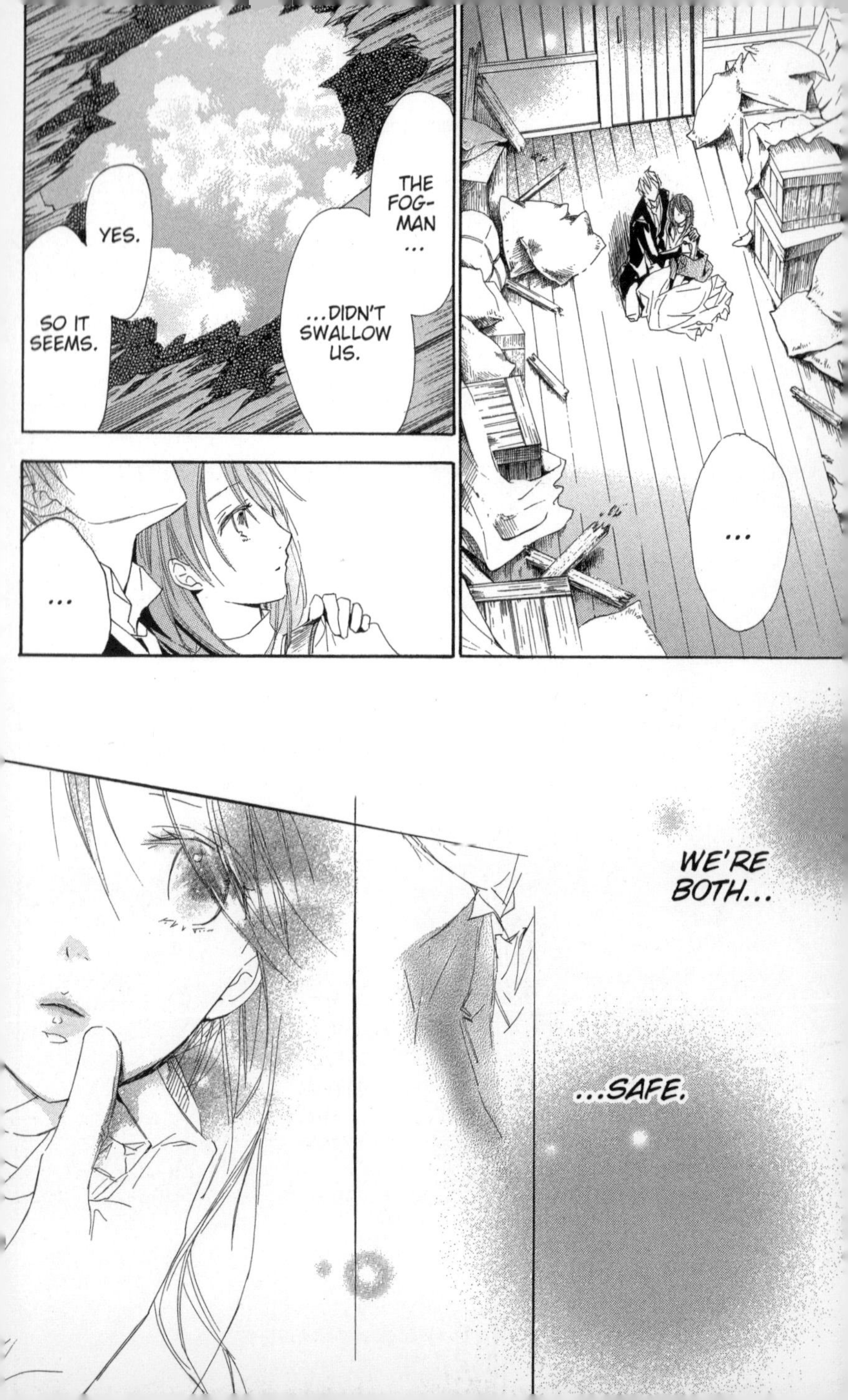
...
THE FOG-MAN...
...DIDN'T SWALLOW US.
YES.
SO IT SEEMS.
...
WE'RE BOTH...
...SAFE.

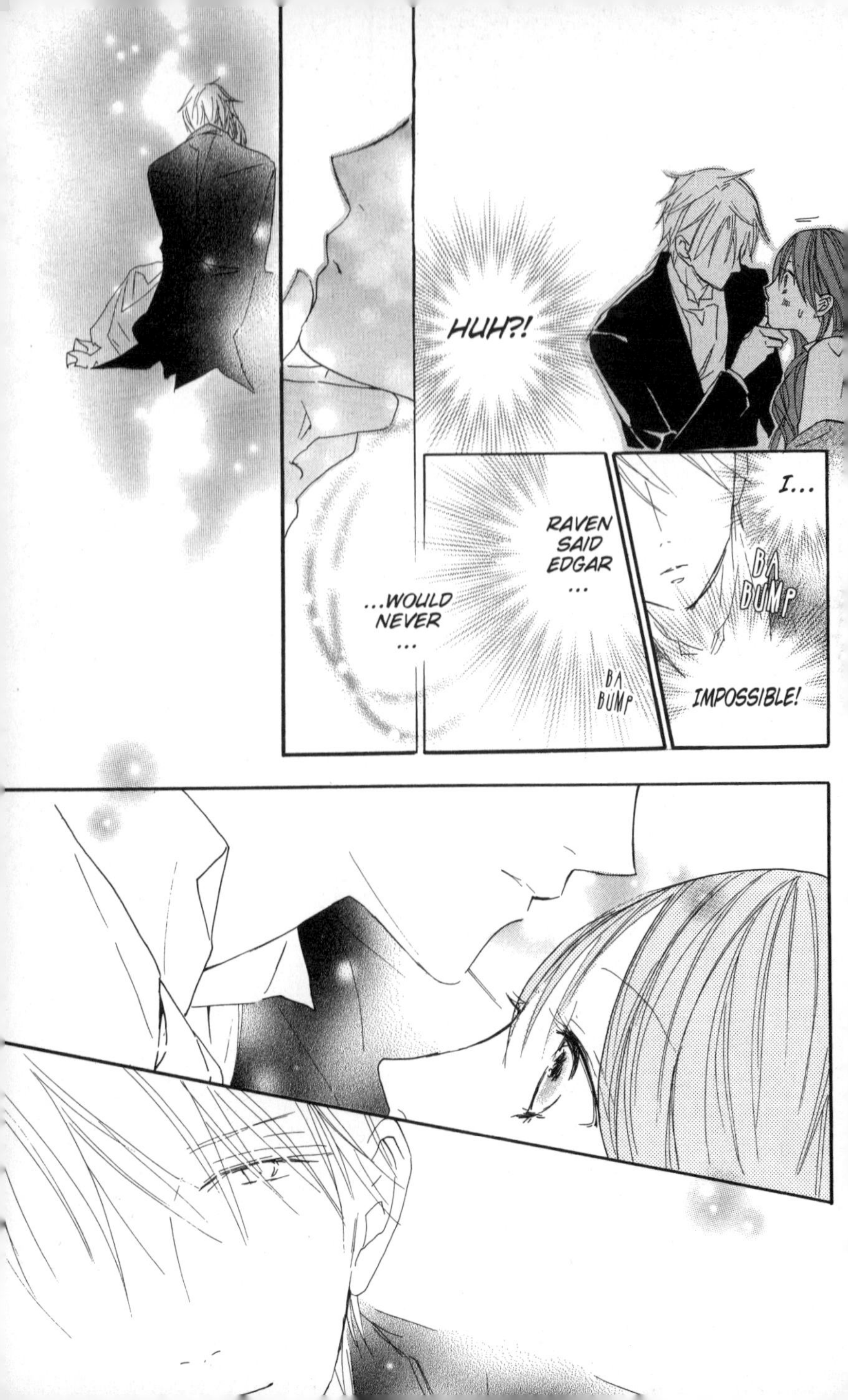
HUH?!
I...
BA BUMP
IMPOSSIBLE!
RAVEN SAID EDGAR ...
BA BUMP
...WOULD NEVER ...

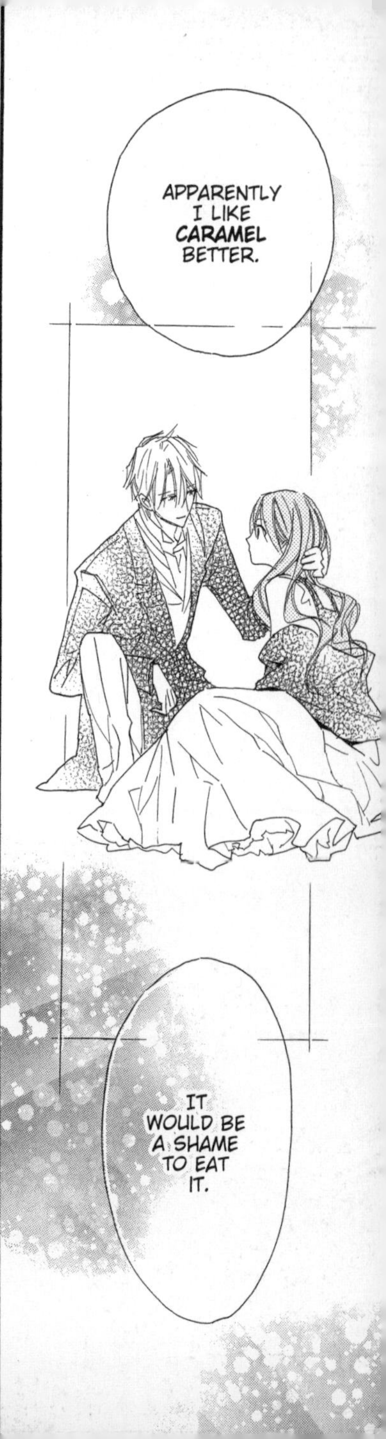
APPARENTLY I LIKE **CARAMEL** BETTER.
IT WOULD BE A SHAME TO EAT IT.

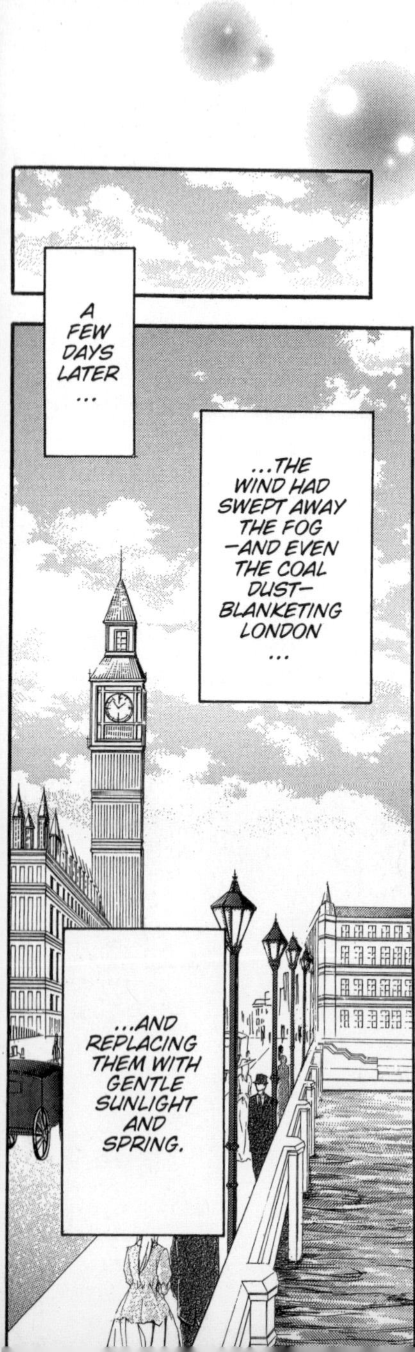
A FEW DAYS LATER...
...THE WIND HAD SWEPT AWAY THE FOG—AND EVEN THE COAL DUST—BLANKETING LONDON...
...AND REPLACING THEM WITH GENTLE SUNLIGHT AND SPRING.

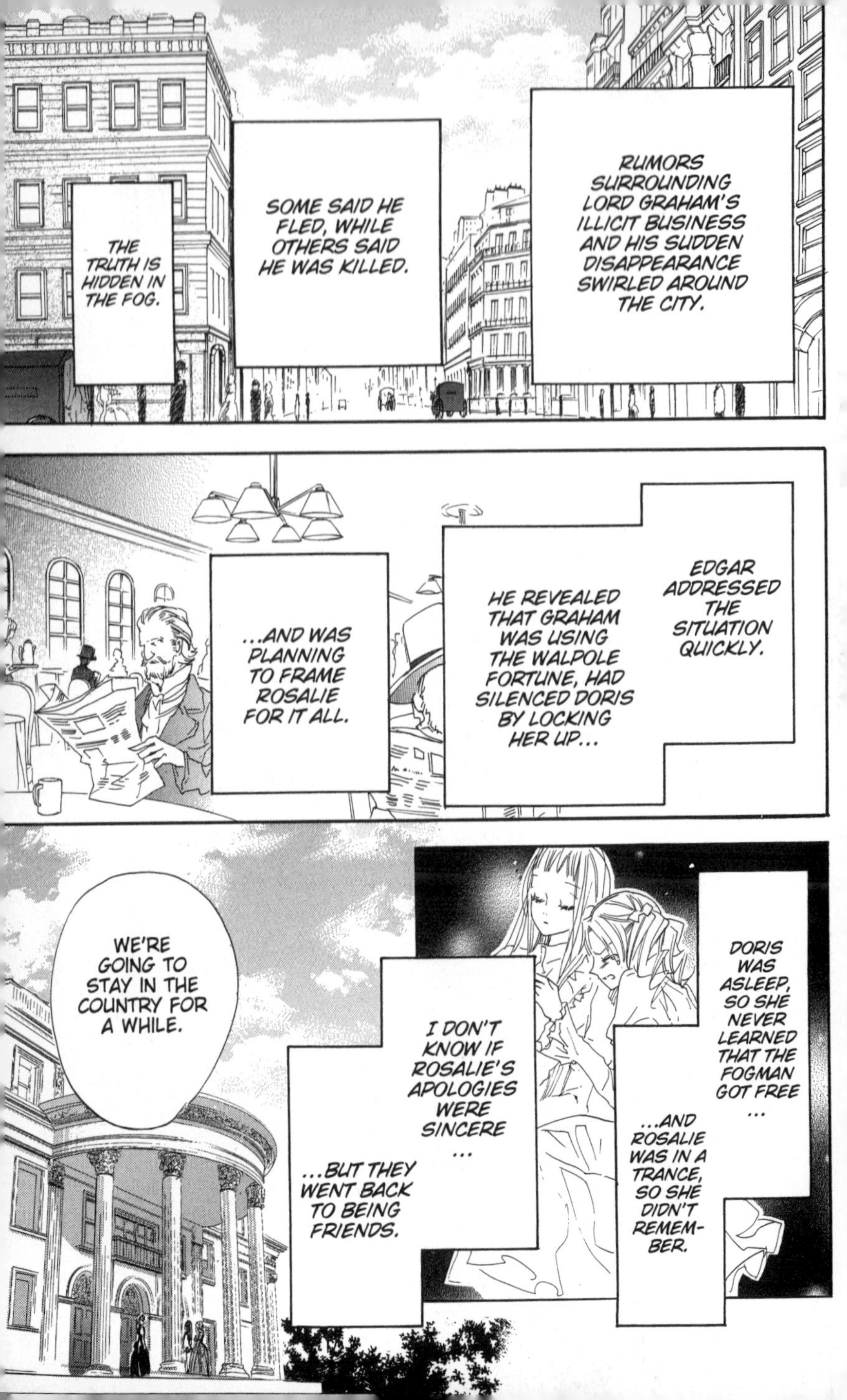
RUMORS SURROUNDING LORD GRAHAM'S ILLICIT BUSINESS AND HIS SUDDEN DISAPPEARANCE SWIRLED AROUND THE CITY.
SOME SAID HE FLED, WHILE OTHERS SAID HE WAS KILLED.
THE TRUTH IS HIDDEN IN THE FOG.
EDGAR ADDRESSED THE SITUATION QUICKLY.
HE REVEALED THAT GRAHAM WAS USING THE WALPOLE FORTUNE, HAD SILENCED DORIS BY LOCKING HER UP...
...AND WAS PLANNING TO FRAME ROSALIE FOR IT ALL.
DORIS WAS ASLEEP, SO SHE NEVER LEARNED THAT THE FOGMAN GOT FREE ...
...AND ROSALIE WAS IN A TRANCE, SO SHE DIDN'T REMEMBER.
I DON'T KNOW IF ROSALIE'S APOLOGIES WERE SINCERE ...
...BUT THEY WENT BACK TO BEING FRIENDS.
WE'RE GOING TO STAY IN THE COUNTRY FOR A WHILE.

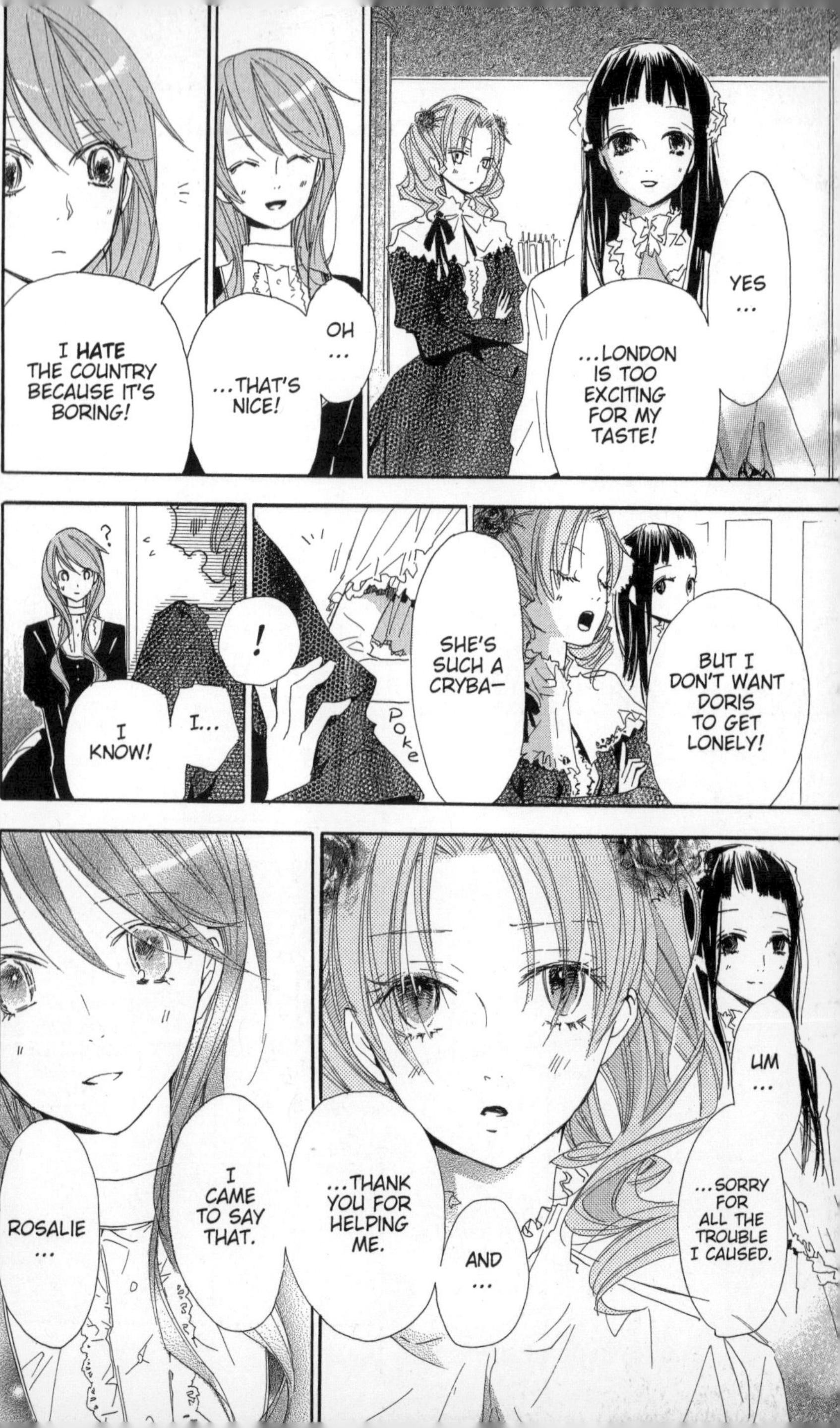
YES ...
...LONDON IS TOO EXCITING FOR MY TASTE!
OH ...
...THAT'S NICE!
I **HATE** THE COUNTRY BECAUSE IT'S BORING!
BUT I DON'T WANT DORIS TO GET LONELY!
SHE'S SUCH A CRYBA—
Poke
!
I...
I KNOW!
UM ...
...SORRY FOR ALL THE TROUBLE I CAUSED.
AND ...
...THANK YOU FOR HELPING ME.
I CAME TO SAY THAT.
ROSALIE ...

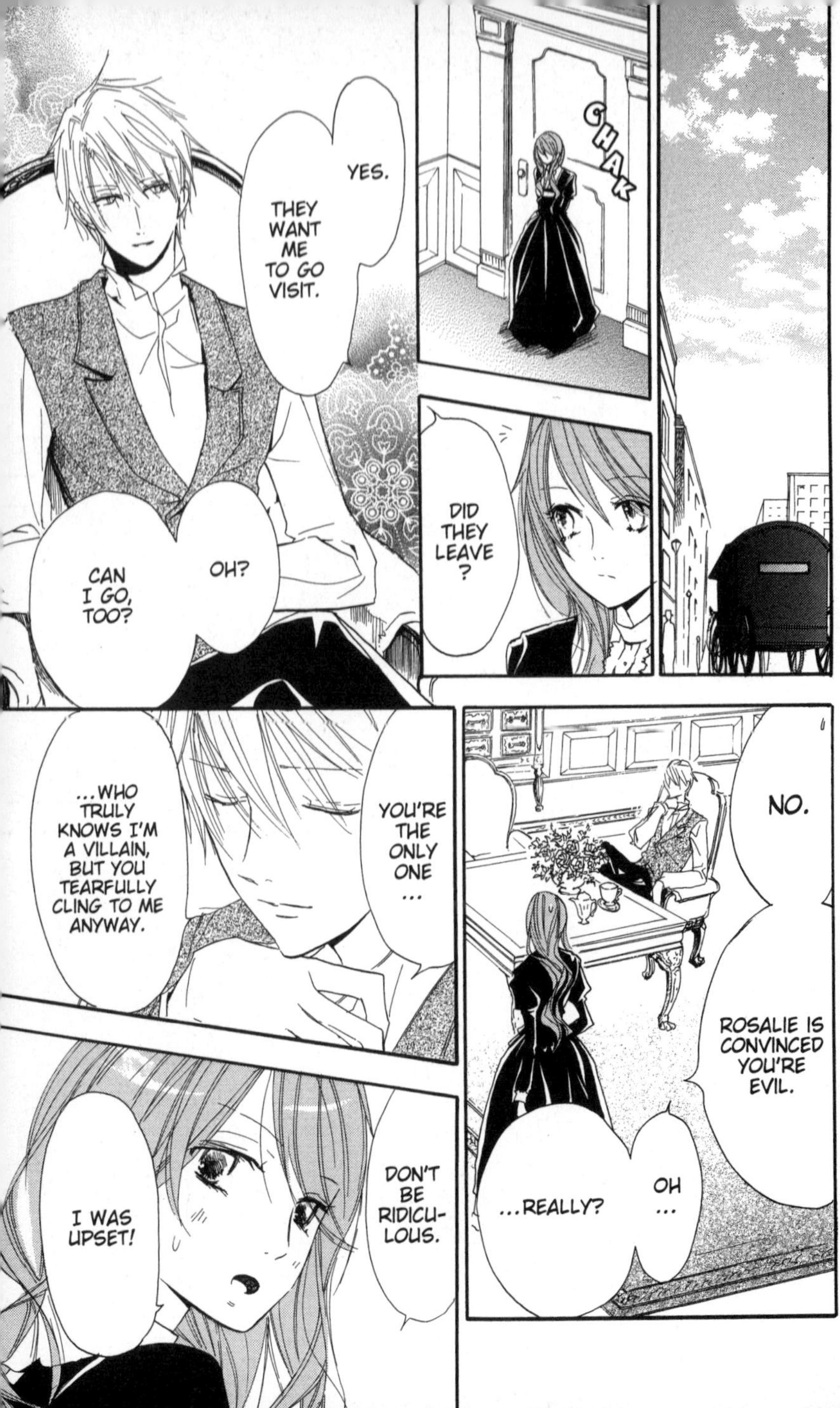
CHAK
DID THEY LEAVE?
YES.
THEY WANT ME TO GO VISIT.
OH?
CAN I GO, TOO?
NO.
ROSALIE IS CONVINCED YOU'RE EVIL.
OH...
...REALLY?
YOU'RE THE ONLY ONE...
...WHO TRULY KNOWS I'M A VILLAIN, BUT YOU TEARFULLY CLING TO ME ANYWAY.
DON'T BE RIDICULOUS.
I WAS UPSET!

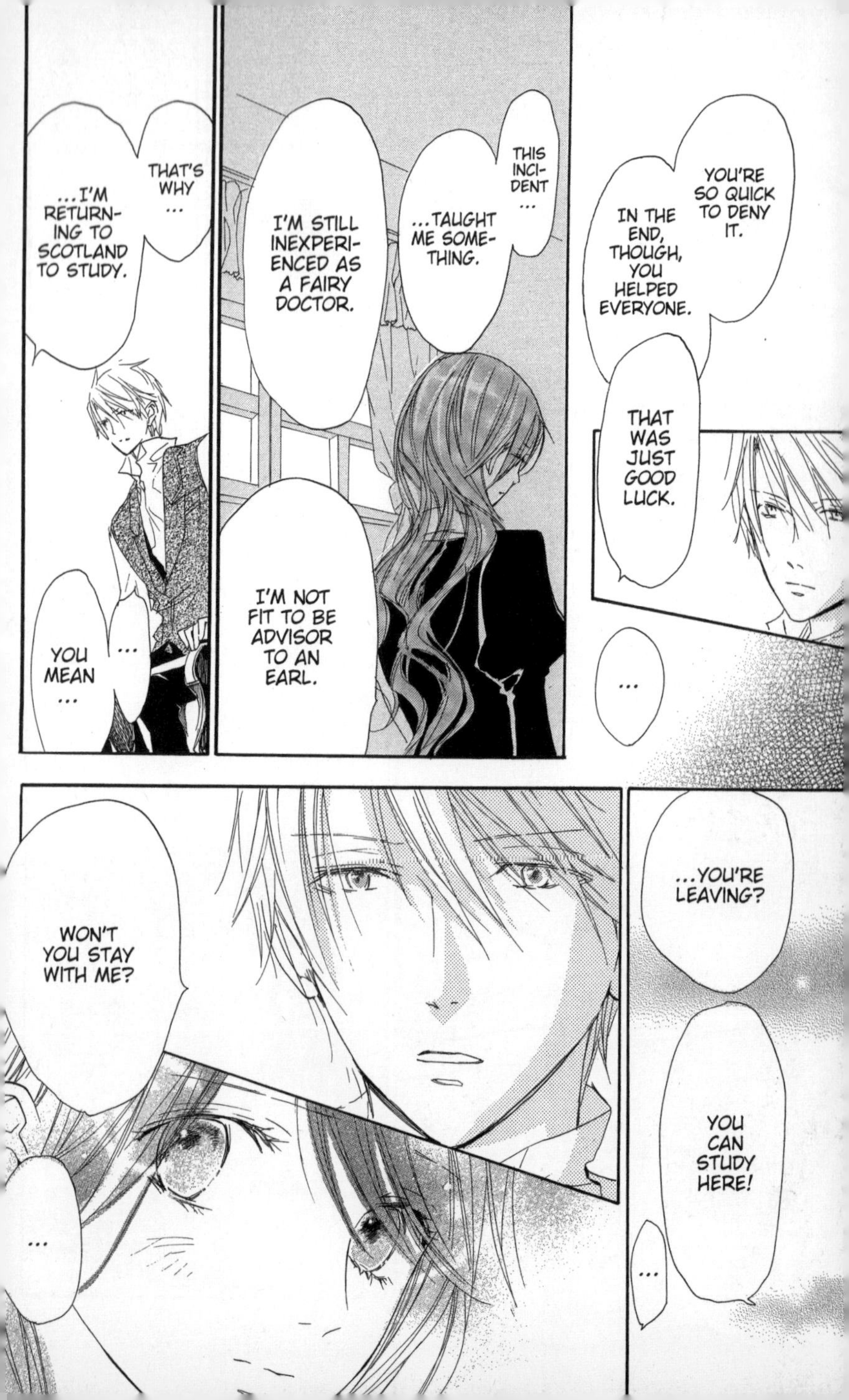
YOU'RE SO QUICK TO DENY IT.
IN THE END, THOUGH, YOU HELPED EVERYONE.
THAT WAS JUST GOOD LUCK.
...
THIS INCI-DENT...
...TAUGHT ME SOME-THING.
I'M STILL INEXPERI-ENCED AS A FAIRY DOCTOR.
I'M NOT FIT TO BE ADVISOR TO AN EARL.
THAT'S WHY...
...I'M RETURN-ING TO SCOTLAND TO STUDY.
...
YOU MEAN...
...YOU'RE LEAVING?
YOU CAN STUDY HERE!
...
WON'T YOU STAY WITH ME?
...

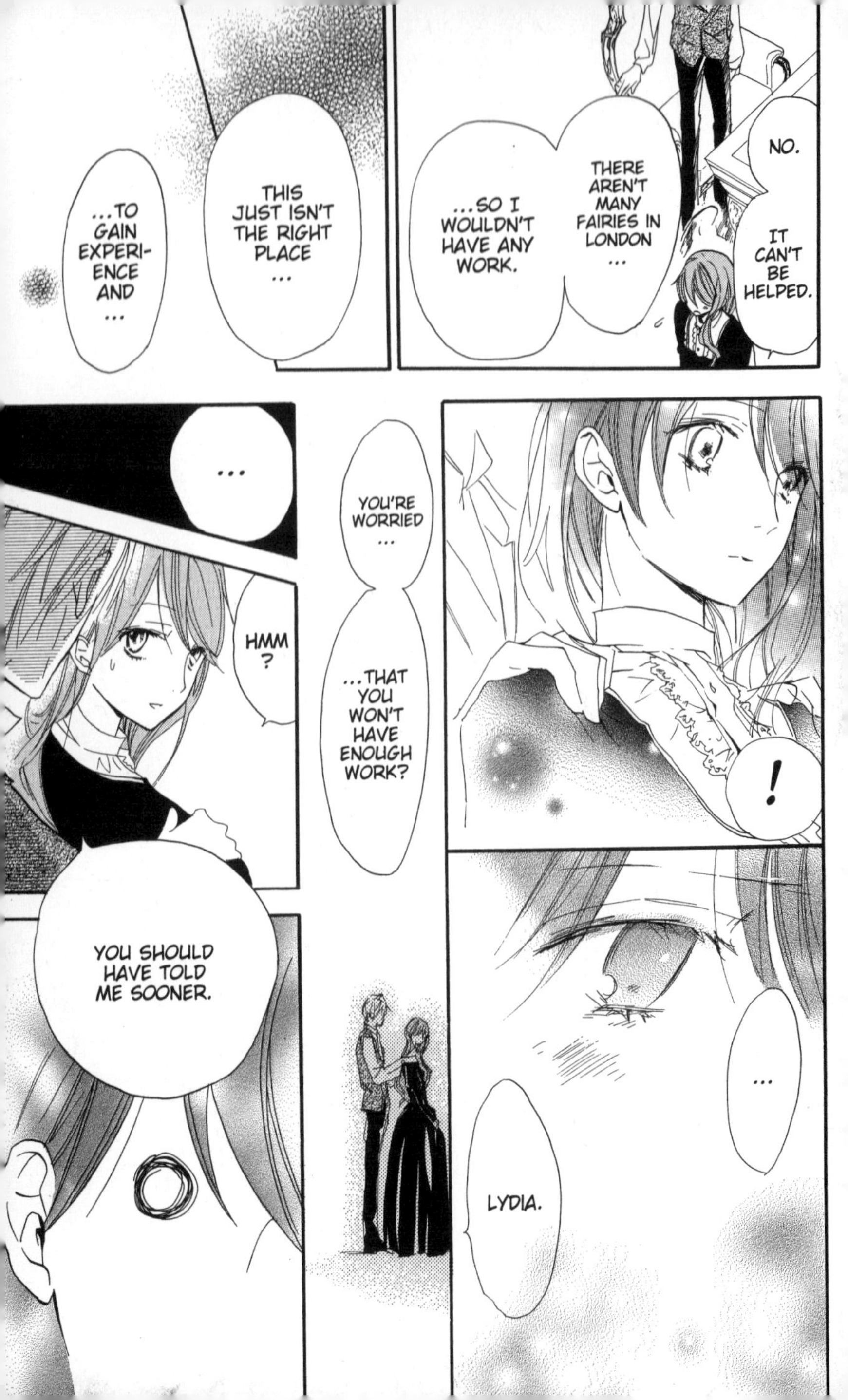
NO.
IT CAN'T BE HELPED.
THERE AREN'T MANY FAIRIES IN LONDON...
...SO I WOULDN'T HAVE ANY WORK.
THIS JUST ISN'T THE RIGHT PLACE...
...TO GAIN EXPERI-ENCE AND...
!
YOU'RE WORRIED...
...THAT YOU WON'T HAVE ENOUGH WORK?
...
HMM?
...
LYDIA.
YOU SHOULD HAVE TOLD ME SOONER.

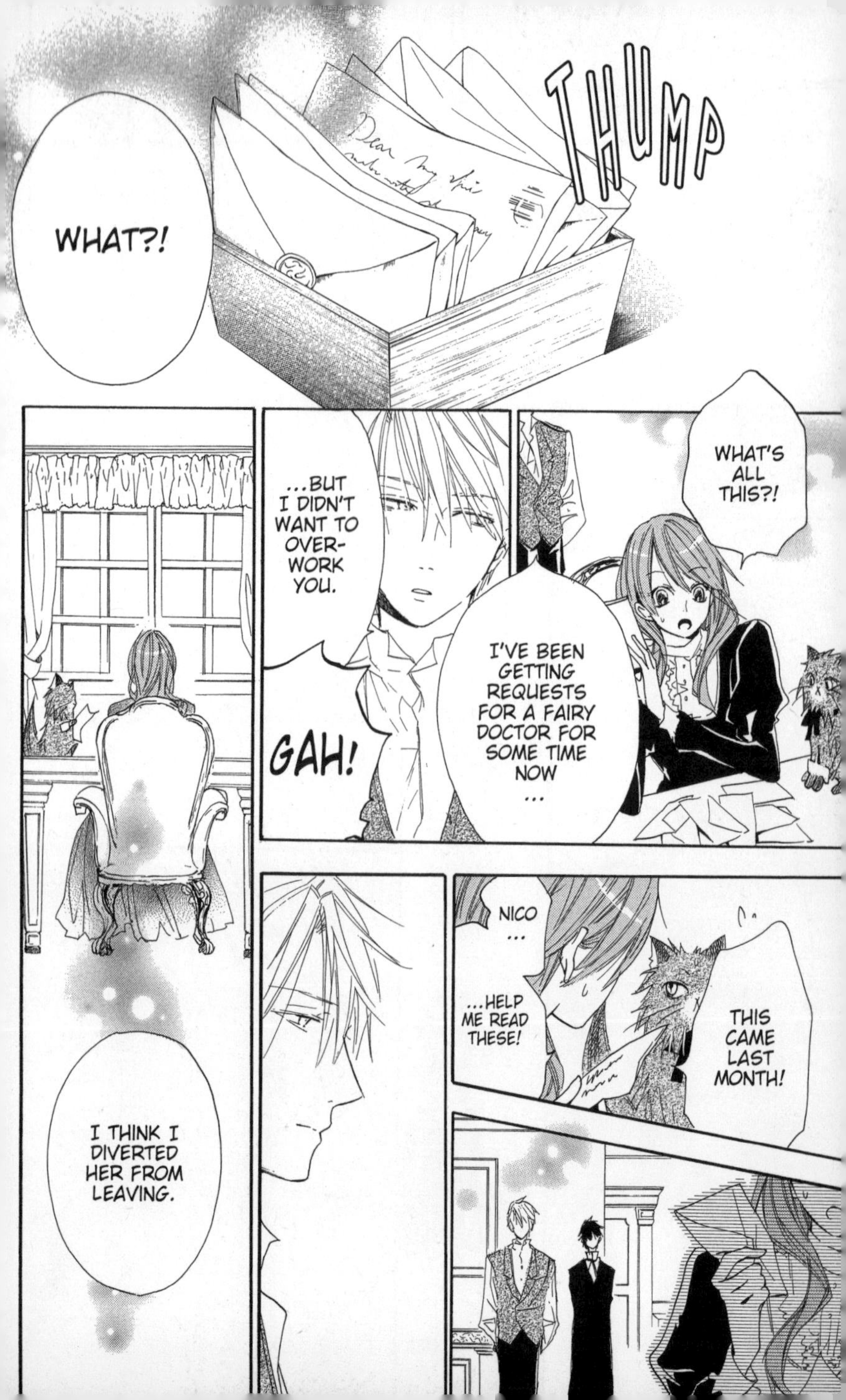

THUMP
WHAT?!
WHAT'S ALL THIS?!
I'VE BEEN GETTING REQUESTS FOR A FAIRY DOCTOR FOR SOME TIME NOW ...
...BUT I DIDN'T WANT TO OVER-WORK YOU.
GAH!
THIS CAME LAST MONTH!
NICO ...
...HELP ME READ THESE!
I THINK I DIVERTED HER FROM LEAVING.

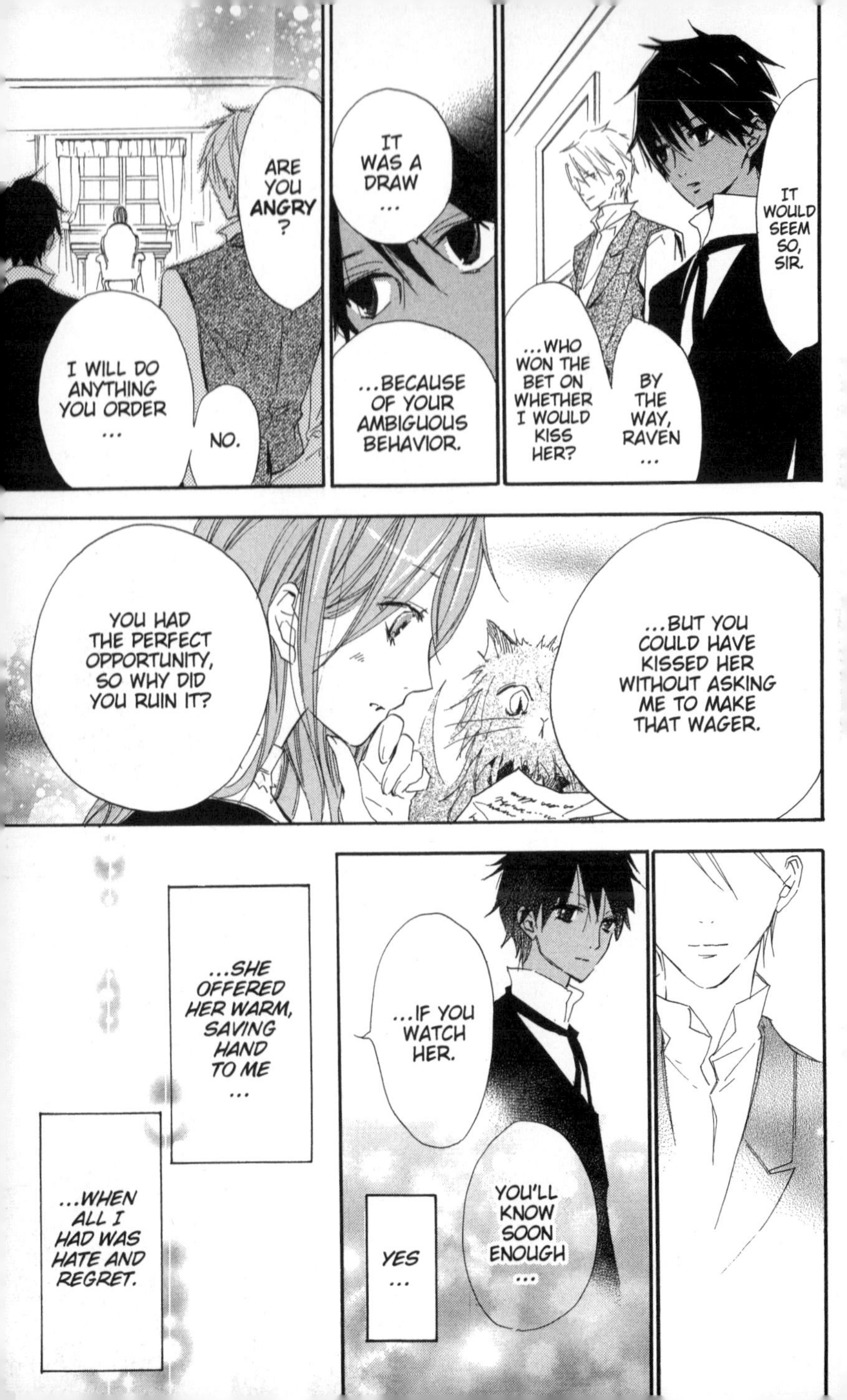
IT WOULD SEEM SO, SIR.
BY THE WAY, RAVEN ...
...WHO WON THE BET ON WHETHER I WOULD KISS HER?
IT WAS A DRAW ...
...BECAUSE OF YOUR AMBIGUOUS BEHAVIOR.
ARE YOU ANGRY?
NO.
I WILL DO ANYTHING YOU ORDER ...
...BUT YOU COULD HAVE KISSED HER WITHOUT ASKING ME TO MAKE THAT WAGER.
YOU HAD THE PERFECT OPPORTUNITY, SO WHY DID YOU RUIN IT?
...IF YOU WATCH HER.
YOU'LL KNOW SOON ENOUGH ...
YES ...
...SHE OFFERED HER WARM, SAVING HAND TO ME ...
...WHEN ALL I HAD WAS HATE AND REGRET.

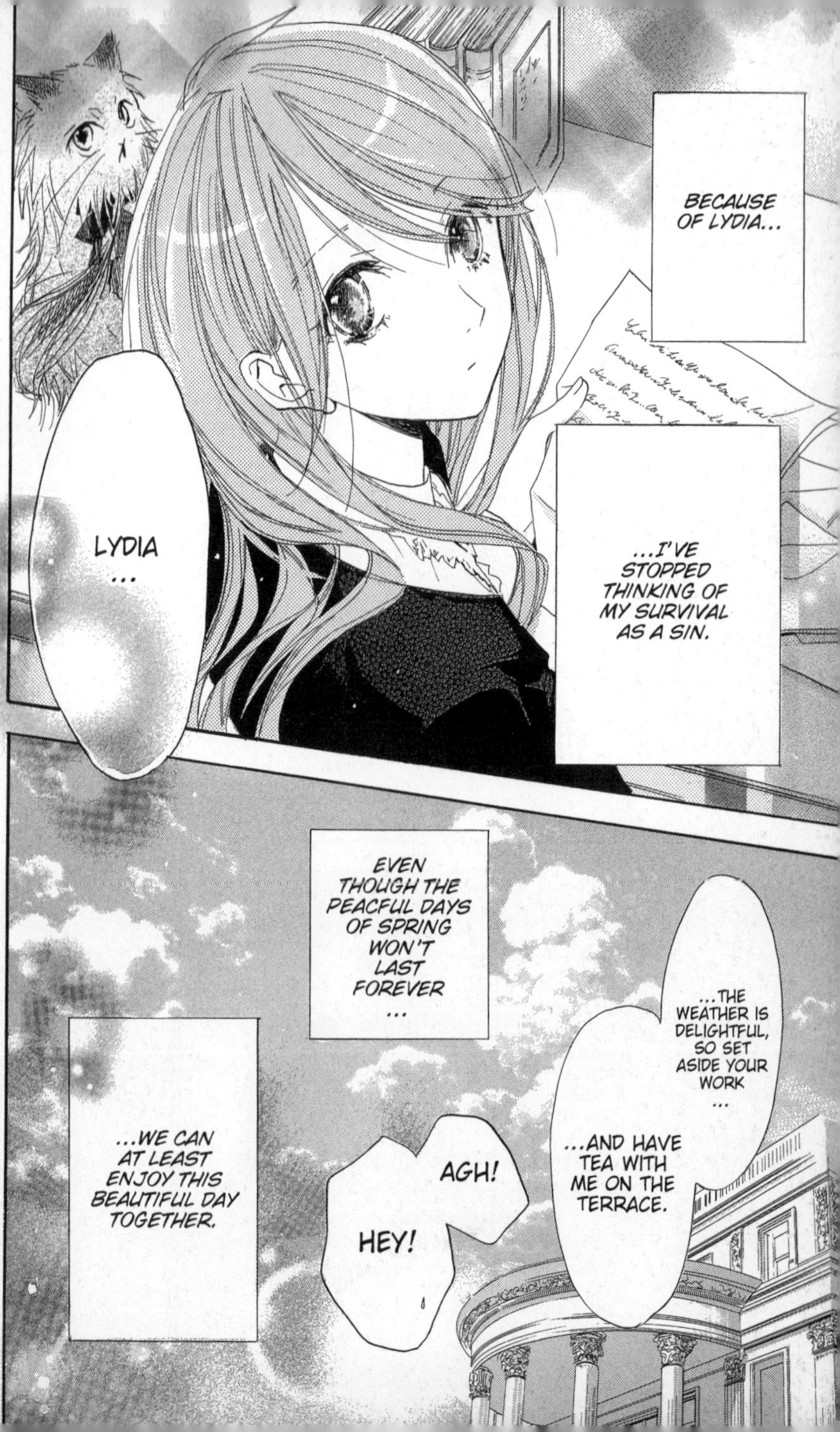
BECAUSE OF LYDIA...
...I'VE STOPPED THINKING OF MY SURVIVAL AS A SIN.
LYDIA ...
EVEN THOUGH THE PEACFUL DAYS OF SPRING WON'T LAST FOREVER ...
...THE WEATHER IS DELIGHTFUL, SO SET ASIDE YOUR WORK ...
...AND HAVE TEA WITH ME ON THE TERRACE.
AGH!
HEY!
...WE CAN AT LEAST ENJOY THIS BEAUTIFUL DAY TOGETHER.

The Earl & the Fairy

Bonus Manga

RAVEN SAW IT!

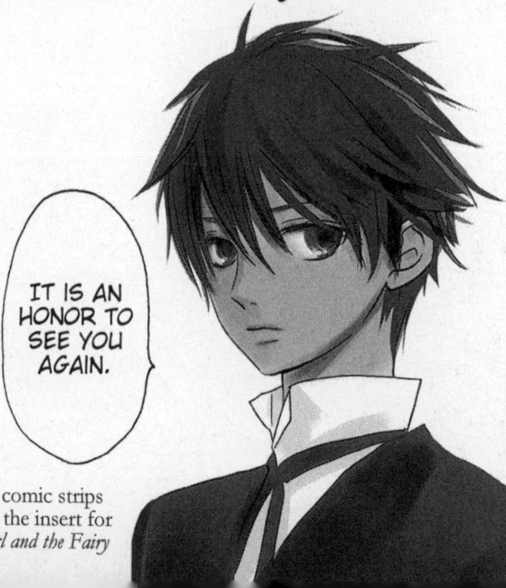
IT IS AN HONOR TO SEE YOU AGAIN.

*These comic strips were in the insert for *The Earl and the Fairy* DVD.

1 SKETCH

It's hard to draw ...
Sorry, Miss ...
...But could you please hold still?
S...
Sorry!
I'm not used to being an artist's model...
Raven ...
...will you model for me sometime?
STARE
Um ...
It's okay to move a little...
Just acting like normal.
?

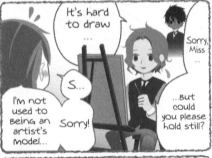

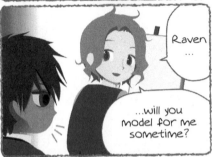

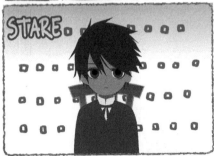

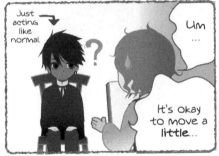

*The name of the artist is Paul. He first appeared in *The Earl and the Fairy: The Soft Proposal* by Cobalt Books.
Edgar likes Paul's drawings of fairies, so he starts visiting the mansion.

2 WHISPERS OF LOVE

Come and get with me, Lydia.
I'll please ya!
I'm so happy when I'm with you.
You're even cute when you're angry!
Argh! Raven!
You're always watching!
Why don't you say something?!
My apologies.
I am incapable of whispering sweet nothings.
That's not what I meant!

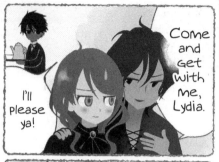

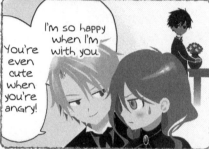

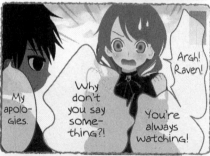

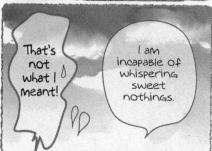

*The man wooing Lydia in panel one is a kelpie. His true fairy form is that of a fierce horse. He appears in *The Earl and the Fairy: The Soft Proposal* by Cobalt Books.

3 RAVEN'S PROBLEM

Raven... are you angry?
No.
I feel quite fine.
Are you worried about some-thing, Raven?
No.
I am not thinking about any-thing in particular.
Raven is staring at himself in the mirror ...
Maybe he's worried about how we mis-understand his expressions.
I had some-thing in my eye ...

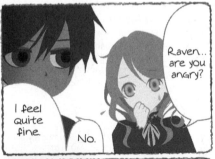

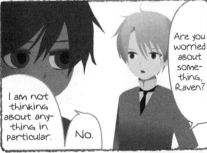

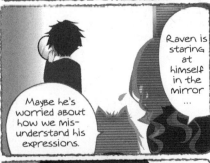

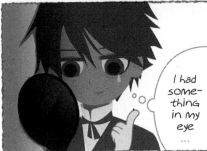

* All six T*he Earl and the Fairy* DVDs now on sale in Japan!

Price per DVD: ¥6,090
Publisher: Delights
Distributor: Pony Canyon

I want a partner like Nico. Even though he says rude things, he'd worry about me and help me when I was in trouble. He's so fluffy! I'm jealous of Lydia.

-Ayuko

Ayuko debuted with the story "Us, You and Me" in *Bessatsu Margaret* magazine and has gone on to publish several manga titles in addition to *The Earl and the Fairy*. Born in Kumamoto Prefecture, she's a Leo and loves drawing girl characters.

Mizue Tani is the author of several fantasy novel series and in 1997 received an honorable mention in the Shueisha Roman Taisho awards. Aside from *The Earl and the Fairy*, her other major series is *Majo no Kekkon* (The Witch's Marriage).

The Earl and the Fairy
Volume 4
Shojo Beat Edition

Story and Art by
Ayuko

Original Concept by
Mizue Tani

English Translation & Adaptation/John Werry
Touch-up Art & Lettering/Joanna Estep
Design/Izumi Evers
Editor/Pancha Diaz

HAKUSHAKU TO YOSEI-COMIC EDITION-
© 2008 by Mizue Tani, Ayuko
All rights reserved.
First published in Japan in 2008 by SHUEISHA Inc., Tokyo.
English language translation rights arranged with SHUEISHA Inc., Tokyo.

The rights of the author(s) of the work(s) in this publication to be so
identified have been asserted in accordance with the Copyright, Designs
and Patents Act 1988. A CIP catalogue record for this book is available
from the British Library.

The stories, characters and incidents mentioned in this publication are
entirely fictional.

No portion of this book may be reproduced or transmitted in any form
or by any means without written permission from the copyright holders.

Printed in the U.S.A.

Published by VIZ Media, LLC
P.O. Box 77010
San Francisco, CA 94107

10 9 8 7 6 5 4 3 2 1
First printing, December 2012

www.viz.com   www.shojobeat.com

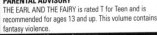

PARENTAL ADVISORY
THE EARL AND THE FAIRY is rated T for Teen and is
recommended for ages 13 and up. This volume contains
fantasy violence.
ratings.viz.com

WELCOME to a private school where trying to become SUPERIOR can make you feel INFERIOR

THE GENTLEMEN'S ALLIANCE †
CROSS

Story and Art by Arina Tanemura
Creator of *Full Moon*, *I•O•N*, *Short-Tempered Melancholic*,
Time Stranger Kyoko

When Haine's father decides to repay a debt by giving her to the Otomiya family, she starts attending the exclusive, aristocratic Imperial Academy. Though she's of proper lineage, will Haine ever really be considered one of the elite?

$9.99 USA | $12.99 CAN *

Read a **FREE** preview at **ShojoBeat.com**
and order the complete manga series at **store.viz.com**
Also available at your local bookstore or comic store.

THE GENTLEMEN ALLIANCE -CROSS- © 2004 by Arina Tanemura/SHUEISHA Inc.
* Prices subject to change

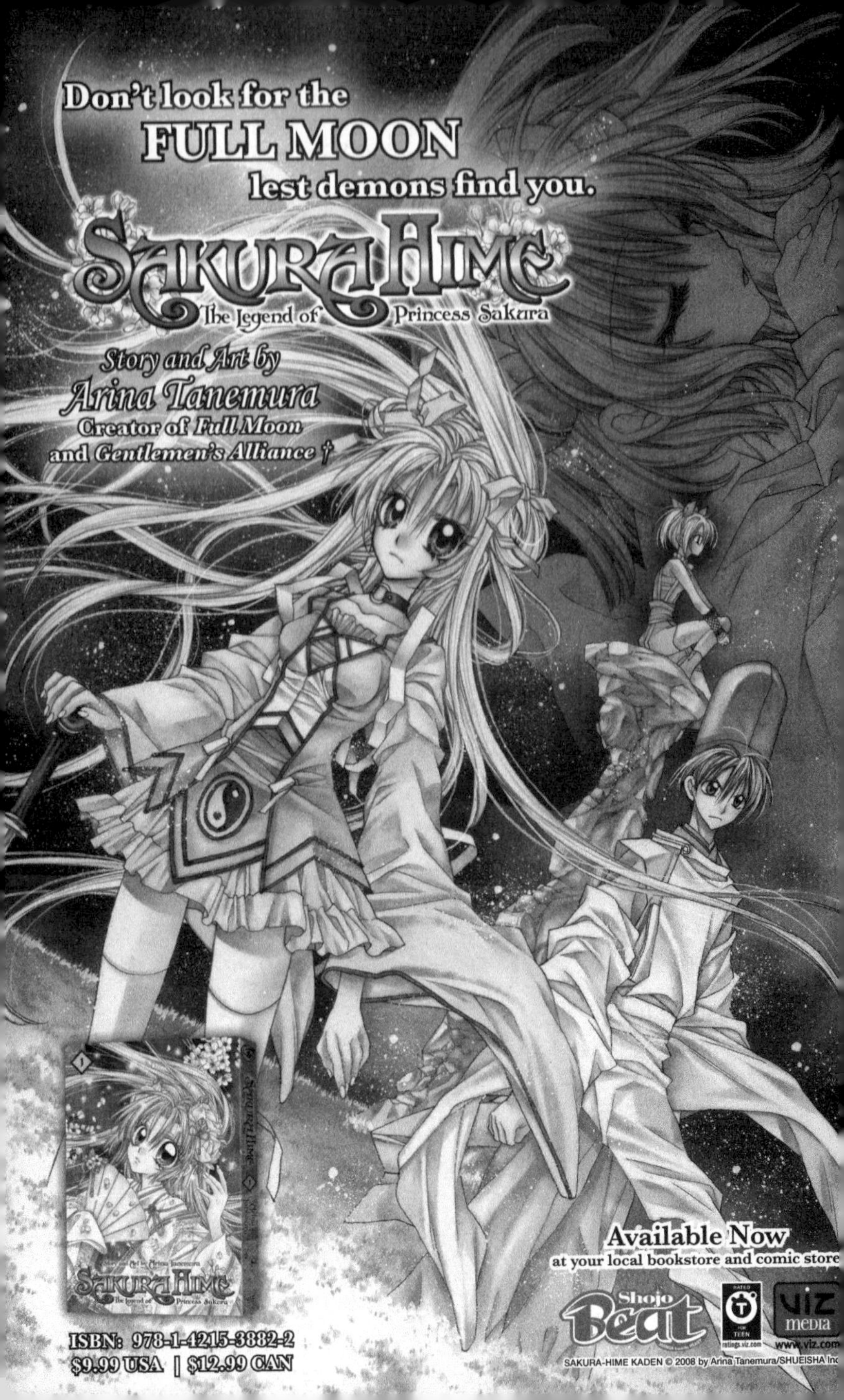
Don't look for the
FULL MOON
lest demons find you.
SAKURA HIME
The Legend of Princess Sakura
Story and Art by
Arina Tanemura
Creator of Full Moon
and Gentlemen's Alliance †
SAKURA HIME
The Legend of Princess Sakura
ISBN: 978-1-4215-3882-2
$9.99 USA | $12.99 CAN
Available Now
at your local bookstore and comic store
Shojo Beat
VIZ media
www.viz.com
SAKURA-HIME KADEN © 2008 by Arina Tanemura/SHUEISHA Inc.

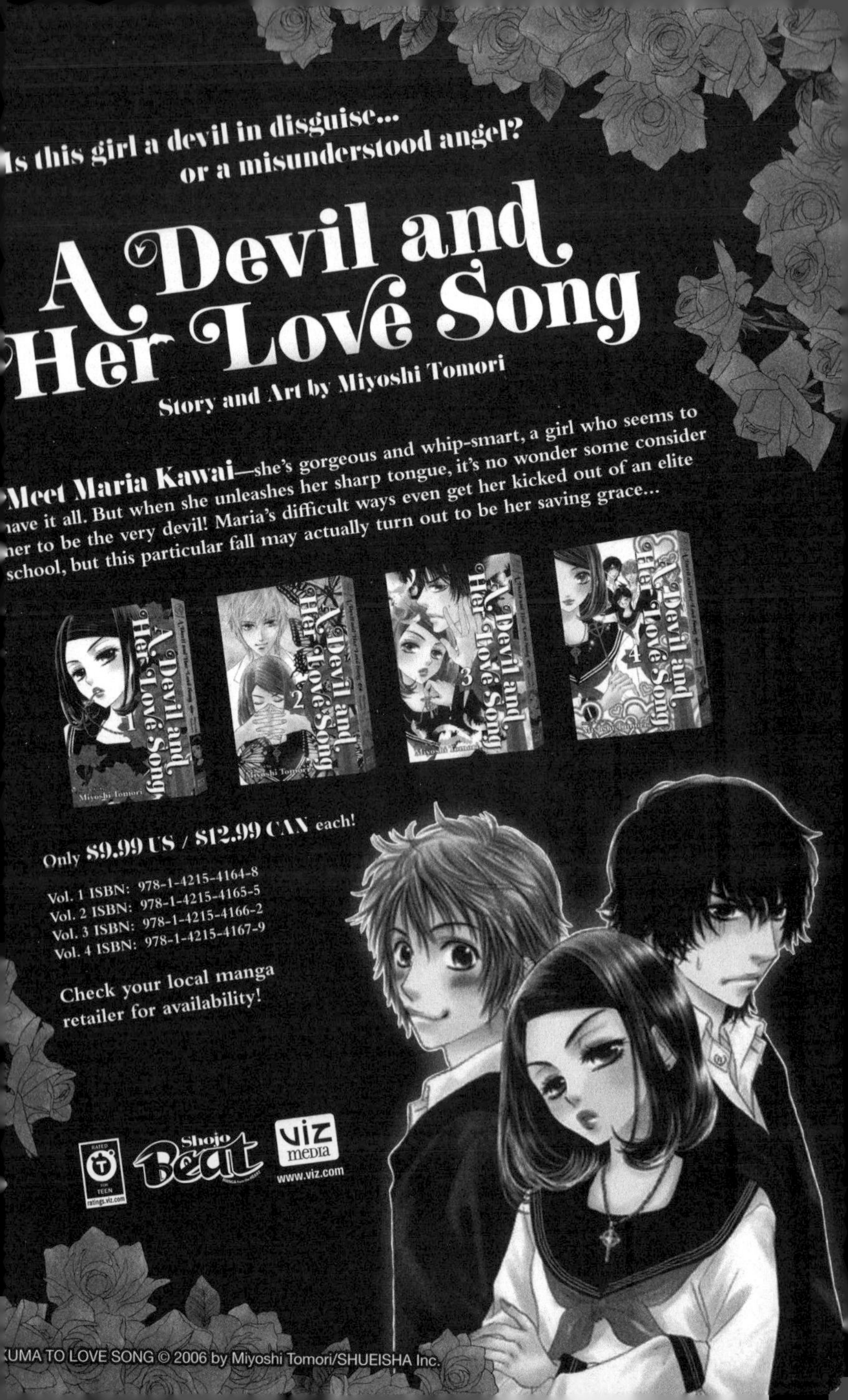
Is this girl a devil in disguise...
or a misunderstood angel?
A Devil and Her Love Song
Story and Art by Miyoshi Tomori
Meet Maria Kawai—she's gorgeous and whip-smart, a girl who seems to have it all. But when she unleashes her sharp tongue, it's no wonder some consider her to be the very devil! Maria's difficult ways even get her kicked out of an elite school, but this particular fall may actually turn out to be her saving grace...
Only $9.99 US / $12.99 CAN each!
Vol. 1 ISBN: 978-1-4215-4164-8
Vol. 2 ISBN: 978-1-4215-4165-5
Vol. 3 ISBN: 978-1-4215-4166-2
Vol. 4 ISBN: 978-1-4215-4167-9
Check your local manga retailer for availability!
RATED T TEEN ratings.viz.com
Shojo Beat
VIZ MEDIA
www.viz.com
KUMA TO LOVE SONG © 2006 by Miyoshi Tomori/SHUEISHA Inc.

ST. ♥ DRAGON GIRL

by Natsumi Matsumoto

WRONGLY POSSESSED

To grow stronger, demon hunter Ryuga Kou summons a powerful dragon spirit. But when that spirit unexpectedly enters the body of his childhood friend Momoka, the unlikely pair finds themselves working together to banish the invading demons! Are they up for the challenge?

Find out in *St. ♥Dragon Girl* — manga on sale now!

On sale at:
www.shojobeat.com
Also available at your local bookstore and comic store.

SAINT DRAGON GIRL © 1999 by Natsumi Matsumoto/SHUEISHA Inc.

RATED T FOR TEEN
ratings.viz.com

www.viz.com

This is the last page.

In keeping with the original Japanese comic format, this book reads from right to left—so action, sound effects, and word balloons are completely reversed. This preserves the orientation of the original artwork—plus, it's fun! Check out the diagram shown here to get the hang of things, and then turn to the other side of the book to get started!